History of
THE DUKE OF WELLINGTON'S
REGIMENT [1st & 2nd BATTALIONS]

Plate 1

After the painting by Sir Thomas Lawrence, P.R.A.

HISTORY
of
THE DUKE OF WELLINGTON'S REGIMENT

[1ST & 2ND BATTALIONS]

1881—1923

BY

BRIGADIER-GENERAL C. D. BRUCE, C.B.E.

LONDON
THE MEDICI SOCIETY, LIMITED

PRINTED IN ENGLAND 1927

FOREWORD

"WELLINGTON THE MAN"
1769—1852

"AN author seeking for a novel subject of universal interest might do worse than choose that of 'decisive conversations of the world.' Probably these would all have some common characteristics. Among such conversations must certainly be reckoned one which took place in some lodgings over a pastry-cook's shop in Oxford Street, probably in the autumn of 1785. Two ladies and a lad were present at it. One of the ladies is only important to us because she heard the conversation and recorded it afterwards. The other was a stately widow, whose husband had died four years earlier, leaving her an embarrassed estate, the title of Lady Mornington, six sons and two daughters. For all these her children, of whom the eldest was nearly of age and now at Oxford, she was anxious by help of family interest to provide. The third who joined in that decisive conversation was her fourth son, Arthur, a sickly, rather gawky boy, 'with a very pronounced nose' as the lady narrator reports. He was about sixteen years of age, had just returned from a short and by no means brilliant career at Eton, and was standing with his back to the fireplace. 'Don't you know my son Arthur?' asked the matron, speaking indignantly after shaking hands with her guest, 'he has been giving us a good deal of trouble lately. I have secured for him the promise of a clerkship in the Irish Excise; he gets £80 a year, and it will rise to £600. He won't have it! Nothing will satisfy him but to go into the army, and idle away his time, as if we had the means of buying him commissions!' 'No, mother,' answered the young man, 'I did not say that, I only asked to be allowed to go to France to study my profession.'

"Fortunately her ladyship's 'ugly son' carried his point. To Antwerp soon afterwards he went. There he remained for about a year, studying such military science as the Marquis de Pignerol, a distinguished Engineer officer of the *ancien régime*, could impart, acquiring also, what in after life was of no small service to him, a good knowledge of French. Napoleon, after spending five years in military schooling at Brienne and in Paris, had just obtained his commission at the time when Wellington entered Pignerol's school at Antwerp.

"Not, therefore, as the 'dunce of the family' was Wellington sent into the army. He was in the eyes of his family the fool of the party because he himself chose his profession, and from the beginning intended to treat it as one requiring serious study. That was his first great advantage in the race of life."[1]

[1] *Cromwell to Wellington*, edited by Spencer Wilkinson.

AUTHOR'S PREFACE

ONE of our best-known military historians has said that the study of history is the study of human nature or it is nothing. "It may and does," he says, "lie principally with documents, on paper, on parchment, on wood, stone, or metal; but unless history is made to speak through the medium of ordinary men—e.g. their activities, their motives, their hopes and fears, and not only through the mouths of kings, queens, ambassadors and so forth—it is not real history."[1]

Any appeal to readers of such a book as this is can only hope to be successful if it speaks a language which they understand, a language which tells of the ordinary trials and troubles of the life of a soldier as well as of its brighter and successful side. It must also make use of light and shade in due proportion and not rely entirely upon the effect of an ever-present limelight.

The writer makes no pretension to be an expert historian. He offers the present volume in hopes that it may and will be found of some interest to all ranks—past, present, and future—of the Duke of Wellington's Regiment, Militia, Territorial and ex-Service Battalions. His only regret is in not being able to include with the record of the 2nd Battalion in the Great War the history of the splendid services rendered to their country by all the other Battalions raised during that period.

Wherever possible the author has made free use of standard works, also of all accessible material such as private diaries, etc., so kindly placed at his disposal, as well as of other records.

Special thanks are due individually to Lieut.-General Sir Herbert Belfield, K.C.B., K.C.M.G., K.B.E., D.S.O.; Brig.-General P. A. Turner, C.M.G.; Colonel J. A. C. Gibbs, C.B., and Major C. W. G. Ince, M.C. The latter has most kindly helped in correcting all the proofs, in the collection of maps, and in many other ways as Hon. Sec. of the Regimental History Committee.

The author's thanks are also due collectively to the Regimental History Committee, and for advice and kind assistance to the Historical Section of the War Office Committee of Imperial Defence.

For the earlier portions of this volume he is indebted mainly to two former works. First, *The History of the 33rd, 1st Battalion the Duke of Wellington's Regiment*, by Albert Lee. Secondly, to the *Historical Records, 76th Hindoostan Regiment*, by Lieut.-Colonel F. A. Hayden, D.S.O., to whom the author is also much indebted for kindly reading through the whole History in final proof form.

The periods to which this present history is confined (1881–1923) may

[1] The Hon. Sir John Fortescue.

seem irregularly divided between the two Battalions. But this is accounted for by the different dates over which the two works just referred to extend.

The History of the 33rd, 1st Battalion the Duke of Wellington's Regiment, by Albert Lee, dates from the original creation of the 33rd in 1702. It ends, practically, in 1902 at the close of the South African War. Lieut.-Colonel F. A. Hayden's *Historical Records of the 76th Hindoostan Regiment* extends from that Regiment's formation in 1787 down to 1881. The object of the present volume has been to bring both previous records up to the same date, viz. 1919, with, in the case of the 1st Battalion, a few later notes up to 1923. For any future record, there is now established—if we may make use of the language of war—a mutual base of operations.

What must any such record aim at? To quote again from Sir John Fortescue:

" The power of bringing back to the senses the impression that past scenes and almost forgotten incidents gave is the most valuable asset of any historian. What then is the quality that is specially demanded of the historian over and above conscientious study, industry, and love of truth?—Imagination. History is not only the story of human nature, it has to be imparted to creatures of human nature. In teaching children history we try, if we are wise, to give them such glimpses of human nature as they can understand. If in telling the story of Samuel to a child we omit the detail ' Moreover, his mother made him a little coat,' we are unfair to the child. The detail may not be very important historically, but a child would recognize in it a link of human nature. The ordinary adult equally calls for such links, and unless he can get them he does not care to read history. To make the story of human nature in the past one with the human nature of the present is the true function of the historian."

Finally, military history is not only for the learned; it is for all sorts and conditions of men who are concerned in the survival of the British Empire. Are we not all of us in greater or lesser degree custodians of the honour, dignity, and self-sacrifice of the British Army? Is it not, in the long run, to the doings of that " Unknown Warrior " " Thomas Atkins " that most of this honour, dignity, and self-sacrifice is due?

To him, therefore, and to his comrades of the Duke of Wellington's Regiment, past and present, officers, non-commissioned officers and men, this book is dedicated.

C. D. BRUCE,
BRIGADIER-GENERAL (*Retired*),
(late The Duke of Wellington's Regiment).

June, 1927.

CONTENTS

	PAGE
FOREWORD	v
AUTHOR'S PREFACE	vii

CHAPTER I — 1
Historical outline of the raising and early years of the 1st Battalion.

CHAPTER II — 9
1st Battalion, 1900–1923: South Africa. York. India. Palestine. Constantinople. Ireland.

CHAPTER III — 24
Historical outline of early years of 2nd Battalion, 1881–1893: The Amalgamation of 1881. Previous regiments under the 76th number. India. Lieut. Hon. Arthur Weslie. 76th under General Lord Lake. Seringapatam. Bermuda, 1886. Halifax, N.S. Barbados.

CHAPTER IV — 36
2nd Battalion, 1893–1913: South Africa. Matabele rising, Mashonaland. India, Rangoon. The South African War. Home Service, Ireland.

CHAPTER V — 51
The embarkation for the front. The British concentration. The beginning of the Battle of Mons.

CHAPTER VI — 67
The Battle of Mons (*continued*).

CHAPTER VII — 82
Mons and after. Battle of Le Cateau and after.

CHAPTER VIII — 95
The retreat to Tournan. The offensive resumed. The River Marne crossed. The advance to the River Aisne.

CHAPTER IX — 110
From the Aisne to Bethune. Ypres, December, 1914.

CHAPTER X — 129
Winter Quarters, 1914. Hill 60, April 18th–May 5th, 1915.

CONTENTS

	PAGE
CHAPTER XI	142

May, 1915–January, 1917: on the Somme. Battle of Arras. Albert, Bertrancourt, Beaumont Hamel. Poperinghe. Back to the Somme. The Flers Line, the attack at Les Bœufs.

CHAPTER XII — 158

February, 1917–May, 1917: Bray. Corbie. Arras. Fampoux. The Chemical Works. Maizière. U.S.A. in the War. A Battalion raid. Back to Ypres, Pilkem. Death of Commanding Officer Lieut.-Colonel A. G. Horsfall, D.S.O.

CHAPTER XIII — 172

January, 1918–November, 1918: German plans for 1918 offensive. March offensive. Transferred to 10th Brigade. Arras. La Bassée Canal, Pacaut Wood. A "Rugger" raid. Vis en Artois. Stipe Copse. St. Servin's Farm. Saultzoir, Verchain, the Pimple and Herman Stellung. Preseau. Back to Mons. The Armistice.

CHAPTER XIV — 186

The Dedication of the Memorial Chapel in York Minster. The Regimental War Memorial.

CONCLUSION — 204

The Regiment during the Great War.

APPENDIX I — 208

The Great War.

APPENDIX II — 210

The Great War.

APPENDIX III — 213

The Roll of Honour.

APPENDIX IV — 217

The Roll of Honour.

APPENDIX V — 237

Army Uniforms 1702–1927.

APPENDIX VI — 240

Pension Fund.

APPENDIX VII — 241

The Death of "The Camel."

APPENDIX VIII — 242

Birth of First Duke.

LIST OF SUBSCRIBERS — 243

INDEX — 245

LIST OF ILLUSTRATIONS

PLATE		
1.	THE "IRON DUKE"	*Frontispiece*
		FACING PAGE
2.	HIS GRACE THE DUKE OF WELLINGTON, K.G., G.C.V.O.	8
3.	OFFICERS OF 2ND BATTALION AT HALIFAX, N.S., 1890	32
4.	OFFICERS OF 2ND BATTALION, CENTENARY BALL, CALCUTTA, DECEMBER, 1902	44
5.	LIEUT.-GENERAL SIR H. BELFIELD, K.C.B., K.C.M.G., K.B.E., D.S.O.	47
6.	OFFICERS OF 2ND BATTALION, DUBLIN, 8TH AUGUST, 1914	52
7.	LIEUT.-COLONEL W. E. M. TYNDALL, D.S.O. CAPT. C. O. DENMAN-JUBB LIEUT.-COLONEL A. A. St. HILL, D.S.O. MAJOR E. C. BOUTFLOWER, O.B.E.	64
8.	Q.M. AND MAJOR A. ELLAM, M.C. MAJOR W. G. OFFICER MAJOR C. W. G. INCE, M.C. CAPT. H. K. O'KELLY, D.S.O.	70
9.	GERMAN "COOKA" TAKEN ON THE AISNE SERGT. J. H. SHAW, D.C.M. THE "CAMEL"	72
10.	LIEUT.-COLONEL A. G. HORSFALL, D.S.O. MAJOR P. B. STRAFFORD LIEUT.-COLONEL R. E. MAFFETT LIEUT.-COLONEL E. G. HARRISON. C.B., D.S.O.	74
11.	COLONEL J. A. C. GIBBS, C.B. BRIG.-GENERAL W. M. WATSON BRIG.-GENERAL P. A. TURNER, C.M.G. BRIG.-GENERAL R. N. BRAY, C.M.G., D.S.O.	80
12.	YPRES, 1914 YPRES, 1919	110
13.	COPY OF THE ORIGINAL ORDER FOR THE ATTACK ON HILL 60, 18TH APRIL, 1915	132
14.	HILL 60	140
15.	R.Q.M.S. E. MOSELEY R.S.M. C. E. METCALFE, D.C.M. AND BAR, M.M. C.S.M. R. GRADY	151

LIST OF ILLUSTRATIONS

PLATE		FACING PAGE
16.	SPLINTER-PROOF SHELTER IN RESERVE LINE, HALIFAX TRENCH, JULY, 1917 THE MILL AT FEUCHY AID POST AT FAMPOUX AFTER BOMBARDMENT ON 11TH APRIL, 1917 BATTALION H.Q., FAMPOUX, APRIL, 1917	164
17.	CAPT. K. E. CUNNINGHAM Q.M. AND CAPT. C. SHEPHERD, M.B.E., D.C.M. CAPT. A. CLIMIE, M.C., R.A.M.C. CAPT. W. O. TOBIAS, R.A.M.C.	168
18.	SERGT. J. BOURN, D.C.M. SERGT. J. R. OGDEN, D.C.M. SERGT. A. BUTTERWORTH PTE. F. HARTE	174
19.	LIEUT. J. P. HUFFAM, V.C.	178
20.	LIEUT.-COLONEL C. J. PICKERING, C.M.G., D.S.O. LIEUT.-COLONEL F. H. B. WELLESLEY	180
21.	OFFICERS OF THE 2ND BATTALION CADRE WHO RETURNED FROM FRANCE IN 1919	184
22.	CADRE OF 2ND BATTALION, HALIFAX, 16TH JUNE, 1919	
23.	MEMORIAL TABLET IN THE CHAPEL OF THE ROYAL MILITARY COLLEGE, SANDHURST	186
24.	MEMORIAL CHAPEL OF THE DUKE OF WELLINGTON'S REGIMENT, YORK MINSTER	190
25.	STAND (d), 33RD REGIMENT, NOW IN POSSESSION OF LORD WHARTON	192
26.	THE ORIGINAL SPEARHEAD ON THE HONOURABLE EAST INDIA COMPANY'S COLOUR POLES FRAMED REMNANTS OF THE ORIGINAL HONOURABLE EAST INDIA COMPANY'S REGIMENTAL COLOUR, NOW IN YORK MINSTER	193
27.	THE HONOURABLE EAST INDIA COMPANY'S COLOURS, NOW IN USE IN THE 2ND BATTALION	196
28.	REGIMENTAL COLOUR 76TH REGIMENT, 1830–1863 REGIMENTAL COLOUR 33RD REGIMENT, 1832–1854	197
29.	2ND BATTALION COLOURS (1906) NOW IN USE	198
30.	1ST BATTALION COLOUR (1925) NOW IN USE	199
31.	1ST BATTALION COLOUR (1925) NOW IN USE	200
32.	3RD (MILITIA) COLOUR (1864–1889), NOW IN YORK MINSTER REGIMENTAL COLOUR 4TH (MILITIA) BATTN., NOW IN YORK MINSTER REGIMENTAL COLOUR 4TH (T.A.) BATTALION (1908–1927), NOW IN YORK MINSTER	201

LIST OF MAPS

	PAGE
GENERAL MAP OF FRANCE AND BELGIUM	1
CHAMAN DEFENCE LINE	20
POSITION ON AUGUST 22ND, 1914	62
MACHINE-GUN POSITIONS ON AUGUST 23RD, 1914	64
THE RETREAT FROM MONS AND ADVANCE TO THE AISNE, 1914	67
TRENCHES OCCUPIED BY BATTALION ON AUGUST 24TH, 1914	74
FRONT NEAR LA BASSEE, OCTOBER, 1914, SHOWING MOVEMENTS OF THE 2ND BATTALION	113
THE YPRES DISTRICT	133
HILL 60	
SITUATION AT 9.0 A.M., APRIL 18TH, 1915	135
SITUATION AT DUSK ON APRIL 18TH, 1915	136
THE FRONT NEAR CARNOY, AUGUST, 1915, TO JANUARY, 1916	144
AREA OF ATTACK, JULY 1ST, 1916	148
LES BŒUFS, OCTOBER, 1916	154
FAMPOUX AND CHEMICAL WORKS, APRIL–MAY, 1917	159
BATTLE AREA N.E. OF YPRES, SEPTEMBER–OCTOBER, 1917	169
PACAUT WOOD	176
DIRECTION OF ADVANCE OF 2ND BATTALION, AUGUST, 1918	178
MOVEMENTS OF THE 2ND BATTALION, OCTOBER–NOVEMBER, 1918	182

ACKNOWLEDGMENT

ALL possible care has been taken to trace the source of the photographs reproduced in this history. The record of indebtedness is printed below and gratefully acknowledged by the Author.

Debenham & Gould (*Capt. C. O. Denman-Jubb*); Elliott & Fry (*Col. E. G. Harrison, C.B., D.S.O.*); Everitt ("*The Camel*"); Gladstone Adams (*Major A. Ellam, M.C.*); Greaves (*Officers of Cadre*, 1919); Hoppe (*Major W. G. Officer*); Lacy (*Capt. W. O. Tobias, R.A.M.C.*); Lafayette (*Lt.-Gen. Sir H. Belfield, K.C.B., K.C.M.G., K.B.E., D.S.O.*; *Col. J. A. C. Gibbs, C.B.*; *Capt. H. K. O'Kelly, D.S.O.*); A. A. Richards (*C.S.M. Grady*); J. Russell & Sons (*Lt.-Col. F. H. B. Wellesley*); Searle Brothers (*Brig.-Gen. R. N. Bray, C.M.G., D.S.O.*); H. Speed (*Memorial Chapel*); Swaine (*Lt. J. P. Huffam, V.C.*; *Lt.-Col. R. E. Maffett*; *Lt.-Col. A. A. St. Hill*; *Brig.-Gen. P. A. Turner, C.M.G.*; *Major C. W. G. Ince*); Winter, Murree & Pinde (*Major A. G. Horsfall, D.S.O.*; *Brig.-Gen. W. M. Watson*).

CHAPTER I

HISTORICAL OUTLINE OF THE RAISING AND EARLY YEARS OF THE 1st BATTALION.

LIKE many others in the British Army the 33rd Duke of Wellington's Regiment owed its inception to a war scare. It may be of interest to recall briefly some events connected with its earliest days.

In the year 1702, over two hundred years ago, Louis XIV of France had it in mind to dominate Europe. In our own day another King and Emperor, this time from East of the Rhine, revived the idea with even more fateful results to his country and dynasty. When Louis of France, in the final period of his extraordinary reign, laid claim to the Spanish succession for his grandson Philip Duke of Anjou, he began—as the saying is—to dig his own grave. William III of England, representing also his own land of Holland, as well as what was then known as Germany, was not prepared to see the balance of power in Europe thus upset. With Spain, the Spanish Netherlands, and that country's great Colonial Empire becoming practically a vassal state of France, England, Holland, Flanders, and the Western German Powers grew thoroughly alarmed. As the Spanish Ambassador of that time remarked: "There are no longer any Pyrenees!" Without this barrier France and Spain would have been one country. Although Russia and Prussia had not yet come on the political stage, they were about to do so.

Thus at the commencement of the eighteenth century we find an European situation not unlike that which ushered in the twentieth century. Amongst such warlike surroundings the 33rd Regiment was born. It was John Churchill, Duke of Marlborough, who led the allied forces, and it was mainly the effect of his unrivalled campaigns which destroyed the position to which Louis XIV had attained in Europe. It may appear strange, but England actually derived little political benefit from these campaigns.

It was under the Duke of Marlborough as generalissimo of the Allies that the 33rd gained its first experience of war. As part of the allied programme war against the French was also prosecuted in the Spanish Peninsula. There, under the immediate command of the Duke of Ormond, the 33rd underwent its baptism of fire: the actual occasion was an abortive and ill-timed attack upon Cadiz.

When in March, 1702, Queen Anne succeeded to the throne of England it was made plain to Europe that England, as William III had hoped and planned, "was to be the soul of the Grand Alliance against France in the war of the Spanish succession." So far as preparation for war was concerned this country was at that time hopelessly unprepared. Here again a historical comparison may be found with our position in 1914. England in 1702 was practically without an army. Not by any means for the last time the policy of Parliament may truthfully be described as—astounding. Whenever a war was progressing money was voted to maintain the army at the requisite fighting strength, and supplies were more or less tardily produced. But as soon as peace was declared there came a wholesale disbandment of troops in order to reduce expenditure. From 70,000 men forming the British Army during the preceding war—figures which to-day almost provoke a smile—it was barely possible to muster 20,000. Of these 20,000 less than half belonged to the English establishment, the remainder being stationed in Ireland.

Like William of Hohenzollern before the Great War, Louis XIV of France reckoned without England. That he gave expression to any such feeling or made use of the same contemptuous language history does not record. But there can be little doubt that with such a meagre standing army in this country as England possessed Louis XIV expected to pursue his policy of aggrandisement unopposed by our forefathers. To provide the 40,000 soldiers considered to be England's fair quota in the coming European war fifteen regiments were hastily raised. Amongst the fifteen, as the following order shows, was the 33rd Regiment.

Order issued to the Earl of Huntingdon on March 14th, 1702:—

"These are to authorise you by beat of Drum or otherwise, to raise volunteers for a regiment of Foot under your command, which is to consist of twelve companies, of two Serjeants, three Corporals, Two Drummers, and Fifty-nine private soldiers, with the addition of one Serjeant more to the Company of Grenadiers. And as you shall raise the said volunteers you are to give notice thereof to our Commisary-General of the Musters, that they may be mustered according to our directions in that behalf. And when the whole number of non-commission officers and soldiers shall be fully as near completed, in each company, they are to march to our city of Gloucester, appointed for the rendezvous of the said regiment. And you are to order such person or persons as you think fit to receive arms for our said regiment out of the Stores of our Ordinance. And all Magistrates, Justices of the Peace, Constables and other our Officers, whom it may concern are to be assisting to you in providing quarters and otherwise as there shall be occasion.

Given at our Court of St. James' this 14th day of March, 1702, in the first year of our Reign.

To our Trusty and Well-beloved
 The Earl of Huntingdon,
Col. of One of Our Regiments of Foot."

THE ORIGIN OF THE 33RD REGIMENT

The names of the officers of the Commission Register stand as follows for the Earl of Huntingdon's Regiment of Foot:—

> George, Earl of Huntingdon, Colonel.
> Robert Duncanson, Lieut.-Colonel.
> John Rose, Major.

That the task laid upon "Our Trusty and Well-beloved The Earl of Huntingdon" was no light one will be realised by anyone conversant with Army conditions two hundred years ago.

The then Earl of Huntingdon was not more than twenty-five years of age when he received the Queen's Commission to form the 33rd Regiment. He was at the time a Lieut.-Colonel of the 1st Regiment of Foot Guards, now the Grenadier Guards.

To attract men to re-enlist as "Voluntiers" who had lately been disbanded was no easy matter. Many of the men had already seen service, and knew the horrors of war as they then existed, entirely different from and in some ways worse than those of to-day. The miseries of a soldier's life two hundred years ago are now almost incredible. The abominable housing with its consequent sickness, the absence of medical attendance, the inadequate provision for creature comforts or even decency, the arrears of pay which affected all ranks. Fortescue[1] has told us how even officers knew what it was to go hungry for lack of a meal. It was not to be wondered at, then, that recruits held back until "levy money," or as we should say a bounty of £3 per man was offered and paid.

The "Voluntiers" for Lord Huntingdon's 33rd Regiment came chiefly from the Midlands and South-western counties, possibly also some companies from Kent. In July, 1702, the whole or a large portion of the Regiment was stationed at and round Hereford and Gloucester.

It is not the purpose of this volume to follow in detail the history of the 33rd Regiment since it was raised, but as far as may be done to link up its glorious past with the no less glorious doings of later days. In order that this idea may be carried out we cannot pass over without reference certain events which link past and present together.

As has already been related, the Regiment's baptism of fire, in 1702, took place under the Duke of Ormond in the Spanish Peninsula. It also suffered in the attack on Valenza under Colonel Duncanson in 1705, where the Regiment lost its gallant Commander. But—to use a hunting expression—it was not really "entered" until 1708. At Alamanza in the Spanish Peninsula, the scene of later glories, it was so copiously "blooded" that it was almost cut to pieces.

As an instance of how *not* to make war the campaign of 1705 in Spain is worth quoting. There are those fully qualified to judge who maintain that victory would not have ensued in 1918 but for unity of command. What are we to think of the following proposition which was seriously made and actually carried out? The proposition was as follows: "To *avoid* (the italics are ours,

[1] The Hon. Sir John Fortescue.

Ed.) friction it was arranged that the three Generals should command alternately for a *week* at a time."[1]

That disaster followed such an extraordinarily unmilitary proceeding is not to be wondered at.

As the Regimental battle honours proudly show, " Dettingen " was the first honour to grace the Colours.

The campaign which included the battle of Dettingen was, as in 1914, fought once more by England to maintain the balance of power in Europe. It is known as the War of the Austrian Succession. At the time when England was committed to fight, a Parliamentary vote for 62,000 men was passed. As in the case of the 2nd Battalion of the Regiment in 1914, the 33rd was in Ireland, when on April 24th, 1742, orders came for its immediate embarkation for Flanders. To carry the parallel still further; after arriving in Flanders, with Ponsonby's 37th Regiment, and Bligh's 20th Regiment, the original 33rd Regiment marched direct to Mons. Who will say that history does not repeat itself?

The battles of Dettingen and Fontenoy have still an interest for soldiers in that they are examples of the early power of British infantry-fire. At the disappointing Battle of Fontenoy it is related that the men of the 33rd and regiments to right and left of them poured in an awful fire on the enemy: " Two Battalions loaded while the third fired." This effective fire occasioned severe losses amongst the French, so that Marshal Saxe was obliged to reinforce the line. One regiment was all but annihilated and the French line was shattered. The reinforcing troops were also unable to stand such a devastating fire, and the advance of the 33rd and other regiments was rendered possible.

The legend that the 33rd Regiment was originally recruited at Sowerby Brig, near Halifax, Yorkshire, dies hard. That there was reason for the belief is no doubt due to the fact that the Regiment was given as its earliest territorial title that of " First Yorkshire West Riding Regiment." An order to this effect was issued in 1782 soon after the return of the 33rd from the disastrous campaign in America under Cornwallis. The idea underlying this order was that a connection between regiments and counties should exist in order to assist recruiting. This county connection was no doubt given to the 33rd because many of the men serving with the Regiment during the American war had been recruited round Leeds and Halifax. The nickname of " Havercake Lads " came to them from the humorous practice of the recruiting sergeants of that time who were in the habit of sticking an oat-cake, locally known as a " Havercake," upon the points of their swords whilst perambulating for recruits the West Riding towns and villages.

The next link with the past worth recalling is the disastrous campaign of 1794 in the Netherlands.

Up to the time of the Netherlands expedition of 1794 the future conqueror of Napoleon had seen no active service. Wellesley's qualities as a commander in the field were entirely unknown. It has even been said that his habits at that time were scarcely such as to give promise of future greatness. A Latin poet and

[1] The Hon. Sir John Fortescue.

dramatist once wrote that " Fire proves gold, adversity proves men,"[1] and of adversity as a soldier Wellesley was to have his full share.

It was as Lieut.-Colonel of the 33rd Regiment, at that time quartered at Cork, that he and they sailed for Ostend in May, 1794. In Flanders, then, as always, the battleground of Europe, was laid the foundation of the future " Iron Duke's " reputation.

To follow the early military career of the future Duke of Wellington reference must again be made to the Netherlands campaign of 1794 which was brought about by the French Revolution. Louis XVI, the unfortunate French King, had been guillotined. This caused Pitt, the great English War Minister, to order the French Ambassador to leave the country. The French response was instant if expected. In February, 1793, the French Convention declared war against England and Holland. The British Army was immediately increased by 25,000 men and troops were at once sent to Flanders.

The Netherlands campaign of 1794, as has already been said, brought the 33rd Regiment under Lieut.-Colonel Wellesley into the war. The campaign was memorable for much hard fighting, also, as in the Crimean War, for considerable mismanagement on the part of the authorities responsible for victualling, reinforcing, and equipping the British Army. But so far as concerns these memoirs, it is memorable because it first brought to notice the young Commanding Officer of the 33rd Regiment, he who was afterwards to earn undying fame as a soldier and a leader of men.

In a later chapter reference is made to Arthur Wellesley's transfer to the 33rd as a Major, also to the coincidence of his early connection with both Battalions which now have the honour to bear his name.

Having in the Netherlands campaign of 1794 already laid a foundation for the reputation he afterwards made, Wellesley and the 33rd Regiment sailed for the East Indies in 1796. Owing to the prolonged delays at the Cape the Regiment did not actually reach Calcutta until February, 1797. Wellesley was ill when they embarked, but rejoined the Regiment in a fast-sailing frigate at Cape Town. The Governor-General of India at that period was Wellesley's brother, Lord Mornington.

The position of the British in 1796 was by no means secure. Tippoo Sahib, Sultan of Mysore, son of Hyder Ali, hated the British. It was known to the Governor-General that he was strengthening his principal stronghold, Seringapatam. At the same time it was to Tippoo that the Emperor Napoleon made his famous offer of assistance to help overthrow British power in the East. In his well-known letter " to the Most Magnificent Sultan our greatest Friend Tippoo Sahib," Napoleon announced his intention of " delivering you from the iron yoke of England." Other troubles were brewing in Southern India. In 1798 a French soldier-of-fortune had taken service under the Nizam of Hyderabad. He had raised, disciplined, and officered with his fellow-countrymen a force of 14,000 men. The French Commander died, but the Governor-General was uncertain as to whether the Nizam would or would not join forces with Tippoo Sahib.

[1] Seneca.

Having made the position easier by securing the loyalty to the British Raj of the Hyderabad potentate, Lord Mornington was in a position to deal with Tippoo. The latter was asked for an explanation of Napoleon's letter, but no reply was received. As Tippoo became more overbearing than ever, war was inevitable.

Wellesley's share in the Mysore campaign was the command of all the Nizam's contingent, a force numbering some 15,000 troops. With these, under General Harris, he took the field.

Surprised by the sudden advance on Mysore, and while waiting help from France and the Maharattas, Tippoo decided to stand in the vicinity of Seringapatam.

Deceived by the idea that General Harris would take the same route as did Cornwallis in 1791, Tippoo moved to bar his advance only to find that General Harris was marching by another route direct upon his main fortress of Seringapatam.

In May, 1799, preparations having been made for an assault, Maj.-General Baird led the attack. This, after hard and severe hand-to-hand fighting, was entirely successful. The Sultan was himself killed and Seringapatam fell to the assault of the British forces, among which was the 33rd Regiment.

The fall of Tippoo's stronghold brought immense booty to the troops engaged, but the wholesale looting which followed the storming of the town was a blot on the otherwise splendid behaviour of the men.

Appointed specially in order to cope with the looting and general chaos following the excesses of the soldiers, Wellesley at once set to work to quell disturbances.

"The scent of a rich booty had for a time subverted discipline. Sepoys and soldiers thronged in from the camp, plundering was vigorously carried on, fires broke out, and the terrified inhabitants fled. Rule appeared to be at an end, unbridled license was seemingly triumphant, but Colonel Wellesley at once made strenuous efforts in the cause of order." He quartered the 33rd and 73rd Regiments within the palace and furnished strong guards over the most important places in the city. Four men were executed before the iron will of the Commandant restored order. By the end of the day he was able to send a message to the General in the following words:—

> "Plunder is stopped, the fires are all extinguished, and the inhabitants are returning to their houses fast. I am now employed in burying the dead, which I hope will be completed this day, particularly if you send me all the pioneers."

It is interesting to note the very large sums distributed to the troops in prize money. "General Harris," it was written at the time, "has something better than three lacs of pagodas (about £125,000). General Floyd, 36,000 pagodas (roughly £15,000). Other generals, 25,000 pagodas (roughly £10,000). Colonels a little more than 10,000 pagodas (roughly £4,000). This is, however, only a first division: they are now in expectation of near as much more."

Such was one aspect of soldiering in the early days of British rule in India.

With all the drawbacks incidental to the looting at Seringapatam there is no doubt that the troops did merit the praise bestowed upon them. They had achieved, as was written at the time, " something which has never been surpassed in splendour by any event recorded in the history of military transactions of the British nation in India."

The fall of Seringapatam placed the whole kingdom of Mysore at the disposal of the British Government. It also extinguished the only power in India deemed formidable, or in any wise disposed to second the dangerous hopes of the French in disputing British control.

For their splendid services in the capture of Seringapatam the 33rd received permission to emblazon " Seringapatam " on their Colours. The capture of the town took place, as has been related, in 1799, but it was not until nineteen years later that the official intimation came from the then Government that the honour was confirmed. So much for the attention paid to the British Army a century or more ago.

Soon after the taking of Seringapatam Sir Arthur Wellesley was again called upon for active service. The Maharatta chiefs were already a growing power in Central India. Holkar at Indore, the Gaekwar of Baroda, Scindia, and the Peishwa were the leaders. In 1800 they were not on the best of terms with each other. Scindia, the head and front of the Maharatta confederacy, had a well-disciplined army under European officers. Holkar was scarcely less powerful either in wealth or in fighting force, but the interests of some of the chiefs conflicted seriously. Holkar and Scindia fell out and the latter joined by the Peishwa was finally defeated. The Peishwa made terms with the British Government in the Treaty of Bassein in 1802. Scindia nettled, prepared for war after making his peace with Holkar and the Rajah of Berar. When requested by Wellesley to explain his preparations, also to what he objected in the Treaty of Bassein, Scindia prevaricated. In a few days, however, he marched to attack the Nizam of Hyderabad.

Early in 1803 Wellesley took the field for the Maharatta campaign. Greatly to the disappointment of his own Regiment, the 33rd were allotted most of the time to the reserve.

In a very brief time Wellesley soon had Scindia suing for peace. Though the campaign had been a short one it was far from an easy one. The seat of war, it was written, " had extended over the continent of India, exhibited in the space of four months as many general battles, eight regular sieges, and storming of fortresses, without including that of Gwalior . . . in all of which British valour prevailed over accumulated obstacles, the combination of formidable powers, and every advantage arising from local position, military means, and numerical strength."

Thus was the future conqueror of Napoleon gaining the experience which later he put to such masterly account. For their part the 33rd had gained the hard-won battle honours of Mysore and Seringapatam.

In 1806 Sir Arthur Wellesley, who for thirteen years had been Lieut.-Colonel commanding the 33rd Regiment, was appointed its Colonel-in-Chief. He succeeded Lord Cornwallis, a distinguished soldier and administrator who had died shortly after being appointed Governor-General of India. Within seven years, Sir Arthur Wellesley—subsequent to his victories in Spain—was created Marquis of Wellesley and appointed Colonel of the Royal Horse Guards. Within ten years the world was ringing with the name of Wellington. Napoleon had risked and lost Waterloo. The glory of that epoch-making victory had been added to the Battle Honours of the 33rd Regiment.

For some forty years after Waterloo Europe was at peace. Then came the Crimean War with Russia. In the meantime in September, 1852, the " Iron Duke " had died. " Alma," " Inkerman," " Sevastopol " were added to the Regimental Battle Honours by the 33rd. Ten years after the death of the " Iron Duke," the turn of events in Prussia brought an unknown diplomatist, Herr von Bismarck-Schönhaussen, better known to the world as Bismarck, to the head of the Prussian Ministry.[1] The rise of modern Germany had begun. Bismarck—as everybody knows—was the maker of modern Germany, chiefly by means of two epoch-making wars. The first of these wars was against Austria in 1866, the second against France in 1870. That Bismarck by his policy was directly responsible for the Great War in 1914 few persons are likely to insist. But we may fairly date the commencement of a European situation which eventually brought about that war from the vindictive peace of 1870.

From the Crimean War to the outbreak of the South African War a series of campaigns occupied the British Army. In only one of them, that in Abyssinia, did the 33rd take part. It was while the 33rd Regiment was once more in India, to where they had gone in 1875, that the Army Order of July, 1881, was issued. By this order the Territorial system of linked battalions came into force. Under Article XVII of the order the 33rd Regiment became linked with the 76th under the then title of

The Halifax Regiment
(Duke of Wellington's).

Almost immediately the designation was altered to " 1st Battalion of the Duke of Wellington's (West Riding Regiment)."

---

[1] *Germany*, Professor Gooch.

PLATE 2

Wellington.

CHAPTER II

1st BATTALION, 1900–1923: SOUTH AFRICA. YORK. INDIA. PALESTINE. CONSTANTINOPLE. IRELAND.

THE war in South Africa of 1899–1902 was yet another milestone on the direct route to the Great War of 1914, for it can hardly be denied that from the date of the Kaiser's "Kruger" telegram that catastrophe became only a matter of opportunity.

It was in December, 1899, at Aldershot, that mobilization orders were received for the 1st Battalion to proceed to South Africa. Under command of Lieut.-Colonel G. E. Lloyd, D.S.O., 1013 officers and men embarked at Southampton. Lieut.-Colonel Lloyd lost his life in November, 1900, during Maj.-General Paget's attack on the Boer General B. Viljoen at Rhenoster Kop. Lieut.-Colonel P. Rivett-Carnac succeeded to the command and under him the 1st Battalion went through the remainder of the war until June, 1902.

After landing at Southampton from South Africa in August, 1902, the 1st Battalion was quartered at York. There, temporarily at any rate, it exchanged the excitement of war for the somewhat humdrum contentment of peace. In April, 1903, the King's South African medals with clasps were presented by Lieut.-General Sir Thomas Kelly-Kenny, K.C.B., under whom the Battalion had fought at Paardeberg. In September of the same year the Battalion was selected to perform a recruiting march through the 33rd Regimental District Area, and in accordance with a general and special idea left York under the command of Lieut.-Colonel P. Rivett-Carnac.

As an example of the value of territorial traditions such marches in the immediate presence of local associations are of great value. The detailed account of the few days spent in marching through the West Riding fully emphasizes this. Even such a trivial incident as the carrying during the march of the traditional "Havercakes" tends to Regimental *esprit de corps*, for it cements territorial feeling. As all the West Riding of Yorkshire knows, the "Havercake" is an oatmeal fritter, oval in shape, about a foot across the widest part, thin, excellent eating, and peculiar to the district. As previously remarked, a couple of hundred years ago it was a custom for the Recruiting Sergeants of the Regiment to scatter these cakes around as they went through Sowerby,

Huddersfield, Halifax, and adjacent districts. Others relate that they carried the " Havercakes " stuck on their sword points presumably to attract the hungry Yorkshireman. Their cry in broad Yorkshire was, " Have a cake, lad ? " whence came the Regimental nickname of " Havercake Lads."

Before reaching Huddersfield on this march, and in order to reproduce the old custom, the Colours were uncased and flew gallantly in the breeze. Each Colour-Sergeant carried a cake stuck on his bayonet at the slope, and a couple of smart drummer boys were told off to distribute others. To a very great extent tradition has made the British Army what it is, and the Duke of Wellington's Regiment has always been great in the observance of traditions.

The ordinary routine of barrack life in England varies little excepting as regards the particular " quarter " a regiment may be occupying. York has the well-deserved reputation of being one of the best " quarters " any regiment could desire. Though war training may seem impossible for troops occupying such a centre, the change from Fulford Barracks to Strensall Camp is easily made. Both Brigade and Battalion training as well as musketry are carried out at Strensall, and the transfer from York is a welcome break in the year's routine.

At York, in the case of both officers and men, the lighter side of soldiering at home is well cared for. Sport nowadays is recognized as not the least valuable portion of a soldier's training. It has lately been said by an eminent politician that nothing is more valuable than sport to teach men the highest virtues necessary to excel in the great adventure of life. And this because it teaches a man to play the game of life. For soldiers his words might well have been extended to cover the other and to them more familiar adventure of death. For in war those most ready to give their lives are most likely to " play the game " in the true spirit of victory.

At York every variety of sport is to be found. From the comparatively inexpensive amusements of cricket and football—the latter always a favourite in both Battalions—to hunting, racing, and shooting, only possible to those blessed with the means for enjoying them.

While at York on September 20th, 1904, the ceremony of the unveiling of the South African War Memorial took place. In the beautiful and historic Minster was dedicated the Memorial to those of the Duke of Wellington's Regiment who gave their lives in the service of their country.

The ceremony was performed by Lieut.-General Sir Thomas Kelly-Kenny, G.C.B., late commanding the 6th Division South African Field Force, under whom the Battalion had fought in more than one severe engagement. Little could any one in that numerous gathering foresee the future and far more awful sacrifices that would shortly be demanded. The Memorial was erected on the wall of the south transept and was subscribed for by past and present officers, warrant, non-commissioned officers, and men of the Regiment and by many friends. It is a work in alabaster, brass, and bronze, and embodies the names of all those who sacrificed themselves for King and country.

1st BATTALION AT YORK, 1904

Above the names on the Memorial is the following inscription :[1]—

"The Duke of Wellington's West Riding Regiment.
To the memory of the officers,
Non-commissioned officers, and
men of the Regiment who lost
their lives during the South
African War, 1899–1902.

Lloyd, G. E.   Lieutenant-Colonel, C.B., D.S.O.
Harris, O.   Major
Wallis, A. F.   Captain
Turner, N. G. H.   Captain
Siordet, F. J.   Lieutenant
Tyler, A. J.   Lieutenant

Moore, R. D.	Col.-Sergeant	2302	Worsnop. Lance-Sergeant	4781
Cook, R.	Sergeant	3619	Hall, F. Lance-Sergeant	5500
Cadman, J.	Sergeant	3520	Newman, G. Corporal	4743
Hill, W.	Sergeant	2709	Finigan, T. Corporal	1199
Cadmore, W.	Sergeant	3294	Hall, B. Corporal	4661
Taylor, J.	Sergeant	4133	Finnigan, E. Corporal	2923
Marks, R.	Sergeant	4868	Mortan, W. Corporal	4774
McGovern, F.	Sergeant	2437	Farrer, G. Corporal	2906
Garney, W.	Sergeant	4737	Cunningham, J. Corporal	2925 "

In addition to the above are the names of 116 Lance-Corporals and Privates, also of one Sergeant and 9 Privates Active Service Companies, volunteers.

Following the names are the lines :—

"Erected by Officers, Non-Commissioned Officers
and Men Past and Present of the two Battalions
(33rd–76th) and by friends of the Regiment."

Other memorials to the gallant dead had already been erected at Pretoria, Winburg (O.R.C.), Rhenoster Kop where Colonel Lloyd[2] was buried, and Bloemfontein. Besides the monuments mentioned hardly a grave has been left unrecognised, even out on the veldt where fell the gallant fellows who could not be moved for interment in any cemetery. On the battlefield of Paardeberg a fine

---

[1] The Memorial has since been transferred to the Regimental Memorial Chapel.

[2] Colonel Lloyd's death was a great loss to the Regiment. His one thought was the efficiency of the battalion and the welfare and happiness of everybody belonging to it. He had won the admiration and even affection of every Officer, non-commissioned officer and private, and will never be forgotten by those who served under him. He never spared himself.

cairn is erected. At Winburg (O.R.C.) the monument takes the form of an obelisk nine feet in height, standing in the local cemetery. Stones have been placed over the graves of those men of the Burma M.I. (2nd Battalion the Duke of Wellington's) who fell at Aliwal N. and at Maitland Cemetery (Cape Colony). At Boshof to the memory of Captain Coode, D.S.O., a granite obelisk has been erected. At Bath, in the parish church, a brass tablet has been placed dedicated to the memory of Private Wilmot, one of the little band of M.I. which did such valuable work in the campaign.

While at York Lieut.-Colonel P. T. Rivett-Carnac completed his period in command of a Battalion. He was succeeded on promotion by Lieut.-Colonel H. D. Thorold. Major C. V. Humphrys became second-in-command.

In the summer of 1905 Battle Honours earned in South Africa were presented by Lady Rundle to the Battalion. The silk scrolls to be sewn on the Regimental Colours were:—

> South Africa 1900–02
> Relief of Kimberley
> Paardeberg.

After presentation, crowned with the symbolical laurel wreaths, the Colours were trooped.

The latter portion of the Battalion's stay at York included various ceremonial parades. These, if of no other benefit, were an opportunity for a display of Regimental efficiency—outwardly at any rate—to a public then curiously ignorant of all matters connected with the inner life of its soldiers. That a well-turned-out man on parade is usually a good soldier is almost a military truism. Few who know will disagree with the statement that much of the fighting efficiency and continued military spirit of all ranks in the Great War was due to the unceasing insistence, wherever possible, on strict personal smartness and cleanliness, and so of increased physical fitness.

In July, 1905, His Majesty the King visited Sheffield and Manchester, upon which two occasions the Battalion was on duty, in the first case lining the streets, in the second forming a Guard of Honour to His Majesty.

When Field-Marshal Earl Roberts, V.C., visited York in order to unveil the Yorkshire South African War Memorial erected near the Minster, the Battalion also provided the Guard of Honour.

In October, 1905, the 1st Battalion left York for India, Lieut.-Colonel H. D. Thorold in command. Previous to embarkation at Southampton the usual " details " under Capt. K. A. Macleod were transferred to Lichfield to join the 2nd Battalion on its arrival from India. On the voyage to India the two Battalions passed in mid-ocean. A somewhat unusual experience. The 2nd Battalion had embarked for England from Calcutta and near Ceylon the two met.

Upon reaching Bombay the 1st Battalion transhipped on board the Royal Indian Marine Steamship *Hardinge* for Calcutta. After being encamped there for some days the Battalion started by train for Seikna, thence by route march to

Lebong. Leaving the train at Seikna the Battalion proceeded by route march to Tindaria 3000 feet up, to Kurseong, to Sonada, and so to Lebong. Here the details left behind by the 2nd Battalion joined the 1st.

Life at an ordinary hill-station in India, if healthy, is usually a dull one, especially for the rank and file. As far as military training is concerned there is opportunity for scouts in hill-climbing, but for musketry, the one thing in which British troops have usually excelled any other nation, there is little scope.

Hockey, soccer, cricket, and boxing helped in keeping all ranks fit, but " the delights " of Darjeeling, as seen by the British soldier, were not inaptly described at the time in the following doggerel lines :—

LIFE AT LEBONG

By Thomas Atkins.

1

They say in an Indian 'ill station
   You all 'ave a clinkin' good time ;
But I don't think Darjeelin's so cushy ;
   I'll try and describe it in rhyme.

2

In the first place we're not in Darjeelin',
   But way down t'Khad at Lebong,
It's only a thousand feet climb up,
   But it seems about twenty miles long !

3

You're sweatin' and puffin' and blowin'
   Before you've got 'alf way there,
And you 'ave to unbotton your tunic,
   And wipe the muck sweat off your 'air.

4

There aint much to do up there neither ;
   There isn't a pub anywhere :
And as for the nursemaids, lor' love me !
   They drives you to utter despair.

Though the above lines seem to have reflected the feelings of the Battalion, yet it was while still under the somewhat depressing influence of Lebong that the " Dukes " began their wonderful series of successes in first-class football in India.

As all the Anglo-Saxon world is aware, the first Duke of Wellington is reported to have said " that the Battle of Waterloo was won on the playing-fields of Eton." By which he meant to imply that the training in teamwork found in school games is the finest training for war either as leader or follower any man can have. We may be sure that the "Iron Duke" would have had words of high commendation for those of his old Regiment who were ready to undergo the intensive training necessary to establish the wonderful record they did at Rugby-football in India.

The "Calcutta" Cup, which ranks as the premier Rugby-football trophy, was first won, as mentioned, by the 2nd Battalion in 1903 and 1905. And if we take these victories into consideration we have the unique record of the Duke of Wellington's Regiment winning the Calcutta tournament nine years out of the ten they entered for it. A remarkable record of which any Regiment might well be proud. In addition, the 1st Battalion won the Cup at Bombay six times, and at Madras on seven occasions.

The following is the complete football record of the Regiment from 1903-1913:—

CALCUTTA CUP RECORD

INDIA

1903. 2nd Battalion beat Madras (2nd round).
　　　　　　　　　　,,　　　,,　the Welch Regiment (semi-final).
　　　　　　　　　　,,　　　,,　the Calcutta F.C. (final).
1904　　　　　　　　,,　　　,,　City (1st round).
　　　　　　　　　　,,　　　lost to the King's Own Regiment (semi-final).
1905　　　　　　　　,,　　　beat Calcutta F.C. (1st round).
　　　　　　　　　　,,　　　,,　the Gloucestershire Regiment (semi-final).
　　　　　　　　　　,,　　　,,　the King's Own Regiment (final).
1906. 1st Battalion beat the Somersetshire Regiment (1st round).
　　　　　　　　　　,,　　　,,　the Gloucestershire Regiment (semi-final).
　　　　　　　　　　,,　　　,,　United Services (final).
1907　　　　　　　　,,　　　,,　　,,　　,,　(2nd round).
　　　　　　　　　　,,　　　,,　the Gloucestershire Regiment (final).
1908　　　　　　　　,,　　　,,　Calcutta F.C. (2nd round).
　　　　　　　　　　,,　　　,,　the Highland Light Infantry (semi-final).
　　　　　　　　　　,,　　　,,　the Gloucestershire Regiment (final).
1909　　　　　　　　,,　　　,,　United Services (2nd round).
　　　　　　　　　　,,　　　,,　South Behar F.C. (semi-final).
　　　　　　　　　　,,　　　,,　Calcutta F.C. (final).
1910　　　　　　　　,,　　　,,　Dalhousie F.C. (1st round).
　　　　　　　　　　,,　　　,,　the Shropshire Light Infantry Regiment (2nd round).
　　　　　　　　　　,,　　　,,　Calcutta F.C. (semi-final).
　　　　　　　　　　,,　　　,,　Madras F.C. (final).
1911　　　　　　　　,,　　　,,　Calcutta F.C. (1st round).
　　　　　　　　　　,,　　　,,　Rifle Brigade (semi-final).
　　　　　　　　　　,,　　　,,　United Services (final).

1912. 1st Battalion beat the Leicestershire Regiment (semi-final).
" " Calcutta F.C. (final).
1913 " " Calcutta F.C. (final).
1914. Owing to the outbreak of the Great War the Calcutta Cup was not competed for by the Battalion.

In 1907, 1908, 1909, 1910, 1911, and 1913 the 1st Battalion won the Bombay Cup, losing in 1912. In 1906 they also won the Madras Cup.

That the " dour " Yorkshire spirit had a good deal to do with this unique list of victories is probably the case. In 1912 the Battalion team had a very hard struggle, having to meet the " Leicesters " four times in the semi-final before qualifying for the final round. To show their appreciation of the sportsmanlike methods of the " Duke's " football team, enthusiasts in Calcutta presented the Battalion with two handsome cups.

Nor was the physical test the only one in which the 1st Battalion made such a mark. In musketry the Duke of Wellington's were equally prominent, having won the Sirhind Rifle Meeting Challenge Cup three years in succession, in 1911, 1912, and 1913.

While still at Lebong it is interesting to recall that the Battalion was inspected by the late Field-Marshal Earl Kitchener, K.G.

In November, 1906, three companies of the 1st Battalion left Lebong for Sitapur, while the following month three more proceeded to Calcutta to take part in the Minto Centenary Fête.

Hardly was the Battalion once more assembled as a unit than four companies proceeded under orders to Ranikhet to occupy the standing camp.

While at Sitapur the distinction "Corunna" was approved by His Majesty the King in recognition of services, and was permitted to be borne upon the Regimental Colours. In the autumn of 1908 the 1st Battalion moved up country to Ambala, where winter training upon modern lines was once more feasible. Polo and Ambala are in India synonymous terms, and the Battalion polo team had plenty of good practice there.

In December, 1908, Lieut.-Colonel and Bt. Colonel H. D. Thorold, on completion of his period of service in command, retired on retired pay. Major C. V. Humphrys succeeded to the Lieut.-Colonelcy and was posted to the 1st Battalion on December 8th, 1908.

In March, 1910, the Battalion was again split up, four companies with Headquarters marching up to Solon, a little hill-station on the road to Simla. In spite of the somewhat dispersed quarters of the Battalion during its first five years in India it was earning, as the following comments show, excellent reports. The G.O.C. Northern Army said of it: " A fine, smart, and eminently satisfactory Battalion with plenty of go and *esprit de corps*"; while the G.O.C. Lahore Division reported it to be " a fine Battalion—well commanded—plenty of *esprit de corps*. Health good. Fit for active service."

Wintering in Ambala, the following summer was again spent in the hills at

Solon, but in November, 1911, a welcome change came with the order for the Battalion to move to Delhi, there to take part in the Coronation Durbar of the King-Emperor. At Delhi the 1st Duke of Wellington's Regiment formed part of the 9th Infantry Brigade of the 3rd Division. During the Durbar the Battalion was selected to give a display for their Majesties at the Military Tournament. On another occasion it furnished the King-Emperor's guard and escort.

In February, 1912, Lieut.-Colonel F. A. Hayden, D.S.O., completed his service in command of the 2nd Battalion and Major W. M. Watson was promoted to Lieut.-Colonel in his place. As Lieut.-Colonel C. V. Humphrys had been appointed Commandant Central School of Musketry at Pachmari in March, Lieut.-Colonel W. M. Watson was transferred to command of the 1st Battalion and Major J. A. C. Gibbs was promoted Lieut.-Colonel in place of Lieut.-Colonel C V. Humphrys.

After the Delhi Durbar the Battalion returned to Ambala and for the hot season was once more at Solon. In November, 1912, Northern Army Manœuvres took place in the vicinity of Paniput, where the 3rd War Division, of which the 9th Brigade formed part, concentrated. The 1st Battalion returned from the manœuvres to Ambala, covering a record distance of one hundred miles in five days. Once again did the little hill-station of Solon claim the Battalion for the hot weather of 1913, after which, in October, it proceeded to Lahore, where the cold weather of 1913-1914 was spent. In April, 1914, Headquarters and four companies entrained for Rawalpindi *en route* to the Murree Hills. Lower Gharial was the Battalion's quarters during the hot weather and a pleasant time was naturally expected in these beautiful surroundings. But the peaceful summer sojourn was rudely broken by the outbreak of the Great War.

In August Headquarters and two companies returned to Lahore, while two other companies were despatched to Ferozepore, where they remained until rejoining Headquarters in December. In October two further companies had been ordered for garrison duty at Amritzar, where they stayed until December.

To the gratification of all ranks, in the King's Birthday Gazette of 1914, the Colonel of the Regiment received promotion to the rank of K.C.B.

"Order of the Bath—Military Division.

The King has been graciously pleased to give orders for the following promotion in the Honourable Order of the Bath :—

K.C.B., Lieutenant-General Herbert Eversley Belfield, C.B., D.S.O., Retired Pay, Colonel, The Duke of Wellington's (West Riding Regiment)."

In order to understand rightly the military and political situation in India, prior to and during the Great War, it is advisable to outline, briefly, the course of events in India from the date of the arrival of the 1st Battalion in 1905.

The revolutionary feeling which permeated the inhabitants of that country had been growing stronger and stronger. Since British rule began the white garrison in India has ever been the deciding factor between peace and anarchy. Unless we understand the political situation in modern India the use and value of its white garrison may easily be under-estimated.

When the 1st Battalion began its tour of service in India in 1905 the whole land was seething with political unrest. The partition of Bengal by the Marquis Curzon of Kedleston, then Viceroy, had given rise to a boycott of British goods and to the "Swadeshi" movement; later on, in 1908, to a revolutionary crusade against the British Government, followed by "Passive Resistance" and by "non-Co-operation."

In April, 1908, political India was startled by a dastardly bomb outrage committed by supporters of the revolutionary movement in Bengal. In itself, historically, hardly worth mentioning, this incident marks the beginning of the attempt at an Indian "reign of terror" akin to that of the French Revolution. Two European ladies, wife and daughter of a leading pleader of the Mozufferpore Bar, Mr. Pringle Kennedy, were brutally murdered. What caused such an overwhelming feeling in the case of this particular outrage was the fact that the bomb was intended for someone else.

Mr. Kingsford, at the time Presiding Magistrate of Calcutta, had become obnoxious to the revolutionaries and it was his murder which had actually been planned. The cry of self-government for India was in full swing in 1909. In 1910 Viscount Hardinge succeeded the Marquis Curzon (as he later became) in the Viceroyalty.

In 1911, as already stated, the King-Emperor's Durbar was held at Delhi. Not long afterwards, in 1912, as if to show the futility of a sympathetic handling of Indian discontent, came the dastardly attempt upon the life of the Viceroy. That the true position of affairs in India when war broke out in 1914—as in Ireland—ought to have been well known to the war-party in Germany seems only natural. Yet nothing could have been further from the real truth than the information upon which Germany acted in the case of both India and Ireland. In these two cases it was supposed that a general rising to drive out the hated rulers was merely a matter of intensive propaganda. In Ireland with the addition of a shipload of arms, Sir Roger Casement's landing was expected to start the long-desired rebellion. In India, German spies were equally sure of a result. The failure must have been as galling to those concerned as the failure in Ireland. Few persons, not excepting many well acquainted with India, would have prophesied the extraordinary response made during the war to British recruiting appeals. Even the unwarlike Bengalees answered the stirring call made to them. What the rejoinder to these appeals from the warlike races of India was during those four fateful years, history will always thankfully recall. Later the local situation altered. In his extremely informing book, *India*, Sir Valentine Chirol has written : " Had the war ended within two years all would have been well, but in India even the strongest waves of emotion are apt to subside suddenly. . . . The politicians of the extremist wing were the first to give any signs of impatience as time passed without any practical attempt in England to give effect to Mr. Asquith's promise of ' a new angle of vision.' " As will shortly be described, the post-war position in India became only too serious.

Such was the political, and in a sense the military situation in India when the war broke out in 1914. At the end of that year the 1st Battalion had been moved from Lahore to Sialkote, 16 officers and 773 other ranks strong. Hardly had quarters been taken over than in December the Battalion received orders to mobilize and two companies were sent for garrison duty to Rawalpindi. On January 1st, 1915, the four-company organization as a permanent measure in Battalions of British Infantry on the Indian Establishment took effect. In the summer of 1915, owing to trouble with Mohmand tribes on the frontier, the Battalion, under Lieut.-Colonel W. M. Watson, moved up to Peshawar. As the Peshawar Division was considered equal to dealing with the tribesmen the 1st Battalion only remained a month at Peshawar, returning therefrom to Sialkote. The Mohmands are a powerful and well-armed tribe of some 22,000 fighting men.

In December, 1915, Lieut.-Colonel W. M. Watson was appointed temporary Brigade-Commander to command the Rawalpindi (Infantry) Brigade. Major R. E. Maffett assumed Command of the Battalion *vice* Lieut.-Colonel W. M. Watson.

In March, 1916, Lieut.-Colonel (temporary Brig.-General) W. M. Watson was promoted Colonel, and Lieut.-Colonel R. E. Maffett was posted to 1st Battalion on promotion. In April, 1917, the Battalion left Sialkote to be stationed at Rawalpindi, moving on once again in May to the hills at Gharial. In August, after a brief stay in the hills, a wing of the Regiment was ordered back to Rawalpindi by route march, thence to Lahore. In November, Battalion Headquarters proceeded to Rawalpindi and afterwards to Burhan Camp, near Attock. Until the date of the Armistice the Battalion remained either at Rawalpindi or Gharial until in March, 1919, it proceeded to Quetta.

Capt. (acting Major) E. C. Boutflower had been promoted acting Lieut.-Colonel while commanding the Battalion *vice* Lieut.-Colonel R. E. Maffett vacated. Hardly had quarters been taken over than the 1st Battalion was ordered back to Lahore for special duty in aid of the civil power in connection with the disturbances then taking place in the Punjaub.

While the war had continued its long-drawn-out course events in India were moving towards a crisis.[1] " In the lurid after-glow of the Great War " the non-Co-operation movement already referred to, gathered deadly force under " Mahatma " Gandhi's persuasive efforts. The revolutionary spirit spread throughout India and when in April, 1919, Gandhi proclaimed his complete *hartal* (abstention from all ordinary business)—practically an anti-British boycott—the match was put to the train. The situation has aptly been described as the most serious since the date of the Indian Mutiny. Commencing in Delhi, collisions between the rioters and the police took place. In Bombay and Ahmadabad, as well as all over the Punjaub, the *hartal* " became the signal for

[1] *India.* Sir Valentine Chirol.

wholesale rioting with pillage and arson, and in some cases murderous outrages on Englishmen and even on Englishwomen, and the movement assumed the undeniable character of an organized revolt against the British Raj."

Then followed the historical " Amritzar " outbreak with its brutal murders of Englishmen and General Dyer's prompt action, the only chance, as he considered, for the restoration of law and order throughout India.

That General Dyer acted in good faith few even among those who abhorred his action will deny. Opinions amongst Englishmen will, probably, always differ as to the necessity for the steps he thought fit to take.

While acting in aid of the civil authorities at Lahore the conflagration which might have spread throughout India was steadily smouldering. The particular duty allotted to the " Dukes " was to prevent any attempt on the part of the native mob issuing from Lahore native city. It was also called in to picket by day and at night the exits from the city and various gates.

On May 15th orders were received for the Battalion to proceed to Quetta, so the following day it left Lahore in two parties to join the 11th Infantry Brigade for service against Afghanistan.

On arriving at Sibi, information was received that the Battalion would proceed to Chaman. Halting at Quetta to take over service ammunition, tentage, mobilization stores, etc., the Battalion in two portions reached Chaman on May 19th and 20th. Lieut.-Colonel E. C. Boutflower was in command.

On May 25th orders were issued from 4th Division that Fort Spin Baldack, situated mid-way between Quetta and Kandahar and some 10 miles north of Chaman, was to be attacked and captured. The Battalion left Chaman early on May 27th to join the General Reserve: 18 British officers and 450 other ranks. Lieut.-Colonel E. C. Boutflower commanded the General Reserve. Major R. H. W. Owen commanded the Battalion. The first assault, after an advance across the open by A and B Companies as firing-line and supports, C and D as local reserves, took place on Tower Hill. This hill was very steep, without any cover, and crowned by a wall 15 feet high. It had three stone towers on it which had been smashed by artillery fire, and the wall had been breached in two places. The hill stood 200 feet above the level of the plain. The breaches had to be climbed. One man at a time, those following were in turn pulled up each man by a comrade. After clearing Tower Hill of the enemy the Battalion then cleared the Fort and another hill where sungars had been built and occupied, and from whence the enemy were eventually bombed by a party under 2nd Lieut. F. L. Foster. The Fort was also cleared, chiefly by bombing in which Sergt. Griffiths distinguished himself. That evening the Battalion returned to Chaman.

From June 1st to July 14th the troops at Chaman constructed the Chaman outer defence line, which consisted of a series of 18 lunettes with supporting strong points in rear. The lunettes were 1000 yards apart with nearly half a mile to each supporting point. The whole perimeter was strongly wired. As the work was done during June and July with a daily average temperature of

20 HISTORY OF THE DUKE OF WELLINGTON'S REGIMENT

105 degrees in the shade, the troops were somewhat highly tried. The enemy were expected to attack during the night of June 2nd/3rd but no attack matured.

On August 8th information was received that peace had been made with the Afghan delegates, and on September 13th the Battalion returned by rail to Quetta.

In the autumn of 1919, on October 17th, orders were received that the Battalion would be reduced to a " Cadre " and that it would then proceed to Palestine, where the " Cadre " would join the Battalion. On November 20th,

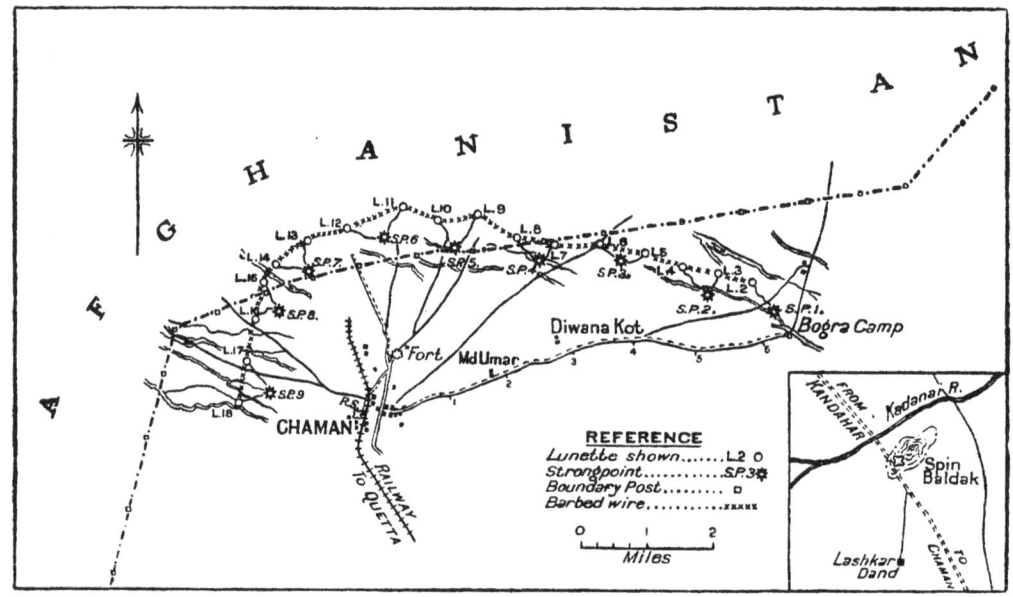

CHAMAN DEFENCE LINE

1919, 7 officers, 3 warrant officers, and 86 other ranks left Quetta for Karachi, preparatory to embarking. But it was not till January 15th, 1920, that the embarkation took place, the intermediate weeks having been spent in a Rest Camp.

In December, 1919, the following Special Divisional Order had been published :—

" On the occasion of the departure of the 1st Battalion The Duke of Wellington's Regiment the G.O.C. 4th (Quetta) Division, Lt.-General R. Wapshare, C.B., C.S.I., desires to record his high appreciation of the efficiency and good conduct of the Battalion during the period that it has been under his command. Though the exigencies of war have ordained that the Battalion should form part of the obligatory garrison of India, and should not take part in any of the major theatres of operations, the G.O.C. observes that it has rendered very valuable services to the Empire. The Battalion took part in the

Afghan operations and distinguished itself in an exemplary manner. The Battalion has trained and despatched numbers of fine drafts for active service overseas. The high standard of military efficiency and splendid soldierly spirit has remained unimpaired in spite of the Battalion's long period of service abroad.

The G.O.C. wishes Lt.-Col. E. C. Boutflower, his officers, and all ranks good luck and every success in the future."

The tour of the 1st Battalion in India was marked by the passing of events as serious to our prestige as any in the history of British India. It is as well to remind ourselves of what the effect might have been had India—in spite of universal unrest—not remained at heart loyal to the British Raj.

How loyally the 1st Battalion taxed itself to supply the wants of the 2nd Battalion in France, also of other units elsewhere, the following list serves to show. Nor does it include the services of numerous N.C.O.'s and men.

A peculiar example of the extraordinary versatility of the war services performed may be gathered from that of C.S.M. R. Grady. This much-travelled N.C.O. came to France in 1914 with an Indian Contingent—returned to India—then went out to Mesopotamia with the Northumberland Fusiliers—crossed Persia, to land up finally at Baku on the Caspian Sea. Another of those who had an equally wide experience was R.S.M. Matthews.

OFFICERS WHO WENT FROM THE 1ST BATTALION IN INDIA TO FIGHTING FRONTS ELSEWHERE DURING 1914–1918

Major J. H. P. Wilson.	Killed in France, 1917, as Lieut.-Colonel.
Major W. E. Maples.	Killed in Mesopotamia in 1917, as Lieut.-Colonel.
Major E. M. Liddell.	Wounded in France, 1917, as Lieut.-Colonel.
Major A. A. St. Hill.	Killed in Italy, 1918, as Lieut.-Colonel.
Major R. M. Tidmarsh.	To 2nd Battalion in France.
Major F. H. B. Wellesley.	Wounded in France, 1917.
Major M. V. le P. Trench.	Invalided from France as Lieut.-Colonel.
Major H. W. Glenn.	To France, acting Lieut.-Colonel.
Major A. G. Horsfall.	Killed in France, 1917, as Lieut.-Colonel commanding 2nd Battalion.
Major P. A. Turner.	To 2nd Battalion. Later Brigade Commander. Wounded in France, 1916.
Capt. W. G. Officer.	Wounded in France, 1917.
Lieut. E. G. Gatacre.	Killed in France.
Lieut.-Colonel W. M. Watson.	Brig.-General Rawalpindi Brigade, India.
Lieut. M. N. Cox.	Wounded in France.
Lieut. R. A. Scott.	Depot Halifax.
Lieut. G. T. Fleming.	To Mesopotamia as Adjutant, Territorial Brigade.
Lieut. C. Wheeler.	To Mesopotamia, R.C.S.
Lieut. J. M. Tidmarsh.	Killed while flying.
Lieut. A. Walker.	Killed in France, 1918.

At the early stages of the Great War in 1914 only eight British Battalions remained to garrison the whole country. And not only to maintain law and order in India but as the sole stiffening against any attack from across her northern frontiers. By January, 1915, fresh British troops to the number of 39 field-artillery batteries and 45 infantry battalions of Territorial troops had been despatched to reinforce the depleted garrison. Later on these in turn were augmented by the inclusion of 18 " Garrison Battalions," all of which came to India between November, 1915, and March, 1917. To these various units the nation may be said to owe a particular debt of gratitude. Originally they had volunteered hoping for employment at the front in Europe. During these four epoch-making years they stood, in Asia, for ultimate peace and security.

Disembarking at Suez on January 26th, 1920, the Cadre of the 1st Battalion, strength 5 officers, 5 warrant officers, and 73 other ranks, under command of Lieut.-Colonel E. C. Boutflower, entrained for Kantara Rest Camp. Early in the following month they proceeded to Ludd *en route* to Surafend.

On February 6th the foreign service details under command of Major R. M. Tidmarsh joined the Cadre from Bir Salem, 31 officers and 908 other ranks.

Later in the same month Lieut.-Colonel R. E. Maffett was placed on the half-pay list upon completing his period of service in command. He was succeeded by Major and Bt. Lieut.-Colonel R. K. Healing, promoted Lieut.-Colonel.

During the stay of the 1st Battalion at Surafend it was twice called upon to provide field service detachments for Jerusalem, thus widening the already somewhat extended scope of its services abroad. The following awards were gazetted at this period for services rendered in India: Capt. (temporary Lieut.-Colonel) E. C. Boutflower, O.B.E. Q.M. Sergt. A. P. Downey, Sergt. E. Lambert, Sergt. J. Palmer, Sergt. B. Coates, Sergt. J. Feather, Pte. (acting Sergt.) R. Drake, the Meritorious Service Medal.

In May, 1921, the 1st Battalion, under command of Major R. M. Tidmarsh, moved from Surafend in Palestine to Cairo, where they took up quarters at Abbassia. Thence, the same month, in two portions the Battalion embarked for England. In June the Battalion took up quarters at Tidworth, where in July Lieut.-Colonel R. K. Healing joined it. In September, 1921, the Duke of Wellington's Regiment suffered a severe loss by the retirement on account of ill health, contracted on active service, of Lieut.-Colonel R. N. Bray, C.M.G., D.S.O. of the 2nd Battalion. During eighteen months in France, as related elsewhere, he had led the 2nd Battalion in many a stubborn fight, never sparing himself, and had well earned and had received the command of a Brigade. Since the end of the war Colonel Bray had not enjoyed the best of health. He died on October 23rd, 1921, and, as truly as if he had been killed on active service, his life was laid down for his country.

After a brief summer at Tidworth a move was made in October to Ireland. There, after an equally short stay at the Curragh in January, 1922, the 1st Battalion found themselves once more at Tidworth. Strength: 18 officers and 672, under command of Major F. H. B. Wellesley.

Lieut.-Colonel Healing had been placed temporarily on half-pay on account of ill health, but in April was well enough to embark with the Battalion for Gibraltar. Early in 1923 the Battalion was sent on to Constantinople, where it arrived in February to augment the British forces then in Turkey. Its quarters were at Bostandjik. It has lately been written by one well-qualified to speak,[1] that "in all the coloured Romance of History there is hardly a story so illustrative of the mutability of human affairs, so fantastic, so dramatic, as that of Turkey during the last eight years." Nor was the period during which the Allied occupation of Constantinople took place by any means the least dramatic. The same authority goes on to state " that the Near East, torn into strips, waited placidly to have its future decided. A great opportunity was given to the Allies, but they showed themselves incapable and unworthy of it. The Ottoman Empire, crushed and defeated, begging only for peace and security, lay at their feet, but that by folly and procrastination and by national jealousies the Allies allowed the fruits of success to rot." " Out of the débris of the Ottoman Empire through a thousand difficulties burst a Turkish Nation. As wild and destructive as any volcano newly in eruption, it rent its way out into the open. It suffered the agonies of a fierce war of self-preservation. As the Allies grew disunited and weak, it grew strong and arrogant, until there came the day when with a mailed fist it threatened the peace of the world and dictated its own terms to the impotent Powers."

Whether, in the autumn of 1922, public opinion in the United Kingdom would have stood for a fresh war in Turkey is now a matter of past history. There is, however, little if any doubt that at Chanak and Mudania the Nationalist Turks were putting up a colossal "bluff." Ghazi Mustapha Kemal Pasha's "bluff" was not called: the evacuation took place: and British prestige fell accordingly throughout the whole East.

In September, 1923, the 1st Battalion embarked at Constantinople for home. It arrived at Southampton on October 10th, from whence it proceeded to Gosport, there to be stationed.

In February, 1924, Lieut.-Colonel R. K. Healing completed his period of service in command. He was succeeded by Major, now Lieut.-Colonel, N. G. Burnand, D.S.O.

---

[1] *Turkey in Travail.* By Harold Armstrong, 1925.

CHAPTER III

HISTORICAL OUTLINE OF EARLY YEARS OF 2ND BATTALION, 1881–1893: THE AMALGAMATION OF 1881. PREVIOUS REGIMENTS UNDER THE 76TH NUMBER. INDIA. LIEUT. HON. ARTHUR WESLIE. 76TH UNDER GENERAL LORD LAKE. SERINGAPATAM. BERMUDA, 1886. HALIFAX, N.S. BARBADOS.

TO the British Army and particularly to what were then known as "Infantry of the Line," the year 1881 brought momentous changes. So far in their history the line regiments of the British Army had claimed, and had enjoyed, an individual existence. Regimental records with their glorious past and their invaluable traditions had belonged to them and to them alone; henceforth, these things were to be shared; so it was only to be expected that where two hitherto quite unknown entities were brought together and suddenly ordered to fuse, the experiment could not at once be successful. It was as if two confirmed bachelors, each highly gifted and efficient as men but living entirely different lives, were suddenly called upon to sink their own differences, to fit in their individual idiosyncracies, and to make an effort to understand a personality in which neither had hitherto taken any interest whatsoever.

That the amalgamation was eventually successful was due almost entirely to the good feeling and wonderful *esprit de corps* of the British Army.

On July 4th, 1881, an important General Order appeared in the *London Gazette*. This order was concerned with Army Organization and it contained among other matters the following extract:—

"II. The Infantry of the Line and Militia will in future be organized in Territorial Regiments, each of four Battalions for England, Scotland, and Wales, and of five Battalions for Ireland, the first and second of these being Line Battalions, and the remainder Militia. These Regiments will bear a Territorial designation corresponding to the localities with which they are connected, and the words 'Regimental District' will in future be used in place of 'Sub-District' hitherto employed."

"VIII. *Honours and Distinctions.* All distinctions, mottoes, badges, or devices appearing hitherto in the 'Army List' or on the colours as borne by either of the Line Battalions of a Territorial Regiment, will in future be borne by both these Battalions."

"IX. *The Uniform.* The uniform of all the Battalions of a Territorial Regiment will be the same (except Scotch Militia Battalions). The title of the Regiment will be shown on the shoulder strap."

REGIMENTAL TITLES UPON AMALGAMATION, 1881

"XVII. The following will show the precedence, composition, title, and uniform of the new Territorial Regiments :—

Precedence.	Titles.	Composition.
33rd.	The Halifax Regiment (Duke of Wellington's).	1st Battalion 33rd Foot. 2nd Battalion 76th Foot. 3rd Battalion 6th West Yorks Militia. 4th Battalion 6th West Yorks Militia.

Headquarters of Regimental District.	Uniform.		Pattern of Lace.
	Colour.	Facings.	
Halifax.	Scarlet.	White.	Rose."

Hitherto the 76th Regiment had worn red facings; but under the reorganization scheme, by a stroke of the pen, these were changed to white. Another change brought about by the new grouping of battalions was the substitution for the "Elephant" badge hitherto worn on the caps of officers and men, of the Duke of Wellington's crest with "West Riding Regiment" below it on a scroll. On the helmet the numerals "76th" were replaced by the same crest. Sentiment, a wise leader knows how to make full use of. It has been said of the French that as a nation they can be led by a bunch of white ribbons. We ourselves are fully aware of the sentiment invoked by the meaning of the kilt. Equally strong is the sentiment attached to the peculiar colour of regimental facings.

Under authority of War Office letter of March, 1905, His Majesty the King approved of the resumption by both battalions of the Duke of Wellington's Regiment of red facings.

Previous to the above orders coming into effect, a change appeared in the *London Gazette* :—

"WAR OFFICE,
"PALL MALL,
"1st July, 1881.

"The Queen has been pleased to approve the following changes in the designation of Regiments of Infantry of the Line, which will take effect on and after the 1st July, 1881.

Present Title.	Future Title.
33rd (Duke of Wellington's Regiment).	1st Battalion of the Duke of Wellington's (West Riding Regiment)."

It was in Ireland, where a considerable portion of its home service had been spent, that the 76th Regiment received the new amalgamation order. June 30th, 1881, was the last day, as an individual unit, of the old 76th Regiment. It was at the Curragh that the new Territorial system came into force under which the 76th Regiment became linked with the 33rd as battalions of the Duke of Wellington's Regiment.

It may be of interest to recall events connected with the birth of the original 76th Regiment.[1] Three regiments of foot in succession have been numbered 76th in the British Army.

The first was the 76th Foot, raised in 1756 and commanded by Lord George Forbes, who came from the 2nd Queen's Regiment. This 76th consisted at first of one battalion, and is shown in the Army List as being on the Irish establishment. In all probability most of the officers and men were natives of Ireland. Here, then, is the first, and what may almost be called the Irish 76th.

In October, 1758, a warrant was issued for the sum of £9500 to be advanced, described as subsistence for "2nd Battalion to Lord George Forbes' Regiment, ordered from Ireland to the coast of Africa." This Battalion did not proceed abroad until July, 1760. The strength on embarkation, exclusive of officers, was 24 serjeants, 24 corporals, 18 drummers, and 600 "Private Men." Colonel Worge was in command. From this date the Battalion was formed into a separate corps and known as "Worge's Regiment." It was eventually numbered "86th Foot." It proceeded to Goree on the north-west coast of Africa, presumably in all the glory of red coats and tight-fitting clothes utterly unfitted to such a climate. To add to the discomforts, not to say the horrors of such a trip in those days, a portion of the Battalion was wrecked *en route* on the Barbary coast, where it was held captive by the Moors. The original 76th, Lord George Forbes' 1st Battalion, was again recruited up to two battalions. It served at the siege of Belle Isle in 1761, was present at the taking of Martinique in 1762, and was finally disbanded at the Peace of Versailles in 1763. At the same time Colonel Worge's Regiment was also disbanded.

The next 76th was a regiment raised in 1777 by a well-known Highland nobleman, Lord MacDonald. It was known as "the 76th MacDonald's Highlanders." Major John MacDonnell of Lochgarry was appointed actual Lieut.-Colonel Commanding, but owing to Lord MacDonald's local influence a good selection of officers to complete the Regiment was made from the families of the MacDonalds of Glencoe, Morrar, Barrisdale, and others of his own clan. The total number of 750 Highlanders was finally reached by the aid of officers representing the Mackinnons, the Frasers of Culduthel, the Camerons of Callart, and others.

Certain companies were raised in the lowlands, among them those of Capt. Cunningham of Craigend, Montgomery-Cunningham, and Lieut. Graham. Together these formed two companies. A separate unit was made up of Capt. Bruce's company raised principally in Ireland. "In this manner," says the original account naively, "each race was kept distinct." The whole regiment amounted to 1086 men, N.C.O.'s, and drummers. They were inspected and reported complete by Lieut.-General Skene at Inverness in March, 1778. "MacDonald's Highlanders" served in the American War of 1781; were involved in the unhappy surrender of Yorktown under Lord

---

[1] *Historical Records. Seventy-Sixth "Hindustan" Regiment.* By Lieut.-Colonel F. A. Hayden, D.S.O.

BIRTH OF 76TH REGIMENT

Cornwallis, and were finally disbanded at Stirling Castle in March, 1784. Here, then, is the second and what might be called the Scottish 76th.

The history of the last and proper 76th Regiment—the English 76th in distinction to the other two—commences in 1787. So far as can be ascertained, it possessed no connecting link with its predecessors. There was a tradition in the 76th—which, however, cannot be confirmed by muster rolls in the Record Office, or by orderly room or other regimental records—that for many years the 76th of 1787 bore a piper upon their establishment to commemorate the 76th (MacDonald's) Highlanders.

The birth of the 76th Regiment, like that of many others of the British Army, was due to an alarm—a not infrequent one even in our own days—that the army was inadequate for the numerous calls made upon it from overseas.

In 1786, Lord Cornwallis, of North American fame, was selected by Mr. Pitt, the great Minister, as "Governor-General and Commander-in-Chief in India." Pitt had earlier decided to put an end to the ambitious schemes of aggression on the part of the East India Company, and Cornwallis was chosen to carry out this policy. Unfortunately for himself and for Pitt's policy, Cornwallis, anticipating by more than a century the League of Nations, declared that henceforward the British would wage no wars in India except those of a defensiv echaracter. But an Indian potentate, one Tippo (usually spelt Tippoo) Sahib, had other views. Tippo had succeeded his father, Hyder Ali, in 1782 and made no concealment of his intention—even though he had just signed a treaty of friendship in 1784—to overthrow at the earliest opportunity the British power in India. To this end Tippo intrigued with another European power—France, at that period a deadly rival to Great Britain in India—and sent ambassadors to Paris soliciting aid.

The ambassadors were graciously received by Louis XVI—later on destined to lose his own head during the French Revolution. Owing, however, to the difficulties in which the unfortunate King was even then beginning to be involved, and which afterwards culminated in the French Revolution, Tippo's mission had no result.

It was, however, owing to the alarm caused by this mission that four new regiments were in 1787 raised for the service of the East India Company. The scare caused by Tippo's mission to France having subsided, mainly owing to Pitt's policy in Europe, the East India Company wished to repudiate the raising of four new "King's" regiments, as they were called in contradistinction to the Company's own regiments. Such was the power, it may almost be said the arrogance of the great "Company," that they even went so far as to refuse permission for the troops to be embarked in their ships for conveyance to India. Pitt, however, that far-seeing custodian of British interests abroad, recognized the absolute necessity for maintaining a strong European garrison in India. He accordingly introduced a Bill, known at the "East India Declaratory Act," by which the Company was compelled to defray the cost of raising, transporting, and maintaining the troops necessary for the security of India.

The 76th Foot was one of the four regiments in question, the other three being the 74th, 75th, and 77th Regiments. It is of interest to note that the 76th at that early period was recruited principally in the counties of Nottingham and Leicester. A point of far greater interest to all members of the Duke of Wellington's Regiment lies in the fact that among the officers borne on the muster roll of March 20, 1788, when the 76th Regiment first embarked for India, was the name of Lieut. Hon. Arthur Weslie, afterwards known to the world as the Duke of Wellington. The name is thus spelt on the muster roll. In December, 1787, the future Duke of Wellington was, as Ensign Weslie, appointed A.D.C. to the then Duke of Buckingham, Lord-Lieutenant of Ireland, so he did not actually embark with the regiment for India.

After promotion to Lieutenant in January, 1788, the Hon. Arthur Weslie was transferred to the 41st Regiment. After leaving the 76th Regiment, the promotion of the young Lieutenant was remarkable. It has already been recorded that in 1788 he was an Ensign at seventeen and that he then transferred to the 41st Regiment. On June 30th, 1791, Wellesley was promoted to Captain. April, 1793, found him transferred to the 33rd Regiment as a Major. In September of the same year he became Lieut.-Colonel, remaining in command (Colonel in 1796) until the year 1802, when he was promoted Maj.-General.

Before passing on to follow the combined fortunes of the 33rd and 76th Regiments, it is of more than ordinary interest to recall in this connection the coincidence of the collateral fighting in the early days of the British conquest in India of the 33rd and 76th. To all ranks of what were then known as " King's " Regiments these small campaigns must have been terribly trying. It is only necessary to remind ourselves, first, of the exceedingly high percentage of killed and wounded at the hand-to-hand storming of besieged towns like Aligarh and Deeg, or in attacks like those at the Battle of Lasswari. Secondly, we should remember the severe toll taken from white officers, N.C.O.'s, and men by fighting through July and August in the Indian plains. Thirdly, the utterly inadequate medical and food arrangements, and finally the totally unhygienic clothing they wore. But they fought and conquered as we know by the despatches of such commanders as Lord Cornwallis, Lord Lake, and Maj.-General Sir Arthur Wellesley, our own " Iron Duke."

Were it here possible to recount fully the famous campaigns under Lake in 1803 against the Maharattas, or of Wellesley in the Deccan, many stirring tales could be retold. And although the relation of such historical events does not come within the scope of these memoirs, a few of the main incidents are well worthy of being recalled. Having received its baptism of fire at the capture of Bangalore in 1791, only a few years after it was raised in 1787, the 76th Regiment under Cornwallis took part in the capture of the very strong fortress of Seringapatam in 1792. In 1803, as related above, the 76th Regiment formed the mainstay of Lord Lake's little fighting force during the severe campaign against the Maharattas. It has been reported of that brave Commander that every morning when he awoke he called out: "*Bring me my boots and the 76th Regiment of Foot and I am ready to do anything and go anywhere.*" That he had a soft spot in his heart for the present 2nd Battalion there is no doubt, for again

THE STORMING OF ALIGARH

and again they received ample and full praise for the gallantry displayed by all ranks during Lake's many heroic attacks against walled forts stubbornly defended. Aligarh, one of the Battle Honours earned under Lake, consisted of a very strong fort surrounded by a ditch 100 feet to 200 feet broad, 32 feet deep, with 10 feet of water in it. There was only one entrance to the fort and that a very narrow and winding one. An episode in the attack is thus related by an eye-witness :—

"The whole line was under arms at 5 o'clock; the storming party formed near Perron's Gardens, and the covering guns were run down during the night. Those destined to cover the left were three eighteen-pounders; those to the right four six-pounders. Four companies of the 76th, with a proportion of men from the Native Corps, formed the storming party, and a quarter of an hour before day broke the whole advanced in silence and in a most steady, becoming manner. I was ordered by the General to accompany the storming party, and to bring him immediate information if any support should be required. The Honourable Colonel Monson, who headed the stormers, advanced steadily at the Head of his column, which was preceded by Shipton, and two twelve-pounders, scaling ladders, etc. We were at the entrance of the Sortie before they could perceive us from the Walls. Our first Salute was from the two half-moon batteries which flanked the gateway, and at the same moment the whole face of the fort was illuminated by the fire of their cannon and musketry. Our covering batteries opened at the same time, and their fire, as we could perceive by the slaughter on the walls, was well directed. In addition to the heavy guns which played upon us in the Sortie, the enemy had also heavy mortars loaded with grape and canister shot, and the leading twelve-pounder of ours was, in the hurry to carry it up to the gate, thrown into a trench which the enemy had made near the entrance of the Sortie. This misfortune detained us considerably, and at this time it was that we lost so many of our officers and men. Never did I witness such a scene before the second gun could be hauled up; the Sortie was become a perfect slaughter-house, and it was with the greatest difficulty that we dragged the gun over our killed and wounded. Nothing could exceed the determined gallantry with which our troops struggled under this most destructive fire. The enemy, too, fought desperately, and many of them actually stepped out upon our own ladders which were placed against the wall to meet our men ascending, but British valour prevailed, and although Shipton, who commanded the guns, was wounded, he kept on his legs until two rounds from the leading gun opened the outer gate, when our troops rushed in, and the slaughter among the enemy, in their turn, became very great. My horse was twice wounded this morning, but I, with my usual good fortune, escaped unhurt."[1]

As indicating an interesting if now obsolete practice of war the same eye-witness adds : "The storming party were allowed three hours to plunder, and we found several tumbrils of treasure in the Garrison."

Again at the Battle of Lasswari under Lake the same eye-witness of events relates : "The Cavalry (our own), we were told, were beaten off, and were then

[1] *War and Sport in India*, 1802–1806. An Officer's Diary.

drawn up out of reach of the enemy's fire waiting the arrival of the Infantry. We were told the loss of our Cavalry had been great in officers and men. About eleven o'clock the attack with the Infantry commenced with great vigour. Our Brigade was drawn up in the rear for the protection of the Park, and when the 1st and 2nd and 3rd Brigades began the attack the enemy's Cavalry immediately came round to attack us, but were soon repulsed. The fire was extremely heavy from the villages of Lasswari and Malpoonah. In about three hours the whole of the enemy's guns, tumbrils, and colours were in our possession, although they cost us dear, as we had 13 officers alone killed in the action and about 40 wounded." Little wars, it may be said; yet such a casualty list for three hours' fighting speaks volumes for the severity of it.

At the battle near Deeg, a third Honour gained under Lord Lake, the losses were equally heavy, nor was it until after a month's fighting that the fortress itself fell. "Possession of a gateway had been obtained with severe loss," writes the eye-witness already quoted; then continues:

"Brigadier MacRie was made acquainted with what we had done, and immediately on learning that Colonel Ball was severely wounded and that we had taken post at the gate which led into the heart of the town he advanced and joined us with a Battalion of the 8th and one of the 15th Regiment, headed by two hundred men of the 76th and European Regiments and eighty men of the 22nd Flankers.

"The enemy had suffered so much in the assault last night that they showed no very strong inclination to oppose any formidable resistance to us this morning; to do them justice, they undoubtedly fought very gallantly, and made a desperate resistance to our cost as well as their own. We met with no serious resistance till we reached the Palace Gardens, which are within half-musket shot distance of the Fort from the walls of which opened a smart and galling fire of grape and musketry. I was with Brigadier MacRie and Colonel Haldane at the head of the column; several men were shot around us, but we all escaped. I advanced with MacRie, for as prize-agent I considered it a point of duty to be foremost—in order to secure any property that may fall into our hands, and prevent the Soldiers plundering it. This check near the Palace Gardens induced us to halt, and we withdrew the troops out of sight and posted them in the Palace, and some were drawn up under the walls of the Garden, which sheltered them from the musketry of the garrison and also prevented their being seen. The Enemy lost no time in bringing some guns to point in the direction of the Palace, but the walls of the fort were so lofty, and we were so close under them, that they found it no easy matter to bring their Artillery to bear on us, and almost every shot whistled over our heads, and made great havoc among the houses of the town. There were many rooms in the Palace nearly full of rose water; the soldiers, some of them, got hold of it, and came out highly perfumed, having thrown it at and over each other. We posted guards in all the different avenues leading to the Palace and Gardens to prevent a surprise; this was one of the sweetest spots I ever beheld. The Palace itself was built of fine stone, very lofty and elegant, and had a most stylish appearance; it was supported within at many places with marble pillars of an immense size, and beautifully inlaid with cornelian, agate, and various other kinds of valuable stones. The rooms were forty and fifty feet in height, and eighty feet long or upwards. On the top of the Palace was a reservoir of water, which supplied the fountains immediately in front of the building; any of which could instantly be set playing by drawing certain plugs. There were numerous fountains in every part of the gardens, which were very extensive and elegantly laid out. It contained ranges of myrtle and orange trees of the finest kind I ever saw; the oranges were hardly ripe, but the men helped themselves plentifully. The walks were all paved with the same kind of stone as the Palace was built of. They were about thirty feet wide, all regularly laid out and kept in the highest possible condition. The Rajah was particularly fond of seeing and feeding fish in the ponds of his garden, and on going from one guard to another I met a soldier of the 22nd Foot with a very fine fish in his hand, just fresh from the water, and on enquiring where he had procured it and how, the answer was: 'With a sharp-pointed bayonet, sir; that's how I catch my fish,' and then pointed out to me a pond about thirty feet square only in which were nearly as many soldiers sticking fish with their bayonets. They had, of course, been preserved, and were as thick in this place of confinement as they could possibly swim. We were told the Rajah himself always fed them daily."

Such were some of the quaint incidents connected with fighting in early days in India. "Tommy" would appear to have been much as he was in the ranks of the "contemptible little army" of 1914. That a glamour now absent was added to the hard fighting of those days may be gathered from an entry in the same diary at the taking of Deeg:—

"Captain Boyce of the 76th Foot, Captain Hay of the Artillery, and myself as prize-agents," writes the diarist, " as soon as everything was secured without, commenced searching the most probable places for treasure, nor were we unsuccessful. In one of the buildings near the Rajah's quarters we found *three lacs of rupees*. It was concealed in a vault, the communication to which was down a very dark, long, winding staircase, covered on the top with a flat board, so contrived that perhaps none but soldiers in pursuit of *plunder* would have discovered it."

As has already been related, the 76th took part in the Siege of Seringapatam in 1792. Seven years later, in 1799, the 33rd under Colonel Wellesley, then commanding a division, repeated this unique experience. Well-earned indeed has been the Battle Honour " Seringapatam " inscribed on the Colours of the Regiment.

But we must follow for the present the fortunes of the 2nd Battalion after the amalgamation order of 1881. From 1881 until the commencement of the South African War the 2nd Battalion of the Duke of Wellington's Regiment carried out the usual tours of alternate home and foreign service. After being at home for five years in 1886 the Battalion embarked for Bermuda, moving on to Halifax, Nova Scotia, in September, 1889, thence to the West Indies.

As " foreign " stations are reckoned, both Bermuda and Halifax compare very favourably with others. Particularly is this the case where officers are concerned, but for both officers and other ranks at Bermuda, at Barbados, or at Jamaica local conditions make serious training for war almost impossible. In maintaining garrisons to safeguard her endless chain of sea communications, Great Britain uses up a large portion of her none too large armies. Whether this system is a sound one or the best that can be organized is open to argument. When it is remembered that modern war needs modern training of the most intensive kind, and that in such garrisons as Gibraltar, Malta, Bermuda, Barbados, Hongkong, and Singapore—to mention only a few—any such training on the necessary scale is almost impossible, there is serious food for reflection. In these strenuous days, training for war in the first place consists in keeping officers and men physically fit to the utmost degree. All the more, therefore, at stations such as those mentioned do outdoor sports stand prominent in the daily routine of every good regiment. In sport, as in war, the " Dukes " have always held their own.

Strategically the Bermudas are a group of islands with a valuable position a little over 500 miles from the American coast. The main island of the group is about 14 miles long by 1 mile in breadth and contains a fine deep-water harbour.

The islands became an important naval coaling station in 1869, when a large iron dock was safely towed across the Atlantic and secured in St. George's Harbour. The Bermudas have a history reaching back as far as the early sixteenth century. In 1612 they were granted by James I to an offshoot of the " Virginian Company," who proceeded to colonise them.

The chief sport at Bermuda is yachting, and so highly is the local rig thought of that it is now equally well known in sailing circles in England. The cedar dingheys were a speciality of Bermuda, being nothing but a shell with centre boards and some loose ballast blocks. The crew had to supply living ballast also by sitting out over the gunwale as was necessary to trim the boat. To race required a thoroughly good skipper. It should be mentioned that the racing masts were approximately three times the length of the dinghey itself and that the silk racing sails (lug-shaped mainsail and jib) were of such a size that the former could be wrapped round the boat two or three times.

The lightest wind was required, and real racing could only take place on a calm-water day. Even then it was no uncommon occurrence to see dingheys on the same day in the same race sink once or even oftener, and on one memorable day in one big race every boat swamped at least once. On these occasions the procedure was as follows : Two of the heavier sailing boats which were always following a race came up over the spot and picked up the crew. One of the latter, for choice an expert swimmer, then dived down and released the mast from its special fitting. The mast and the pig-iron ballast were then reclaimed with the aid of life-lines with cork floats which were always attached in readiness to mark the position. Two ropes having been made fast to the dinghey by diving, the two heavy yachts sailed off on opposite tacks, each with one rope, so bringing the dinghey up to the surface. Having been baled out and her mast re-stepped and ballast replaced, the dinghey then rejoined the race. Unless the accident happened in very deep water this operation took about twenty to thirty minutes. The winter season from November to May was, and probably still is, enlivened by the presence of various " floating palaces " in the shape of American yachts.

While the 2nd Battalion was quartered at Bermuda in 1886–1887 there occurred the renewal of the Regimental Colours ; also a fresh presentation of what are known as the Honorary Colours carried by the Battalion. In a letter dated August, 1886, the Secretary of State for India, Lord Elgin, had intimated that the " Secretary of State in Council was pleased to grant the petition of the officers then serving by presenting them with a new stand of ' Honorary Colours.' " The Colours were to replace former ones already renewed in 1830 which had been found to be beyond repair. On the occasion of the trooping of the Colours, the " King's " and " Regimental " were respectively carried by Lieut. N. G. H. Turner and 2nd Lieut. J. A. C. Gibbs.

The remnants of the former stand were mounted in canvas and framed, the " King's " Colour being placed in the Officers' Mess and the " Regimental " Colour presented by the officers to the Sergeants' Mess. Most unfortunately the former was destroyed in 1901 when the Officers' Mess was burnt down at Rangoon. The latter still survives.

The new " official " Colours to replace those presented to the Regiment at Aldershot in 1863, and now in the Parish Church, Halifax, Yorkshire, were also received at Bermuda in 1888. They were presented to the Battalion by His Excellency Lieut.-General T. L. Gallway, R.E., Governor and Commander-in-Chief of Bermuda.

Upon this occasion Lieut.-Colonel E. G. Fenn was in command of the 2nd Battalion of the Duke of Wellington's Regiment. The old Colours were carried by Lieuts. H. W. W. Wood and Robert Marshall; the new Colours by Lieuts. H. C. Suft and F. H. H. Swanson.

From Bermuda in the autumn of 1889 the 2nd Battalion arrived at Halifax, Nova Scotia. Few who know the beautiful harbour and entrance to Halifax are likely ever to forget it. For soldiers quartered there in the days when it was still a " regular " garrison before being taken over by the Canadian Forces Halifax, N.S., will always recall the happiest memories. As a matter of history Nova Scotia was discovered, possibly only re-discovered, as early as 1497 by the Cabots, the well-known navigators, though no attempt at permanent colonisation took place until 1604. At that time a French expedition landed and began colonising. Settlements were made at what is now Annapolis, at St. Croix in New Brunswick, and elsewhere. But quarrels broke out, and in 1613 the English colonists of Virginia made a descent upon the French, claimed their territory in right of the Cabots' discovery and expelled most of the French inhabitants. In 1621 a certain Sir William Alexander obtained from James I a grant of the whole peninsula, which was then first called Nova Scotia instead of the old French name of Acadie or Acadia. For some time French and English colonists fought over Nova Scotia, the Indians taking part, until in 1710 the province was finally captured by Great Britain and formally ceded to her at the Peace of Utrecht in 1713.

At the time when the 2nd Battalion took over the Wellington Barracks at Halifax—the name a curious coincidence—no finer quarters for ordinary sport were to be found. Fishing of all kinds—salmon, trout, and sea trout—was to be had almost for the asking. Duck and wild fowl shooting in wonderful profusion was there for any sporting subaltern who cared to put down his name for three days' leave. Moose and caribou both rewarded those prepared to go a little way farther afield, and compared to present-day prices, first-class sport was to be obtained at a very small outlay.

Cricket, football, and polo were all to be had for those who cared to play, and it was probably the presence of His Majesty King George V, at that time Prince George, Commander of the gunboat *Thrush*, which helped to make the latter game popular. His Majesty the present King was a frequent and honoured guest at the Wellington Barracks, and played polo whenever *Thrush* was in harbour.

Nor were the younger Haligonian sportsmen, " Blue Noses " as they were sometimes irreverently called, by any means prepared to take lying down the cricket and football reputation of a regiment or battery. Far from it. One of the most exciting of regimental efforts is associated with a football tour made by the rugger team of the 2nd Duke of Wellington's in the autumn of 1890.

" The Dukes' " football team had a reputation which Nova Scotia declined to accept on hearsay ; and as the Regiment were prepared to put its reputation to any fair test, some very strenuous football was the result. Could better physical training be found in that rigorous climate ?

The Halifax winter with its outdoor tobogganing and skating, and indoor ice-rink skating, afforded such amusements as only Canada can provide. It was as well, perhaps, that such opportunities for keeping fit were to be had, for the hard winter and deep snow were all against military exercises of an intensive kind. Company training as laid down in the then syllabus, especially where entrenching work was its object, suffered under serious drawbacks. Apart from the fact that neither picks nor shovels could be handled—except in huge fur gloves—without the fingers becoming frostbitten, the ground was generally frozen to a depth of at least three feet. The usual routine on parade was to break two picks and then to report the ground " too hard for digging." Route marches were the winter method of putting in soldiering time, but on many days these were only rendered possible for all ranks by wearing with their brown-leather knee boots a sort of glorified climbing-iron termed a " creeper." This was supposed to prevent, and did, slipping about on frozen roads or ice, but thus handicapped naturally few " records " were set up in the way of marching. Another drawback in frosty weather and one which interfered to some extent with route marches was the inability of the Regimental Band to play. As the Battalion would emerge from the barrack-square on to the slippery roadway owing to the moisture in the wind instruments they began to freeze. The result was a horrible cacophony of discords which usually irritated the C.O. Then the Adjutant would be ordered to " go and stop that —— band " and the music would cease. Such were some of the amenities of a soldier's life in Canada in the

PLATE 3

OFFICERS OF 2ND BATTALION AT HALIFAX, N.S., 1890

Reading left to right.—2nd Lieut. W. M. GRIMLEY, 2nd Lieut. A. J. M. HIGGINSON, Lieut. T. S. SMITH, Lieut. W. EXSHAW, Surg.-Capt. G. E. WESTON, Lieut. R. MARSHALL, Sergt.-Major C. HYDE.

Back row.—Lieut. H. W. BEECHER, Lieut. J. A. C. GIBBS, Capt. A. R. HUME, 2nd Lieut. N. W. FRASER, Lieut. F. H. A. SWANSON, 2nd Lieut. F. J. THURSBY-PELHAM.

Second row.—Lieut. H. W. W. WOOD, Lieut. & Adjt. S. C. UMFREVILLE, Q.M. W. FITZPATRICK (Hon. Lieut.), Capt. P. T. RIVETT-CARNAC, 2nd Lieut. P. A. TURNER, Capt. H. C. SUFT.

Front row.—Lieut.-Colonel E. NESBITT, Major S. J. TRENCH, Capt. C. D. BRUCE, 2nd Lieut. J. LEWIN (*sitting*), Major C. W. GORE, Lieut. A. F. WALLIS, 2nd Lieut. W. K. TROTTER, Lieut. E. M. K. PARSONS.

year of grace 1890. Yet Halifax, N.S., will always keep fresh in the hearts of those who had the good fortune to soldier there a memory of generous hospitality on the part of its very loyal inhabitants.

In March, 1891, from Halifax the 2nd Battalion proceeded to Barbados in the West Indies. In Nova Scotia at that season the long winter was far from over, and the sudden jump from an ice-cold frying-pan into the West Indian fire was far from pleasant. The Battalion's relief, the Leicestershire (17th) Regiment, arrived from Bermuda in their thin red serge jumpers with two feet of snow on the ground. The departing Battalion was still wearing, and glad to be wearing, the picturesque and comfortable Canadian winter uniform. This consisted of a grey fur cap with ear-flaps, and gloves, thick fur-lined and collared overcoat, and brown knee boots. Within forty-eight hours a glassy tropical sea with a brazen sun overhead made the very thought of such a costume almost unbearable. Commanded by Lieut.-Colonel E. Nesbitt, who had passed most of his service in the 1st Battalion, the 2nd landed at Barbados in March, 1891.

Headquarters and five companies were stationed in Barbados, with the other three at Jamaica under Major C. Gore.

Later one company was sent to the little island of St. Lucia under Capt. J. Gould. Even less than at Halifax could war training be carried out at Barbados, but officers and men kept themselves as fit as possible by means of polo and cricket. During two uneventful years in the West Indies trips were made to Trinidad and Demarara in British Guiana to take on the respective residents at cricket and polo. Such opportunities for seeing all parts of the Empire are one of the prerogatives of the British Army. And to these opportunities a well-known German writer upon military affairs has rightly attributed much of the adaptability and resourcefulness of British officers and men.

CHAPTER IV

2ND BATTALION, 1893–1913 : SOUTH AFRICA. MATABELE RISING, MASHONALAND. INDIA, RANGOON. THE SOUTH AFRICAN WAR. HOME SERVICE, IRELAND.

IN April, 1893, the 2nd Battalion, under Lieut.-Colonel E. Nesbitt, embarked for Wynberg, Cape Colony, dropping one company in lonely isolation at St. Helena. From Wynberg, in October, a detachment had the good fortune to proceed as a unit on active service. This party consisted of 3 officers and 51 non-commissioned officers and men who were despatched up-country to do duty during the Matabele rising with the Bechuanaland Border Police. The Matabele Expedition of 1893 was conducted by the Chartered Company of South Africa, not by the British Government, and was directed against Lobengula, the paramount chief whose main " Kraal " was at Buluwayo.

That some difficulty arose over the use of the services of British regular troops is apparent from the fact that they had to be temporarily incorporated with the Bechuanaland Border Police, the well-known B.B.P., a Government force.

At the time of the rising the Chartered Company applied to the British Government for the services of the B.B.P. Small detachments of British Regular Infantry were sent from Cape Town to be temporarily incorporated with the B.B.P. The detachments sent were :—

50 men and 2 officers.	Capt. W. M. Watson and Lieut. W. K. Trotter of the 2nd Battalion Duke of Wellington's Regiment.
50 men and 1 officer.	Capt. Woolridge-Gordon, the Royal Highlanders.
1 officer.	Lieut. P. A. Turner, the Duke of Wellington's Regiment.

Upon arrival at Mafeking these detachments formed the nuclei of two fresh troops of the B.B.P., each being made up to 100 men. One troop was under the command of Capt. W. M. Watson, the other under that of Capt. Woolridge-Gordon. A third troop, of which the nucleus consisted of 50 men of the Cape Mounted Rifles, was commanded by Capt. Woon.

All three troops were equipped and paid by the S.A. Chartered Company. They were commanded by Major Raleigh Grey, Inniskilling Dragoons, and as soon as the equipment was completed marched north.

Meanwhile, the troops of the Chartered Company moving from Salisbury had already defeated Lobengula's Matabele in two fights. The main body of the B.B.P.—who had advanced from Macloutsie—their Headquarters—had also fought an engagement, so that the back of the rebellion was already broken. When the troops of the 2nd Battalion the Duke of Wellington's Regiment, under Capt. Watson, arrived in Matabeleland they were detached to watch and cover the Mungwe Pass, to patrol the country, to round up cattle, and to disarm the Matabele.

After collecting many hundred head of cattle, quantities of assegais, and a few rifles without much resistance, their work came to an end. Towards the end of the operations, owing to horse-sickness (*sic*), the horses of the troop were almost decimfiated, and it became difficult to send out patrols of any strength.

A curious coincidence, if such it may be called, occurred during the above-mentioned brief campaign. It has already been related that the regular detachments sent to join the Chartered Company's forces included troops of the 2nd Duke of Wellington's Regiment and of the Royal Highlanders. Strange as it may sound, another unit known as the " Dukes and the Highlanders " also took part. *Neither* of the two units composing it were regulars nor had any connection with the regular detachments. The first unit was composed of the Duke of Edinburgh's Own Volunteer Rifles, Cape Town, the other of the Cape Town Highlanders, also volunteers.

In September, 1894, the 2nd Battalion, under Lieut.-Colonel C. W. Gore, embarked for Pietermaritzburg, the capital of Natal. As a colony Natal has two main divisions, Natal proper and Zululand. Up to the time of the South African War Natal had always been a thorn in the side of Imperial unity. For the British Army, Natal will always be connected with such names as Isandhlwana, Rorke's Drift, Majuba, Laing's Nek, Spion Kop, Colenso, and Ladysmith. Also with the names of such well-known fighting soldiers as Chelmsford, Colley, Evelyn Wood, Garnet-Wolseley, Buller, Ian Hamilton, Kitchener, and Roberts, not to mention many others of lesser fame. Natal has also its tragic page of history connected with the death in early youth of the Prince Imperial of France who at that time was the last hope of French Imperialists. So late as May, 1910, Natal's stormy past was finally merged in the Union of South Africa.

Upon arrival in Natal six companies of the Battalion were posted at Pietermaritzburg. One of these was a mounted infantry company. Two others were stationed at Eshowe in Zululand, of which again one was a mounted company.

Sir Walter Hely-Hutchinson was at this period Governor of Natal, and as one of his aides-de-camp had taken Lieut. Robert Marshall of the Duke of Wellington's Regiment. As all the pre-war theatre-going world knows, " Robbie " Marshall became later one of the most successful playwrights of his day. His first play to secure public notice and favour was one entitled, " His Excellency the Governor." " Robbie " Marshall had for some time been the popular and gifted actor-manager of many regimental productions. In co-operation with another equally popular performer on the local boards, Lieut. H. W. W. Wood, known throughout the Battalion as " Charles," he had raised the standard of regimental acting to a very high point.

Had not Capt. Marshall died prematurely he would undoubtedly have stood in the very front rank as a writer of English light-comedy. Few of the tens of thousands of theatre-goers who saw his most popular play, "The Second-in-Command," are likely to consider such an estimate exaggerated.

Cricket and football filled in spare hours and helped to keep men fit while the Battalion was at Pietermaritzburg. Lieut. P. A. Turner and Drummer Nourse were selected to play for Natal in the "Currie" Tournament of 1895. Drummer Nourse's discharge from the Army was afterwards purchased by Natal sportsmen interested in cricket. As Mr. A. D. Nourse, the well-known Natal and South African cricketer, he has since amply justified their selection.

During the second rising in Matabeleland, known officially as the "Rhodesian Campaign" of 1896-1897, detachments of the Battalion took part, on the Mashonaland side. During this period 13 officers and 320 non-commissioned officers and men proceeded on active service. Some served on the staff, some with Mounted Infantry, others with service companies, the remainder on "odd jobs."

The following officers were employed:—

Staff:	Major H. D. Thorold.
	Lieut. P. A. Turner.
Mounted Infantry:	Major P. T. Rivett-Carnac.
	Capt. W. M. Watson.
	Capt. E. M. K. Parsons.
	Lieut. A. F. Wallis.
	Lieut. T. S. Smith.
	Lieut. A. J. Tyler.
Service Companies:	Capt. F. H. A. Swanson.
	Capt. H. W. W. Wood.
	2nd Lieut. P. Coode.
Special Service:	Lieut. N. W. Fraser.
Staff Officer to B.S.A. Company:	Lieut. J. A. C. Gibbs.

Major Rivett-Carnac was later appointed Staff Officer to Sir Richard Martin, the Imperial Commissioner.

The operations in Mashonaland in 1896 were under the command of Maj.-General C. Carrington, who had as his Chief of Staff Colonel—now—Sir Robert Baden Powell, G.C.V.O., K.C.B. The 7th Hussars embarked at Durban for East London, proceeding thence by rail to Mafeking. Under Lieut.-Colonel Paget, 7th Hussars, they and the M.I. formed a mobile mounted column, marching from Mafeking via Macloutsie on Gwelo in Mashonaland.

The campaign of 1896-1897 was fought in country in many parts both rough, hilly, and bushy, and the total force concerned was very small compared with the area of the country in which it operated: some 2000 men to over 100,000 square miles. As has been said, the area in which the small column, under Lieut.-Colonel Paget was operating, was mainly bush and low hills. The

Mashonas were never met in large numbers, so that operations were mainly carried out by a series of patrols. In this rough country M.I. on their hardy, small cobs could be more effectively used than the Cavalry on their bigger horses.

Though written for a later occasion, Kipling's immortal lines were equally applicable :—

"M. I."

" I wish my mother could see me now, with a fence-post under my arm,
And a knife and a spoon in my putties that I found on a Boer farm ;
Atop of a sore-backed Argentine with a thirst that you couldn't buy—
I used to be in the Hampshires once,
(Glosters, Lincolns, and Rifles once),
Sussex, Scottish and Yorkshire once ! (*ad lib.*)
But now I am M.I. ! "

Shortly after leaving Gwelo, Major Rivett-Carnac had to go on the sick list from dysentery, and Capt. Watson took over the command of the M.I. During the latter part of the operations, the M.I., reinforced by about eighty " friendlies," were detached to round up the elusive chief " Boonga." For some six weeks he and his remaining followers were harassed and hunted in the bush country, until Boonga was finally cornered and surrendered.

In the light of present-day warfare such bush fighting is, of course, of no great account. It may be as well to remember, however, that it makes no difference to the individual soldier how he goes " West," if " West " he must go. Whether that departure is due to the agency of a native assegai costing a shilling or two, or whether it is expedited by a modern high-explosive gas shell costing some hundreds of pounds, the final result is identically the same. Be he left unburied and unwept outside some native kraal, or interred with almost regal pomp and ceremony in Westminster Abbey, to the " Unknown Warrior " it is a matter of supreme indifference.

To " Thomas Atkins " the " fun of the fair " is all the same, as the following little incident may help to show. In the above-mentioned campaign a body of Rhodesian Horse had just started to attack some native kraals near which a famous witch-doctor had his cave. When the cave was at last located and surrounded, unfortunately the bird had flown. To show the white man's entire disregard for witch-magic it was decided that the cave should be blown up. On this being done, the party turned for camp. The sun was low and as the troops moved off a terrible sight met their view. Behind them a figure suddenly appeared. It looked like the witch-doctor. The figure was partially nude, covered with blood and dirt, and crying out for water. A more pitiable object could hardly be imagined. For a minute or two no one in the retiring column could think who the figure represented ; then it seemed that he must be one of their own people who had been left behind and in some way injured in the explosion. This proved to be the case.[1] It eventually transpired that the figure was one of the Salisbury Rifles, a man named Day. Also, that he had been doing a bit of loot-hunting in the cave, and had found an English five-pound note.

[1] *With the M.I. and the Mashonaland Field Force in 1896.* By Lieut.-Colonel Alderson.

Quite innocent of his danger he was searching diligently for more when the explosion came. Day had been blown out of the cave and had fallen through a tree a distance of at least 30 feet, which, no doubt, saved his life. Curiously enough Day had put the five-pound note in his breeches pocket, and these garments had been blown almost to shreds by the explosion! As soon as Day's loss became generally known it was curious to find how many friends he had, anxious ostensibly to go to his help and aid him find his lost rifle. There may have been also the fond hope of picking up another five-pound note.

To all ranks who remained, and took part in the 1897 operations in Mashonaland, a " Mashonaland 1897 " clasp was awarded.[1] The honours list included the names of Major Rivett-Carnac, promoted to a Brevet of Lieut.-Colonel, of Lieut. Norman Fraser, granted the D.S.O. for conspicuous gallantry when wounded in the Matoppo Hills, and of Lieut. P. A. Turner, mentioned in despatches for excellent staff service.

Under the command of Lieut.-Colonel H. E. Belfield, now Lieut.-General Sir H. E. Belfield, K.C.B., K.C.M.G., K.B.E., D.S.O., the 2nd Battalion left South Africa for India in December, 1897, arriving at Bangalore early in 1898. The ship in which the Battalion made the passage had the unique experience, off Madagascar, of passing through the centre of a cyclone.

After arrival at Bangalore, in the Madras Presidency, the Battalion had to face a severe plague epidemic. " Plague " duty, no pleasant one at best, occupied a large number of both officers, N.C.O's. and men.

From India the Battalion was transferred to Rangoon, Burma, in October 1899. While stationed at Rangoon (1899–1902), far from the scene of the South African War, units of the Battalion were once more lucky enough to be selected for active service. What was known as the Burma Mounted Infantry Regiment was drawn for service from the three regular battalions quartered at that time in Burma. The quota from the 2nd Duke of Wellington's Regiment consisted of 1 company M.I., total 5 officers (2 attached from other corps), and 103 N.C.O.'s and men. The officers who served with this M.I. company in South Africa were :—

Capt. J. A. C. Gibbs (in Command).

Section Officers :

Capt. N. G. H. Turner.
Lieut. P. Coode.
Lieut. E. Tatchell (Lincoln Regiment).
Lieut. N. G. B. Forster (Royal Warwick Regiment).

In addition to the M.I. company, the 2nd Battalion was also represented at the front by their Commanding Officer, Lieut.-Colonel H. E. Belfield, who was appointed A.A.G. to Maj.-General Tucker, C.B., commanding 7th Division. On Christmas Day, 1899, Lieut.-Colonel Belfield sailed to take up his staff duties in South Africa.

[1] Major and Bt. Lt.-Col. P. T. Rivett-Carnac and Capt. J. A. C. Gibbs awarded clasp " Mashonaland 1897."

THE BURMA MOUNTED INFANTRY

Other officers on special service in South Africa were: Lieut. A. J. Tyler, on the staff of Colonel (now Field-Marshal Lord Plumer, G.C.B., G.C.M.G., G.C.V.O., G.B.E.). Capt. H. W. Becher and Lieut. R. E. Maffett were attached to the 1st Duke of Wellington's Regiment. 2nd Lieuts. Jenkins, Oakes and Maples, who had been posted to the 2nd Battalion on joining, but who had not at the time started for Rangoon, were in December, 1899, transferred to the 1st Battalion in England in order to proceed to South Africa. In 1902 Capt. A. G. Horsfall took 150 N.C.O.'s and men from Burma in relief of a similar number of men serving with the 1st Battalion. Eight officers and 254 N.C.O.'s and men were thus included among those who took part in the South African War from the 2nd Battalion.

The part played by the M.I. detachment sent from Burma by the 2nd Battalion was an experience of very considerable value to all ranks concerned. Though the total numbers were comparatively very small the work they did and the fighting they saw were far from negligible.

Arriving at De Aar on February 22nd, 1900, the Burma M.I., as the little force was known, served almost continuously until the armistice made with the Boers by Earl Kitchener in May, 1902. Apart from the weary marches trekked —in all some 7000 odd miles—the Burma M.I., not counting the usual Boer sniping, was under fire on over two hundred occasions. The detachment earned the following medal-clasps: Driefontein, Johannesburg, Diamond Hill, Wittebergen, Cape Colony, and the King's Medal with the two clasps. Among other quaint experiences must have been those of the tiny Pegu ponies brought from Rangoon. Early in June, 1900, as many as 50 per cent had already to be replaced by local remounts. Two of the little ponies were kept by Colonel Gibbs as pets, and for the next eighteen months they followed the "Duke's" M.I. Company like dogs.

Early initiation into M.I. field service began with the advance on Pretoria. Then followed Sir Archibald Hunter's "drive" after Prinsloo, in which the other columns, those of Generals Paget and Clements, took part. In November of the same year the famous Boer leader, de Wet, was contemplating one of his lightning raids on Cape Colony. General Knox, having learned of his intention, set various columns in motion. One of these, under that well-known soldier and sportsman, Le Gallais, of the 8th Hussars, all but rounded up a whole Boer laager. Lieut.-Colonel Lean, commanding the 5th Battalion M.I., and later in command of the Duke of Wellington's Regiment, found himself looking down from a rise upon a whole Boer laager, guns, waggons, and horses, within 300 yards, quite unconscious of their danger.

The Boer picquet had already been "done in." Doornkraal Farm lying in a hollow was nearly the undoing of the whole commando, but, as so often happened, the surrounding cordon was not complete, so many of the Boers, scattering, pushed through and escaped. Unfortunately, the British casualties were heavy from hidden Boer marksmen, and among them was the gallant leader himself, Colonel Le Gallais. January, 1901, found General Knox with his three mounted columns, including the Burma M.I., still hunting de Wet, but a rest at Winburg came as a welcome change to all ranks. So the "drives" went on all through the early portion of 1901. Bloemfontein, then Bethulie, and later the bleak Karroo country were the next experiences. Following this "round up" came fresh instructions as to the collecting of Boer cattle and the searching of farmsteads for the menkind, who played hide-and-seek with the British columns and got their women folk to shelter them.

The slaughtering of a considerable number of cattle did not improve the hygienic amenities of the country-side, added to which, there was the constant danger from Boer snipers concealed at these farms.

At the end of May the Burma M.I. joined Colonel Thornycroft's column working in the Aliwal North district. So the summer passed. The beginning of 1902 found the column under a new temporary leader, Colonel Ternan, moving along the Basutoland border. Some kraal fighting where Boers had taken cover once again revealed their elusiveness. It was during this little fight that Capt. Gibbs—as he then was—got a bullet through the left elbow-joint. He was at the time lying flat on the ground directing the advance of one of the M.I. sections by signalling with his arm to Sergt. Allen, its commander. The latter himself soon after got a bullet-graze on the side of the head. He was afterwards killed in the Great War. As usual, the Boers were able to clear, and the unusual sight was seen of wounded men of their party being carried off in hammocks slung between two horses.

The following table is of interest :—

Two Years' Wastage in 2nd Duke of Wellington's Company B.M.I.

	Officers.	Sergts.	R. & F.	Total.	
Strength on leaving Rangoon, January, 1900	5	5	98	5 O. 103 R.&F.	
Strength, 1st January, 1902 Present with Company	2	4	46	2/50	
Hospital S.A.	—	—	10	10	Never rejoined—but went to 1st Bn.
Cape Town (unfit)	—	—	2	2	
Killed in action	—	—	1	1	Wilmot
Died of disease	1	—	2	1/2	Capt. N. G. H. Turner at Winburg, 25th May, 1900, of enteric—Crabb and J. Harrison.
Invalided England	—	1	14	15	
To 1st Bn. unfit for further column duties	—	—	6	6	
To England on promotion	2	—	—	2	Lieuts. Forster (Warwicks)—Tatchell (Lincolns).
Convalescent Camp, etc.	—	—	16	16	Never rejoined, but went to 1st Bn. later.
Storeman C. Town	—	—	1	1	
Total	5	5	98	5/103	

THE BURMA MOUNTED INFANTRY

The B.M.I. became 29th M.I. about March, 1902.

In June, 1902, the "fit men" went to the 1st Battalion—leaving 4 Sgts., 17 other ranks at Headquarters, Brandfort, to clean up prior to return to England.

The following casualties occurred:—

Lieut. A. J. Tyler. Killed in action. Crocodile River, March, 1900.

BURMA MOUNTED INFANTRY.

Killed in action:
  Capt. P. Coode, April 8th, 1902. Near Bullfontein, Orange River Colony.
  No. 2302 Col. Sergt. R. D. Moore, March 9th, 1902. Near Bloemhof, Orange River Colony.
  No. 3175 Pte. F. Wilmot, March 10th, 1900. Battle of Driefontein.

Died of disease:
  Capt. N. G. H. Turner, May 25th, 1900. At Winburg, Orange River Colony.
  No. 3461 Pte. W. Crabb, June 6th, 1900. At Cape Town.
  No. 3476 Pte. J. Harrison, December 15th, 1900. North, Cape Colony.

Wounded:
  Capt. J. A. C. Gibbs, Sergt. L. Taylor, Sergt. W. Allen, Corpl. G. Whitefoot, Corpl. W. Gibson (twice), Ptes. M. Moorhouse, J. Parry, A. Bevan, W. Birkett, D. Donoghue, J. Atkinson, E. Harrison, W. Burton, H. Spalding, J. Sanderson, J. Shepherd, J. Johnson, D. Burke.

Mentioned in Despatches:
  Staff: Colonel H. E. Belfield (twice).
     Capt. H. W. Becher
     Capt. J. A. C. Gibbs (twice).
     Capt. P. Coode.
  No. 2215 Col. Sergt. A. Butterworth (twice), No. 2302 Col. Sergt. R. D. Moore, No. 2879 Sergt. O. Buckley (twice), No. 5004 Sergt. W. Allen, No. 3549 Sergt. C. Sims, No. 4127 Pte. J. Parry, No. 3439 Pte. D. Donoghue.

C.B.: Colonel H. E. Belfield.

D.S.O.: Colonel H. E. Belfield, Capt. P. Coode.

Medal for Distinguished Conduct in the Field:
  Col. Sergt. A. Butterworth, Pte. J. Parry, Pte. D. Donoghue.

Promoted Brevet-Majors:
  Capts. H. W. Becher and J. A. C. Gibbs.

While the 2nd Battalion was quartered at Rangoon, Burma, the officers suffered a severe loss by the burning of their mess bungalow. In less than half an hour the mess, a large wooden building, was completely destroyed.

At the time the Battalion was out at musketry camp at Tokine. The whole of the regimental plate, both stands of Colours, as well as many almost irreplaceable pictures and books, thus perished. Though the actual loss was partly covered by insurance, and replicas of some of the modern trophies, including the centre-piece, were procurable, other losses were irreparable. Amongst these, in addition to the Colours, was the elephant snuff-box presented by the " Iron Duke " himself, also Lord Lake's original despatches presented to the Regiment after the Maharatta Campaign.

In October, 1901, the 2nd Battalion was armed with the Lee-Enfield rifle.

While in Burma one company of the Battalion was sent to the Andaman Islands as guard to the penal settlement. It was in these islands whilst on tour that the then Viceroy, Lord Mayo, was murdered by a convict in February, 1872.

Life under British regime in the islands was in those days an interesting experiment. There were some 20,000 convicts, all " lifers " or " long " sentences, and the interest of the experiment lay in the endeavour to turn these criminals into honest, self-respecting, men and women.

After ten years' graduated labour the convict was given a ticket-of-leave, and became self-supporting. He could farm, keep cattle, marry, or send for his family, but he could not leave the settlement or be idle. There are those—to their shame be it said—who sneer at the " Pax Britannica " and the " White Man's burden " ; but British soldiers in all parts of the Empire are proud to help in keeping that peace and in shouldering that burden.

In December, 1902, the 2nd Battalion returned to India. After wintering in Calcutta, with one company at Lebong, it proceeded to that hill station, sending another company to Jalapahar.

An amusing incident befel the Royal Indian Marine transport in which the Battalion had embarked at Rangoon. Lieut.-Colonel S. J. Trench, at the time commanding the 2nd Duke of Wellington's Regiment, happened to be away acting as umpire at the Delhi Manœuvres of 1902. Major F. M. H. Marshall was in temporary command. When the Indian Marine transport anchored in the Hoogli, by a mistake in a code message the authorities in Calcutta were informed : " Mutiny on board; send help." The message should have read : " Hope to be up on afternoon tide."

Whether the mistake was owing to ignorance in the use of the code, or as was generally supposed to the use of an obsolete code, is a matter of no great moment. The result of the mistake was, first, that a heavily-armed posse of agitated staff officers boarded in a gingerly manner the transport on its arrival at the quay : secondly, that the innocent soldiers on board were amazed to find themselves received by two strong companies of another regiment fully armed with ball ammunition. That the two companies were cleverly camouflaged behind some coal stacks, later on only added to the amusement. On such occasions that priceless gift " humour " is the only resource.

In December, 1903, Lieut.-Colonel S. J. Trench was placed on half-pay on completion of his period in command, and Major F. M. H. Marshall was

PLATE 4

OFFICERS, 2ND BATTALION, CENTENARY BALL, CALCUTTA, DECEMBER, 1902

Capt. H. P. Travers. 2nd Lieut. J. C. Burnett. Lieut. G. R. Hartley.
Capt. H. W. Cobb. 2nd Lieut. T. M. Ellis.
Major F. M. H. Marshall. Lieut.-Colonel S. J. Trench. Lieut. J. Y. Greenwood.
Capt. R. K. Healing.

THE RESTORATION OF RED REGIMENTAL FACINGS 45

promoted in his place. In February, 1904, Headquarters of the Battalion left Lebong for Dinapore, sending one company to Barrackpore and three companies to Dum Dum. In April of the same year Major F. A. Hayden, D.S.O., took over command *vice* Lieut.-Colonel Marshall, granted sick leave to England. In June two companies left Dum Dum for Benares. By Presidency Brigade Orders, dated Calcutta, February, 1905, the 2nd Battalion Duke of Wellington's Regiment was adjudged to be the best British Battalion in the Presidency Brigade. The Drill and Instruction test—Annual Training—is, as is well known, by no means a matter of " eye-wash." To have secured pride of place in the tests carried out in accordance with India A.O. 726 of 1904, shows the very high standard the 2nd Battalion had reached before its return to England. In December, 1904, two companies rejoined Headquarters from Benares, while two others proceeded to Dum Dum on detachment.

In March, 1905, Lieut.-Colonel Marshall rejoined from sick leave, and in September orders were received from the War Office that the 2nd Battalion was to proceed home, leaving 500 men behind to be posted to the 1st Battalion. It may be of interest to note that among these were included most of the Battalion Rugby Football team, which had already laid the foundation of the record later on created by the 1st Battalion.

Under War Office authority dated March, 1905, His Majesty the King approved of the facings of the Regiment being changed back from white to the old red facings.

In October, 1905, the Headquarters companies left Dinapore for Calcutta. Here they were joined by the companies from Dum Dum and Barrackpore. On the 26th of October, 1905, after nineteen years' foreign service, the 2nd Battalion embarked for England on the R.I.M.S. *Dufferin* at Calcutta. At Bombay they transferred to the hired transport *Plassey*, which took them home, arriving at Southampton on November 27th. It is of interest to note, as already mentioned, that the 1st and 2nd Battalions passed each other in the Indian Ocean, the one going out to, the other returning from, India.

After returning to England, Lichfield was the first quarter occupied by the 2nd Battalion. At that period, though clouds were already gathering upon the European horizon, the tension between Germany and Great Britain was perceptible only to the politically initiated. Agadir, as well as the abortive 1905 revolution in Russia, were merely straws indicating the way a war-wind was blowing. That German military pride, unrestrained by the common-sense of her merchant princes, would set Europe ablaze had not as yet become clear to many of our politicians.

It was true that some of our leading soldiers were preparing for what they already considered more than a possibility of war with Germany, but outwardly Europe was still lulled in the lap of peace and commercial prosperity.

In May, 1906, the 2nd Battalion was re-armed with the new short magazine Lee-Enfield rifle. The same summer it underwent its first experience of home manœuvres. In October of the same year at Lichfield the Duke of Wellington, K.G., presented new Colours to the Regiment. These Colours were to replace those destroyed in the fire at Rangoon, Burma, in 1901. Upon this occasion four Colours were presented, viz., the set of Colours usually carried, also a set presented by the India Office to replace those formerly given to the Regiment by the Hon. East India Company in 1807. These Colours were for service in the Maharatta Campaign of 1803-1805. The ceremony of consecration was performed by the Right Reverent the Lord Bishop of Lichfield, assisted by the Rev. M. W. Churchward, Chaplain to the troops at Lichfield. Amongst the officers on parade on this occasion was General Sir Hugh Rowlands, V.C., K.C.B., Colonel of the Regiment. In referring to his own connection with it the Duke of Wellington spoke of the early history of the 76th, the "Hindoostan Regiment" in India. The Duke also recalled the fact of his predecessor, "the Iron Duke," having served for a short period in the 76th, and for most of his regimental service in the 33rd. It was probably owing to this fact that these two regiments became linked.

In January, 1907, Lieut.-Colonel F. M. H. Marshall was placed upon half-pay. He was succeeded in command by Lieut.-Colonel and Bt. Colonel Kenneth E. Lean, transferred from the Royal Warwickshire Regiment.

After serving for a brief period in command of the Battalion, Colonel K. E. Lean, on completion of command, was succeeded in February, 1908, by Lieut.-Colonel F. A. Hayden, D.S.O.

During the same month the distinction "Corunna," to be borne upon the Regimental Colours, was approved by His Majesty the King. This distinction, though earned in 1809, was none the less welcome as marking the part played by one battalion of the Regiment in a fine feat of arms. Every soldier knows that during the engagement at Corunna Sir John Moore was killed. During this retreat the British forces were able to make use of British sea-power, so frustrating Marshal Soult's attempt to drive them into the sea. This is merely one more instance of what sea-power means to the British Empire. It may also be of interest to recall that the same harbour at Corunna gave shelter in 1588 to the "Invincible" Spanish Armada.

In the autumn of 1908 the 2nd Battalion moved to Tidworth on Salisbury Plain, taking over quarters in Candahar Barracks. In 1909 there were further changes in fighting equipment, when the Battalion was armed with the new pattern bayonet. During the summer of 1909 the Regiment suffered a severe loss by the death of their Colonel, General Sir Hugh Rowlands, V.C., K.C.B., at the age of eighty years.

Appointed Colonel of the Regiment in 1897, Sir Hugh Rowlands, V.C., was one of the few surviving links with Crimean days. He was present at the Battle of Alma, was severely wounded at Inkerman, took part in the siege and fall of Sevastopol, the assault on the Redan, where he was wounded, and the attack on the quarries. He was awarded the Victoria Cross at the Battle of Inkerman for saving the life of another officer. Sir Hugh Rowlands also took part in the South African War of 1877-8-9.

He was succeeded as Colonel of the Regiment by Maj.-General Herbert Eversley Belfield, C.B., D.S.O., as he then was, General Officer Commanding

LIEUT.-GENERAL SIR H. BELFIELD, K.C.B., K.C.M.G., K.B.E., D.S.O.
(Colonel, The Duke of Wellington's Regiment.)

4th Division Eastern Command, whose record of army service up to the year 1909 is of more than passing interest.

> Lieut., 101st Royal Bengal Fusiliers, 26.2.76.
> Capt. Royal Munster Fusiliers, 2.5.85.
> Passed Staff College, 89.
> Brigade Major, 1st Infantry Brigade, 8.90.
> Major, Royal Munster Fusiliers, 1.2.93.
> D.A.A.G., Aldershot, 5.93.
> Chief Staff Officer, Ashanti Expeditionary Force, 11.95.
> Bt. Lieut.-Colonel, 25.3.96.
> Lieut.-Colonel, West Riding Regiment (2nd Battalion), 28.7.97.
> Colonel on appointment as A.A.G. 7th Division, S. Africa, 18.12.99.
> Transferred as A.A.G. to 1st Division, S. Africa, 2.00.
> Brig.-General as Inspector of Imperial Yeomanry, S. Africa, 23.1.02.
> Brig.-General Commanding 4th Infantry Brigade, 23.1.02.
> Colonel as A.A.G., 1st Army Corps, 11.12.02.
> Maj.-General, 1.12.06.
> Commanding 4th Division, 12.5.07.
> Colonel, Duke of Wellington's Regiment, 2.8.09.
> Lieut.-General, 10.8.12.

Garrison life at home is not an existence which usually appeals to the born soldier. The latter, by instinct, is usually a wanderer, averse to being bound by rule of thumb, almost certainly one upon whom the somewhat monotonous duties he is called upon to perform quickly pall. To obtain the best results from men of this type they must be well cared for and well looked after.

As the new Colonel of the Regiment said after his first inspection of the 2nd Battalion, "In my opinion the turn-out was excellent, the men were steady in the ranks and looked strong and healthy. I never saw anything better in the way of institutions in my life, and the barrack rooms were admirably kept.

"All the care and attention to details which were evident to me must be productive of good results, in that the soldier finds himself well looked after and cared for, and thereby the discipline and general good comradeship are strengthened, thus the conduct of the Battalion in the field and its ability to carry out correctly its allotted duties is materially influenced for good."

Prophetic words these, though the speaker was unaware how soon they would be proved true. "Mons" and "Hill 60" were in the womb of the future.

In these pre-war years at home the 2nd Battalion was maintaining the high reputation which it had brought back from India, a reputation which it afterwards justified to the full during those four long years of such fighting as the world had never yet known. Both on manœuvres and in barracks it earned praise from men who could speak with authority. From the civil authorities at Lichfield the following official letter was received :—

"Lichfield, October 9th, 1908.

"DEAR COLONEL HAYDEN,

"On behalf of the city, and myself personally, I write to say how sorry we are to lose your Regiment, for during the time it has been quartered among us the conduct of the men has been excellent, and all that could be desired; in fact, the Battalion has been very popular in every way—the goodwill between it and the civilians has been of the most cordial description, and as Chief Magistrate I can unhesitatingly say I scarcely ever remember one of your men appearing before me. A proud record for any regiment to have.

"In the name of the city I wish you, the officers, N.C.O.'s and men every prosperity and happiness in your 'new home.'

Yours very truly,
(Sgd.) W. R. COLERIDGE ROBERTS
(Mayor).

Lieut.-Colonel F. A. Hayden, D.S.O.,
Commanding 2nd Duke of Wellington's Regiment."

Through the Lieut.-General Commanding-in-Chief, Southern Command, the Battalion with the other troops on manœuvres was commended by the Director of Operations in 1909 for "its efficiency and soldierly bearing." The Lieut.-General himself expressed his "appreciation of the marches performed, and the cheerfulness of the men under strenuous circumstances." He considered "the performances of all ranks remarkable," which, he added, "had elicited the admiration of the civil population."

In 1910 the British Empire was so much the poorer by the grievous loss sustained by the death of His Majesty King Edward VII. The 2nd Battalion proceeded to London in order to take part in the funeral. It is a curious coincidence, if unpremeditated, that the portion of the streets to be lined by the Battalion should have been from Apsley Gate (Hyde Park Corner), to Hamilton Place.

Among the unpleasant duties connected with home service is that in which troops are called upon to preserve law and order in such matters as the coal strike of 1910.

In June, 1911, the coronation of His Majesty King George V once more took the Battalion for service in London. Later in the summer it was warned for duty in connection with the London Dock strike and, following this, for railway strikes at Birmingham and Wolverhampton.

Before quitting Tidworth for Ireland the Battalion was inspected by Brig.-General Lawrence Drummond, C.B., M.V.O. In the course of his remarks the Brigadier made the following statement: "As we all know events may occur which will alter the present arrangements, but they are in the future and we must not waste time looking too far ahead: you must, however, remember that it is the Army, and the Unit, and the individual soldier in the ranks who is the most

INDICATION OF THE COMING WORLD WAR

intelligent and most highly-trained, who will come out top-dog in time of war." The cause of the trouble referred to was the very strained relations in Morocco between France and Germany. The quarrel was usually known as the "Agadir incident" from the name of the port to which the *Panther* was sent to represent the "mailed fist" in Morocco. Once more the words were prophetic. They were also probably the first reference to the near approach of war which most of the men of the Battalion had heard.

In September, 1911, the Battalion moved by rail and steamer to Dublin. Early the following year it was re-armed with the S.L.E. rifle, mark IV and with mark VII high velocity ammunition. In February, 1912, Lieut.-Colonel F. A. Hayden, D.S.O., was placed on retired pay on completion of his period of service in command. The vacancy was filled by the promotion of Major W. M. Watson who, after being posted to the 2nd Battalion, was transferred to the 1st Battalion. In March, Major J. A. C. Gibbs was promoted Lieut.-Colonel and posted to the 2nd Battalion. It was in 1912 that the new "Duke of Wellington's" shoulder strap superseded the old "West Riding." An additional scroll, "Duke of Wellington's," was also added to the officer's helmet plate.

The years immediately preceding the outbreak of the Great War will always remain as landmarks in the training, not only of the British Army, but of all armies, for war. For fifty years England had been at peace in Europe, and, however strenuous battle training had come to be, there was always in the minds of certain serious students of war the possibility of its being off the true line.

Would the next war be one in which mechanical methods would more than ever predominate? Would it be fought in the air? Were cavalry to be once more the eyes and ears of advancing armies? That there were to be no longer advancing armies hardly entered the mind of man. Would musketry as of old be one of the decisive factors when troops joined issue? Would modern war be a matter of weeks, sharp, short and decisive?

Such were a few of the questions troubling the minds of serious soldiers in those pre-war days. Troubling, it is safe to say, the mind of Brig.-General T. Capper, C.B., D.S.O., as he then was, commanding the 13th Infantry Brigade in Ireland.

As an instance of pre-war training carried out by the 2nd Battalion while belonging to the 13th Brigade, it may be of interest to recall their first inspection. This was by their new Brigadier, afterwards Major-General Sir T. Capper, K.C.M.G., C.B., D.S.O., killed, in 1915, at the battle of Loos. Owing to pouring rain the original programme had to be altered. At 10 in the morning three companies, with the Battalion first line transport complete, paraded at Long Meadows training ground with orders to cross the Liffey by such improvised methods as local stores allowed.

One of the companies constructed a Wilmer boat and swam all the horses over. The other two companies constructed a tarpaulin and hay raft by means of which all the waggons and carts were floated across. The time occupied was $3\frac{1}{4}$ hours.

The official report on the whole inspection was received later. Amongst other remarks the G.O.C. wrote :—

> "The inspection was thoroughly satisfactory in all material points. I am convinced that all ranks are trying to attain a very high standard of efficiency."

To the armies of Europe the year 1913—though they were, of course, unaware of the fact—was merely the proverbial calm before the storm. In Ireland the year was passed in the usual peace routine. Musketry, battalion, brigade and divisional training, Irish Command exercises, and the Annual Inspection.

In Ireland the year 1914 began with labour unrest in Dublin. This, as is now realised, was part of the German propaganda against any settlement in that unhappy country. The troops in garrison were highly complimented by the Chief Commissioner of Police through the Commander of the Forces for the manner in which they performed the many disagreeable duties which fell to their lot.

CHAPTER V

THE EMBARKATION FOR THE FRONT. THE BRITISH CONCENTRATION. THE BEGINNING OF THE BATTLE OF MONS.

ON August 12th—a day usually devoted by Englishmen to the celebration of a less stirring occasion—orders were received for embarkation the following morning.

On August 13th Battalion Headquarters and the right-half Battalion paraded at noon and embarked upon H.M. transport *Gloucester*, upon which ship 13th Brigade Headquarters, the 2nd Battalion K.O.S.B.'s, and the 1st Battalion The Queen's Own Royal West Kents had already found place. At 4 p.m. the left-half Battalion joined the right, but as the tide was falling it was found that there was not enough water for the ship to leave the basin, so that the *Gloucester* could not move until the early hours of the 14th. The crossing was uneventful, though the *Gloucester* was more than once challenged by French gunboats, who cheered heartily when they found British troops were on board.

Havre, where the Brigade were to disembark on the 16th, was not reached until dusk had almost fallen, so for that night, in pouring rain, the troops were ordered to make the best of it in large warehouses on the quay. At 6 a.m. on 17th, guided by French Boy Scouts, the Brigade set out for Bleville rest-camp, some five miles distant.

Here the 2nd Battalion encountered their first and very mild foretaste of what was to come in the way of weather conditions in Flanders. The camp at Bleville was a muddy field in which half the saturated tents had been blown down in the previous night's gale. But soon after the arrival of the Battalion the sun came out in full force, tents and clothes were dried, the former repitched, and the men soon settled down. Another foretaste of the future was met with for the first time in the immense piles of tinned rations heaped up on the camping-ground. The brightly-painted labels of hundreds of tins of strawberry jam, the property of a very well-known firm, called forth special cheers from the younger ranks.

August 17th was spent in final preparations for an immediate move towards the Belgian frontier. " Mobilization " maps were distributed. " Secret " road books and other publications showered upon Commanding Officers during the last few days of mobilization at home began to be digested. It may be worth consideration whether an earlier and less-hurried study of the future war *terrain* would not have been advisable. So far as the chances of secrecy were likely to have been upset by an earlier distribution, the decision for a late distribution falls to the ground. In any case, a considerable number both of maps and books must have been in the enemy's hands within barely a week, taken from the dead or badly wounded at Mons.

Before attempting to follow in detail the fortunes of the 2nd Battalion in France some outline is necessary for the *general* trend of military events immediately prior to the outbreak of the Great War. Nowhere has the sequence of events been more clearly stated than in the *Official History of the War* (Military Operations, France and Belgium, 1914) and these are freely drawn upon in the early portion of this chapter. But the events therein related refer primarily to the general conduct of the war, to the doings of the Allied Armies, Corps, and Divisional Units, as well as to General Orders for the various movements of these vast forces.

To link up connection between minor units such as battalions, companies, or even platoons with these armies is no easy task, but only by so doing can right values be arrived at of why minor units fought or were sacrificed, for—to them at the time—no apparent reason.

In the first volume of "Military Operations" referred to, the narrative "to a large extent, treats the battalion, squadron and battery records as the basis of the story. For this volume the scale adopted seems appropriate, in view of the importance of small units in the early operations; of the lessons to be derived from the study of the work of these units in open warfare; and of the desirability of leaving a picture of what war was like in 1914, when trained soldiers were still of greater importance than material, and gas, tanks, long-range guns, creeping barrages, and the participation of air-craft in ground fighting were unknown."

The wider the individual grasp of any situation where fighting is concerned, the more likely the chance of success. To throw light on the fog which enveloped the action of both sides in August, 1914, is now a comparatively easy task. In the study of the fighting during the early days of August, 1914, we have, perhaps, the key to the subsequent victory of the Allied Powers.

The British Expeditionary Force of 1914 owed its inception to the changes made in War Office administration when the General Staff came into being in 1905 under the guidance of Mr. (now) Lord Haldane. The latter had become Secretary of State for War in December, 1905, and "was charged with the duty of reorganizing the land forces not only of the country but of the Empire.

"The need of reform was urgent, for even twenty years ago the Germans made little concealment of their intention to enter the lists for the domination of the world, and were not only perfecting vast military preparations, but quietly insinuating themselves into the control of the most important financial and commercial undertakings of their neighbours."

In 1908 British reorganization began in earnest and "the first step was to build up a General Staff which should be the brains of the Army." The Staff College, Camberley, was greatly enlarged and further instruction for officers was provided at the new Indian Staff College founded at Quetta by Lord Kitchener. After considerable changes in the various branches comprising the

PLATE 6

OFFICERS OF 2ND BATTALION, DUBLIN, 8TH AUGUST, 1914

Back row.—Lieut. F. R. THACKERAY, Lieut. R. H. OWEN, Lieut. C. BATHURST, Capt. W. E. KEATES, Lieut. L. E. RUSSELL, Capt. J. C. BURNETT, Lieut. J. H. THOMPSON, Capt. R. M. TIDMARSH, Capt. H. P. TRAVERS, Lieut. H. K. O'KELLY, Capt. T. M. ELLIS.

Middle row.—Capt. E. R. TAYLOR, Capt. R. K. HEALING, Capt. E. V. JENKINS, D.S.O., Major K. A. MACLEOD, Lieut.-Colonel J. A. C. GIBBS, Capt. C. O. DENMAN-JUBB, Major P. B. STRAFFORD, Major E. N. TOWNSEND, Capt. H. GARDINER, Capt. R. C. CARTER.

Front row.—2nd Lieut. E. J. Y. GREVELINK, Lieut. G. W. OLIPHANT, Lieut. W. M. OZANNE, Lieut. M. C. B. K. YOUNG, 2nd Lieut. F. H. FRASER. (Lieut. C. W. G. INCE absent on duty, escorting the Regimental Colours to Halifax.)

LORD HALDANE'S WORK FOR THE EXPEDITIONARY FORCE

home Army such as reorganizing into and renaming the Militia and Garrison Artillery Militia the Special Reserve, organizing the Field Artillery into brigades, rebalancing Lord Cardwell's system that for every battalion almost at least one should be at home, came the reorganization of the Regular Army, or First Line into an expeditionary force of six divisions of all arms and one cavalry division. "Each of the six divisions comprised three Infantry Brigades, or twelve battalions altogether, with divisional mounted troops, artillery, engineers, signal service, supply and transport train, and field ambulances. The total war establishment of each division was thus raised to some 18,000 of all ranks and descriptions, of whom 12,000 were Infantry, with 24 machine guns, and 4000 artillery with 76 guns (54 18-pdrs.; 18 4·5-inch howitzers; and 4 60-pdrs.). The Cavalry Division comprised four brigades of three regiments each and cavalry divisional troops consisting of artillery, engineers, signal service, and medical units. The strength was some 9000 of all ranks and 10,000 horses, with 20 guns (13-pdrs.) and 24 machine guns.

"Although the nucleus of the corps-staff was maintained in time of peace at Aldershot, and corps had been formed at manœuvres, it was not originally intended to have any intermediate echelon between the General Headquarters of the Expeditionary Force and the six divisions. The decision to form corps was —in order to conform to French organization—made immediately on the formal appointment on mobilization of Field-Marshal Sir John French, G.C.B., G.C.V.O., K.C.M.G., as Commander-in-Chief. Thus it happened that two out of the three corps-staffs had to be improvised; and even in the divisional staffs the Peace Establishment allowed for only two out of the six officers given in the War Establishment.

"The Yeomanry became the second line of Cavalry and was reorganized into fourteen brigades.

"The Volunteers were treated according to the precedent of Lord Castlereagh, who had invited them to convert themselves into Local Militia, on pain of disbandment. So, too, Mr. Haldane bade them either become Territorial troops or cease to exist. . . .

"The old Militia Garrison Artillery was replaced by Territorial Coast Artillery. The Field Artillery of Territorial Divisions was armed with 15-pdr. guns converted into quick-firers, and 5-inch howitzers used in the South African War; its heavy artillery consisted of 4·7-inch guns.

"So much for the reorganization of the Territorial forces on paper. Unfortunately, before 1914 both Special Reserve and Territorial troops sank so far below their establishment as to cause some anxiety at headquarters; but it was not doubted that many old Territorials would rejoin the force at the approach of danger; and this confidence proved to be well justified. It is true that it was not anticipated that the Territorials would be ready for the field in less than six months; but they had at least some training: and, since their organization was identical with that of the First Line, they could be employed to reinforce the Regular Army, either by units or by complete divisions as they became ready."

Of the Army's training for war—such a war as that of 1914—much has since been written. At the time, however, no military student of war could possibly have envisaged " trench warfare " as exemplified by continuous lines of trenches reaching from the Swiss frontier to the North Sea near Ostend.

" The first text-book issued after the South African War for the instruction of the Army was *Combined Training*, dated 1902, written by the late Colonel G. F. R. Henderson. This, in 1905, became Part I of *Field Service Regulations*. In 1909 the book was superseded by the issue of *Field Service Regulations*— 'Part I (Operations),' and 'Part II (Organization and Administration) '— published for the first time. These manuals dealt with the general principles governing the employment of the army in war." Tanks, poison-gas, aircraft in battle, and " big Berthas " were as yet undreamt of.

" The great feature of British infantry training for the attack and counter-attack was combination of fire and movement. Ground was gained as the enemy was approached by rushes of portions of a battalion, company, or platoon, under cover of the fire of the remainder and of the artillery.

"All the above-mentioned reforms were pushed forward under the inevitable disadvantages which have ever hampered the British Army. Recruits were dribbling in at all times of the year. Trained instructors were being withdrawn for attachment to the auxiliary forces, and drafts of trained men were constantly leaving their battalions during the autumn and winter for India. The Commanders, again, could never tell whether their next campaign might not be fought in the snows of the Himalayas, the swamps and bush of Africa, or the deserts of Egypt—a campaign in Europe had hardly entered into their calculations. . . . Nevertheless, British regimental officers, to use their own expression, ' carried on,' although confronted with two changes uncongenial to many of the older men among them. The cavalry was trained to an increasing extent in the work of mounted infantry, and was armed with a rifle instead of carbine. And the Regular infantry battalions were organized into four companies instead of eight.

" In every respect the Expeditionary Force of 1914 was incomparably the best-trained, best-organized, and best-equipped British Army that ever went forth to war." It was to a very large extent due to the personal influence of Mr., now Lord, Haldane, that the British Expeditionary Force of 1914 was so well equipped with transport as it turned out to be. That this work was carried out in the face of considerable uninformed opposition with practically no help from other members of the then Government was all the more to the credit of Lord Haldane. " Except in the matter of co-operation between aeroplanes and artillery and use of machine guns its training would stand comparison in all respects with that of the Germans. Where it fell short of our enemies was first and foremost in numbers, so that, though not ' contemptible,' it was almost negligible in comparison with continental armies even of the smaller states. In heavy guns and howitzers, high-explosive shell, trench mortars, hand-grenades, and much of the subsidiary material required for siege and trench warfare, it was almost wholly deficient. Further, no steps had been taken to instruct the

Army in a knowledge of the probable theatre of war or of the German Army, except by the publication of a handbook of the Army and of annual reports on manœuvres and military changes. Exactly the same, however, was done in the case of the armies of all foreign states. *The study of German military organization and methods was specially forbidden at war games, staff tours, and intelligence classes* which would have provided the best opportunities for such instruction.

" The last of the preparations for defence that requires mention here is the formation of the National Reserve, initiated by private enterprise in August, 1910, with the approval of the Secretary of State for War and the Army Council. Its object was to register and organize all officers and men who had served in and left any of the military or naval forces of the Crown, with a view to increasing the military strength of the country in the event of imminent national danger. . . . By 1914 the National Reserve numbered about 350,000. On mobilization many of the members rejoined military and naval service. The remainder formed eventually the nucleus of the Royal Defence Corps.

" In India, the reorganization of the Army on modern lines into nine divisions, six cavalry brigades and a certain number of independent brigades by Lord Kitchener in 1903 was designed to meet the Russian menace and make India independent of assistance from overseas for twelve months. As a consequence of the Anglo-Russian agreement in 1907, and the state of Indian finance, this reorganization was never completed. The 'Army in India Committee' of 1912-13 recommended that the field army should consist of seven divisions, five cavalry brigades, and certain army troops, a force sufficient to deal with Afghanistan and the mountain tribes combined, till reinforcements could arrive. This was the authorized Field Army when war broke out in 1914, but even this had not been provided with all its mobilization equipment. Not till August, 1913, was the Government of India invited to consider the extent to which India would be prepared to co-operate with the Imperial Forces in the event of a serious war between Britain and a European enemy. It was agreed that the Army Council might count upon two—possibly three—divisions and one cavalry brigade. Actually in 1914, as will be seen, two infantry divisions and two cavalry divisions were sent to France, a division to the Persian Gulf, the equivalent of the infantry of two divisions to Egypt, besides minor detachments, and all but eight battalions of British infantry, of which the 1st Battalion The Duke of Wellington's Regiment was one, were withdrawn from India, their places being filled by British Territorial troops.

" In 1895 a Defence Committee of the Cabinet had been formed, which after changes in 1902 developed into Mr. (now Lord) Balfour's ' Committee of Imperial Defence.' The Committee was placed under the direct control of the Prime Minister and a Secretariat was provided to record its deliberations and decisions, to collect information, to outline plans necessary to meet certain contingencies, and to ensure continuity of policy. . . . Lastly, the essential steps to be taken immediately upon the outbreak of war were all of them studied exhaustively, and the distribution of the consequent duties among the various departments and among even individual officials was arranged in the minutest detail so that there should be no delay and confusion.

"Altogether, Britain never yet entered upon any war with anything approaching such forwardness and forethought in the preparation of the scanty military resources at the disposal of the War Office.

"From 1911 onward the French and British Staffs had worked out in detail a scheme for the landing of the Expeditionary Force in France and for its concentration in the area Maubeuge-Le Cateau-Hirson, but though there was an 'obligation of honour' there was no definite undertaking to send the whole or any part of this force to any particular point, or, in fact, anywhere at all."

We now know under what a terrible handicap the conduct of the war suffered in its very early days owing to the lack of co-ordination between the Services and Cabinet Ministers.

Presiding this year (1926) over a lecture at the Royal United Services Institution, Field-Marshal Sir William Robertson mentioned that the machinery when the war began was utterly out of gear. "They began on 5th August," he said, "by calling a Council of War. It was attended by twenty Cabinet Ministers, seven soldiers, and, he presumed, some sailors. It was not surprising to know that there was great disagreement as to what should be done. After a time there was nothing definite left but the Cabinet. The Cabinet set up a body which was called the Joint Naval and Military Committee for Considering Combined Operations in Foreign Territory—a rather long name which, for shortness, was called the Offensive Committee. That lived until about November, 1914, and then it disappeared and a War Council was formed of Cabinet Ministers, which lived until May, 1915, and gave way to the Dardanelles Committee, which lived until the end of the year and gave place to the War Council."[1]

As a unit of the "Contemptible," though as it turned out far from negligible British Expeditionary Force, the 2nd Battalion Duke of Wellington's Regiment left Havre by troop train in the early morning of August 18th. Before the train started two French interpreters, to act as *liaison* between the population and the Battalion, reported for duty. They were Corpl. Boutard and Pte. Guérin, Reservists of the 133rd Regiment of the French Infantry. The former subsequently gained the D.C.M. for service with the Battalion.

Pursuing the general route via Rouen and Amiens, the Battalion reached "railhead" at Landrecies about 6 p.m. on the 18th. Their reception *en route* was such as to leave no doubt of French enthusiasm at the presence at the front of British troops. Two miles north of Landrecies the Battalion went into billets at Marouilles, a pretty old-world French village.

The "fog of war" has rarely hung more densely over any military situation than it did during the time of the British concentration in France.

As a German journalist with a world-wide reputation has since written :—

"Europe stumbled into this war as a child walks upon thin ice, believing it will bear its weight and suddenly finding itself struggling in a torrent."[2]

[1] Report from the *Times* newspaper.
[2] *My Contemporaries.* Maximilian Harden, 1926.

THE FOG OF WAR

While the 2nd Battalion, all unconscious of their danger, lay at Marouilles the Germans were rapidly approaching in overwhelming force. It is easy to be wise after the event, as all the world knows, but a curious and perhaps unprecedented part of the August situation was that both sides were almost equally ignorant; equally unaware what enemy forces they were about to meet.

On August 4th German cavalry had crossed the Belgian frontier and moved upon Visé, north of Liège. By evening of August 5th six small German columns of all arms had passed the frontier and were nearly two miles into Belgium. Then came the siege and capture of Liège (August 5th/16th).

On August 10th German cavalry and Jäger battalions extended north as far as Hasselt (18 miles north-east of Tirelemont) and Diest (12 miles north of Tirelemont). On the 18th, for the second time, the Germans attacked and carried Haelen and entered Tirelemont. " They then fell upon the front and left flank of the Belgian 1st Division and only by hard fighting were held at bay. As neither French nor British were as yet ready to give assistance it was hopeless for the Belgians to think of contending against odds of four or five to one. On the evening of the 18th the five Belgian divisions were skilfully drawn off northwestward to Antwerp, which they entered on the 20th without being seriously molested.

" Further south about Namur, where the 4th Belgian Division was stationed, German cavalry patrols were in touch with the Belgian cavalry on August 5th. But it was not until nearly a fortnight later that the main bodies of the enemy approached. On August 20th the Germans drove in the Belgian outposts and on 21st opened fire upon the east and south-east forts of Namur. Within twenty-four hours the forts were practically destroyed, the Belgians being powerless to reply to the monster German howitzers. At midnight on the 23rd the Namur garrison withdrew south-west into France, whence later it rejoined the main Belgian Army at Antwerp. Thus for eighteen days the Belgians had faced the German invasion, delaying the hostile advance during a most critical period, and gaining time which was of priceless value to the Allies."[1]

During these early and fateful days of August the French Commander-in-Chief, General Joffre, ordered the following moves :—

On August 3rd General Sordet's Cavalry Corps began to move forward east of Mezières, and on the 5th, with King Albert's consent, it was ordered to enter Belgium. The idea was that Sordet's Cavalry should ascertain the direction of the enemy's advance and delay it. Sordet crossed the frontier on the 6th and moved first towards Neufchateau (36 miles east of Mezières). Then striking north Sordet's Cavalry arrived eventually within 9 miles of Liège. Finding that the Belgian field troops had already withdrawn from the area of the fortress the cavalry retired in the direction of the Meuse.

To assist the Belgian Army and support the cavalry, the I Corps of the French Fifth Army was sent forward on August 12th from Mezières

---

[1] *Official History*, Vol. I, Military Operations France and Belgium 1914.

northwards " to oppose any attempts of the enemy to cross the Meuse between Givet and Namur."

" Between August 6th and 8th it became certain that an enemy force containing units belonging to five different German Army Corps was operating against Liège, but the main group of the German armies appeared to the French General Staff to be around Metz in front of Thionville and Luxembourg."

" The enemy," continues the *Official History*, " was thus, it was thought, in a position either to advance westwards if Liège fell, or if Liège held out to wheel southwards pivoting on Metz. A decision was, therefore, made by General Joffre, and communicated to the French Armies on August 8th, to the effect that his intention was to bring the Germans to battle with all his forces united as in the original plan, with his right extended to the Rhine. If necessary, the left of the line would be held back, so as to avoid the premature engagement of one of the armies before the others could come to its assistance. If, however, the enemy's right were delayed in front of Liège, or turned southwards, the left would be advanced. As the concentration would not be finished until the 18th, it was still too early to give detailed movements; but the instructions provided for the armies gaining ground as soon as they were ready to move."

Meanwhile a French offensive on a small scale began in Alsace on August 6th. The French forces soon found themselves in the presence of superior enemy forces and were withdrawn. On the 14th the offensive was renewed with a stronger force. On the same date the First and Second French Armies began their forward movement across the frontier (south of Metz).

" On the afternoon of August 15th news came from the Belgian Army that 200,000 Germans were crossing the Meuse below Visé and from the I French Corps of the attack at Dinant. The Fourth French Army then occupied the ground vacated by the Fifth (the III and X Corps, Fifth Army, having joined I Corps) and the Third Army took over the objectives lately assigned to the Fourth. There was thus a general taking of ground to the left."

" General Joffre's general plan of operations now began to take definite shape as cumulative evidence showed that the main German advance was in progress through Belgium.

" The situation as it presented itself to him on August 16th (the day the 2nd Duke of Wellington's landed at Havre) was as follows :—

> " In the north, seven or eight German army corps and four cavalry divisions are endeavouring to pass westwards between Givet and Brussels, and even beyond these points."

South of Metz the Germans appeared to be on the defensive.

Joffre's " intention now was to make the principal attack with the Third and Fourth French Armies through Luxembourg and Belgian Luxembourg, so as to strike at the flank and communications of the enemy faces which had crossed the Meuse between Namur and the Dutch frontier, and, if possible, attack them before they could deploy for battle by wheeling south.

"To support this offensive the First and Second French Armies were to make only a secondary attack between Metz and the Vosges, for the purpose of holding the enemy, who seemed to be gradually shifting westwards, and who otherwise might be able to take in flank the French armies operating in Luxembourg. Lastly, the left wing, consisting of the Fifth French Army, the British Army *when* it should arrive, and the Belgian Army, was to move up so as to hold in check any German forces that might advance from the Meuse, and so gain sufficient time to allow the attack of the Third and Fourth French Armies to become effective. In order to give weight to the attack the Third and Fourth Armies were considerably strengthened. In brief, Joffre's first object was to break the enemy's centre, and then he intended to fall with all available forces on the right or western wing of the German armies."

This general advance was to take place on August 21st.

The Allied positions on the morning of the 20th (while the 2nd Duke of Wellington's was resting at Marouilles) were:—

The French Army of Alsace had reached Mulhausen.

The First and Second Armies were across the frontier in front of Lunéville and Nancy.

The Army of Lorraine observed Metz.

The Third and Fourth Armies were close up to the Belgian frontier astride the River Chiérs.

The Fifth Army was disposed:—

I Corps and 8th Infantry Brigade on the Meuse facing east, near Dinant.

51st Reserve Division marching up from the south to act as a link between Fourth and Fifth Armies.

X and III Corps each with an African division attached to it lay along the Sambre near Charleroi facing north.

XVIII Corps was echeloned to the left rear on the line Guzée-Thuin (6 miles and 9 miles south-west of Charleroi).

General Valabrégne's two remaining Reserve divisions were on the left of the XVIII Corps north-east of Maubeuge, in the gap into which General Joffre intended the British Army should move up.

Further to the west and beyond the space to be occupied by the British were three Territorial Divisions under General D'Amade, 84th near Douai; 82nd near Arras; 81st between Hazebrouck and St. Omer.

Such being the actual disposition, let us now examine the result of French movements. A glance at the map will show that the front of the Fifth French Army (General Lanrezac's) formed a dangerous salient along the Meuse and Sambre. At the apex of the salient stood Namur. By the evening of August 20th the Germans, as already related, were closing upon Namur. Consequently, any failure on the part of the French right to hold its ground on the Meuse would place the centre in a very dangerous situation, rendering it liable to be cut off.

Before the general advance ordered for the 21st had begun misfortune had already overtaken the French. "The First and Second French Armies tired by several days of marching and fighting, came up against strongly organized positions, armed with powerful artillery, whose fire was admirably prepared and directed by aeroplanes."

"After being violently counter-attacked the Second French Army was compelled to retire and the First had to conform to its movements.

"On August 21st, in spite of this reverse to the right wing, the Third and Fourth French Armies crossed the frontier and advanced from 10 to 15 miles into the difficult Ardennes country, hilly, wooded, and with marshy bottoms. They were met by the Germans in superior force and compelled to fall back towards the Meuse. The attempt to break the German centre before the right wing could deliver its blow against the Allied left wing had thus failed."

General Lanrezac with the Fifth Army had considered it inadvisable to advance simultaneously with the armies on his right. He preferred to wait until his reinforcements should have arrived, which would not be until the 23rd. He wished also that the "Fourth Army should have cleared the gorges of the Semoy and shortened by its advance the eastern face of the salient which the front of his army presented to the enemy."

He intended also to wait until the British Army should have come up on his left.

On August 21st, as we already know, Sir John French's two Corps were approaching the line of the Mons-Condé Canal.

The general situation in which it was about to play its part may be thus summarized:—

The French First and Second Armies were retiring.
The Third and Fourth "had failed and the reverse seemed serious."
The Fifth was in a salient about to be attacked by two German armies.
Namur was on the point of falling.
The Belgian Army had been driven into Antwerp.

The 13th Brigade (including the 2nd Battalion the Duke of Wellington's Regiment) remained at Marouilles until August 21st. With the exception of an advanced line of observation outposts the time was chiefly spent in preparing for the coming advance into the war zone. On the left of the 13th Brigade was the 14th and on its right the 19th Brigade. At Marouilles connection with home seemed to be once more established by the passing of miles of London motor omnibuses and tradesmen's motor-vans, which on August 19th were *en route* to try and find and join the Cavalry Brigade as their transport. A few days later these same familiar "buses" gave rise to the reflection what a lot of wounded men could have been got away instead of being left behind as prisoners of war if only some motor transport had been substituted in Infantry Brigade for the old-fashioned G.S. wagons.

On August 20th the Brigade and each battalion in it was visited and addressed by its Divisional Commander, Maj.-General Sir Charles Fergusson,

Bt., C.B., M.V.O., D.S.O. All that the 5th Divisional Commander could say to relieve the dense fog of ignorance of the general situation he told; but the information was almost entirely negative. Nothing was known so far of the enemy or of the movements of our allies, the French. The Divisional Commander was as yet unaware of the arrival of other British troops or of British artillery. Nor had he then any orders for a forward advance, though by 11.30 p.m. the same night they arrived. The "fog of war" was at its thickest.

On August 21st reveillé sounded at 4.30 a.m. and by 7 a.m. the advance of the 13th Brigade had begun. After an uneventful march of some 10 miles the route taken led through the north-east corner of the wonderful Forêt de Mormal. Penetrated by broad, good roads intersected by glades every few hundred yards and cut at right angles to the main road for purposes of timber-hauling, this cool and peaceful forest was a delightful change. How soon it was to be devastated few that day dreamed.

Debouching at Obies, the Brigade continued its march through Mecquignies to Bavai, which was reached by 3 p.m. The Battalion went into billets south of the town as escort to the II Corps and 5th Division Headquarters there. The rest of the 13th Brigade went on to Houdain to take up an outpost line facing north.

Even at Bavai on August 21st nothing definite had come through about German movements. A few patrols had been localised well to the north-east in the direction of Hasselt-Liège, but the "fog" continued. Were the German movements north of the British only those of small bodies, or were enemy "friends" in Northern France numerous and anxious not to give away information? Whatever the cause of this blank ignorance, it still continued when on August 22nd the 2nd Duke of Wellington's crossed the Belgian frontier just south of Athis, moving via Dour and Boussu to St. Ghislain. Here at 2 p.m. the Battalion outspanned in a field allotted to the 13th Brigade. On August 22nd, as known to Battalion Headquarters, the general disposition of the British troops in France was as follows:—

The II Army Corps, 3rd and 5th Divisions, under General Sir Horace L. Smith-Dorrien, G.C.B., D.S.O., to hold a line Condé-Mons.

The I Army Corps, 1st and 2nd Divisions, under Lieut.-General Sir Douglas Haig, K.C.B., K.C.I.E., K.C.V.O., to hold a line from Mons eastward to connect with French armies. Cavalry at Binche.

Immediately north of St. Ghislain the 2nd Battalion K.O.Y.L.I and the R.W. Kents took over outpost duty along the Mons-Condé section of the canal. The actual detail covering from the bridge at Les Herbieres to La Marette, both inclusive. The 2nd Duke of Wellington's were detailed to work in support and relief of the 1st Battalion R.W Kents section, while the 2nd Battalion K.O.S.B.'s were to perform the same service for the 2nd Battalion K.O.Y.L.I.'s.

At 3 p.m. on August 22nd the 13th Brigade Commander went round his battalions as well as the ground they were occupying. (*Vide* map.) He was accompanied by the Officer Commanding 2nd Duke of Wellington's, Lieut.-Colonel J. A. C. Gibbs. The R.W. Kents had one company pushed out in advance (under Major P. Hastings) on the Tertre road. This company was in support of the Divisional Cycling Company operating to the north. Even so late as 3 to 4 p.m. on August 22nd little, if any, news of a German advance had reached the foremost British troops, which goes to explain the practical "wash-out" of Major Hastings' Company during the subsequent twenty-four hours and the death of its gallant commander. Curiously enough, Major Hastings had for a brief period been attached to the 2nd Duke of Wellington's Regiment at Rangoon in 1899. Returning through the section of the front line occupied

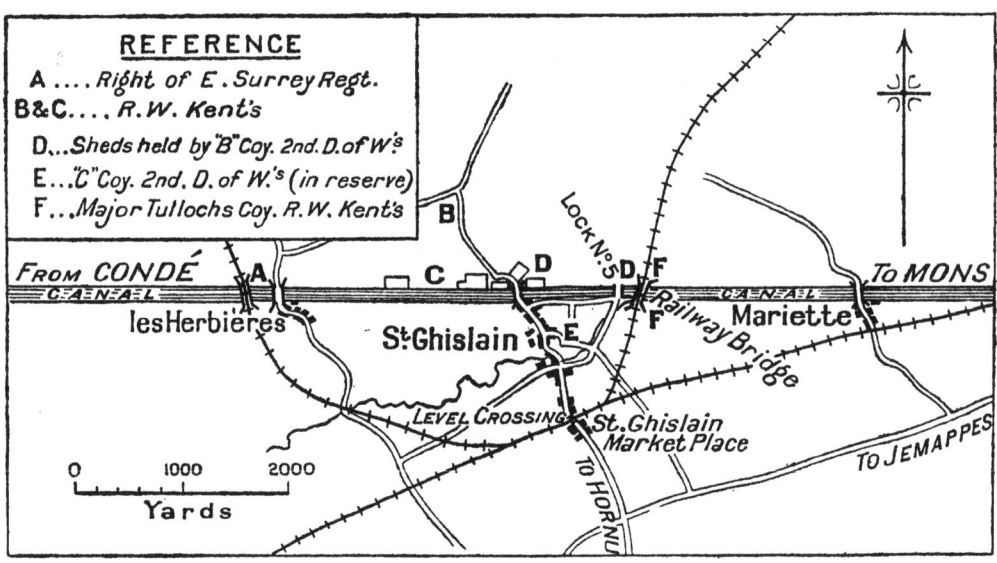

POSITION ON 22ND AUGUST, 1914.

by the 2nd Battalion K.O.S.B.'s the Brigadier met the 1st East Surreys (14th Brigade), under Lieut.-Colonel J. R. Longley. They were moving up to prolong the 13th Brigade line to the west.

As viewed by those ordered to occupy it, the advanced outpost line of the 13th Brigade was almost as bad as could be. Two of the most necessary qualifications for a line of outposts were entirely absent. These being, first, a free and extended field of infantry fire for the defenders, secondly, good artillery positions for the supporting guns. Everywhere, too, the front of the outpost line gave good cover for an enemy to move up to close quarters with the defenders.

Upon reaching the Battalion bivouac, Lieut.-Colonel Gibbs found that orders had been received for the 13th Brigade to go into billets at Hornu, a mile south-east of St. Ghislain. The Battalion were also ordered (subject to cancellation) to relieve the 1st Battalion R.W. Kents on outpost duty on the evening of

August 23rd, the 2nd Battalion K.O.Y.L.I. being also detailed to relieve the 2nd Battalion K.O.S.B.'s.

By 5.30 p.m. on August 22nd the Brigade reached Hornu, where the billets allotted to the 2nd Duke of Wellington's were found to be in the market place.

"I shall always remember," writes the Machine Gun Officer[1] of the Regiment, " crossing the frontier line where many Belgians had collected, to greet us as it were, and who showered upon us boxes of matches, chocolates, and fruit, etc. Being ahead of the Battalion I presume I came in for more than my share of these attentions ; matches were particularly welcome as French matches were scarce and of very bad quality. Billets were good and plentiful at Hornu, consequently there was no difficulty in getting everything cut and dry by the time the Battalion arrived the same evening. My anticipations of a good night's rest were far from realized, as at about 8.30 p.m., I received orders to proceed on outpost duty with my M.G. section. My orders were to proceed immediately to Lock 5 on the Mons-Condé Canal and to supplement with my guns the defence of the railway bridge in that locality. I was informed that I should find a Company of the Royal West Kents there and that I was to coordinate my plans of defence with those of the Company Commander.

"It was a particularly dark night and I found it no easy matter getting my gun limbers along the somewhat rough tow-path. I arrived at Lock 5 about 10.30 p.m. to find Capt. H. D. Buchannan-Dunlop was commanding the Royal West Kent Company. Being pitch dark it was impossible to site gun positions. I decided, therefore, to bivouac immediately and commence defence arrangements the following morning as soon as there was sufficient light.

"At about 4 a.m. on August 23rd some Belgian civilians (cyclists) passed through our lines with information as to the approaching enemy, stating they had seen large numbers of infantry and guns.

"As soon as there was sufficient light I sited gun positions, on the north side of the canal, one gun on each side of the railway embankment (see rough sketch, p. 64), so that each gun could bring fire to bear on the embankment itself and on to the open country both east and west of the embankment. Both guns had a wonderful field of fire up to about 1200 yds.; the ground was void of cover except for corn stooks and the moderately thick scrub skirting both sides of the railway embankment. While the gun positions were being dug I prepared defence range cards for each gun.

"At about 10 a.m. both gun positions were completed (with overhead cover). It was at this moment I saw my first 'boche.' I had gone out about 200 yards in front of my left gun position, to view it from the enemy side to ensure that it was well concealed. I might add that I had foolishly gone out unarmed, otherwise I might have 'bagged' a Uhlan very early in the day. I had approached to within about 20 yards of a track which ran under the railway embankment (marked x on sketch) when I came face to face with a Uhlan. He appeared about as surprised to see me as I was to see him ; before I had time

[1] Capt. W. M. Ozanne, wounded August 23rd, 1914.

even to weigh up the situation he had turned about and galloped back along the track under the embankment. I in turn made off as fast as my legs would carry me to my right gun position; the gun by this time was mounted and all in readiness for action. On arrival at the gun position I saw a party of about 6 Uhlans making off at the gallop towards a small wood (y on sketch). Rightly or wrongly, I ordered fire to be opened on them. I felt justified in taking this action, partly because I had taken several key ranges, and I felt there was every chance of inflicting casualties; on the other hand, by opening fire we gave away

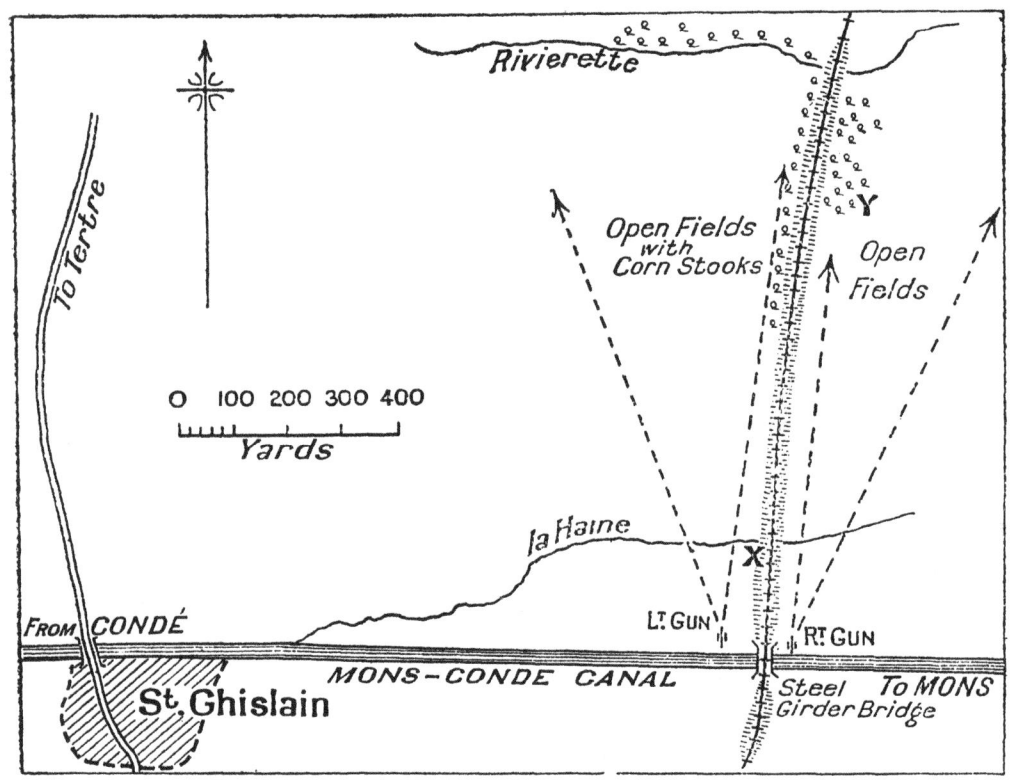

MACHINE-GUN POSITIONS ON AUGUST 23RD, 1914.

the fact that we had machine guns in this locality. The Uhlans were about 500 yards away when we commenced to open fire, but I'm sorry to say the gunner rather lost his head in the excitement of the moment; as a result we did not inflict any casualties whatsoever.

"I think I am right in saying that these were the first shots fired on this front.

"Having one gun each side of the embankment, it was impossible to command both guns. I therefore put Sergt. Smith (my Senior Sergt.) in command of the right gun and I myself remained with the left gun.

"The first enemy attack developed about 12 noon as far as I can recollect. It was not pressed with much determination, consequently we didn't have much

PLATE 7

LIEUT.-COLONEL W. E. M. TYNDALL, D.S.O.

CAPT. C. O. DENMAN-JUBB

LIEUT.-COLONEL A. A. ST. HILL, D.S.O.

MAJOR E. C. BOUTFLOWER, O.B.E.

difficulty in breaking it up. Small bodies of enemy reached the open fields to our immediate front; they were, however, soon checked by our M.G. and rifle fire; as a result they scattered in small groups behind corn stooks, where they remained for the rest of the day. Their rest, however, behind these stooks cannot claim to have been peaceful, as we hotted them up with gun fire at irregular intervals throughout the day.

"In this attack I engaged (with my left gun) an enemy field-gun battery which endeavoured to come into action more or less in the open about 1100 yards from my left gun position. We had the desired effect of forcing them to cover, but I don't think we inflicted many casualties. No serious attacks developed on our immediate front during the rest of the day. Practically all our casualties were a result of enemy shelling. This was very consistent and accurate, particularly after about 3 p.m., when our guns appeared to stop firing, the enemy then traversed along the general line of the canal continually until night-fall.

"It was about 3 p.m. that I myself was wounded. A shell burst at the front of the M.G. emplacement; we were lucky, however, as regards casualties. I fared worst with a shattered arm, the No. 2 had a slight wound in the hand, the No. 1 and the gun itself were not touched. I was able to make my way to the railway bridge and remained under cover of the bridge until nightfall. From this position I was able to a limited extent to command my section. There were several wounded under the bridge and we had many anxious moments owing to a charge which the R.E.'s had laid with a view to blowing up the bridge if and when necessary. In the course of their shelling the enemy registered many direct hits on the bridge, and consequently a direct hit on this charge would have meant the end of the bridge and all of us underneath.

"The worst, fortunately for us, did not happen.

"At about 6 p.m. the enemy were seen to cross the canal at the crossing about a mile east of Lock 5, but an immediate counter-attack drove them north of the canal again. What troops were responsible for this counter-attack I don't know. Fortunately, at nightfall the enemy shelling ceased. As I was then no longer able to command my section, I took the opportunity of making my way back to St. Ghislain, where I thought I might be able to get my wound attended to. It was slow going, but eventually I reached the village and there found detachments of my Regiment (D Company, I think). I was conducted to a school which had been converted into a hospital; the latter was being run entirely by Belgian civilians. Several of my Battalion were in this hospital, including Capt. Carter, who had been wounded in the leg.

"At about 11 p.m. Colonel Gibbs visited us and gave us the 'cheering' news that orders for retirement had been received; as there was no means of moving us, everything pointed to our being made prisoners in an unpleasantly short space of time. About two hours later a Belgian civilian came into the hospital with the astounding announcement that there was a train at the station siding if anyone could get there. Personally, I thought this was a hoax as it seemed too good to be true. However, train or no train, we had no hesitation in deciding that the risk was worth it. We at once organized our small party. We only had one stretcher and were, therefore, only able to take one stretcher case with us (Capt. Carter). It was hateful leaving others behind, but this was unavoidable. With the Belgian guide and others assisting us, we were conducted through some back streets to a railway siding on the south side of the village. Here, to our astonishment, was an engine with steam up and about half a dozen carriages. Within a very few minutes we were on our way to Amiens.

" After the war I met a Lce.-Corporal of the Regiment (Lce.-Corpl. Hart, I think). He was in the same hospital at St. Ghislain and was unfortunately one of the more serious cases left behind. He told me that we hadn't quitted the hospital more than about five to ten minutes when the Germans entered the village and made them prisoners."

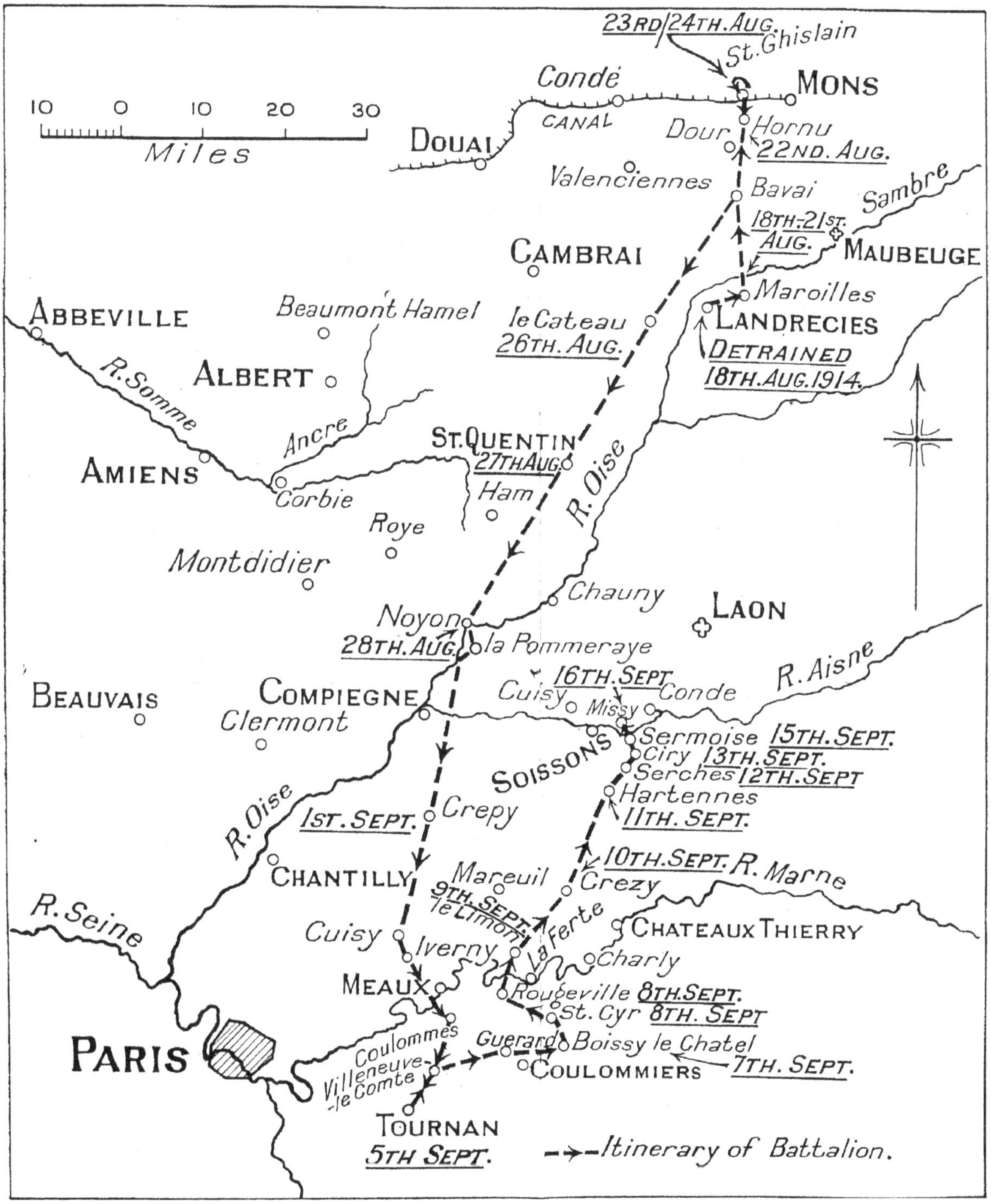

23RD/24TH. AUG.
St. Ghislain
Condé
MONS
CANAL
DOUAI
Dour
Hornu
22ND. AUG.
10 0 10 20 30
Miles
Valenciennes
Bavai
Sambre
18TH-21ST. AUG.
MAUBEUGE
CAMBRAI
Maroilles
ABBEVILLE
Beaumont Hamel
le Cateau
26TH. AUG.
LANDRECIES
DETRAINED
18TH. AUG. 1914.
R. Somme
ALBERT
Ancre
ST. QUENTIN
27TH AUG.
AMIENS
Corbie
Ham
R. Oise
Roye
Montdidier
Chauny
LAON
Noyon
28TH. AUG.
la Pommeraye
16TH. SEPT.
R. Aisne
BEAUVAIS
COMPIEGNE
Cuisy
Missy
Conde
Clermont
Sermoise
15TH. SEPT.
SOISSONS
Ciry
13TH. SEPT.
Serches
12TH. SEPT
Hartennes
11TH. SEPT.
Crepy
1ST. SEPT.
R. Oise
10TH. SEPT.
R. Marne
CHANTILLY
Mareuil
Crezy
9TH. SEPT.
le Limon
R. Seine
La Ferte
CHATEAUX THIERRY
Cuisy
Iverny
Charly
MEAUX
Rougeville
8TH. SEPT.
St. Cyr
8TH. SEPT
Coulommes
Guerard
Boissy le Chatel
PARIS
Villeneuve-le Comte
COULOMMIERS
7TH. SEPT.
TOURNAN
5TH SEPT.
Itinerary of Battalion.

CHAPTER VI

THE BATTLE OF MONS (*continued*).

FOR survivors of the British Expeditionary Force in France, Sunday, August 23rd, is a date they will remember to their dying day. It must also be, for all time, a memorable date to the Regiment. The Sunday morning broke sunny and peaceful, as seemed appropriate, but the fates ruled otherwise. Church bells were sounding and the neat black Sunday clothes, so universal in France, were everywhere in evidence. Not even yet did anyone seem to realize the smashing blow which was to fall upon the " Contemptible " Little Army. By the kindness of the local coal-miners their large baths had been put at the disposal of the 2nd Battalion this Sunday morning. A welcome luxury indeed it was, and arrangements had been made over-night to take advantage of the opportunity for a real clean-up. As luck would have it, B and C Companies had finished bathing when an order came for two companies to go up at once to the canal to support the R.W. Kents. With these two companies Major Strafford proceeded to carry out instructions, A and D Companies (A having missed its bath) being ordered to stand-by. This was at 9 a.m. Wagons were packed and all preparations made for a move. By 10 a.m. orders came for the rest of the Battalion to move up to the canal, leaving the first-line transport, except S.A.A. carts, under the Headquarters party as escort. After the Battalion had moved off a Uhlan patrol wandered into Hornu. This, with his usual efficiency and by aid of the Headquarters party, Q.M. and Major A. Ellam promptly " did in."

With A and D Companies the C.O. proceeded towards St. Ghislain, and at the level railway-crossing south of the village, half a mile from the canal, the sound of firing was first heard.

An officer of the Regiment thus aptly describes his first impressions of modern war :—[1]

" We had left Marouilles on the 22nd, and on the 23rd August went into action for the first time at Wasmes. My feelings I cannot say were of the happiest and I remember that my first actual experience of shell-fire was a German shell bursting over Wasmes whilst I, with several others, was enjoying a cup of coffee and some chocolate outside a small estaminet. I can only say I did not enjoy that coffee and chocolate. However, with the general excitement, the noise and one's responsibility (I was commanding No. 1 Platoon) I soon settled

---

[1] Lieut. (now Major) C. W. G. Ince, M.C., later severely injured.

down, and I think one's fear was more of oneself in case one did the wrong thing.

"We were very soon in action along the canal at St. Ghislain. Unfortunately, my platoon-sergeant (Sergt. Greenhalgh) was wounded by a shrapnel bullet in the square of St. Ghislain, just before we moved off to take up our position on a slag dump near the canal facing north. It was very hot, and we were very soon a dirty-looking crowd after climbing about on the coal dump. Fear was put into us very shortly after we had moved into position, by a German shell making a direct hit on one of the overhead trolleys that run the slag from the coal pit-head to the slag heap. The trolley fell rolling down the heap very nearly on top of us. We remained in position most of the afternoon, and in the evening I received orders to join the rest of my Company (A) (Major Townsend's). They were situated in a natural entrenchment on a low slag heap. It was whilst in this position that I had one of the best targets in the shape of the enemy to fire at that I saw during the whole of the War. I think it was about 8 or 8.30 p.m., when at about 500 yards we saw a German company in fours marching down a road on our right flank towards the British positions. We immediately opened fifteen rounds rapid into them, together with one of our Vickers guns. We practically wiped out the German company, though they did the only thing they could do, that was to extend and immediately open fire on us. Most of them were either killed or wounded, and a few retired rapidly. Our casualties were unfortunately two killed and one or two slightly wounded. I remember that the fact of seeing one of my Company killed had a very heart-breaking effect, which in later days wore off as one became used to seeing so many of one's comrades knocked over.

"In my own experience the first few days of the War were far the most trying. As time wore on one got hardened to all the agony of it. In fact, one became callous and looked upon all the bloodshed, etc., as quite the natural thing.

"In the evening (August 23rd) we received orders to retire, and during the night we snatched a few moments of sleep on the sides of the road. Early in the morning (24th) we relieved the Dorsets in some trenches, which we occupied until about 4 p.m. in the day until we were ordered to retire. This day was the great day on which we took our part in the Battle of Mons.

"It was, I think, early in the afternoon when we saw the masses of German Infantry advancing on us, into which we poured as much rifle fire as we could, and it was not until I saw the platoon on my right retiring in extended order, just as one might see it on a field-day at home, that I realized that something was up. Very shortly one or two men came to our position running hard, saying that they had received orders to pass the message to retire. Fortunately for my platoon, I had lost very few men (very few killed that day, as far as I can remember). We left all our wounded in cottages close by, and I am afraid, poor fellows, they eventually became prisoners. I should have said that some of those wounded earlier in the day were eventually evacuated as they were able to be removed before the general retirement commenced."

THE FIRST CLASH IN THE OPEN

To the above may be added another little incident, the recital of which, by Lieut. O'Kelly, gives a vivid picture of those early lessons of the Great War. The story also exemplifies how entirely ignorant the individual officer, N.C.O., or private soldier often is of why he is ordered to do this, or to refrain from doing something else.

"On Sunday morning" (August 23rd), Lieut. O'Kelly, D.S.O., relates, " I attended Mass and just as it was nearly over I was sent for and told that the enemy had been reported marching in very large numbers towards Hornu, that they were unopposed, and that, as far as we knew, our division was the only one about. No French troops had been seen. We were pushed forward very hurriedly, and after about a five miles march shells began to drop amongst us, doing some little damage. At that time I commanded a platoon, 54 men strong. I was told that there was a canal in front of me and that I was to line the bank between two certain points. Soon after I got into position I found myself enfiladed by rifle fire coming from our right. Assuming I had been given a wrong front I doubled the platoon out across the open and faced them the other way. In doing this manœuvre I lost a few men. When I and my platoon were lying out in the open, a very heavy rifle fire opened on us, also shells whistled over our heads, but so far no damage had been done. I saw a sort of natural bank some distance in front of us and moved on, getting the men lined up in it. About an hour later (3 o'clock afternoon) we saw the enemy advancing in a great mass several hundreds strong, while we were about 50 only. We opened rapid fire and did terrible damage, the enemy's front ranks falling fast, but always filling up. Each man must have fired some hundreds of rounds that evening. I had sent several messages back to say unless help came very soon we would be wiped out, as, of course, had we retreated into the open we would have been shot down at once. The enemy advanced very slowly, but towards 5 o'clock were within 300 yards of us, at which time I got a message from Major Townsend, our Company Commander, telling me that there was no possible hope of escape, and that we must sell ourselves as dearly as possible as he was also preparing to do. We fixed bayonets and waited patiently, the men behaving admirably. I told them that our retreat had been cut off and that we could not expect to rejoin our regiment any more. This was the one and only time during that War that I prayed for a bullet, and hoped that it would soon come. Of course, had the Germans known our numbers they would have come on at once. About 5.30 a lot of bugles sounded the ' cease fire.' I concluded that this could not possibly apply to me, so every time the enemy jumped up to advance we continued the fire. This I afterwards learned was treachery on the part of the Germans. They never got nearer than 200 yards, as suddenly they started to retreat. They either suspected a trap, cavalry charge, or something else, but imagine our delight when we found they retreated, and we still kept up our fire until we could not see in the dark. Later that night Townsend sent for me and told me to retire. I had 3 men killed and about 12 wounded. We joined the Battalion and found the total losses were very few, Capt. R. C. Carter being the only officer wounded."

For the Duke of Wellington's, as for the other regiments of the 13th Brigade, this was the actual commencement of four years of the most terrible and destructive fighting the world has ever known. For most of those engaged it was also their first taste of the horrors of modern war. It may for this reason, then, be worth while to attempt to describe in some detail these first forty-eight hours round Mons. Fortunately this can be done, and in the C.O.'s own words up to the time when Colonel J. A. C. Gibbs, C.B., was himself wounded at midday on August 24th.

"Halting the two companies," writes Lieut.-Colonel Gibbs, "and leaving our horses at the level crossing I walked on with Macleod[1] and Jubb[2] to take stock. Things were getting very 'warm,' and it was difficult to locate the enemy or his numbers owing to the flat country to the north of the canal and the natural cover afforded by hedges and deep ditches. The field of fire in front of D Company was barely 300 yards in depth. I visited Lieut.-Colonel A. Martyn (C.O. Royal West Kent Regiment), who told me he would be glad to have Tulloch's[3] Company reinforced near the railway bridge. He also told me that, with the exception of an odd cyclist or two who had come back with reports and who gave somewhat conflicting stories, he did not know what was in front.

"I sent back to the railway crossing and ordered the two companies up to St. Ghislain market square, telling Jenkins[4] on arrival there to send two platoons to Tulloch.

"It was now about 1 p.m. and oppressively hot. I went to where B Company was in fairly good cover behind some banks just beyond the sheds at D. (see map on page 62), and from which we could get a fairly good view with glasses. Occasional glimpses of Germans creeping along hedgerows at from 400 to possibly 700 yards were now to be had, but Carter[5] had warned his men not to fire till a really good target offered itself, so as not to give their position away. When they did begin I think it fairly staggered the enemy, who went to ground at once. Shrapnel was soon opened on the buildings along the canal, but luckily without any serious effects to our men. It soon ceased. The hopelessness of having no guns to reply with was most galling, but I can't help thinking it puzzled the 'Bosche,' and certainly as far as our part of the line went they had evidently made up their minds to wait till dark before making any further advance, although rifle fire was kept up pretty regularly. Carter got a bullet through the calf of his leg, necessitating his removal to the dressing station at the town hospital. Pte. Shellabear was killed close to me, about 3 p.m., and was, I believe, the first man killed in the Regiment.

"The Brigadier-General came out during the afternoon and told me he heard they were entrenching a position near Wasmes, to which we should probably fall back after dark. He had no news as to what was in front, but in common with the rest of us felt sure that the German forces were not the small force of two or three Army Corps we had been given to understand it was. He told me

---

[1] Major Kenneth A. Macleod (Second-in-Command).
[2] Capt. C. O. Denman-Jubb (Battalion Adjutant). Killed on August 24th.
[3] Capt. R. M. C. Tulloch, p.s.c., 1st Battn. Queen's Own Royal West Kent Regt.
[4] Capt. E. V. Jenkins, D.S.O.   [5] Capt. R. C. Carter.

Q.M. & MAJOR A. ELLAM, M.C.

MAJOR W. G. OFFICER

MAJOR C. W. G. INCE, M.C.

CAPT. H. K. O'KELLY, D.S.O.

the rest of the Brigade had had a hot time on our left. Before leaving, the Brigadier-General directed me, should things get too hot, to send back a special report.

"About 4.30 p.m. I received an order to make good the right flank of the Brigade—as the 9th Brigade (on our right) was shortly going back—so I sent the following order to Townsend[1] at 4.40 p.m. : 'Take your Coy. and proceed and get touch with 9th Brigade at Mariette AAA. Should this brigade be withdrawn you must protect our right flank on line of road running Quaregnon–La Cordellette AAA.' I also sent an order to Jenkins to stay in reserve on the square (St. Ghislain) with his 2 platoons and particularly to watch the right flank.

"About 5.30 p.m. we heard Townsend having rather a busy time on our right towards Mariette, so I sent Strafford[2] with his remaining 3 platoons to support him, and Macleod went off with them to find out how things were going there.

"About dusk firing ceased, and shortly we could distinctly hear the Germans entrenching and moving up guns to fairly short ranges. I went along to where Martyn and the West Kents were, and he agreed with me that the position would be untenable at dawn. I sent back a report to this effect to Brigade Headquarters. Martyn had had bad news of poor Hastings'[3] Company—odd men who had got back told him the former was dead and a large number of the Company either dead or wounded in the enemy's hands.

"At 9.55 p.m. I received the following order :—

'O.C. DUKE OF WELLINGTONS.

'B.M. 43. 23rd.

'The Division will retire to the prepared position on the Wasmes–Bois de Boussu line. The 13th Bde. will hold the line from the 2nd S in Wasmes to the Hornu–Champ des Sarts road inclusive. aaa. 14th Bde. will continue this line Westwards. aaa. All Bridges are to be blown up before leaving the Canal. Retirement to commence as soon as possible. aaa. The 2nd Dukes will hold the line from the right to the westernmost of the two roads running S from the W of Wasmes (inclusive). 2nd K.O.Y.L.I. will hold the left section from above road exclusive. aaa. 1st R.W.K. will withdraw through the 2nd Dukes into a position in support.

2nd K.O.S.B. will start by withdrawing through the 2nd K.O.Y.L.I. aaa. It is not necessary to occupy trenches to-night but to take up a more or less concentrated position behind them covering works with outposts. aaa. The trenches will be fully occupied by dawn. aaa.

Brigade H.Q. will be at road junction about $\frac{3}{4}$ mile South of W in Wasmes. Report when your withdrawal is complete. O.C. 2 D. of W. will be responsible that 2 Coys. 15th Bde. retire with him. These two companies are on the Chaussée near Hornu.

13th Inf. Bde.
9.30 p.m.

(Sd.) C. C. EGERTON, Lt.'

---

[1] Major E. N. Townsend, D.S.O., wounded on 24th.
[2] Major P. B. Strafford.   [3] Major P. Hastings (Queens Own R.W. Kent Regt.).

"Owing to it now being very dark and no lights being allowed in the town, and also to the extent of front we were spread over, I knew it would be difficult to assemble the whole Battalion before moving to Wasmes. I therefore told Ellis[1] (now in Command of B Company) to collect his men and move as soon as possible to the market-place where Jenkins was.

"I sent written messages to Macleod, Strafford, and Townsend to collect and retire direct to Wasmes railway station, and also stating the position of our trenches.

"Before leaving the Canal, I saw the R.E. C.S.M., who had been in charge of a party sinking barges and preparing demolitions in our section, who told me everything was ready to destroy the bridges after the West Kents had all got across the Canal.

"The town seemed very quiet as Jubb, Graham (M.O.), and I walked back to the 'Place,' and none of the inhabitants seemed to know what was going on. I met Jenkins and told him the situation and also that I had arranged with Martyn to bring Thompson's[2] platoons back with Tulloch's Company. Jenkins had taken up a position with his remaining platoons covering the streets leading from the 'Place' to the Canal, so I gave him an order to remain in observation until the West Kents came back and then to join me at Wasmes.

"I also found an orderly of the Cheshire Regiment who had come to tell me where the O.C. detachment 15th Brigade was (Capt. Stapylton),[3] and I sent a message telling him I would meet him shortly at the level railway crossing on the Hornu road.

"It was now after 11 p.m., but as Ellis had not yet arrived I left Jubb to bring him on to the above crossing and went with Graham to the hospital to see if any evacuations had taken place. To my dismay, I found that except the horse ambulances having been used to their full capacity, no further transport had been arranged. I went at once to the station (about $\frac{1}{4}$ of a mile away) and was lucky in being able to arrange for an engine and a few trucks to be ready in half-an-hour's time.

"Hurrying back I gave the order out that any officers or men who were not dangerously wounded and who could manage to get to the train could get away. Many did succeed, I am glad to say I afterwards learnt, including Carter and Ozanne.[4]

"I got to the railway crossing about midnight, and found Jubb—B Company—and the two Cheshire Companies, and, to my great joy, as I was very legweary, Shaw with my horse, 'The Camel.' Shaw[5] told me Dapple (my second horse) had been hit by a fragment of shrapnel, but was luckily not bad. He had left her in a stable close by, and went off to bring her along.

"We moved off, and on passing through Hornu I knocked up Monsieur

---

[1] Capt. T. M. Ellis. Killed at Hill 60 later.
[2] Lieut. J. H. L. Thompson.
[3] Major B. H. Chetwynd-Stapylton (1st Battn. Cheshire Regt.).
[4] Lieut. W. M. Ozanne, M.C.
[5] Pte. Shaw (C.O's. groom).

Plate 9

GERMAN "COOKA" TAKEN ON THE AISNE

SERGT. J. H. SHAW, D.C.M.

THE "CAMEL"

DEATH OF CAPTAIN AND ADJUTANT DENMAN-JUBB

Croissiaux, my host of the day before, and told him what was happening—poor fellow, he was very perturbed.

"It took some time from Hornu to Wasmes owing to the number of by-streets and roads not shown on the map, and we had constantly to knock people up to ask the best way. I left guides at cross roads to bring on the others.

"On arrival at Little Hornu the Cheshires went off to join their brigade. Passing through this mining village I reached the rendezvous given at Wasmes railway station bridge, north-west of the town, about 3 a.m., with B Company, where I left them whilst Jubb and I went to look for the trenches.

"Crossing the road over the bridge, Jubb went down it to the market-square where Brigade Headquarters was, to report, etc., whilst I moved off the road in a north-east direction up a stubble field slope, to locate our trenches. Thanks to the glare from a colliery, I saw British uniforms, and on getting up to them found two companies of the Dorsets occupying the trenches on high ground, which the K.O.Y.L.I. were to take over. Capt. Maxwell-Hyslop[1] was with them. I soon got the direction of the 'dividing' road specified in our orders (local name, Rue d'Hornu), and on arrival found Townsend with A Company, and also Thompson and his platoon. It was still dark, so leaving them to rest I walked down towards the town, meeting Currie[2] (our Brigade Major) who could give me no information of any dispositions outside those of our Brigade—Jubb came up and told me he had found the trenches to be occupied by B and D Companies, and had them ready to go into and relieve the Dorsets and Bedfords, and also that he knew a way to get them there under cover. He added the original extent of front to which the Battalion was detailed (about $\frac{3}{4}$ of a mile) had had to be considerably increased by the 15th Brigade, owing to a large gap on the right and dead ground, and he supposed we had better conform to what the Dorsets and Bedfords had done. I concurred. I arranged with him to move them in whilst I went and put A Company into their trenches on the left of our section, and told him I should then go on to the 'bosquet' knoll about the centre of our Battalion, where he should join me there as soon as he could.

"Poor fellow, he never rejoined me. I learnt later he had been killed whilst watching our machine guns away to the right.

"I returned to A Company as dawn was just breaking, so we got the men into their trenches as quickly as possible. These were in the open to the north of a powder magazine and some cottages, which were now empty.

"C Company and Macleod came up just then, much to my relief, as I didn't know where they were.—Apparently they had lost their way among the coal pits in the dark.—This Company I sent down to the 'bosquet' as battalion reserve.

"(*N.B.*—On meeting Lieut.-Colonel R. C. Bond, K.O.Y.L.I., about two years later in Germany, he told me that on arrival at Wasmes on August 24th, 1914, just at daybreak, when near the railway station bridge, he was told by the Staff Captain that his *right* was now to rest on the bridge.

---

[1] Capt. R. G. B. M. Hyslop, 1st Battn. The Dorset Regt.
[2] Capt. R. A. M. Currie, Somerset Light Infantry (Brigade Major 13th Bde.).

This, of course, accounts for the K.O.Y.L.I. not taking up their proper position ordered. I received no intimation of this change, and can only imagine the Staff Captain seeing troops on the high ground took them for my battalion (these were the two companies of Dorsets) and also as the K.O.Y.L.I. were late in arriving he therefore thought this was the best thing to be done.)

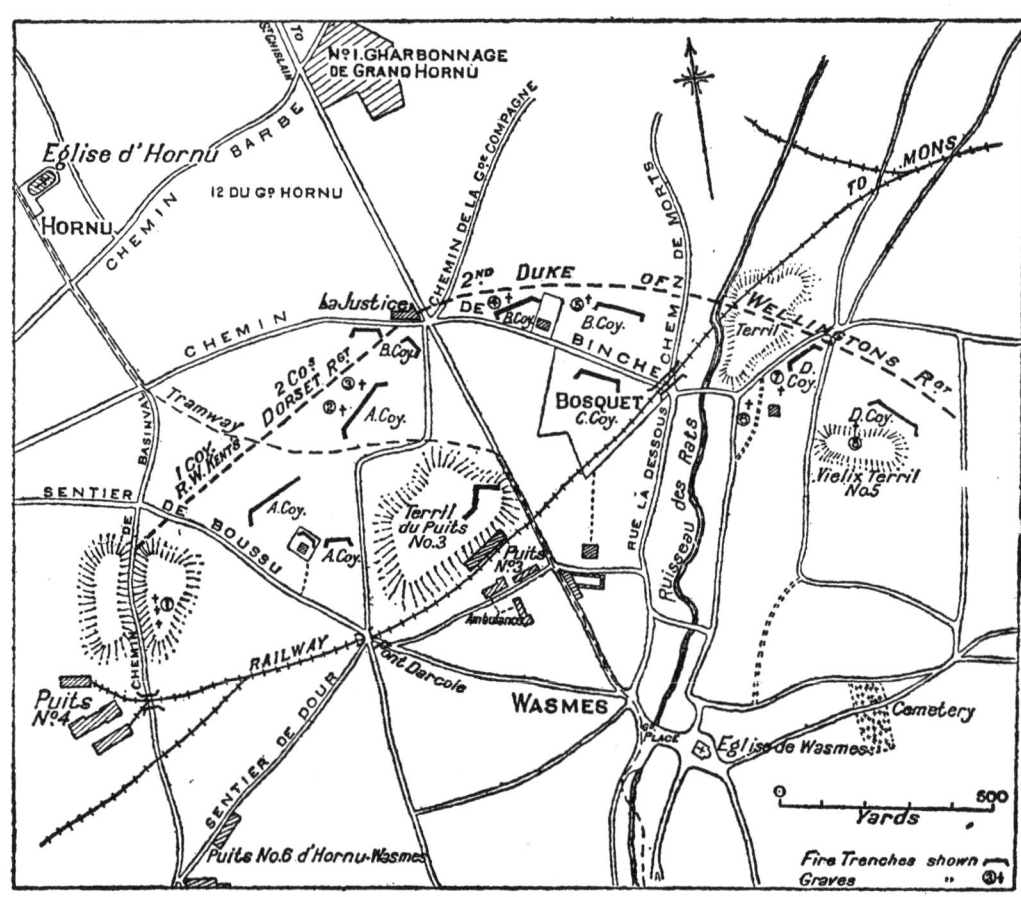

TRENCHES OCCUPIED BY BATTALION ON AUGUST 24TH, 1914.

" Before returning there myself, I went again to our left flank and found the Dorsets still there awaiting relief by the K.O.Y.L.I. There appeared to be a big gap between them and where the rest of their brigade (15th), on their left, was. I was glad afterwards I had gone, as this ground was higher than where our section began, and commanded us; also later on, when things began to get warm, I was able to send and ask for a company from the brigade reserve to be sent up to the exact place. I also sent Russell's[1] platoon from C Company (Battalion Reserve) to work round on to this high ground to keep touch with our left in

[1] Lieut. L. E. Russell.

PLATE 10

LIEUT.-COLONEL A. G. HORSFALL, D.S.O.

MAJOR P. B. STRAFFORD

LIEUT.-COLONEL R. E. MAFFETT

LIEUT.-COLONEL E. G. HARRISON, C.B., D.S.O.

case the K.O.Y.L.I. had not arrived, giving orders that if that Battalion was in position he was to work back to me under cover.

"(*N.B.*—The accompanying map (page 74), made from the original prepared for me when in the ambulance at Wasmes by the Colliery's Engineer, Monsieur Hermann Capiau, shows the trenches occupied by the Battalion on August 24th, also the graves of those buried on the 25th.

All these graves were subsequently opened and the remains moved by the Germans to a cemetery at Hautrage, but at the time those killed in the vicinity of the 'bosquet' and Powder Magazine were collected into one grave, to which also by special arrangement I had the bodies of poor Jubb and Russell taken so as to be buried with poor Strafford.

The graves to the left, marked on map (2)†[1] and (3)†[2] are where poor Pack-Beresford[3] (W. Kents) and his men and some of Russell's platoon, all of whom were killed in hand-to-hand combat (mentioned later on), were originally interred.)

"At daybreak the battle began by 2 15-pounder guns dug in near Townsend's trenches (Terril. No. 3), and a howitzer battery (which was complete, I believe) in rear of the slag dump of the 'Hornu et Wasmes' Colliery, opening fire on the enemy, but they did not get many rounds off before an overwhelming reply by German guns forced them to go back—presumably to find other positions which, unfortunately, did not exist. This opening fire was the only gun-fire in our section that morning.

"About 8 a.m. our Brigadier, also the Brig.-General[4] R. A. (Headlam), Tulloch,[5] C.R.E., and Cameron (G.S.O. 2nd Grade[6]) of the 5th Division came up to 'La Bosquet' to have a look round, but all soon left except General Cuthbert,[7] who had a look round our trenches before returning to Brigade Headquarters. I walked with him part of the way back, and he said he could tell me nothing new, but that as *existing* orders went we were to hang on at all costs.

"Returning through a large garden leading to the 'bosquet,' I found Jubb had not yet returned, and as Russell had sent no word as to the K.O.Y.L.I. having arrived, I got Macleod to make out a message asking for a company of the Brigade Reserve to be sent up to the high ground where the Dorsets were. Major Pack-Beresford and his company of the West Kents were detailed, and moved up in fine style, crossing one open bit of ground well extended at the double, and before the Germans could 'sprinkle' them with shrapnel.

"A German 'Taube' sailed high over us about 11 a.m., but I would not allow the men to fire and disclose our position. It moved along to the left of our section, where rapid rifle fire was opened on it without hitting it, but with the

---

[1] The grave of 36 British R. & F. (D. of W., R. W. Kent, and Dorsets).
[2] The grave of Major Pack-Beresford.
[3] Major C. G. Pack-Beresford (1st Battn. Queen's Own R. W. Kent Regt.).
[4] Colonel (Temp.-Brig.-General) J. E. W. Headlam, C.B., D.S.O. (C.R.A., 5th Div.).
[5] Lieut.-Colonel J. A. S. Tulloch, R.E., C.R.E. (5th Div.).
[6] Major (Temp.-Lt.-Col.) A. R. Cameron.
[7] Colonel (Temp.-Brig.-General) G. T. Cuthbert, C.B. (cmdg. 13th Bde.).

result of its dropping white discs near Townsend's trenches, which led to an immediate burst of gun-fire on the spot indicated. The range, however, was luckily over-estimated, and the shells burst on the road in rear of A Company.

"Things were now getting fast and furious as far as enemy gun-fire went, and it became evident that our guns must be out of action as there was no reply. It rather looked as if the Germans were preparing for an advance, so I sent a message back at 11.30 a.m. asking if it would be possible to have some artillery support. I can't tell if this message ever arrived, as my messenger did not return before the Regiment began to retire."

Another account of this withdrawal is related by an officer serving with the Regiment.[1] Graphic, yet entirely unadorned, the description serves to bring vividly home the horrors of modern war.

"We marched all that night (August 23rd) and took up a position behind a long wall which ran along the edge of a wood. The other three companies dug trenches behind us in the wood at about fifty yards intervals. At about 3 a.m. on Monday morning artillery fire poured into the wood from two directions. This fire lasted all day till 5 o'clock, when we saw infantry advancing. It is too long an account to tell how that artillery fire almost wiped us out; suffice it to say that before 5 o'clock I commanded half our own company and half a company of Bedfords, my platoon, which before 3 o'clock was depleted, leaving myself, 1 N.C.O., and 17 men the only survivors. I then moved down to the wall and joined the remainder of my company, found that Major Townsend was wounded and several junior officers, and that I had to take command of C Company. I was also given by Count Gleichen about 100 Bedfords, who had lost their officers about 4 p.m. The shelling became so heavy that the wall was being fast knocked down and many men were being killed. After the Colonel was hit, Major Macleod sent me down word at once to say I might retire, and that he thought I had better not do it through the wood as the further back trenches would stay on till later. There was a place, a hole in the wall made by a shell. Through this hole I started the retirement. There was another position I wanted to get back to, so told the men to double through the hole and round. Unfortunately a machine gun opened fire the moment they appeared, killing a lot of men, and by the time I was to go, the hole was blocked up with bodies. This suited us as it turned out, for myself and about 4 men left crouched under these bodies, and so got cover from the machine guns whose bullets dumped about, making a most sickening noise on the poor bodies. Of course, we had to leave all the wounded behind the wall and all near the hole. As we ran up the road, myself and the other men, about 12 Uhlans (Cavalry men) rode at us. We turned round, the men's rifle fire frightening the horses though they fired well up in the air. I myself let off four revolver shots, only nailing one Uhlan, though they were quite close to us. Had we only fixed bayonets we would have 'done them' all in. They fled anyway, leaving the one dead, and we continued running up the road under a perfect hail of rifle bullets. I had my water bottle shot off. It was a very sad sight to see the long line of wounded (and dead) here who

[1] Lieut. H. K. O'Kelly, D.S.O.

begged us to help them, which was, of course, impossible. When I got back very few of my men were left. That night the Battalion retired 8 miles back—its losses being very heavy indeed."

Before noon on the 24th the flank of the 2nd Duke of Wellington's was practically in the air. German infantry had advanced beyond their right and were almost in their rear. The extreme right flank of the Battalion was for the time being held by No. 12 Platoon of C Company, commanded by Lieut. Russell.

A survivor from that day's fighting, Corpl. J. G. Williams, also of C Company, gives a simple but extremely interesting account of how this gallant young officer and all that were left of his brave platoon met their end.

"About midday," writes Corpl. Williams, " I was sent by my Platoon Officer, the late Lieut. Thompson, to try and find Major Macleod and to tell him that our Company Commander, Major Strafford, had been wounded. Lieut.-Colonel Gibbs, our C.O., had already been wounded and Major Macleod was in command. My platoon was in support and entrenched just inside a small plantation on top of a little hill.

"The other platoons had their trenches below us and Mr. Russell's Platoon was on the extreme right flank. I could not see any British troops further to the right. When scouting round to find Major Macleod I came quite close to Mr. Russell. He had only 9 men with him. He was not properly entrenched, as he had only just previously been moved further to the right in order to try and get in touch with the brigade on our right.

"The Germans were all round his front, right, and rear, and at very close quarters. More Germans were advancing across the cornfield in which the platoon was situated, carrying stacks of corn as shields in front of them. Mr. Russell and his platoon were all firing the 'mad minute' with their bayonets fixed.

"I saw the Germans charge the platoon, who fought to the last with the bayonet, and were all either killed or wounded. The Germans were piled up in heaps all round them. I managed to get back to my platoon under cover of a railway embankment. The other two platoons had fallen back and joined us. All our officers were either killed or wounded and the Germans were all round our rear. Sergt. Spence ordered us to fix bayonets and to cut our way back. I bayonetted a German but was clubbed on the head with a rifle before I could get my bayonet free, and that is all I remember until I came round a German prisoner. I had earlier in the day been shot through the foot, but not badly."

When the Red Cross party went out late on August 24th, two of the regimental stretcher-bearers accompanied them to collect discs and identify bodies. They reported that Major Pack-Beresford (Royal West Kents) and Lieut. Russell with 21 men were found dead side by side with fixed bayonets, some still in the bodies of 16 dead Germans whose advance they had evidently received shoulder to shoulder. Most of our dead had evidently been shot down by other Germans, as in some cases the bodies were riddled with bullets, and there were no signs of bayonet wounds. Thus died " Boy " Russell and the remnant of his gallant platoon, their only thought just to do their duty, and in that last desperate scrimmage to worthily uphold the name and honour of their beloved "Duke's."

"About noon," continues Lieut.-Colonel Gibbs, "a platoon of C Company, which had been holding a loopholed wall on the east side of the 'bosquet,' came back as the wall was getting so knocked about by shell fire and I told Healing[1] to get them up into the higher trenches on the slope.

"The fire, although now 'hellish,' had up to date done practically no damage to the Reserve Company, thanks to the concealed position of the trenches, etc., but at 12.15 p.m. three shells burst in quick succession, the first getting into the advanced trench on the east side of 'bosquet,' killing and wounding several; the second burst close to where Strafford and myself were talking. He fell dead with a piece of shrapnel through his temple, and at the same time I got three pieces in my left side and a small piece through my left wrist. A small trench in front of us had several casualties also.

"The third shell went over our heads and burst in a field in rear of the 'bosquet.'

"Taylor,[2] who was near me, tied me up, and with the help of another man got me into the shade behind a trench, from which I could more or less see what was going on.

"I sent word to tell Macleod I was hit and to carry on.

"It was now evident the retirement had begun, although I had never received any orders, as we could see the troops on our right going back.

"Thompson and his platoon, being in good cover, hung on, giving great assistance to those on our right to cross exposed ground.

"At about 1.10 p.m. Taylor came and told me all had now gone back except Thompson and his men, and that Thompson was hit. I therefore ordered the former to take all the remaining men back via the garden in rear of the 'bosquet' in the direction of the market square (Wasmes).

"The Germans could be seen about 1000 yards to our front.

"With the assistance of one of the men I dragged myself through the garden in rear of the 'bosquet,' and on emerging into the side street in rear, I was just in time to see Sergt. Spence, who had collected a handful of men, charging down the road after some Germans who had worked round from the left. The latter turned and made off down another street. This action on Sergt. Spence's part without doubt did much to enable the rear platoons to get away without further loss."

The following casualties occurred on August 23rd and 24th, during the fighting on the Mons–Condé canal. Also during what is known in official British records as the Battle of Mons.

August 23rd.

>   *Officers*: Wounded, Capt. R. C. Carter, and Lieut. W. M. Ozanne, 2nd Lieut. G. W. Oliphant.
>
>   *Other ranks*: 7 killed, 24 wounded, 1 missing.

---

[1] Capt. R. K. Healing.   [2] Capt. E. R. Taylor. Killed at Hill 60 later.

August 24th.

Officers: Killed, Major P. B. Strafford, Capt and Adj. C. O. Denman-Jubb, Lieut. L. E. Russell.
Wounded, Lieut.-Colonel J. A. C. Gibbs, Major E. N. Townsend, Lieuts. J. H. L. Thompson,[1] M. C. B. K. Young.
Missing, Capt. E. V. Jenkins, Lieut. O. Price.

Other ranks: 33 killed, 39[2] wounded, 244 missing.

Few incidents in the long-drawn-out history of the Great War make a more stirring appeal to the imagination than the wonderful devotion shown by Belgians to British wounded and temporarily missing during the retreat from Mons. Belgian women of all classes were foremost in these courageous efforts to save life. Only a few months ago His Majesty the King paid a well-earned tribute to their devotion. The experiences which befell two officers of the 2nd Battalion during those never-to-be-forgotten months of August and September may be of interest, particularly to survivors of the Old Army.

Capt. Ernle R. Taylor and Capt. T. M. Ellis were the two officers concerned. Capt. Taylor's escape can hardly be better told than by quoting from a letter recalling the incident. Madame Barbier, the writer, was one of that band of heroines who risked not only their safety, but, as we well know, their lives in 1914 to save British soldiers.

" . . . Here are the recollections I am able to give you," Madame Barbier writes, " with regard to that brave Captain Taylor.

"Towards the middle of the month of September, 1914, when he had barely recovered from the wound in his shoulder, he had but the one desire and that was to rejoin his regiment. He communicated his plan to us, and we helped him to escape. Monsieur Capiau, Engineer, gave him a suit of plain clothes, and I handed him a certain sum of money and provisions for the journey. We put a trustworthy guide at his service, and preceded by him he started very early one morning. Captain Taylor only remained a few weeks with us, but we learnt to appreciate his fine qualities and his heart of gold. So soon as he arrived at our Ambulance station he told me that everything that was left in his haversack—cigarettes, chocolate, soup tablets—were for his men and that he no longer needed them. Every day when I distributed cigarettes and *de la friandises* I had to compel him to accept something: he never considered himself, but thought always of his men. It was the same thing on the occasion of his escape, he showed just such fineness of feeling about accepting money.

"I forgot to say that when he left the Ambulance he walked as far as Peruwelz, and there he had the good fortune to catch the last train that ran to Tournai and Ostend. Since then we had had no news of him, and we have been very much grieved to hear of his death."[3]

In case of being caught Capt. Ernle Taylor carried his uniform over his

---

[1] Died of wounds 17th Sept., 1914. Buried in Wasmes cemetery.
[2] Four died of wounds. Buried in Wasmes cemetery.
[3] Madame Barbier's letter of March 31st, 1926. (Translation.)

shoulder wrapped in a peasant's large handkerchief. The name of the brave guide was Alexandre Brenez, who was a miner living at Hornu.

This other record of an escape is also during the memorable retreat in August–September, 1914. Sad to say both these very promising young officers gave their lives not long afterwards for King and Country. Both were killed on Hill 60 on April 18th, 1915. A day of supreme sacrifice for the " Duke's " as for those other battalions who fought with them.

Capt. T. M. Ellis also escaped, thanks to the courage and devotion of Belgian peasants and to the bravery of a Belgian priest.

During the last week in August, 1914, at the beginning of the retreat, Capt. Ellis and a corporal of the Regiment had become separated from their unit. On the particular day referred to, as far as is known, two companies including some of the " Duke's," the " West Kents," and the " Dorsets," had " dug in " while acting as rearguard. By midday, no orders had been received either in Capt. Ellis's trench or in that occupied by Capt. Jenkins. German artillery were already dropping shells freely two miles in rear of the trenches, and German Infantry had worked round both flanks.

The vicinity of a wood to the original front offered a chance of escape. Capt. Ellis and some fifty men of the Regiment took cover there, and had various local encounters with Germans trying to surround the wood. During these the men got scattered, and finally Capt. Ellis and Corpl. H. E. Kerman got away in the dark. For twelve days Capt. Ellis and Corpl. Kerman were cut off. Bavai, St. Ghislain, Hornu, and Maubeuge, were places they touched. Some nights were spent concealed in woods, and three times Capt. Ellis had to turn on his tracks. On the 27th a kindly peasant's hut afforded shelter, and on the night of the 30th Capt. Ellis was taken to the Priest's house. This brave man, who spoke English, hid him in a disused lime-kiln for two days and nights while he communicated with a Belgian who had offered to assist any English soldiers. This Belgian hero was a middle-aged man who had promised[1] that if Capt. Ellis would take the risk and discard his uniform for peasant's clothes he would lead him through the German lines to safety. The man was as good as his word. Armed with a card given by the good priest asking all who could to help them in any way in return for the aid British soldiers had brought to Belgium, the two set out on their long tramp for the coast.

For many weary and nerve-racking miles Capt. Ellis followed thirty or forty yards behind the brave Belgian. On the way he picked up two privates in the " Manchesters " and took them along. Through villages, past German troops they made their way, hiding in ditches or anywhere when necessary. On one occasion the Belgian signalled to Capt. Ellis to take shelter suddenly, and for five hours he was forced to stand behind the door of a barn while German troops tramped endlessly by. In the end the brave guide led the British officer to Leuze, from whence other Belgians passed the little party by train to Ghent and finally to Ostend. From there they crossed in a destroyer on September 5th, and Capt. Ellis at once reported at the War Office in London.

[1] Worked in a merchant's office in London.

COLONEL J. A. C. GIBBS, C.B.

BRIG.-GENERAL W. M. WATSON

BRIG.-GENERAL P. A. TURNER, C.M.G.

BRIG.-GENERAL R. N. BRAY, C.M.G., D.S.O.

ESCAPE OF CAPTAIN ELLIS

Capt. Ellis was taking a serious risk when he decided to bury his uniform and rifle before starting to try and escape. Had he been stopped, not dressed in uniform, as a spy there could only have been one end to his adventure. Such, however, is the spirit of the British officer that, as Capt. Ellis afterwards confessed, the only two things which worried him as militating against his escape when he changed into peasant's clothes were, that his hair was red and that the Regimental crest was tattooed on his arm.

CHAPTER VII

MONS AND AFTER. BATTLE OF LE CATEAU AND AFTER.

IN order that the sequence of these momentous events may be clearly fixed in the minds of readers about these early days it is necessary to recapitulate briefly what has so far happened.

On the evening of August 23rd the British position is thus officially described:[1] "Altogether the British Commanders were not ill-satisfied with the day's work. The unsatisfactory position on the canal had been imposed upon them fortuitously; but it had been held for a sufficient time, and had been evacuated without great difficulty or disaster in favour of a second position only a mile or two in rear. The men were in high spirits for they had met superior numbers of the most highly renowned army in the world and had given a good account of themselves."

At 8.40 p.m. on August 23rd Sir John French issued the following message to the II Corps: "I will stand the attack on the ground now occupied by the troops. You will therefore strengthen your position by every possible means during the night."

The withdrawal from the first position on the Mons Canal was in accordance with the known intention of Sir Horace L. Smith-Dorrien, G.C.B., D.S.O., G.O.C. II Corps. A loop in the canal round the town of Mons itself made any position facing north unsatisfactory, so that another upon which it was intended to stand had been prepared on a line west to east—Boussu-Wasmes-Paturages-Frameries. When, then, the unexpected order for a further retirement upon Bavai arrived from Sir John French at 2 a.m. on 24th August, the whole of the II Corps' local dispositions were thrown completely out of gear.

Dawn of August 24th found the British Army occupying a line 17 miles long, the centre some 3 miles south of Mons and the line facing roughly north-east.

The right of the I Corps was near Grand Reng, Rouveroy, Givry; its left near Bougnies.

The right of the II Corps, 3rd Division, was at Nouvelles, its left at Frameries.

The right of the 5th Division, including 2nd Duke of Wellington's, was at Paturages. Its left, consisting of the 19th Infantry Brigade and a Cavalry Division, was round Thulin, Elouges, Audregnies, Quiévrain.

[1] *Military Operations: France and Belgium*, 1914.

As we know by Lieut.-Colonel Gibbs's narrative, the 13th Infantry Brigade, of which the 2nd Duke of Wellington's formed part, did not reach the position assigned to it much before dawn on the 24th. About midnight of August 23rd/24th the senior General Staff Officers of the I and II Corps and the Cavalry Division had been summoned to General Headquarters at Le Cateau. There the Chief of the General Staff explained that it was the intention of the British Commander-in-Chief to continue retiring for another 8 miles. The line it was proposed to take up lay east and west from La Longueville (5 miles west of the fortress of Maubeuge) westward through Bavai to the hamlet of La Boiserette. This was a front of some 7 miles. In addition, it was ordered that the I Corps was to cover the retirement of the II Corps, while the Cavalry was to simultaneously make a demonstration. The I Corps was able to withdraw with comparative ease. Not so the II Corps. It became apparent by 5.15 a.m. on the 24th that the Germans were moving westward in an endeavour to outflank the British left. At about the same hour they also developed a general infantry attack against the front of the II Corps. By 6 a.m. they had also evidently made up their minds to try and pin the left of the I Corps round Frameries to the ground they were then occupying. This they failed to do.

Immediately west of Frameries and towards Wasmes at an early hour a German artillery bombardment began. Still further west the 13th Brigade were hotly engaged. St. Ghislain and Hornu were German local objectives. On the front of the 14th Brigade on the left of the 13th Infantry Brigade all was quiet. Still further west the 19th Infantry Brigade had been ordered from G.H.Q. at midnight to fall back on Elouges, 6 miles south-east, and by 2 a.m. had begun to retire. They were followed by the French 84th Territorial Division which evacuated Condé and began its retirement towards Cambrai. At dawn also the British Cavalry Division in rear of the left began to move south. Then, hearing from the G.O.C. 5th Division, Sir Charles Fergusson, that that Division was to hold its ground, Major-General Allenby agreed to cover its flank.

The Dorsets and Bedfords at Paturages were still covering the right of the 13th Infantry Brigade, which was endeavouring to hold up the German southern advance out of Hornu. When the 5th Infantry Brigade of the I Corps retired the right of these two battalions was in the air and their withdrawal was well effected none too soon.

About 11 a.m. Sir Charles Fergusson received a message from the II Corps giving him discretion to fall back as soon as the troops on his right had retired. Finding that this had already occurred and that he was being outflanked he proceeded to follow their example. The 13th Infantry Brigade was holding on, though the 2nd Duke of Wellington's on the right were being somewhat severely punished by shell fire. The 14th Infantry Brigade on the left of the 13th were left in comparative quiet, though the 2nd Manchesters supporting the 2nd Battalion K.O.Y.L.I. were under heavy artillery fire. The 14th Infantry Brigade began the retirement by successive battalions unpunished by the enemy, and were able to form up at Blaugies to cover the retirement of the 13th Infantry Brigade. By some mishap the order to retire did not reach the

2nd Battalion The Duke of Wellington's, which accordingly remained in position with one battery of the 27th Brigade R.F.A. close to it. Before noon (August 24th), just when the 2nd Duke of Wellington's should have begun to retire, the Germans suddenly concentrated an overwhelming fire upon this battery at close range. A sharp fight followed, says the official account, and for the next hour and a half it was only the rifles of the 2nd Duke of Wellington's which saved the battery. About 1 p.m. the Germans attacked from the Boussu-Quiévrain road in thick skirmishing formation. They were followed by dense masses from the left front of the Battalion, but being met by a rain of bullets from rifle and machine-gun fire at 800 yards, and a severe salute from the battery, they were stopped dead. The guns were thus able to limber up and the 2nd Duke of Wellington's to withdraw south-west into Dour, but the Battalion had suffered heavily. Though the casualties reached nearly 400 of all ranks, the Duke's had driven back six German battalions.

By 2 p.m., August 24th, the 13th and 14th Infantry Brigades had assembled at Warquignies and Blaugies respectively, ready to continue their retreat to their places in the new position at St. Waast and Eth. But the 5th Division had not even then got clear. Hardly had the 13th and 14th Infantry Brigades begun their retreat when Sir Charles Fergusson realized that the premature withdrawal of the Cavalry and 19th Infantry Brigade uncovered his left flank to strong German forces advancing due south between Thulin and Condé. Sending an urgent message to the Cavalry Division to come to his assistance, Sir Charles Fergusson pushed forward a rescue force of the 1st Cheshires and 1st Norfolks with the 119th Battery under Colonel C. R. Ballard of the Norfolks with orders to advance north and counter-attack. Meanwhile Major-General Allenby had acted instantly upon the message from Fergusson and sent back two Cavalry Brigades with L Battery R.H.A. Thanks to the aid of these supports and Colonel Ballard's force, the Germans, after some fine cavalry attacks and good work by L Battery were temporarily held up. While this action was going on the II Corps troops to the eastward resumed the retreat. The 3rd Division marched on Bavai and the main body of the 5th Division struck south from Blaugies through Athis upon Bavai and St. Waast. Meanwhile, a German attack east of Colonel Ballard's force was beginning to be felt and the 119th Battery suffered considerably. By the gallant action of Major E. W. Alexander, who received the V.C., and a few of the Battery, aided by the fine conduct of some of the 9th Lancers under Capt. Francis O. Grenfell, who also earned the V.C., the guns were saved. The 1st Norfolks and L Battery also got away in good order, but the 1st Cheshires, who had failed to receive the order to retire, were eventually mostly either killed or cut off after fighting until nearly 7 p.m.

It was finally due to the indefatigable "gunners" of the 5th Divisional Artillery that the survivors were able by 9 p.m. to reach St. Waast. The losses during the fighting on 24th August exceeded those of the 23rd. They were roughly a total of 2500, including I Corps losses. By far the heaviest toll taken was that from the 5th Division, which alone lost 1650 of all ranks. But it had worthily endured its baptism of fire, having been called upon to defend and hold

6 miles of front against the most highly trained troops in the world. The 5th Division with the Cavalry Corps and the 19th Infantry Brigade had also parried the enveloping attack of Von Kluck's vast forces upon the British left. It may be of interest to recall that the strength of the 3rd and 5th Divisions, those principally engaged at Mons, was just under 36,000 men. The strength of the British Army under the "Iron Duke" at Waterloo was 31,585 men.[1]

The night of August 24th found the British Army disposed as follows on a line east to west through Bavai, and unless the subsequent positions occupied in the retreat are carefully checked no real understanding of those wonderful days can be grasped.

5th Cavalry Brigade	Feignies.
I Corps—	
1st Division	Feignies, La Longueville.
2nd Division	Bavai.
II Corps—	
5th Division	Bavai, St. Waast.
3rd Division	St. Waast, Amfroipret, Bermeries.
Cavalry Division } 19th Infantry Brigade }	St. Waast, Wargnies, Jenlain, Saultain.

In order to shorten the length of the retirement of the 5th Division that unit was ordered to fall back due south instead of south-west. The 3rd Division, for the same reason, had crossed the line of retreat of the 5th from east to west and was now upon the latter's left, the 5th Division forming the right of the II Corps.

At 8 p.m. on August 24th the German Army Commander, General Von Kluck, issued the following orders to his troops for August 25th:—

> "Enemy's main position is believed to be Bavai-Valenciennes. The first army will attack it with envelopment of the left flank, II Cavalry Corps against the enemy's rear."

At 8.25 p.m. the same night Sir John French issued his orders for a further retirement of the British forces on Le Cateau, where another division, the 4th, had just arrived from England and detrained. A glance at the map will suffice to show to any soldier the interest of knowing in advance what moves are in process of being carried out by opposing forces. Of course, neither Von Kluck nor Sir John French were aware of the other's dispositions, nor had Sir John French any alternative as may be gathered by considering the information at his disposal on the night of August 24th. From Von Kluck's method and the direction of his attacks it seemed clear to Sir John French that he was endeavouring to drive the British back on to the old fortress of Maubeuge, as well as to turn their left flank and to cut, as Von Kluck thought, their communications with

---

[1] *Military Operations: France and Belgium,* 1914.

the Channel ports. In fact, to make of Maubeuge another Metz of 1870. Sir John was also aware that, already, the left of the French XVIII Corps was 10 miles in rear of the British right. There was nothing to be done, therefore, but to conform.

The retirement of the 5th Division took it on to the so-called Roman road immediately west of the well-nigh—for formed troops—impassable Fôret de Mormal. For Sir John French the forest was an unpleasant problem upon his line of retreat. But he finally elected to move south, the I Corps to the east of it, the II Corps to the west of the forest. Nor was the retirement rendered any easier for the I Corps by the presence of a French Division crossing its line of march, and by the tail of General Sordet's Cavalry Corps using the same road on its way to Le Cateau.

It was not long after Sir Douglas Haig had established his Headquarters at Landrecies that he was ordered from G.H.Q. through his Chief G.S.O. to continue the retirement. Sir John French considered this was absolutely necessary owing to the further withdrawal of the French Army on his right and the presence in strong force on his immediate front of German troops. He decided on withdrawing to St. Quentin and Noyon. Haig, therefore, ordered the retirement of the I Corps to begin at 2 a.m. on August 26th, the rendezvous being given from G.H.Q. as Bussigny, 7 miles south-west of Le Cateau.

The II Corps had also been hampered by the passage across its front of General Sordet's Cavalry. Roads to the south had become badly congested by traffic so that when midnight on the 24th came—the time ordered to begin the retreat—the whole of the transport was late in getting away. The fighting troops were also an hour behind time, and the rearguard of the 5th Division had to be pushed north nearly to Bellignies to cover the withdrawal of its guns from St. Waast through Bavai.

Further to the west the 3rd Division began its retirement at 5 a.m., covered, as was the British left flank, by Allenby's cavalry. The operations on the west of the II Corps may be summarized as a running fight during which the Germans closed in following the II Corps and Cavalry Division, so that at night German advanced troops were practically in contact with the troops of the II Corps. During August 25th the newly arrived 4th Division under General Snow had been ordered forward to Solesmes, where immediately south of that place the infantry began to dig in. So prolonged were the cavalry running fights that when darkness closed in the troops round Solesmes were still in position to engage the enemy or were actually fighting him. The infantry of the II Corps had reached the vicinity of Le Cateau much earlier after a day of sweltering heat, ending in a heavy thunderstorm. Between 3 p.m. and 5 p.m. the 5th Division got in and the 13th Brigade took up a position for bivouacking between Le Cateau and Troisvilles. The Germans were closing in on the British left flank and front, though at a respectful distance.

By dusk on August 25th the I Corps at Landrecies and Marouilles were settled in and around these two main crossing places over the Sambre River. Extraordinary as it may appear, the advanced guard of the German IV Corps,

UNCERTAINTY AT LANDRECIES AND LE CATEAU

an infantry brigade with a battery, were actually marching towards Landrecies for the purpose of billeting there, quite ignorant of the presence of British troops. Early in the evening stories were brought in by refugees of the close advance of German troops. Both at Landrecies and Marouilles fighting occurred and, to quote from the official account verbatim: " As it was impossible in the dark to discover the scope of the attack the information sent back to G.H.Q. from the I Corps was somewhat alarming. It stated at 1.35 a.m. that the situation was very critical, and at 3.50 a.m. it was suggested that the troops near Le Cateau should assist by advancing straight on Landrecies. Although the situation was soon restored and better news sent, all this, and the uncertainty as to what the Forest of Mormal might conceal, tended to confirm the view of G.H.Q. that the continuation of the retirement was the proper course."

Up to midnight the congestion on the roads in and around Le Cateau remained almost hopeless. It even included French Chasseurs marching in from Valenciennes. For one mile north of Le Cateau the road to Montay rises very steeply and becomes, from a military point of view, practically a defile. Down this road, says the official account, " infantry, cavalry, guns and wagons, in places three abreast, were jammed together in what seemed irremediable confusion. Had the Germans pushed on, even with a small force supported by guns, they might have done terrible damage." But what " might have " happened is no longer war. The Germans, as a matter of fact, were as weary as the British and possibly, by then, somewhat cautions of the rapid rifle fire of British infantry, so fortunately the II Corps were left alone to disentangle at their leisure. As it was, the Germans bivouacked in force only 5 miles away. While the small, in numbers " contemptible," British Army lay as already outlined on the night of August 25th, it is profitable to lay stress on the German dispositions and particularly on their overwhelming numerical superiority. The German II Cavalry Corps and IV and III Corps were close enough to the British to be able to strike in force the following morning early, whilst the IV Reserve, II and X Reserve were within a march of the position. Parts of the IX and VII Corps drawn from the investment of Maubeuge were also available in case of need, and such was the enemy the British were up against.

At 7.30 p.m. on the night of the 25th from G.H.Q. at St. Quentin Sir John French issued his orders for the British retreat to be continued 10 to 15 miles to the south-west the following day. Sir John, of course, was without the exact information as to German movements or of the situation at and around Le Cateau in the hands of General Smith-Dorrien. The British Commander-in-Chief was influenced, too, by his information from French G.H.Q., viz.: that General Joffre's attempt at the offensive had failed and that the latter intended retiring to the line Laon-La Fère-St. Quentin, whence he meant again to take the offensive.

With the historic conference at General Smith-Dorrien's Headquarters after midnight on August 25th all who served in the war are now familiar. Allenby—no man better—was in a position to sum up the situation in front of the II Corps. Also to forecast plainly the work his cavalry would have to do the following day, work which he frankly owned could not adequately be expected from them, so worn out were men and horses. Hubert Hamilton, an equally fine soldier, stated clearly the position and condition of his own 3rd Division, and, bluntly, that as many of his units were only just coming in, if an imminent retreat were attempted they could not possibly be formed up under many hours.

Thus runs the official record: "General Smith-Dorrien, after a full discussion of the situation with Generals Allenby[1] and Hamilton,[2] reluctantly came to the decision that he must stand his ground."

There are other factors which it is as well should be recalled when memory goes back to that momentous decision. The first is the doubts there must have been in the mind of the II Corps Commander as to the safety of even his right flank should he commence to retire. We now know that at 3.50 a.m. that same night Sir Douglas Haig asked for assistance for the I Corps from the II Corps. We have also Sir John French's own despatches (September 7th, 1914) in which he wrote: "The I Corps was equally exhausted, and could not get further in without rest"; and therefore could not come "further west so as to fill the gap between Le Cateau and Landrecies."

"The die having been cast," says the *Official History*, "it remained only for General Smith-Dorrien to inform his subordinates." But this, under existing conditions, was the one thing it was practically impossible for him to do. So far as the 5th Division was concerned the 13th Brigade did not hear of the decision to stand until about 6 a.m. on the morning of the battle, at which time other brigades had already been fired on by attacking German troops. It is not the purpose of this brief account to attempt to describe in detail the varied phases of that bloody battle. But a brief outline of the position in which the II Corps were compelled to fight is necessary to a proper understanding of the wonderful part played that day by the "Contemptible" Little Army.

That the Battle of Le Cateau was fought on the anniversary of that of Crécy did not probably occur to any one present that hot misty August day. They had other things to think about—especially their commander—for few men have ever had to face a like predicament.

It is seldom that any participator[3] takes pains to give any account of the meterological conditions under which battles are fought. It may be of interest, therefore, to quote from the narrative of an officer of the "Duke's" present at Le Cateau. Few who experienced one are likely ever to forget a February day, or night, in the trenches when trench-warfare had finally superseded the warfare of Mons and Le Cateau. But this day, August 26th, was the kind of day anyone would have selected to fight if fight he must :—

"I received orders, or rather Capt. Tidmarsh my Company Commander did," writes Lieut. Ince, "to proceed as escort to the 108th Battery, Royal Garrison Artillery (60-pounders). Unfortunately Major Townsend was

[1] Major-General (now Field-Marshal) The Viscount Allenby, G.C.B., G.C.M.G.
[2] Major-General H. I. W. Hamilton, C.B., C.V.O., D.S.O.
[3] Lieut. (now Major) C. W. G. Ince, M.C.

severely wounded on the 24th at Mons and had had to be left on the field. We took up a position in support of the Battalion and as an escort to the Battery. The remainder of the Battalion had taken up a position in trenches on the northern slope of the high ground south-west of Le Cateau. The 26th was a beautiful day. The corn was lying on the ground in stooks, and during the night of August 25th/26th we had been able to sleep out in the open in real comfort.

"The companies not on outpost had done their best to improve the shallow trenches in preparation for the great battle which little did we individuals realize was to take place that day. When the German attack commenced they were seen advancing on the slopes north of Le Cateau and never shall I forget the 108th Battery shelling the German column at long range. The country in the vicinity of Le Cateau was fairly open and consequently from the position of our support line we were able to obtain a very fine view of the commencement of the battle."

Fighting began almost at dawn, when at 5 a.m. German guns opened upon troops of the 4th Division, the 1st Rifle Brigade, from north of Beauvois almost on the extreme left of the British position. It was not until 5.30 a.m. that General[1] Snow received notice that the II Corps was going to stand fast, which notice he passed on at once to his brigades, only to hear that already they were "at it hammer and tongs."

To the east at the other end of the British position, very soon after 6 a.m., German batteries from the vicinity of the Fôret de Mormal opened fire upon British units immediately west of Le Cateau. A little later, about 6.30, the Duke of Cornwall's Light Infantry, who were waiting in column of route by the railway bridge in Le Cateau, were surprised by being fired upon from the windows of the neighbouring houses. Between the two places where these incidents occurred lay the British position at Le Cateau. Not, it should be remembered, a selected position chosen as one upon which to fight, but one on to which the various units were more or less sorted in the dark, and under conditions as to choice of ground greatly handicapped by the use of the only maps, French maps, available. As has been said already it is only possible here to follow in detail the fortunes of the troops with which this narrative is concerned, and so far as refers to the 5th Division a glance at the map is sufficient to show the serious disabilities under which it fought. That the troops were able to hold off the attack of vastly superior numbers so long is a wonderful tribute to the fighting qualities of those concerned. From 5 a.m. until 2 p.m. that day the British position was hammered by artillery and attacked by superior masses of German infantry. The gallant Suffolks, who up till then on the right flank had borne the burden and heat of that never-to-be-forgotten stand, were, with the Argyll and Sutherland Highlanders, finally overwhelmed. They died fighting, needless to say, after they had "for nine hours been under an incessant bombardment which had pitted the whole of the ground with

---

[1] Major-General (now Lieut.-General), T. D'O. Snow, C.B. (commanding 4th Division).

craters, and they had fought to the very last, covering themselves with undying glory."[1]

All that long hot morning the 13th Infantry Brigade had made its stand immediately to the west of the 2nd Suffolks, but about 2 p.m. Sir Charles Fergusson issued orders for the retirement of the 5th Division. Already by 1 p.m. Sir Charles could see from his Headquarters at Reumont that a German division was working round his right flank, but it was not until 3 p.m. that his orders to retire would seem to have reached any of his battalions. To send up orders into the firing line was practically impossible, so fierce was the hand-to-hand fighting, the ground in rear of the firing line being also swept by shell fire. As a result of this extraordinary position no orders at all reached Lieut.-Colonel R. C. Bond, D.S.O., and the companies of the K.O.Y.L.I. in the firing line. These, again, were enfiladed upon their right flank by German infantry advancing over the ridge which the Suffolks had so gallantly held.

In the meantime the West Kents and the Duke of Wellington's, both of whom had been in the support line, had begun to retire. Shortly after 3 p.m. General Smith-Dorrien was able to re-strengthen his right flank and before 4 o'clock reported by telegram to G.H.Q. that his retirement had begun. By 4.30 p.m. in the immediate front of the 13th Brigade the Germans were not pressing so hard as was to be expected. Shells from the 61st Howitzer Battery and 108th Heavy Battery constantly broke up German formations trying to attack, and both the 2nd Duke of Wellington's and the West Kents suffered little harm, though the former was heavily shelled. As the various battalions from the right flank retired, Bedfords, Dorsets, Cheshires, and Scottish Borderers all overflowed into the Roman road near Reumont or Maurois, but without the slightest pressure from German cavalry or infantry.

That no two persons ever described alike an experience both have undergone is a well-authenticated fact. In the present case, however, their experiences after, if not at Le Cateau, were for these two officers very different. Of the battle itself Capt. O'Kelly, attached to the 2nd Duke of Wellington's, writes in almost similar terms to those used by Lieut. (now Major) C. W. G. Ince. But the after-account by the former officer of getting astray during the early part of the retreat has an interest of its own. Were there not, unfortunately, scores of brave fellows, wounded or otherwise, who were never able to rejoin their units at all ?

"We had a good night's rest before Le Cateau," writes Capt. O'Kelly, " were wakened about half-hour before dawn, and started to dig trenches where we had been sleeping. We had a splendid field of fire and could see a low-level plateau for about 1200 yards. At Le Cateau we did not see infantry advancing at all except at a great distance. Just as we were dug in, shells began to burst over our heads. Personally, I had made quite a good trench for myself. I was at the time in command of half a company. We stayed there all day under very awful shell fire, with our guns firing right beside us. I saw that day the gunners doing the most extraordinary feats of bravery. I saw one officer with his arm

[1] *Military Operations: France and Belgium,* 1914.

blown off still riding his horse giving instructions. Of course, he soon fainted from loss of blood, but just imagine doing your duty with your arm blown off in most awful agony, knowing that you had only a few minutes more to live. I also saw batteries blown to pieces, one gun being left intact in one battery; immediately a team of gunners galloped out with their horses and hooked in and galloped back with their gun safe. I saw an artillery major blown high in the air and falling down in pieces. I am sorry to say an order to retire too soon was given. This would have meant that the German cavalry would have come up across the gunners, but the General, riding about amongst the shells, quite calmly asked our fellows to return and volunteer to try and save the gunners; this they did. Messages were repeatedly coming along to say French divisions and four cavalry brigades were coming up on our left to help us. Unfortunately, they never came. About 4 o'clock we were told to retire on to the main road. I happened to be the last to leave the front trenches. When the Major and myself got on the road we found huge columns of transport, guns, wagons, ammunition columns, etc., etc., all struggling to get on, and infantry crowded up in hundreds. I got the Major on to an ambulance wagon and trekked on myself, when I came up with one of our Captains. We were the only three officers left of my old company. When we had gone about 3 miles we were stopped by a General, who asked for the senior officer. The General told him he wanted an officer to stay behind on the crest of the hill with some men to protect the column which he feared would be followed up by cavalry. The Captain was ill, so of course there was nothing but for me to say I would do it. The General stopped about 130 men of all regiments, and pushed them into a field. I found that we had a machine gun with us and another very young officer. I don't know what regiments were with us. I was too beat to notice particulars, only I saw about seven men of our own Regiment, whom I called together and asked to show a bold front and give a good example. I also told them that they would probably be motored back. Well, it was getting on towards twilight, with no sign of the enemy in sight. The infantry and cavalry had mostly, except stragglers, passed on, when I saw Germans bringing a big gun down a laneway with twelve horses attached. I got the machine gun on them and shot most of the horses. They brought up another lot and tried to harness them; of these we also shot some and were beginning to enjoy it when a shell burst amongst us. This came from a gun they had brought from the other side of the road. This shell blew up the machine gun and killed seven or eight men, including the little officer. Immediately three other shells burst in our midst, doing frightful havoc, and everyone ran for cover, myself included. When we collected together I halted them about thirty yards back in a cave and found only eleven men and myself; we sat there until it was dark, and then I crept back and found a good many were only wounded but found none who could walk. We then started to try and rejoin our units and I decided to do so across country. The first village we came to was deserted, and as I had neither map nor compass I had not the slightest idea where we went. We must have gone in a ring and, of course, very slowly. Anyway, the next village I came to was full of Germans and some of our prisoners. I set off again in the opposite way and so kept going all night, sometimes passing quite near Germans, always afraid to approach a peasant, as on one occasion I rode up to one to ask the way and she called her husband and the two together cried out most hysterically, 'Vive l'Angleterre,' which brought Germans who were feeding in her house out after us. Towards morning I decided that we must hide in some place and sleep all day and creep out at night again. We were only nine, two having fainted during the night. We were too tired to keep a watch, so just fell asleep. That night one of the men appeared to be going off his head. Next daylight we hid in a cave, and when I woke up it was just getting dark. I found of the seven men only three remained, four having left us in the day. That night (the third night) we did not see a single German, and all I can remember is trekking along by myself. When I woke up I found myself in an ambulance in charge of a Lieutenant of the R.A.M.C. He told me the next day that he had picked me up, looking a wreck, and that he was with the 4th Division, which had been only three days out in France. He was a very nice chap and wanted to report the thing to Headquarters, but after two nights' rest I was all right, so he did not report the matter. He eventually handed me over to Headquarters with a report that I was picked up by one of his ambulances, very fatigued after several days' marching. I gave General Snow (4th Division) a slight account of why I stayed behind and he very kindly placed a motor-car at my disposal, in which I got to the 5th Division, and rejoined the Regiment. I was absent four days and four nights, not including my three days' motoring with the 4th Division."

"The withdrawal of the 5th Division," says the official account, "from a broad and scattered front on to a single road at right-angles to that front naturally brought about as a consequence a thorough mix-up of all units except in the case of the 15th Infantry Brigade, which entered it as a formed body."

By 6 p.m., in a drizzling rain, the enemy's pursuit seemed to die away. As darkness fell the whole of the 5th Division and the 19th Infantry Brigade were in retreat along the Roman road. Between 9 p.m. and midnight the bulk of the 5th Division and of the 19th Infantry Brigade reached Estrées, 15 miles from Le Cateau. Why Von Kluck's Cavalry did not press the pursuit it is difficult to say, but they made little if any effort except by shell-fire. As the official account points out, "the whole of Smith-Dorrien's troops had done what was thought to be impossible. With both flanks more or less in the air, they had turned upon an enemy of at least twice their strength; had struck him hard, and had withdrawn, except on the right front of the 5th Division, practically without interference, with neither flank enveloped, having suffered losses certainly severe,[1] but considering the circumstances by no means extravagant. The men looked upon themselves as victors, some, indeed, doubted whether they had been in a serious action; yet they had inflicted upon the enemy casualties which are believed to have been out of all proportion to their own; and they had completely foiled the plan of the German commander." Of the correctness, or the reverse, of the decision to stand at bay at Le Cateau this

[1] 7812 of all ranks and 38 guns.

MILITARY VALUE OF THE BATTLE

narrative is not concerned, though the ampler knowledge of events we now possess tends not only to confirm, but strongly to endorse it. That the after-effect of the battle at Le Cateau was not at first clearly understood, even by students of the higher strategy, will probably now be allowed, and this the following extract tends to make plain. Writing in the *Journal of the Royal Artillery*, the January issue, 1915, Brig.-General C. De Sausmarez, C.B., C.M.G., D.S.O., who himself commanded a heavy battery at Le Cateau, says:—

" It is, of course, a mistake to dogmatize concerning the consequences of a supposititious happening, but it is not unreasonable to assume that the battle of the Marne would not in these supposititious circumstances have been the victory for the Allies, which in truth was the case. The German sledge-hammer plan of moving ruthlessly forward, each column attacking and knocking out everything that withstood it, came perilously near to success as it was, but the machine was thrown out of gear by the blow it received at Le Cateau, which was one of the chief causes of the war not being won by the Germans off-hand, ' according to plan.' Had this blow not been dealt and had the German machine not been thereby thrown out of gear, it is unpleasant even to contemplate what might have happened. That all the tactical dispositions for the battle were perfect and could not have been improved upon, no one who has studied the subject seriously could possible assert; but it is contended that the strategical conception of the battle was the correct one, and that General Sir Horace Smith-Dorrien made a great and right decision when he determined to stand and fight. . . .

" The German plan of advancing in numerous columns, attacking wherever opposition was met and never stopping, must have formed part of the military creed of all ranks from general to private. They were taught to believe that this was the only sure road to victory. With their numbers, their iron discipline, the bravery and physical fitness of their troops, they came near to justifying their creed. It is pleasant to think that they were taught at this early stage that the British Army of 1914 was good enough to thwart them, and we may be thankful that Sir John French's ' Great Subordinate ' recognized this important fact, and utilized his knowledge by standing up to them and striking them a crippling blow, instead of retiring with those of his troops who could march, and leaving the remainder to their fate."

We left the bulk of the 5th Division, having reached Estrées, 15 miles south of Le Cateau, late on the night of August 26th, though some units had not yet rejoined. From the 23rd to 25th many of the men had received no rations owing to the confusion over the divisional transport. On top of this had come the Battle of Le Cateau, so some of the troops were utterly worn out. Two miles beyond Estrées the sorting out of units was begun by Staff officers, and in spite of the tremendous difficulties of darkness, weary, dead-beat men and disgruntled transport animals, by 2 a.m. on the 27th order had been restored. By 4 a.m. the 5th Division marched off in good fettle. South of St. Quentin somewhat after sunrise a further reorganization of different units of the Division took place.

From St. Quentin the 5th Division was directed to move south-west on Ham, to billet at Ollezy, 4 miles east of Ham. Sir H. Smith-Dorrien had himself visited Noyon, to which place Sir John French, with G.H.Q., had gone. Earlier on the 26th General Joffre also visited Sir John French, who, after hearing the French Commander's plans, agreed to make the British retirement as deliberate as possible.

On the 28th at 4 a.m. the retreat was continued in great heat on Noyon, thence to Pontoise, where billets instead of a bivouac in the open were most welcome.

On the night of August 28th/29th the British Army was in position as follows: The I Corps south of the Oise River. The II Corps had one division south of the river, whilst the remainder of the Corps and the 4th Division were still north and east of Noyon and north of the river. A dangerous gap of 11 miles still separated the two Corps. On the right British troops were 6 miles in rear of the left of the French Fifth Army, but on the left they were in touch with the French Cavalry of General Sordet, and General Manoury's new Sixth Army had its Headquarters at Montdidier. At 11.30 p.m. on August 28th Sir John French issued orders for the British troops to halt for a badly needed rest on the 29th, though all units were to be south of a line east and west through Nesle and Ham. He also arranged with General Joffre that for purposes of rest and recuperation the British Army would fall back to a line a little south of the Aisne between Soissons and Compiègne. At this period the British advanced base at Amiens had to be evacuated owing to the German sweep westward.

On the 29th spasmodic fighting with British cavalry occurred, but by midnight practically the whole of the II Corps had crossed the Oise River. General Joffre was anxious to attack from the line Rheims–Amiens, but as it was imperative that the British Commander should have a breathing space to rest and reorganize his forces, the latter issued at 9 p.m. on the 29th from G.H.Q. orders for a further retirement to the line Soissons–Compiègne, behind the Aisne River. The 30th saw the retreat continued in weather so intensely hot as to add seriously to the exertions of the troops. Fortunately, there was practically no interference by German cavalry. In order to help as far as he could to fall in with General Joffre's plans, Sir John French agreed to contrive to fill the gap between the Fifth and Sixth French Armies. At 5.15 p.m. on the 29th orders were issued for the British Army to move south-west, the I Corps and 5th Cavalry Brigade to the area round Villers Cottérêts, and the II Corps to the west of the I Corps to the area Feigneux–Crépy en Valois, the new III Corps to the area St. Sauveur–Verberie, and, west of all, Allenby's cavalry.

August 31st was a repetition of the preceding day so far as the intense heat was concerned. So oppressive were the conditions to marching infantry heavily weighted and with the added difficulties of the new country south of the Aisne River that the day's route of the Army Corps had to be curtailed.

The I Corps halted for the night north of the Forest of Villers Cottérêts; the II Corps at Coyolles and Crépy en Valois.

CHAPTER VIII

THE RETREAT TO TOURNAN. THE OFFENSIVE RESUMED. THE RIVER MARNE CROSSED. THE ADVANCE TO THE RIVER AISNE.

ON September 1st, a collision occurred with German cavalry at Nery, where the 1st Cavalry Brigade with L Battery R.H.A. had some difficulty in extricating themselves, thick mist early having delayed their march. At Crépy and Villers Cottérêts other small encounters took place. The 13th Infantry Brigade had held an outpost line due north of Crépy en Valois, where they were attacked about 6 a.m. by German cavalry: later on by infantry from Bethancourt. By noon, the outposts having become the rearguard, they had fallen back south of Crépy en Valois.

Here occurred an incident very creditable to a young officer of the "Duke's,"[1] and one which caused some amusement at a time when life on the whole was taken somewhat seriously. As a plain, unembroidered account of a minor affair, of which there were, of course, hundreds during the war, this story is worthy of being related.

"The next occurrence of any interest I can remember," writes the officer referred to, "was the capture of some 'Death's Head' Hussars. We were retreating about a week from the date of Le Cateau, and on arrival at a village we were informed that a Cavalry Division had pushed on very rapidly and were about 4 miles behind us. We were told this about 7 o'clock p.m. C Company was on duty, and at that time I was in command of it. I had no other officers. As you know, a senior Captain or Major, a second Captain and four subalterns are the correct number of officers to a company. I was sent on outpost duty, which means that my company had to stay on watch all night while the other three companies slept. I got the men stretched across our front for about a mile, made the usual arrangements and lay down to sleep with instructions that I was to be called on anything being seen. At dawn on September 1st some cavalry were pointed out to me on the crest line. I judged them to be a patrol sent on, so gave instructions not to fire on anything without orders. I sent down a message to Battalion Headquarters saying I might require reinforcements later, and started the company digging themselves in. A road ran through my front, and this was where I selected my own trench, putting some of the company on each side of the road. I got a message to say B Company was 800 yards in my rear, and if I wanted reinforcements I was to send for them. About 900 yards in front of

[1] Lieut. (now Capt.) H. K. O'Kelly, D.S.O.

my trenches there was a thick wood. About two hours later we shot at some cavalry approaching from our left. A little later two motor-cars came spinning down the road towards our trenches. I had the greatest difficulty in keeping the men from firing until they got to close range. Other troops did open fire on them. At about 300 yards we loosed off and succeeded in stopping the motor-cars, which were armoured. Immediately we came under a veritable hail of bullets from the wood. We had not thought the enemy had infantry so near. I then noticed a man signalling from the rear motor-car, so determined, as we could not make sure of them with bullets, we would have to charge them. I then sent back a message to B Company asking them to come up and support us as I was going to charge and wanted covering fire, but they were a long time coming, so I decided not to wait and called for volunteers. We charged out with fixed bayonets and reached the motor-cars right enough. There was an old General potting at me with an automatic pistol, and I determined not to miss him, so, as I am a hopeless shot with a revolver, I shoved it in his face and pulled the trigger, nearly blowing the poor old chap's head off. The men prodded most of the others, and some had already been hit with rifle bullets. I tried to start the cars but could not get either going, so was obliged to leave everything as we were under very heavy fire from the edge of the wood. We first burst up a gun which they had mounted on the rear car. I also took all the dispatches and relieved the old general of his revolver, which I still have, and some good cigars and cigarettes. I also took a few other things, which I afterwards lost. There were two serio-comic things about the affair. No. 1—An officer in great agony was waving his arms; nothing would persuade one of our fellows that he was not signalling, so he bayoneted him. A second was a young aide-de-camp who spoke English quite well, begged of me not to kill him and offered me a lot of jewellery as a bribe. I don't know what he took me for. On the return journey we came under a rifle fire from the direction of our own trenches. It turned out to be the ——— Regiment, who mistook us for Germans. Unfortunately, they shot two of my seven volunteers, and as three had already got wounded from German fire I was extraordinarily lucky to escape. The capture turned out to be some of the Headquarters Staff of the 1st German Cavalry Division, which was composed of 'Death's Head' Hussars, and was of some importance. I am glad to say the five survivors of the volunteers have been recommended for the D.C.M."

Between 7.30 and 9 p.m., on the night of September 1st, the 5th Division reached Nanteuil after another march of intense heat. The rest of the II Corps were in the vicinity.

Upon the same day, owing to information that the British Commander-in-Chief intended retiring past Paris further south, Lord Kitchener, on behalf of the Cabinet in London, crossed the Channel to discuss the general situation with Sir John French. As the result of this interview Lord Kitchener informed the Cabinet as follows by telegram :—

> "French's troops are now engaged in the fighting line, where he will remain conforming to the movements of the French Army, though at the

same time acting with caution to avoid being in any way unsupported on his flanks."¹

Upon returning to his own Headquarters at Dammartin from the meeting with Lord Kitchener, the British Commander-in-Chief was satisfied with the situation at the front, also that the reunion of the I and II Corps had finally taken place. They had remained separated since August 25th. Finding, however, that the heads of strong German columns had reached Villers Cottérêts and Crépy en Valois, it seemed desirable to Sir John French to withdraw the British troops still further south out of reach of a night attack by the enemy.

Soon after midday on September 1st, Corps Commanders were warned of a further retreat on the following day, " but by 7 p.m. that evening, realizing that the enemy was so near and in such force, and that some enemy cavalry were already actually behind the British front, Sir John French decided to continue the retreat earlier than he had intended, and all the Corps were ordered to get clear by a night march."²

At the same time G.H.Q. was moved south to Lagny, only some 15 miles east of Paris.

In suffocating heat on September 2nd the retreat was continued to the line Meaux–Dammartin. Round Mouy, on the British extreme left, lay the French Sixth Army of General Manoury. To its right, though some 25 miles away and a good march north, was the French Fifth Army.

When the British Commander-in-Chief ordered a further retreat on the night of the 1st/2nd September, there were good reasons for his action. There is now little doubt that the Germans intended to attack in force that night and to cut off and surround, if possible, the British forces. At 10.15 p.m. on September 1st, Von Kluck issued orders for his armies to attack next day, but, thanks to the prescience of Sir John French, he was too late. " The possibility of dealing a decisive blow against the British could no longer be reckoned on," says the official account.³

It was now that the German commander made the first great and initial error of the war, one which may possibly have entirely altered its final result. Having allowed the " Contemptible Little Army " to withdraw without being annihilated—for that had been Von Kluck's first aim and intention, he turned to strike against the French. Wheeling his two left Corps south-east against the Fifth French Army, soon after midday on September 2nd Von Kluck issued orders for this new movement.

On September 3rd, to comply with General Joffre's plans, Sir John French withdrew his corps south of the Marne slightly south-east, to avoid the perimeter of General Galliéni's command at and round Paris.

The 5th Division crossed the river at Îles les Villenoy, all bridges over the Marne being blown up as British troops passed. The evening of the 3rd, after a toilsome march on roads heavily blocked by the transport of refugees, the army lay south of the Marne River on a line Jouarre–Nogent. Sir John French was in touch on his right with the French Fifth Army, also south of the river, and on

---

¹ *Military Operations: France and Belgium*, 1914.   ² *Ibid.*   ³ *Ibid.*

his left with the Sixth French Army, but north of the Marne. By noon on the 3rd Sir John French was assured by his intelligence that the Germans were still moving rapidly south-east against the French, whom they struck at near Chateau-Thierry. By 4.35 p.m., convinced of Von Kluck's new plan, the British Commander-in-Chief informed his Corps Commanders that unless the situation changed the troops would remain in their billets and probably have complete rest the following day. But as General Joffre was not yet ready with his counter-stroke, and proposed to retire still further behind the Seine, Sir John French issued his order at 11.50 p.m. on September 3rd to continue moving south.

Upon the very early morning of September 4th the retreat continued south of the Grand Morin. The same day Sir John French received from his air-reconnaissance full and further confirmation of Von Kluck's position and intentions. Upon the 4th also the French Military Governor of Paris, General Galliéni, came to visit Sir John French. With him was General Manoury, commanding the French Sixth Army. From these two the suggestion was made that the opportunity had now come and should not be missed for the British, with what available French armies there were, to turn and strike hard at the right flank of Von Kluck's eastward-wheeling Corps. Sir John French happened to be absent from G.H.Q., so nothing definite was decided. General Galliéni waited until 5 p.m., then left British G.H.Q. on his return to Paris. There, awaiting him, was a telegram from General Joffre giving somewhat different views. The latter preferred to see General Manoury's army on the south bank of the Marne River before he himself struck back at the wheeling German troops, also the British armies between the right bank of the Seine and the Marne. Having informed Sir John French of his views, the latter at once decided to comply with General Joffre's suggestions, and to retire still further south. At 6.35 p.m. on September 4th the British Commander-in-Chief issued his orders from Melun on Seine for the army to move south-west on the following day. The new line to be held by the rearguards was to be roughly east and west through Tournan. The British Cavalry Division transferred from the British west to its eastern flank on the 6th. The 5th Division of the II Corps lay just east of Tournan.

From the day of the arrival of the British round Tournan, through all ranks there seemed to run the same feeling of relief that at last the retreat was over. " I remember," writes an officer of the Regiment,[1] " Sunday, September 6th, was our turning point and a red-letter day, as it was on this day that we received orders to turn round and advance against the enemy instead of continuing our retreat. I remember Capt. Tidmarsh and I walking up to the top of some high ground near by, and having a glimpse of Paris some 15 kilometres to the south-west of us. We had an excellent view of the Eiffel Tower and the dome of Nôtre Dame. I think it struck us somewhat forcibly then as to the distance we had covered since Mons in so short a time, and the fact that we had approached so near Paris. At 12 noon, on the 6th, we had a Church Parade in the square of Villeneuve, and in the afternoon we moved off in pursuit of the enemy. You can imagine the moral effect on us all of having the enemy *on the run* after our run

[1] Lieut. (now Major) C. W. G. Ince, M.C.

of several days. We all felt as fit as ever and began to think the war was near its end. False hopes, I'm afraid."

"Our run," thus described in the language of the camp, was one of the most notable retreats in the history of the British Army, and as such is worthy of closer scrutiny.

"The retreat of the B.E.F.," says the *Official History*,[1] "had continued with only one halt for thirteen days, over a distance, as the crow flies, of 136 miles, and as the men marched, at least 200 miles, and that after two days' strenuous marching in advance to the Mons canal. . . .

"The troops suffered under every disadvantage. The number of reservists in the ranks was on an average over one-half of the full strength, and the units were, owing to the force of circumstances, hurried away to the area of concentration before all ranks could resume acquaintance with their officers and comrades, and re-learn their business as soldiers. Arrived there, they were hastened forward by forced marches to the battle, confronted with greatly superior numbers of the most renowned army in Europe, and condemned at the very outset to undergo the severest ordeal which can be imposed upon an army. They were short of food and sleep when they began their retreat, they continued it, always short of food and sleep, for thirteen days as has been told; and at the end they were still an army, and a formidable army."

But that the troops required breathing space was perfectly clear to those in high command at the time.

"On September 5th," continues the official account, "there were some 20,000 men absent of the original numbers of the B.E.F., but, as in all great retreats, a large proportion of these rejoined later; the official return shows a figure of a little over 15,000 killed, wounded, and missing. The loss of war material is difficult to set down exactly. Some transport was abandoned, as is inevitable at such times; many of the valises and great-coats were discarded or burnt, and a very large proportion of the entrenching tools were left behind. As to guns, forty-two fell into the enemy's hands as the result of active combat, and two or three more, through one mishap or another, were left behind. Such a casualty list can, in the circumstances, be only considered as astonishingly light. Its seriousness lay in the fact that whether in guns or men, the loss had fallen almost wholly upon the left wing, the II and III Corps and, above all, upon the II Corps."

The retreat of the British forces with the rapid advance of the German armies had rendered necessary a change of sea-base. Thanks to the power of the British Navy, this change was at once made. By September 5th, St. Nazaire, on the Loire, instead of Havre had become the British sea-base. "In four days," says the official account, "20,000 officers and men, 7000 horses, and 60,000 tons of stores had been shipped from Havre to St. Nazaire."

It was on September 6th, the Sunday already referred to, that General Joffre issued his instructions for the long-hoped-for offensive. So far as concerned our own army, the intention was that the British troops facing east were to attack

[1] *Military Operations: France and Belgium*, 1914, Vol. I.

from the front Changis (7 miles east of Meaux,)—Coulommiers in the general direction of Montmirail, French cavalry ensuring connection with the Fifth French Army. Unfortunately, Joffre's instructions did not reach British G.H.Q. until early on the 5th, when, acting on the French Commander's previously issued instructions, the British troops had already commenced carrying out the further retirement. Thus, at nightfall on the 5th the British Army was 12 to 15 miles in rear of the position General Joffre expected it to be occupying.

At 5.15 p.m. on September 5th Sir John French issued orders for the advance east with a view to attack. A preliminary movement was ordered to bring the British Army on to a line from near Rozoy—5 miles south-east of Crécy, this line being parallel to the course of the Grand Morin and 7 miles south of it. The British Cavalry Division, with the 3rd and 4th Cavalry Brigades were to cover the front and flanks of the force, and connect with the French armies on either wing. These movements to be completed by 10 a.m. on September 6th.

Progress was slow when the leading troops of the I Corps were held up near Rozoy, while the II Corps had not progressed much beyond La Houssaye (6 miles north-west of Rozoy), so Sir John French issued orders for the II Corps to close in on the I Corps to Lumigny (4 miles north of Rozoy). At 3.30 p.m. he followed these with further orders for the I Corps to advance almost up to the line of the Grand Morin, for the II Corps to come up to the west of the I Corps, and for the III Corps to move up into the loop of the Grand Morin, south-west of Crécy. Thus, on the night of September 6th, when the combined Anglo-French advance commenced, the British Army lay as follows along the line of the Grand Morin :—

Cavalry Division	Jouy le Chatel.
I Corps	Vaudoy–Pezarches.
Gough's Cavalry	Pezarches–Lumigny.
II Corps	
3rd Division	Lumigny to Faremoutiers.
5th Division	Mortcerf to La Celle-sur-Morin.
III Corps	Villiers-sur-Morin southwards to Villeneuve le Comte and Villeneuve St. Denis.

On September 7th it became fairly clear that the German armies were withdrawing north. Air-reconnaissance having confirmed the information, Sir John French at 8 a.m. issued orders for the continuation of the British advance across the Grand Morin towards Rebais. The ground over which the advance was to take place is part of the great plateau east and north-east of Paris. It is cut from east to west as the map shows, deeply cut by the following streams whose sides are precipitous, in places almost ravines, the Grand and Petit Morin, the Marne, the Upper Ourcq, the Vesle, the Aisne, and the Ailette. These streams are only passable by bridging or where bridges exist.

On the night of the 7th the British Army lay north and south of and along the line of the Grand Morin. General Joffre's instructions, issued at 5.20 p.m. on the evening of the 7th, were for a general pursuit of the enemy, also with the possibility of enveloping his right wing. The British share in these plans was " to endeavour to get a footing in succession across the Grand Morin, the Petit Morin, and the Marne."

In pursuance of these instructions the British Commander-in-Chief ordered a further advance against the line of the Marne, before reaching which the Petit Morin had to be crossed, and this, from a military point of view, was not by any means an easy proposition. There were only six bridges in the section of operations. The stream ran through a narrow valley whose steep, wooded sides were only approachable through close country studded with innumerable copses as well as villages and hamlets. The valley of the Marne is of similar character.

Desultory fighting up to midday on September 8th showed that the north bank of the Marne, as well as the main bridge-head at La Ferté sous Jouarre, was held in force by the enemy. Before 2 p.m., after further fighting, the passage of the Petit Morin had been forced at the eastern extremity of the British line. Further west, as early as 9 a.m., two battalions of the 13th Infantry Brigade 5th Division were deployed for attack on St. Cyr. Even with reinforcements little progress was made until nearly 3 p.m., when the German position round St. Cyr became untenable owing to the British crossing near Orly. Orly itself was captured about 4 p.m. At the same time the Cyclist Company of the 5th Division, under Major J. C. Burnett, D.S.O., reached the main road, La Ferté sous Jouarre–Montmirail where they caught 200 Germans. Unfortunately a British battery turned its shrapnel on to the spot, so creating a diversion which allowed more than half the prisoners to escape. By 5 p.m. both divisions of the II Corps were within less than a mile of the River Marne. Practically the whole of September 8th was spent in forcing the passage of the Petit Morin. That night the British Army halted all south of the Marne.

Cavalry Division	Replunges.
I Corps	Bassevelle–Hondevillers–Boitron.
II Corps	Les Feuchères–Rougeville–Orly.
III Corps	Grand Glairet–Venteuil
3rd Cavalry Brigade	Chateau-Signy Signets.
5th Cavalry Brigade	Between Gibraltar and Rebais.

On the evening of the 8th, Sir John French issued orders for the army to continue its advance north next day at 5 a.m., and to attack enemy rearguards wherever met. Why the Germans did not stand on the Marne position is not known. But it was already evident, from air reports on the 8th, that they intended not to do so. Early on the 9th British Cavalry seized possession of the two bridges at Nogent and Charly, and by 9.30 a.m. British Infantry of the 1st Division were across the Marne. The II Corps found no opposition, so the 3rd and 5th Divisions crossed at Nanteuil and Saacy. Some interesting and human reminiscences of that day's work are given by an officer of the Regiment.[1]

[1] Lieut. (now Major) C. W. G. Ince, M.C.

"Wednesday the 9th September was a wet day," he wrote. "I was sent out on a patrol to try and find a crossing over or the best means of passing the River Marne. Fortunately, there was a repaired bridge so we had no difficulty in getting across.

"We stopped at Le Limon for the night. On the way we passed a captured German Field Battery of 8 guns. Nearly all the gunners lay dead by their guns. I was told that the battery had held up our advanced guard for several hours before it was silenced. I believe the 15th Brigade were acting as advance guard on this day. Before we arrived at Le Limon we passed a long German convoy which had been captured by our advanced cavalry. The 17th Lancers, I believe, actually captured it. At any rate, we were able by their kindness to supply ourselves with a very efficient German travelling cooker which served the Battalion a long time afterwards!"

There was considerable fighting before the Marne was crossed, especially opposite to the III Corps at the west end of the British line of advance, and when darkness fell on the 9th, ten of the sixteen battalions of the III Corps were still on the south side of the Marne, but the three days' battle was over. That the Battle of the Marne was one of the deciding issues of the war is now a matter of history. That Von Kluck made his initial error in high strategy is also generally allowed, but it is not so well known and is a matter of great interest that Von Moltke, Chief of the German General Staff, was held also to have been heavily at fault. "Von Moltke," says the official account,[1] " seems to have conceived two separate battles, one near Paris and the other near Verdun. So important did he consider the attack in Lorraine, that when the threat from Paris began to materialize, he still persevered there, instead of sending every man who could be spared from the left to the vital right wing in accordance with the original plan. For this purpose there were trains actually waiting on the sidings. It was not until the 9th September that orders were given for the transfer of the XV Corps from the Seventh (German) Army to the west."

Hoping to be able to intercept the retreat of the German First Army across the British front, Sir John French at 8.15 p.m. on September 9th ordered his troops to continue the pursuit northwards at 5 a.m. the following morning. Intermittent fighting and a general pressure from the British kept the German troops on the move during the 10th, but the 5th Division and the III Corps met with no opposition. Montreuil was reached early, but the Germans had slipped away. By the evening of the 10th the four divisions of the I and II Corps were astride the River Alland, the cavalry in front astride the upper Ourcq, and the III Corps behind the left flank.

Operation orders for the 11th directed a further pursuit north-east, at 5 a.m. to cross the River Ourcq and to make for a line from Bruyeres north-east through Cugny to St. Remy, and thence west to La Loge Farm. The actual billet of the " Duke's " that night was at Chezy. The 11th was quite uneventful, " but on the 12th, when we left for Hartennes," writes an officer of the Regiment, " very wet." " G.H.Q. orders for the 12th were that the pursuit should

[1] *Military Operations: France and Belgium*, 1914.

be continued, and that the crossing-places of the Aisne should be seized and the high ground on the northern side of the river secured."[1]

But the situation was by no means clear. So far it was uncertain to what extent the German retreat had demoralised their troops, and the heavy rain and weather conditions of the 11th and 12th had prevented any but cursory air reconnaissance. By 1.30 p.m. the Vesle River was crossed by troops of the 2nd Division near Courcelles, and British Cavalry had occupied Braisne, but when darkness fell not a single bridge over the Aisne was in British hands. That at Vailly was reported by British Cavalry as destroyed, and the bridge at Condé, 1¾ miles west of Vaizy, as strongly held by the enemy.

By 3 p.m., on the British extreme left, the III Corps had pushed on to the heights at Septmonts, 3 miles south-east of Soissons on the Aisne, from whence the troops overlooked the valley and the bridge at Venizel. British infantry, the Inniskilling Fusiliers, had even advanced as far as the bridge and had reconnoitred the crossing, but only to find it still held by the Germans. On the night of September 12th the B.E.F. rested as follows :—

Cavalry Division } I Corps	Longueval, Dhuizel, Courcelles.
3rd and 5th Cavalry Brigades	Chassemy, Ciry Salsogne.
II Corps	Brenelle, Serches (The Duke of Wellington's), Braisne.
III Corps	Septmonts, Buzancy.

Although the complete story of the fighting included under the title the Battle of the Aisne cannot be told here, it is advisable to try and understand some of the characteristics and complexities connected with that three days' battle. First, it should be remembered that the severe fighting on the heights north of the Aisne—the Chemin des Dames—was practically the end of open-fighting as hitherto practised in war. Also, that it marked the commencement of those heart-breaking years of trench warfare which may or may nor remain the chief characteristic of all future wars.

As has been pointed out above, at the crossing of the Marne there were certain points which still remained obscure as to whether the enemy's forces were retreating as a beaten army, or merely were forced to withdraw for reasons of strategy. Before the crossing of the Aisne, as well as during the heavy fighting accompanying that successful feat of arms, the general conditions were equally, if not more, obscure. As it happened, the fierce stand made by the Germans north of the Aisne had not been expected, for as the official account of the fighting on September 14th tells us : " The British Divisions came piecemeal on the battlefield to the support of the advanced guards already across the Aisne. They found the enemy not only in position, entrenched and supported by 8-inch howitzers, but in such force that so far from manifesting any intention of continuing his retreat, he made every effort to drive the British back over the river. Thus September 14th passed in alternate attack and counter-attack and ended

[1] *Ibid.*

in no decisive result. It was the first day of that 'stabilization' of the battle-line that was to last so many weary months—the beginning, as it turned out, of trench-warfare."

Let us return to the actual position on September 12th and glance for a moment at the physical difficulties the British had to face. "The Aisne," says the official description of the *terrain* fought over, " offers great facilities for defence. The river, winding and sluggish except when in flood, and some two hundred feet wide, is unfordable; it runs through a valley which has steep sides covered with patches of wood, but with a gently sloping or level bottom from a mile to two miles in breadth and over three hundred feet below the level of the plateau through which the course of the stream has been cut. As in the case of many other valleys in the north of France, the sides form a series of spurs and ravines, wooded on the toes of the spurs and sides of the ravines, and the stream passes first close to one side and to the other in its winding course. There is little cover on the low ground in the valley itself for infantry seeking to force a passage from the south, and no position for artillery to support it, except on the southern heights. The German Artillery could harass British troops in the valley at a range of 3000 yards and yet have no British battery within closer range than 5,000 to 6,000 yards.

"In the section opposite the British, from Bourg to Venizel (both inclusive), there were seven road bridges, an aqueduct carrying the Oise–Aisne canal over the river at Bourg, and a railway bridge east of Vailly, where a narrow-gauge railway, which runs along the southern bank from the direction of Rheims, crosses the river to the northern bank on its way to Soissons. All these bridges, except that at Condé, were eventually found to be more or less unserviceable."

So much for the difficulties British troops were called upon to face and overcome.

General Joffre's Special Instructions, issued on September 12th, were for the B.E.F. to move north between Bourg and Soissons supported on both flanks by French armies. Sir John French issued his orders at 7.45 p.m. the same evening. These directed that the heads of the three British Corps should reach a line about 5 miles north of the Aisne: Lierval–Chavignon–Terny ($4\frac{1}{2}$ miles north of Soissons), starting at 7 a.m. on September 13th.

"The destination of the B.E.F. was thus roughly the top of the plateau, at this point little more than a ridge, which lies between the valleys of the Aisne and Ailette, and is traversed from east to west by the now well-known Chemin des Dames."[1]

In passing over the Aisne the II Corps and Gough's cavalry were allotted the bridges at Vailly, Condé, and Missy, in the centre of the British line of advance, and the 3rd Division were sent against the bridges (canal and river) at Vailly, the 5th against the bridge at Missy and that at Condé. About 6 a.m. two companies of the leading battalion of the 13th Brigade, the West Kents, approached the Missy bridge, but were compelled to retire by fire from the northern bank. Thereafter the two companies entrenched to the east of the bridge, the

[1] *Military Operations: France and Belgium*, 1914.

Battalion remaining at Sermoise. "After dark had set in, a small boat without oars was found on the south bank, and some sleepers were brought from a railway line a quarter of a mile away, with which a small raft was constructed. No rope was available so barbed wire was used to lash the rafts and to tow the boat and raft to and fro across the river (40 yards wide). Neither boat nor raft could accommodate more than four or five men at a time. The Germans gave no sign until about forty men were across. Then a patrol of five men came down to within about two hundred yards of the river. Three were killed, and the other two badly wounded."[1]

Before daylight on the 14th two battalions of the 13th Brigade had been ferried across on larger rafts constructed under R.E. supervision. These were the 1st Royal West Kents and the 2nd Battalion K.O.S.B.'s. For their gallant work at the rafting, Capt. W. H. Johnston and Lieut. R. B. Flint, R.E., were awarded respectively the V.C. and D.S.O. The other two battalions of the Brigade, the 2nd Duke of Wellington's and 2nd K.O.Y.L.I.'s, remained south of the river, the one at Sermoise, the other at Ciry. By noon of September 13th the British position was roughly this: The passage of the Aisne had been won at both extremities of the British line, by the I Corps and cavalry on the right and by the III Corps on the extreme left. Before dawn on the 14th a precarious footing had been gained at several points on the north bank, though there still remained on the south side of the river some six British brigades, which included, as has been said, half of the 13th Brigade, the 2nd Battalion Duke of Wellington's, and 2nd Battalion K.O.Y.L.I.

As Sir John French's information appeared to indicate that the whole German line was still retiring in a north-easterly direction, he decided he was justified in making a great effort to carry out General Joffre's instructions for an energetic pursuit. His order for September 14th, therefore, directed an advance northward to the line Laon–Fresnes (the latter 12 miles west of Laon), cavalry covering both flanks. But when night fell on some of the most severe fighting of the war along the Chemin des Dames, the British objective was as far off as ever.

The operation orders for the 5th Division for September 14th directed the continuation of the pursuit northwards, via Missy, but it was soon evident that so long as the high ground on the Chivres spur was held by the enemy, progress would be exceedingly difficult, if at all possible. Until the late afternoon severe, and at times confused, fighting took place to obtain possession of the Chivres spur, but thick woods and trenches protected by wire netting and fencing led to both overcrowding in the attack and confusion. As the official account relates, "Confused advance gave place to confused retirement, and Brig.-General Count Gleichen, the senior officer on the spot, decided to abandon the attack, called back his battalions and broke off the fight."

A line was then taken up and held by the 5th Division for the night from Bucy le Long on the west to Missy village on the east, across the mouth of the

---

[1] *Invicta.* With the 1st Battn. the Queen's Own Royal West Kent Regt. in the Great War, by Major C. V. Molony

Chivres valley. The West Kents and K.O.S.B. of the 13th Brigade prolonged the line to the Missy bridge.

In spite of the heavy losses sustained—those of the III Corps alone amounted to 3500—and of the audacity displayed in the British attack, the situation on the night of September 14th was far from reassuring. There were gaps in the line between divisions; the 4th and 5th Divisions only held a precarious position on the north bank, and were also separated from the rest of the army by the Chivres promontory. Two battalions, the Duke of Wellington's and K.O.Y.L.I., were still on the south bank at Sermoise. The Germans might decide to counter-attack and sweep the British south of the river. The British were extended on far too wide a front for their strength, except in defence, and practically every battalion was already in the firing-line and there was no general reserve whatever. Permanent bridges over the Aisne there were none, and the greatest difficulties occurred in bringing up supplies and disposing of the wounded.

On the night of September 14th/15th Sir John French conferred personally with his Corps Commanders, the I Corps being represented by a G.S.O.[1]. Though orders issued from G.H.Q. contained only information as to the general situation, it was decided to order all troops to entrench in the positions they then occupied.

At 1.15 a.m. on the 15th, Sir John French received from General Joffre a copy of a telegram addressed to all his Army Commanders. The telegram ran thus:—

> "It seems as if the enemy is once more going to accept battle, in prepared positions north of the Aisne. In consequence it is no longer a question of pursuit, but of a methodical attack, using every means at our disposal and consolidating each position in turn as it is gained."[2]

That these instructions were not carried out is due to the fact that September 15th was a day of German attacks. The 5th Division was not left in inaction, for a final attempt was made to gain the Chivres spur. The 14th and 15th Brigades were ordered to renew their attacks from the south and south-west as before, whilst the 13th Brigade, reinforced by the "Duke's" and K.O.Y.L.I.'s from the south bank of the river, struck from the south-east simultaneously. The "Duke's" crossed over at Missy on rafts, but were punished by German high-explosive shells while approaching and crossing the river. The K.O.Y.L.I.'s also suffered, though owing to the rafts not being ready for them the Battalion had to remain south of the river.

Owing to new German defences in the woods, and a wire-netting fence 6 feet high, the attack of the 14th and 15th Brigades of the 5th Division came to a standstill, nor could the 13th Brigade reach its assigned position for the attack on the Chivres spur, as the Condé road was swept by German artillery. The whole movement was checked and Missy, overcrowded with some battalions of the 14th and 15th Brigades, was almost overwhelmed by a storm of German

---

[1] *Military Operations: France and Belgium, 1914.*   [2] *Ibid.*

shells. The 15th Brigade was eventually ordered to retire south of the river, which it did just before dawn on the 16th.

"It now seemed established beyond doubt that the capture of the promontory of Chivres was beyond the strength of the British force.

" . . . Everything pointed to the probability, if not the certainty, of a deadlock on the line of the Aisne which could only be resolved by a decisive action on the one open flank towards the west."[1]

In accordance with this principle, one which both sides had worked out in detail as the most likely road to success, preparations were mutually commenced for prolonging their lines westwards and northwards. This was done by withdrawing troops from other parts of the front. In furtherance of this idea General Joffre on September 18th informed Sir John French that "the general offensive would be resumed as soon as a new army that he was concentrating in the west was in a position to move forward."

For September 16th Sir John French issued orders that the line held by the army was to be strongly entrenched, though he added that it was his intention to assume a general offensive at the first opportunity. Next day he ordered the line to be strengthened by every available means, thus inaugurating trench-warfare. Henceforth the general situation remained unaltered.

From September 16th to the 24th the "Duke's" remained at Missy. Some notes by an officer of the Royal Engineers[2] who was with them give an interesting account of the original crossing of the Aisne.

"*The Battle of the Aisne.*

"No. 2 Sec. 17th Fd. Coy. R.E., having rafted continuously on the 13th and 14th September (1914) in passing the 14th and 15th Infantry Brigades over the Aisne with their first line transport, at 3.0 a.m. on 15th received orders to move the raft from Moulin des Roches to the site of the old Missy–Sermoise bridge and there raft over the remainder of the 13th Infantry Brigade.

"The old bridge was reached about 4.30 a.m., and just as it was getting light the first battalion of the 13th Infantry Brigade arrived and the rafting commenced.

"The men were rafted over on a standard pontoon raft which took fifty men each journey, the trip taking about $6\frac{1}{4}$ minutes. The river here was some 70 yards wide.

"The situation on the north of the river was rather obscure, and no one appeared to be quite certain as to where the Germans were. As soon as it became light the Germans started shelling us with 5·9 H.E. and shrapnel. The former were short and the latter burst high. There was also considerable activity from enemy snipers. Losses were, however, very slight.

"After two battalions had been rafted across, one of which was the Duke of Wellington's Regiment, a small maintenance party was left to deal with the ammunition and wounded, the remainder of the section moved through Sermoise and bivouacked.

---

[1] *Military Operations : France and Belgium,* 1914. [2] Capt. K. B. Godsell, R.E.

"The approaches to the raft from Sermoise were in fair condition, but no transport was taken across at this time, a pontoon bridge having now been completed at Moulin des Roches. On the north bank the ground was marshy and thickly wooded, which made progress and the forming up of the troops difficult.

"The men were very tired and rather shaky.

"The weather was bad, being cold and wet."

The same officer continues:—

"*September 17th–24th, 1914.*

"Missy normally had a two-battalion garrison. During this period the 2nd Battalion Duke of Wellington's Regiment were on the right, that is, from the eastern outskirts of the village to the Missy–Chivres road (exclusive).

"The position in light of modern knowledge was distinctly sketchy. It consisted for the most part of shallow trenches behind the loosely-built local walls. The trenches had a field of fire of some 200 yards. The village was dominated by the German position some 200 yards away, which made any movement difficult. The main streets through the village provided good lateral communication as it had a high stone wall and houses on each side, most of its length. There was practically no depth, for lack of men and for lack of any position.

"Supports were entrenched in long, deep trenches south of the main streets, but could only assist in the defence by thickening up the front trenches.

"Elaboration of the defence works was not encouraged as it was generally thought the advance would be continued.

"Each day Missy received its dose of shelling in varying quantities and unequal doses. The houses became dilapidated, offering less and less cover. The last of the inhabitants left about September 23rd. It became unsafe even for the troops to use the houses as billets, but this practice was continued to a much later date. The only effective cover against the shell fire were the trenches. These were dug 5 to 6 feet deep for the troops in support, but were not as a rule traversed. The weather was very wet and these trenches filled with water, and had to be drained.

"In the front line there was even less cover as the men had to be able to fire over the rickety walls which only gave them 2 feet of trench behind.

"Much labour was spent in building up these walls as many fell down at a bullet's strike.

"We tried to wire the position, but as all the wire had first to be collected from local fences and used again, although something was done, it could not be considered satisfactory.

"To add to our joys, our shrapnel was continually bursting over our heads and behind us.

"During the nights the Germans used a searchlight from near Chivres, but I do not think it showed up much to them. I do not remember any Very Lights being used. Perhaps this accounts for the following amusing incident.

"A sentry of the 'Duke's' in the barricade on the Missy–Condé road was stirred from stupor one night by seeing a black object approaching slowly with long horns. He fired and killed it. In the morning it was discovered he had shot an ass.

"Another sentry of the same company from behind his wall saw a round black object silhouetted against the sky and gradually rising above the wall. Thinking it was a German's head he shot it and a cat fell dead at his feet.

"One morning, in walking along the main street, I met a private of the Duke of Wellington's Regiment who seemed tremendously pleased with himself. He was carrying a helmet in each hand, one silver, one brass. He showed them to me and said they were German helmets he had just found—Prussian Guards' ones, he believed. An inspection of the helmets proved them to be those of the local fire brigade. The man was so pleased I had not the heart to undeceive him.

"There was a good stock of 'meat on the hoof' in the shape of fowls, rabbits, etc., and all messes and stock-pots did well. The rabbits were a nuisance as one was continually stepping on them when prowling about at night."

Another account of the time spent at Missy is given by an officer of the Regiment.[1] Once more the fact is emphasized that an army "marches on its belly."

"We had quite an interesting time in Missy," he wrote, "as although we were shelled pretty heavily daily we had our first real experience of trench warfare and preparing a position for defence. The village was still occupied by its inhabitants and we defended the northern and eastern edge of the village, our right flank running down to the river.

"The ground in front of us was enclosed and was high, so that except for about a distance of 200 yards we could see nothing more. At first we loopholed the walls, but later, as these got knocked about by shell fire, we dug trenches. We even had a cow which supplied fresh milk daily in the front line. The civil population were able to live in the very deep cellars under their houses. These were often some 20 feet underground. In them were the wine vats and presses. Needless to say, we made use of these for our reserves, etc., when the village was heavily shelled. The weather kept fairly fine so that our time at Missy was not so bad, though, of course, we had to be ready to move at a moment's notice, the position of affairs being somewhat obscure. We were very well fed during our time in Missy. We were also able to obtain fresh bread in the village as the village bakery continued working, and when we left it was still carrying on, although it was hit by shells on more than one occasion."

---

[1] Lieut. (now Major) C. W. G. Ince, M.C.

CHAPTER IX

FROM THE AISNE TO BETHUNE. YPRES, DECEMBER, 1914.

"THE scale and intensity of the First Shock in 1914 have not been fully realized, even by the well-instructed French public, and are not at all understood in England. At the beginning all totals of casualties were suppressed in every combatant country by a rigorous censorship. Later on in the war, when more was known, no one had time to look back in the midst of new perils to the early days; and since the war no true impression has ever reached the public. British eyes have been fixed upon the vivid pictures of Liège, Mons, and Le Cateau, that part of the Battle of the Marne which occurred near Paris, and the desperate struggle round Ypres. The rest lies in a dark background, which it is now possible to illuminate.

"In the first three months of actual fighting, from the last week in August to the end of November, when the German drive against the Channel ports had come to an end and the first great invasion was definitely arrested, the French lost in killed, prisoners, and wounded 854,000 men. In the same period the small British Army, about one-seventh of the French fighting strength, lost 85,000 men, making a total Allied loss of 939,000. Against this, in the same period, the Germans lost 677,000."[1]

During the pause on the Aisne—though to the troops who were occupied in learning how to avoid casualties in trenches there seemed to be no pause in the persistent shelling of their positions—a new type of warfare was being initiated. Nor must it be forgotten, initiated under conditions far more favourable to the Germans than to the British. "September, 1914," says the official account, "found them (the Germans) equipped with heavy guns (8-inch howitzers), trench-mortars, rifle-grenades, hand-grenades, searchlights, illuminating pistols, and periscopes designed for the attack of fortresses but practically comprising all the apparatus of trench warfare."

At this period of the war how many British officers knew what a periscope was? Some may have heard of, most had never seen, a hand-grenade or a trench-mortar, a flare-ball or an illuminating pistol.

Pride of position, so far as the siting of trenches was concerned, was in most cases almost always in favour of the German troops. During the third week in September the redistribution of the British Air Force and the equipment of British 'planes with wireless somewhat redressed the balance. It also enabled British batteries to try and reply more effectively to the heavy shelling

---

[1] *The World Crisis* 1916–1918, Part V. By the Rt. Hon. Winston Churchill, C.H., M.P.

PLATE 12

YPRES, 1914

YPRES, 1919

of the German gunners. But the British field-howitzers were a poor substitute for the German guns of large calibre. Until the end of the third week such operations as took place were mainly confined to small attacks to screen the withdrawal of troops required for the " race to the sea " in the western section of the opposing lines.

It was on September 25th that the 2nd Duke of Wellington's were withdrawn from the fighting line. " We recrossed the Aisne," writes Lieut. C. W. G. Ince, " and went into reserve near Sermoise on the south bank. Actually we were bivouacked in Goebin Wood in rear of the village, lying about a kilometre from the river bank. During our period in this wood-bivouac, which lasted until October 2nd, the Battalion was mainly occupied in patrolling the south bank of the Aisne at night and in furnishing outposts. Frequent warnings were received to prepare for a sudden enemy raid across the river, but nothing ever came of them. Our time waiting near Sermoise was broken by at least one amusing incident. Our outpost company on the right had its position concealed by a belt of trees some 1500 yards from the river. The outpost faced northwards towards Fort de Condé with the bridge at Missy on its left. Between the outpost and the river was a burnt-out farm consisting of several dilapidated buildings. Fairly late one evening two Germans were seen approaching the farm, about 1000 yards from the outposts. The soldiers were noticed entering the farm and were shortly after seen leaving it again with a fat old sow in tow. This was altogether too much for the outpost sentries, who promptly opened with rapid fire on the German soldiers. They immediately let go the old sow and made a bolt for the river. Unfortunately, owing to the failing light, both got away, though one was seen to be hit."

During the stay of the Battalion in Goebin Wood slight casualties kept occurring. Towards the end of September Capt. R. M. Tidmarsh having to go on the sick-list, Lieut. C. W. G. Ince assumed the duties of Adjutant. Major Kenneth McLeod, who had succeeded Colonel J. A. C. Gibbs in command of the Battalion after Mons, was also obliged to go to hospital, so Major H. K. Umfreville took over as Commanding Officer on September 16th.

At and during the retreat from Mons the " Duke's " had, of course, suffered heavy casualties, but these were practically made up by the arrival of various officers and drafts between September 5th and the beginning of October. Capt. W. E. Keates with 102 other ranks was the first party of reinforcements to join the Battalion. Later arrivals were: Lieuts. D. F. de Wend and Yates with 172 other ranks. On September 16th at Missy-sur-Aisne the following officers reported for duty: Capts. H. K. Umfreville, B. J. Barton, C. A. J. S. Langdale, and N. H. Moore; Lieuts. G. Williamson, W. R. Downey, H. G. Henderson, and Lieuts. M. M. Elrington, Essex Regiment, F. A. Rippingille, and R. F. Gosset of the East Yorkshire Regiment.

Two days after his arrival Lieut. R. F. Gosset was wounded by a shell bursting close to him on the road. On September 23rd another draft of 2nd Lieuts. C. St.T. Phillips and C. F. Whittaker with 162 other ranks joined up.

On the date when the 2nd Duke of Wellington's, together with the rest of the 13th Infantry Brigade, 5th Division, left their precarious position on the Aisne nothing was known of their new destination.

In order that the sequence of events can be intelligently followed it may be well to anticipate what happened in the light of later knowledge. By early October French armies had occupied a line of position as far north as Béthune. French Territorials were also holding a rough line northwards to a point east of St. Omer and west of Hazebrouck. French efforts to turn the German right flank had been in each case successfully held up. German efforts in the shape of von der Marwitz's huge cavalry forces had also failed to break through the French past Hazebrouck. "By October 9th, 1914, after severe and heavy fighting chiefly by the French Second, Sixth, and Tenth Armies, the battle line had been extended from the Aisne westwards and northwards to within thirty miles of Dunkirk and the sea."[1]

Three years of stalemate had begun. The following account of how Germany envisaged the war in the autumn of 1914 is of extraordinary interest to-day. The writer, Maximilian Harden, whose reputation as editor and journalist was world-wide, was throughout the war the most outspoken and honest critic of the Kaiser and Supreme War Staff. Towards the end of the war he was—mainly for this reason—more read in the German newspapers than any other journalist. In his interesting book of post-war memories[2] he writes thus :—

"It was autumn, 1914. The people of Germany were hearing of nothing but victories in the west and in the east—not a word of their army's enforced retreat on the Marne. They were confident that, long before the leaves turned yellow, Paris would fall and that before Christmas their victorious army would return home.

"An official circular-letter signed by the Prussian General von Viebahn from the front requested information as to the number of windows in Berlin on the Pariser Platz and Unter den Linden that could be reserved for special guests to witness the triumphal entry of the troops into the city."

So near was the final victory, thought the recipients of Von Viebahn's letter!

On being relieved at Goebin Wood by the Durham Light Infantry the 2nd Duke of Wellington's marched to Violaines, October 3rd, then via Hartennes and Largny, October 4th and 5th, to Fresnoy, and on October 7th to Verberie. Entraining at Longueil next day, the Battalion found itself by noon at Abbeville. Detraining the Duke's marched to Noyelle, where they billeted. Marching on via Guescart and Harravesnes the Battalion halted on the 9th just south of the Conchy–Hesdin road. The following day motor-buses conveyed the companies via St. Pol to billets at Dieval, and on October 11th the Battalion reached Béthune, going into Corps reserve with the rest of the 13th Brigade near Vaubricourt.

[1] *Military Operations: France and Belgium*, 1914, Vol. I.
[2] *My Contemporaries*. By Maximilian Harden, 1926.

A brief idea must now be given of what the 13th Brigade, 5th Division, were sent to do at La Bassée. All through October, 1914, as at Ypres in October–November, the plan of the German Supreme Command was to pierce the allied weakly held, irregular battle-line. To further this object German reinforcements were constantly arriving.

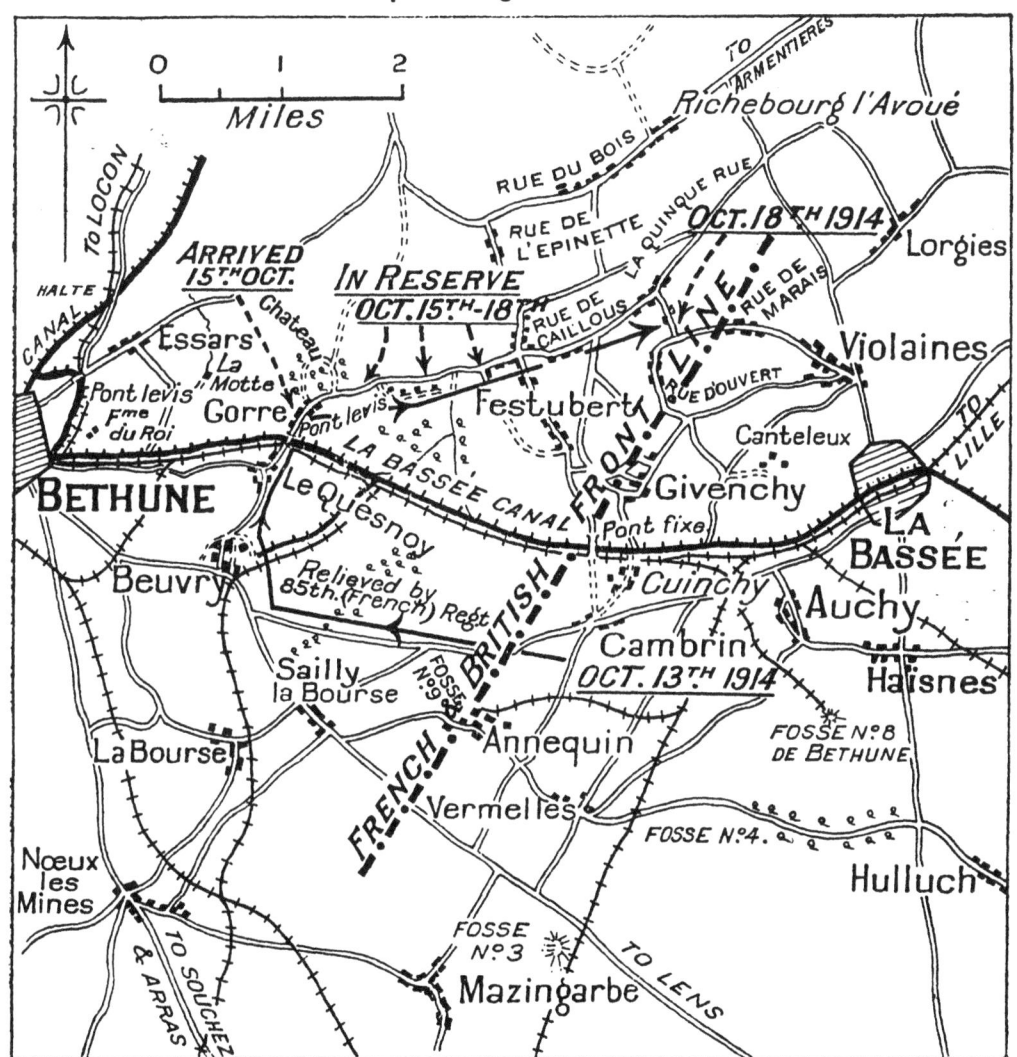

FRONT NEAR LA BASSÉE, OCTOBER, 1914, SHOWING MOVEMENTS OF THE 2ND BATTALION.

"The fighting on the La Bassée front," says the official account,[1] "so far as the valour and determination of the troops on both sides are concerned, was as desperate as that of Ypres, but it never had the same strategic or sentimental importance. The capture of the Béthune district, with its coalfields and

[1] *Military Operations: France and Belgium*, Vol. II.

resources, would undoubtedly have been a very serious loss to France, but not an irreparable one like that of the Channel ports."

Luckily for most men during the Great War sufficient for the day was the evil thereof, though the II Corps' arrival at Béthune was understood to mean being once more on the war-path. Nor were the prophets disappointed. October 12th saw the 13th Brigade ordered to move in the direction of Vermelles and La Bassée against the Germans entrenched. Reaching Annequin they were found to be in force, so the 13th Brigade took up a line north of the Givenchy-Noyelles road. All day on the 13th Annequin was heavily shelled, but on the next the Battalion was relieved by a French battalion. A French attack had been arranged for that day but did not take place, so the "Duke's" marched to Le Quesnoy, where they billeted. October 15th was fairly quiet, so the opportunity was taken for holding a Regimental concert. On the 16th and 17th a forward move was made as far as the little village of Rue d'Ouvert, where trenches were occupied in which the Battalion remained for two days, October 18th and 19th.

Major E. G. Harrison, C. B., D.S.O. (as he then was), who later was three times wounded with the Battalion, took over command at Rue d'Ouvert from Major H. K. Umfreville. Various casualties occurred at this time. Capt. W. E. Keates, Capt. N. H. Moore, and Lieut. C. W. G. Ince had to go into hospital, while Capt. Travers, Royal Munster Fusiliers, Capt. Owen T. R. Crawshay, and Lieut. J. Bennett and 57 other ranks joined for duty.

On October 20th/21st at 4 a.m. Headquarters of the 13th Brigade moved to Festubert. In his diary written at the time Colonel Harrison adds this very interesting account of October 19th and subsequent days spent in trying to hold up German attacks round Givenchy and immediately north of the La Bassée Canal.

"*Monday, 19th October.*—A fine day. Our Brigade, viz. 13th, now on extreme right of the British Army. The French are in position on our right, and for two days have been trying to take the Canal Bridge (La Bassée Canal) which is strongly defended. Yesterday they failed and lost a lot of men. Our left Brigade, the 14th, made a night attack at dark on Violaines, a largish village or town on our right front. We are in so-called reserve but only 400 yards in rear of first line, so get a full share of shells, especially as there are battery positions on each side and just behind us. Nothing much up to 10 p.m. except heavy firing on our left, i.e. the 3rd Division. We are in a comfortable farmhouse."

"*Tuesday, 20th October.*—Shelling started 6 a.m. and went on hard all day. We still remained in support of the Norfolks and got a lot of shrapnel We only lost three men, two of these officers' servants in their billets. The Brigadier sent for me at 3 p.m. The Germans are attacking all along the line from the coast to Arras, but were repulsed everywhere."

"*Wednesday, 21st October.*—Hard shelling still going on all day here, the artillery observation post got knocked out at 2.30 p.m. on top of a haystack on left of A Company. The shell appears to have burst as it struck the man, and set fire to the rick. The Cheshires on our left front seemed to be busy from

7 o'clock or so for about an hour. Night attack on our half-right front 8.45 p.m. to 9.45 p.m. No result as far as can make out up to 11.30 p.m., and only a few casualties."

Most of the day was spent in digging. B Company, after dark, relieved a company on outpost near St. Roch. C Company was in support. A and D in reserve.

Thursday, 22nd October, turned out a busy day with much hard work. Just before dawn B Company was relieved by C and returned to its former billets in Rue d'Ouvert. Then came orders to turn out immediately as the Cheshires having been rushed at dawn in Violaines, the Germans had broken through and caused the Dorsets to retire also. As the latter were on the left of the "Duke's" this made a gap of about one mile between battalions. The 13th Brigade received orders to attack houses in Rue de Marais, but owing to confusion the attack was unsuccessful. Three companies—A, C, and D—of the "Duke's" attacked north-east towards Violaines. About 2 a.m. on October 23rd the companies were withdrawn. The casualties were small.

B Company had been ordered to assist the Manchesters and Bedfords in their attack on Violaines, and dug itself in alongside the Bedfords, finally withdrawing to Festubert unmolested by the enemy, who failed to keep in touch with our troops.

Colonel Harrison writes: "A very heavy day, being shelled practically without ceasing. Extended our firing line right along the Violaines road. At midnight got orders to retire about a mile and to dig in a new line of trenches. We did not get into position until 4.30 a.m. in an open ploughed field and had great luck not to lose one company, but owing to the good management of the company officer who got into his place just before daylight very few hit and none killed."

On October 23rd the Germans appeared about 8 a.m. Could be seen through trees and houses 500 yards west of Rue d'Ouvert. The companies of the "Duke's" had only been able to partially dig in. There was no connection between groups of trenches and many men were lying down behind. 2nd Lieut. Yates was badly wounded in the head. Other casualties were 6 killed, 13 wounded, 2 missing. The Battalion was temporarily attached to the 15th Infantry Brigade. Battalion Headquarters moved to the end of the village of Givenchy.

Colonel Harrison's diary continues :—

"Had a horrible day, being under both high explosive and shrapnel from 7 a.m. till 4 p.m. with hardly any cessation. Lost 24 men and 1 officer, Lieut. Yates, killed. The Germans advanced to within 400 yards in the evening and entrenched themselves, so we expected a night attack for certain, which, however, did not come off. . . ."

The fighting of October 22nd and 23rd may be taken as showing the heavy wear and tear inflicted on the troops near La Bassée. Casualties so far as concerned the Battalion were few, 2nd Lieut. Phillips was wounded on 26th, but there was never any rest, never any respite from the eternal shell fire of the Germans. On October 24th for the first time, except for some German 8-inch howitzers used on the Aisne, really heavy H.E. shells poured over the troops. They came at the rate of some 200 shells a day. That they were not all so dangerous as they appeared may be gathered from the fact that of 31 H.E. field howitzer shells counted as falling behind B Company in one day, at least 26 were " duds."

On October 29th the " Duke's " were relieved by the Black Watch, who had arrived from India, and got back to billets in Rue de Béthune after midnight on the 30th, though they were not left long in their well-earned rest.

Of October 30th Colonel Harrison notes :—

" Got into our new billets Rue de Béthune about 1 a.m., having handed over our trenches to the Black Watch. Took boots off and had a good sleep. A tremendous battle started about 7.45 a.m. and continued to 2 p.m., the right front being engaged. Got order about midday to have two companies ready to send up to support the firing line, and took the rest of the Battalion to support the Bedfords in the trenches at Festubert. Stayed all night, during which time the Sikh Battalion, who came up late, lost their C.O. and Adjutant in taking a solitary house held by a few Germans just across the road on our extreme left. The Gourkhas also lost more than half their officers, including their C.O., whom I met wounded on the road."

On this day a good piece of work was performed by Lieut. F. R. Thackeray, who with his platoon managed to get 60,000 rounds of S.A.A. from Festubert up to the Devons, who were in need of replenishing.

On Saturday, October 31st, Colonel Harrison continued :—

" In trenches in support of the Sikhs. Unfortunately, our rations could not get up last night, so everyone was down on their luck. Lost Elrington and 8 men killed taking a trench in front of the Sikhs. Also Whittaker wounded by a sniper on returning in early morning. A very anxious day, though we were chiefly in support trenches, but I had a distinct feeling that everything was in a very critical state. At one point there was only about 15 yards between our trenches and the Germans. They could be seen and heard continually sapping, and at night I quite expected them to blow up a mine. This I afterwards heard was done some days or more afterwards when we had gone to Ypres."

After what may be described as a foretaste of real trench-warfare, though since the arrival of the 5th Division on the extreme British right the fighting had been neither one thing nor the other, the " Duke's," with the Division now under Maj.-General T. L. N. Morland, C.B., D.S.O., were moved still further north. During the October fighting the II Corps had nearly 14,000 casualties.

" In Flanders' fields the poppies blow
Between the crosses, row on row,
That mark our place ; and in the sky
The larks still bravely singing, fly
Scarce heard amid the guns below.

> "We are the Dead. Short days ago
> We lived, felt dawn, saw sunset glow,
> Loved and were loved, and now we lie
> In Flanders' fields."
>
> JOHN McCRAE, Colonel.
> Killed in Action.

No officer, N.C.O., or private soldier who fought round Ypres is likely ever to forget that historic town. There are memories connected with the name and the now hallowed ground men will carry with them to their graves. It was on November 5th, 1914, that the "Duke's" got their first sight of the beautiful old Town Hall, and during the remainder of that month of mud and drenching wet put in some as severe fighting as occurred during the whole course of the war. The day-to-day happenings of these nerve-racking days it is more or less simple to record. The ceaseless strain both physical and mental of such fighting is best left to the imagination of the reader.

The plan of campaign, if such hand-to-hand fighting as occurred can be said to be planned, may be summed up as a supreme effort on either side to break through: the British towards Menin, the Germans towards and past Ypres.

A French general and very gallant soldier[1] has wittily summed up the Allied effort as "always twenty-four hours and an army-corps behind the enemy." Be this as it may, the fighting qualities of the individual soldier, nothing else, turned the scale in favour of the Allies.

From October 19th to November 22nd is the period officially described under the title "the first Battle of Ypres." It is one of the crucial, perhaps the most crucial in the long history of the Great War. The never-to-be-forgotten horrors of those ceaseless days and nights of long-drawn-out fighting stand out clear as daylight in this plain and unvarnished account. It is a splendid record worthy of the part played by the Duke of Wellington's Regiment in the historic salient of Ypres. It can best be realized from the account of an eye-witness. We quote once more from Colonel E. G. Harrison's diary:—

"*Sunday, 1st November.*—Returned 5 a.m. to our old billet and arrived 7 a.m. I went to Brigade Headquarters 9 a.m. and received orders to move out again at once. Got order after much difficulty cancelled, our men had had no rations for 48 hours. Again Headquarters 2 p.m. and met General Anderson, moved out one company 7.30 p.m., but got relieved at Festubert by the 15th Sikhs. Lieut. R. J. A. Henniker returned to billet 10 p.m. Heavy firing all along the line till late at night, especially on the French side.

"*Monday, 2nd November.*—2 a.m. received orders to march to Estairs, from whence we could get motor buses to Bailleul. Marched 10 a.m., arrived Estairs 2.45 p.m. Left in buses 8.30 p.m., arrived Bailleul 10.30 p.m., and got into billets about midnight. There has been heavy fighting for the last several days, and I am told that we have lost about 5000 around Ypres. The dismounted cavalry seem to have done well, doing continual trench work.

---

[1] General Galliéni, Military Governor of Paris.

"*Tuesday, 3rd November.*—A real peaceful night, the first one spent out of reach of shell fire and the noise of rifle fire since my arrival. Slept till 8 a.m. Reported Headquarters 10 a.m. Told to have a complete rest to-day if no urgent call for reinforcements. Our Brigade Headquarters now 15th Brigade are 2 miles on Locre–Ypres Road. Large reinforcements of French Artillery and Cavalry are here, also Zouave Infantry marched through Bailleul all day. Most picturesque in their large red pantaloons and blue short jackets. The French Artillery horses are very bad compared with ours, in fact the same applies to both Cavalry and Transport. All our horses are really looking splendid, and not even fine drawn.

"*Wednesday, 4th November.*—Got rid of all our Court-martial prisoners in the morning, and received order to move out $2\frac{1}{2}$ miles to rejoin the 15th Brigade at Dranoutre. Marched 2.30 p.m. to the place appointed exactly on the Belgian frontier. Wet drizzly rain and got into billets in a small estaminet 5 p.m. Orders came to march to Ypres to-morrow to join the I Corps. We were here 15 officers and 800 rank and file. I tried my best to get hold of a photographer at Bailleul so as to have an officers' group taken, we also had two officers on the staff to add to this number; unfortunately orders came to move before it could be done. Less than three weeks later we were 2 officers and 380 men.

"*Thursday, 5th November.*—Marched 6.45 a.m. Were delayed three-quarters of an hour at Dranoutre, where a French Cavalry Division passed us. About noon heavy artillery fire was going on in front of us, so the whole Brigade turned left-handed and we spread ourselves out over a largish area behind some woods and hedges, where we stayed for two hours, when the shelling ceased. Roads very bad and knee-deep in mud except on the pavée. Arrived Ypres 5 p.m. As we passed the fine old Town Hall and Cathedral it looked splendid in the twilight, and though a few shells had been dropped in various buildings in the town there had actually been no damage done to these buildings. Later on, however, I believe the greatest part of this place has been destroyed. Marched on till 7.30 p.m., and took over the trenches from the General Commanding 22nd Brigade, of which only some 900 men remained. An attack about 10 p.m. died out, and the fire trenches were taken over by the Bedfords and Cheshires. We remained in support in edge of wood.

"*Friday, 6th November.*—Enemy shelled us all morning from 9 a.m., and again 2 p.m., lasting most of the afternoon. Reported advance on our left flank. Lost 3 officers wounded and 12 men, from shells mostly. Ordered to relieve Regiment in Brigade reserve in 7th Brigade 3 miles off. Marched 10 p.m., arrived midnight. The road we marched after leaving the main Ypres Road was through a large wood about 1 mile of thick mud, at many places 18 inches deep, also many shell-holes which we kept bungling into, so we arrived absolutely drenched and clogged with mud. Hear the Guards' Brigade and the French on their right had retired during the day, and that we hope to recover the ground to-morrow.

"*Saturday, 7th November.*—5.30. a.m. operation order came re Brigade on our right whose trenches were lost yesterday, a very sharp engagement started 6 a.m. Half of them were retaken and 3 machine guns. Heavy shelling all day, lost 1 officer—Owen—shot in leg as we were marching off to relieve 9th Brigade, which were heavily pressed. We started back through the wood where we marched last night. After a short halt at General MacCracken's Headquarters at the end of the wood I found that the left half of the Battalion was missing, they had got separated in the wood. After a quarter of an hour they fortunately turned up, it was pitch dark, foggy, and wet, and literally one could not see 3 yards. We stayed in some old dug-outs on right-hand side of the Ypres–Menin Road at the entrance to Hermitage Château, about 1 mile short of the position we had been in yesterday. On the left Royal Fusiliers and Northumberland Fusiliers stood to arms all night but we did not reinforce. Lincolns supported.

"*Sunday, 8th November.*—Very heavy shelling all day from 9 a.m. Ordered to send two companies 2 p.m. to reinforce the Zouave Regiment on our left. We retook the trenches, but at dark I sent word to retire the company if they could do so without giving the Zouaves the idea that we were clearing off, and if the officer in command of the company was satisfied that the trenches were properly occupied again. Soon after dark Sergt. Taylor reported himself to me at the dug-out with what remained of the two companies. Only half returned without any officer. Travers killed, Henderson missing, and Williamson died at night. Got about 12 prisoners. Am afraid our losses are heavy, but cannot tell till morning. A quiet night. Total killed, wounded, and missing, 3 officers, 87 men. On further enquiries I found that the first advance in the morning the companies had been driven back, and all the officers knocked out. Sergt. Taylor and Sergt. Pogson, however, rallied the companies between them, also collected some Zouaves and after a lot of opposition recovered and re-occupied the trenches, remaining there until they received my message to retire. For this very fine performance these two Sergeants received the D.C.M. and I promoted them C.S.M.'s in place of the two killed in action that day.

"*Monday, 9th November.*—I hear the Germans are massing just north-east of us 10 a.m. Heavy shelling started 10.30 a.m. and lasted with little interval all day. Several minor attacks were made by the enemy on our Brigade (now the 9th). At 6.15 p.m. very heavy fighting occurred to our right, viz. 8th Division. Sent up B Company 4.30 p.m. to dig trenches and reinforce the Lincolns, who have had a very rough time of it. I went up with them past the Hermitage Château and they dug themselves in about 100 yards in rear of the Lincolns in a young plantation, they are practically on the left of the trenches we occupied on the 6th inst. Everything was fairly quiet whilst I remained with them with the exception of the continual sniping which goes on all day and all night incessantly in these huge woods, where the German sniper, who anywhere is a marvel at his job, gets well behind our lines, and very seldom gets caught. While on the subject of sniping I may as well mention that wherever we are this continual sniping on the part of the Germans goes on, they are good shots, evidently picked men, and lie up in ditches or turnip fields and keep at it all the time. They always mark our Battalion Headquarters or places where waggons are known to pass and evidently fire their rifles at night on these objects, having fixed them to a post or tree.

"*Tuesday, 10th November.*—Shelled as usual all day. The French on our right about 4 miles off made an attack all day where there was heavy rifle fire. Not heard result. 4 p.m. received order to move to the Veldoek Château and take up one company firing line, rest in support to be attached to 1st Brigade, got into position 2 p.m. Relieved by Royal Scots Fusiliers in our old dug-outs and just before leaving, about 6 p.m., Lieut. G. Osborne, 20th Hussars, with 2 Maxim guns arrived to be attached to us, as both of ours were out of action. The Veldoek Château and Hermitage Château are close together, the woods, which are very large, belonging to each property are divided by the Ypres–Menin Road, and the drive gates are exactly opposite each other on this road. All we had to do this evening was to cross the main road, and the Headquarters dug-out that I took over was only about 100 yards from the entrance gate to a long drive up to the Château. The fire trenches we took over were some 450 yards through the wood and well past the house, support trenches being just short of there and on the near side of the lawn. D Company, under Lieut. Carey with 2nd Lieut. Rippingille and 2nd Lieut. Bennett, with one platoon C Company, were in the firing line; A Company, under Lieut. de Wend and remainder of C Company in reserve with about 40 men of the Royal Scots under Lieut. Alexander. Lieut. Osborne with his 2 Maxims was also in the fire trenches.

"*Wednesday, 11th November.*—Exceptionally heavy shelling started 7 a.m., practically all shrapnel, covering the whole position from the firing line to the reserves, continuing the bombardment till 8 a.m., when it abated. At this time a message came to me by an orderly from Lieut. R. O. D. Carey, saying, ' Am very hard pressed but will hang on as long as possible.' I then advanced with the remainder of my force. We found the Germans had advanced past the Veldoek Château, but we managed to repulse them, gaining back the ground, being nearly as far as our old firing line, which Lieut. R. O. D. Carey with D Company had been driven out of. We could have actually regained these trenches if the troops on the right and left of us had been up, but in this position behind a small rise in the ground our right rested on the Ypres–Menin Road, the next troops being about 300 yards in rear on the south side of the road. On our left a company of the Zouaves occupied a position between us and the next British troops on our left, but immediately after the advance, in which they materially assisted, they vacated the position, thus leaving both our flanks exposed. At 10 a.m. I sent back a message saying I could retake my original trenches if I had another company in support, but got no reply till 3 p.m. I also sent two more messages, which, however, were never received. By this time we had dug ourselves in under a small bank some 60 yards from the Germans, who were occupying our old trenches. During the action, lasting the whole day, Lieut. Thackeray had command of the reserve company, and owing to his energy and gallantry in pushing forward, not only his own men but also a number of Zouaves who were on our left, contributed considerably to our success. Capt. H. K. Umfreville, my Adjutant, although wounded, continued for several hours looking after the left flank. Our losses during the day were 8 officers and about 300 men; Lieuts. de Wend, Bennett, Rippingille, and Osborne killed, Umfreville, Fraser, and Henniker wounded, Carey a wounded prisoner. After a most anxious day went at 11 p.m. to Brigade Headquarters to report our precarious position as regards our flank.

"*Thursday, 12th November.*—Had a very anxious night but fortunately I received reinforcements last night, consisting of 100 cavalry, viz.: 15th Hussars, 19th Hussars, and Queen's Bays, who occupied our support trenches and the Veldoek Château, the cellar of which I made my headquarters. It rained heavily all night and everywhere the mud was ankle deep. My new firing line, when I came to look into them by daylight, consisted of a mixed force of Royal Sussex, my own Regiment, and Royal Scots, also at 9 a.m. a platoon of Irish Guards was sent up to secure my right flank at the Menin Road. I had to withdraw Lieut. Thackeray from the firing line to do Acting Adjutant in place of Umfreville, wounded. This was my only remaining officer except 2nd Lieut. W. O. Edwards, who joined on the 10th inst., a promoted drill Sergeant from the Coldstream Guards. At 9 a.m. I again went to the Brigade Headquarters regarding my flank. A half-hearted attack was attempted about 11 a.m., which, however, came to nothing. I stayed at the Château cellar as my Headquarters, but as the enemy had a machine gun trained on the approach right down one of the large drives, it made communication rather precarious. Capt. R. P. C. Milbank arrived with a reinforcement of 75 recruits, but as I could not put them straight into the firing line I sent him back 2 miles with them to some dug-outs at Hooge Château to spend the night.

"*Friday, 13th November.*—A quiet night in the Château cellar, again heavy shelling as usual after 8 a.m. till 3 p.m., but a strong attack was made about a mile to our right, which was repulsed with heavy loss. We had, however, to withdraw our advance part of firing line at night, as it was in danger of being outflanked. It took all night to withdraw and finally adjust our support line. This was naturally a very ticklish operation, as the enemy only being 60 yards from us on the right flank it would have been fatal if they had known we were withdrawing, and a panic might easily have been caused. For this reason, men were sent back by squads of 5 or 6 men at a time, and we did not lose a single man. In this way we were at least able to divide up the men of the different regiments in the support line, which was being held by cavalry and Royal Sussex. At 4 a.m., having completed the movement, I took up my headquarters in a dug-out at the entrance of the Veldoek Château drive, some 300 yards in rear.

"*Saturday, 14th November.*—Got back to our new dug-outs at 5 a.m. after completing withdrawal to support line. Enemy shelled us out of some new trenches made last night in front of the Château at 9 o'clock, so most of the men had to retire into the building during the day. Heavy fighting all day on left, but we got off with only 12 casualties. Enemy sapped up close on our right front. Hodson, Royal Fusiliers, turned up with the King's Own Yorkshire Light Infantry. The Royal Scots lost heavily, including Commanding Officer and

Adjutant, also Gordon of Royal Scots, who had been in East Africa with me in the King's African Rifles and also during the last few days here. Heavy firing up to midnight. I sent back to Hooge for Capt. Milbank and his draft of 75 men to march up to join the Regiment. Unfortunately on their road up about 4.30 p.m. they came under shell fire and they scattered so much that he only turned up with 42. This is an example of what may happen where there are a scratch lot of men without any N.C.O.'s or cohesion of any kind. The only Sergeant got a bullet in his stomach next morning and died.

"*Sunday*, 15*th November*.—5th Fusiliers retook building occupied by the enemy near Hermitage Château south of the road at dawn. Our trenches on the east of the Château were shelled so heavily that we had to evacuate them, but we reoccupied at dark without much loss, 2 killed and wounded. 11th Hussars relieved us in the trenches at 11 p.m. and we moved out to the Ypres Road about 2 a.m. Wet and cold, but we got a good cottage to lie down in, when there was a storm. Two abortive attacks were repulsed during the day. We are now attached to the 1st Cavalry Brigade, under my old friend General Briggs.[1]

"*Monday*, 16*th November*.—Brigade Office 8 a.m. reorganized Battalion at 9 a.m., and fell all in, dividing the Battalion into two companies, total about 300. Barring a little shelling had a peaceful day in reserve 1½ miles in rear, which is the first real day off since we passed Bailleul. Our total losses in 9 days are 15 officers and 387 men, including 4 killed and 4 missing officers, the only remaining officer except myself being Lieut. F. R. Thackeray and 2nd Lieut. W. O. Edwards, who joined from the Coldstream Guards 3 days ago. This was the first opportunity since the 6th inst. that we have had to fall in the Battalion and really check our casualties. After the rough handling that we have had for some days with no chance of a rest of any kind, they look uncommonly fit. Unfortunately, poor chaps, their rest in the so-called reserve this time means nothing but very wet dug-outs, and it is bitterly cold.

"*Tuesday*, 17*th November*.—Orders came 11 p.m. last night to move back into the support dug-outs where we were the day before yesterday, horrid, cold, wet night, and men dog tired. It took 1¾ hours to get them fallen in, and then nearly 100 men were absent. The fact was that it had been pouring wet most of the day, and as there were a few cottages within 200–300 yards where some other troops were billeted, our men being in miserably wet dug-outs had in many cases gone into these cottages, and the platoon Sergeants when warned at 11 p.m. in pouring wet rain could not find their men. We, however, arrived in the support dug-outs about 2 a.m. A miserable job too in all this mud. It appears the French did not turn up to take over this section of the trenches as had been arranged. We spent the whole day in the old dug-outs with the 11th Hussars in support, but did nothing and were relieved by the French at 11 p.m., returning to our old spot in Ypres Road.

"*Wednesday*, 18*th November*.—In our cottage all day, and barring considerable shelling had a peaceful day. We had 4 casualties, 2 from shell. We are again transferred to the 7th Brigade. The French are said to be taking over the

[1] Col. (Temp.-Brig.-Gen.) C. J. Briggs, C.B.

section of the trenches south of Ypres Road to-morrow, and not to-night as expected. Hard frost last night, and ground white till sun came out. It is very interesting to see the old woman and her daughter of about 16 who live in our cottage. Poor things, they have hardly anything to live on and they sit quite cheerily in the kitchen listening to the shells bursting quite near, without any apparent fear. There is one of our howitzer batteries about 250 yards behind the cottage, and all the morning the enemy have been trying to find them, and shelling with high-explosives.

"*Thursday, 19th November.*—Moved over to 7th Brigade Headquarters under General MacCracken[1] at 7.30 a.m., and stayed in reserve till 4 p.m., when we moved up into trenches, firing line and support to relieve the King's Own Scottish Borderers. It snowed most of the afternoon, and by 4 p.m. all was quite white and wintry, though not so very cold. A good deal of shelling all day, but not as much as usual.

"*Friday, 20th November.*—After a cold night and hard frost a beautiful bright winter day. A quiet day on the whole, and not quite the usual amount of shelling. We unfortunately lost 5 men with one shrapnel as they were bringing up rations. The French came to relieve us about 11 p.m. after keeping us waiting since 8 o'clock. We did not get relief finished till midnight. We had received orders before leaving to collect all spare rifles and ammunition, and for this purpose I sent 3 patrols of 3 men each to search the woods just around our support and reserve trenches. I could hardly believe it when they brought in 62 rifles and 14,000 rounds of ammunition. These had all been chucked away and lost by wounded men. This shows how careful one must be to check these sort of things. Wounded men, if possible, should carry their rifles to the dressing station and stretcher bearers take them if no one else available. Rifles of dead men should be taken back to Headquarters and sent back with the ration waggons at night. I must add that none of these rifles picked up belonged to men of my Regiment.

"*Saturday, 21st November.*—Marched 1.15 a.m., and went through Ypres, which had been shelled a good deal. A great pity, as it is such a fine old town with beautiful Town Hall, which, however, has not suffered much as yet. Stopped to have tea at 6 a.m. with our cookers, which could not go on any further without having their horses roughed. We then marched on, arriving Locre 9.15 a.m. Very cold and hard frost, snow lying on the ground. Rejoined our real Brigade, the 13th, after drifting 17 days from one Brigade to another. Met two old friends in Bates and Fairfax. The town is full of troops as the French have been taking over a large section of our line near Ypres, thus relieving many regiments who have had a rough time like ourselves.

"*Sunday, 22nd November.*—I slept like a log in a real bed till 8.30 a.m. We have billets in a comfortable cottage. Hot tub and a thorough wash all round made me feel a different person. General Morland came round to see me at 11 a.m. and tells me that we may look forward to 2 or 3 days' rest, and then, after

---

[1] Col. (Temp.-Brig.-Gen.) F. U. N. MacCracken, C.B., D.S.O.

the 13th Brigade have been reorganized, we are to have a much smaller area to hold, and we shall have alternative weeks out of the trenches.

"*Monday, 23rd November.*—Another peaceful night, stayed in bed till 8 a.m. Got men equipped with a good deal of clothing and arranged for 130 men to have hot baths at Bailleul Lunatic Asylum. This was a great idea, and we hope the whole Brigade will be able to avail themselves of it. Orders came to us about midday about officers being given one week's leave if they can be spared, and I hope that in another month I may get it; at present we are so short that no one can get away. I must try to get Thackeray off as soon as possible. More snow and sleet which turned into rain; however, I got an hour's ride over Locre Hill in the afternoon, which I thoroughly enjoyed. Our trenches in this part of the world are about 4 miles due east of the town, and we have heard very little artillery fire all day, and of course no rifle fire, so hope things are quieter down here.

"*Tuesday, 24th November.*—Another real comfortable night in bed, boots and breeches off. Slept till 8 a.m. Not so cold, and a thaw set in about midday. The Prince of Wales turned up at Locre to-day and was seen by several people walking through the town. I went for a walk in the afternoon to get a little exercise, and wrote letters. Understand we may expect to be here till 27th inst., the men's billets are fairly good and some of them very nice cottages; anyhow they appreciate anything in the way of a house or fires as they have had neither of them for a long time, and the whole Regiment is literally tired out and stale.

"*Wednesday, 25th November.*—Feeling rather seedy, the results of no exercise and stuffy billets. Went into Bailleul in the morning in one of the company carts to get my spectacles mended. No success, so wired home for another pair. I went a long ride with Thackeray in the afternoon, and met General Gleichen at St. Jean Capelle. Dull and foggy weather.

"*Thursday, 26th November.*—A cold, damp, foggy day. A draft of 13 men arrived from the base with Capt. E. R. Taylor, who had been a wounded prisoner and escaped at Mons, and 2 Subalterns, A. H. Cheetham and T. Hutton, arrived 11 a.m. Rode down to 14th Brigade at Dranoutre 3.30 p.m. to see General Maude about taking over the trenches to-morrow, the most affable General I have ever met. Had tea with him and met Phillips[1] of the Duke of Cornwall's Light Infantry, one of my old Subalterns in East Africa, who is acting Staff Captain to the 14th Brigade. Currie came over about 2 o'clock to discuss our moving out to-morrow to go to the 14th Brigade, and hopes to see us back to his Brigade and our proper one after this next turn of trench work.

"*Friday, 27th November.*—Parade at 11 a.m. and Commander-in-Chief Sir John French came round 1 p.m. and gave us an address saying what fine fellows we were. Myself and the Adjutant left with Company Officers 3 p.m. and rode over to reconnoitre our position in trenches to-night at Wulverghem, about 6 miles via Neuve Eglise. Marched at 4.30 p.m., and we returned 6 p.m. to Neuve Eglise and had tea before going to take over the trenches from the Manchester Regiment at 8.10 p.m. Clear moonlight night.

[1] Captain G. F. Phillips.

"*Saturday, 28th November.*—At 4.30 a.m. there was a heavy cannonade of German guns to the north, but a long way off. Barring a little shelling at odd times, we spent a quiet day. Our dug-out was very comfortable, and the largest one I have been in except some of those of Brigade Headquarters; I got an oil-stove installed, which keeps it warm and dry. Went round trenches in evening 5 p.m. 2 killed, 5 wounded from snipers who were busy all day and most of the night. They must have our Headquarters dug-out well marked and a couple of rifles tied to trees sighted on it, as so many shots fall our way.

"*Sunday, 29th November.*—Were shelled incessantly from about 11.30 a.m., but not much damage done, except to the right fire trench, where 1 sergeant was killed and 2 men wounded. We were relieved 5.30 p.m. by the King's Own Scottish Borderers, and got back to billets in Neuve Eglise 7.30 p.m. This was almost a record in the way of reliefs, the King' Own Scottish Borderers had occupied the same trenches as before, so knew all about them. The actual relieving only took a very little over an hour. Wolverghem is about 2 miles from Neuve Eglise and is the village (or remains of one) where all ration carts are taken for distribution to the Battalions occupying this section of trenches, practically 1 Brigade. Heard that Carey was not killed on the 11th, but a wounded prisoner, so I still hope Bennett, Rippingille, and Osborne may be with him.

"*Monday, 30th November.*—A quiet day in billets at Neuve Eglise. I have not heard a single shell bursting the whole day long. Cox and I rode round for exercise, and also to look for some faggots for making fascines, with good results, as we came across 3 large stacks of them about 3 miles off. We sent carts for them in the afternoon, and put on nearly half the Regiment making fascines to place at the bottom of the trenches, which are now in such a dreadful state with mud.

"*Tuesday, 1st December.*—Completed confidential reports all morning. Rode 12.30 p.m. to relieve King's Own Scottish Borderers in trenches 5 p.m. Went round firing trench about 5.30 p.m. Heavy rain 7 p.m. to 8.30 p.m. We had a record in taking over, completing the whole job in just an hour. I went round 7 p.m. to 8.30 p.m. with Major E. W. Singer, Royal Engineers, to some new support trenches and to see about sandbagging and recutting fire trench. The waggons brought down 4 loads of the fascines we have been making and left them just beyond Wulverghem village.

"*Wednesday, 2nd December.*—A quiet day, enemy began sending a few high explosives round us at 8.15 a.m., and continued for about an hour, then quietened down. Visited Headquarters West Kent Regiment, who have got a very comfortable cellar in a farm house, close by our dug-out, it is really quite palatial with an adjoining room for their telephone operator. Arranged scouting section, as all the old lot are knocked out. A lot of sniping during the evening, and could not get new support trenches dug, as the moon was so bright. Did some work on communicating trench.

"*Thursday, 3rd December.*—The Germans fired 30–40 Black Marias 8.30 to 9.30 a.m., then kept fairly quiet except sniping. At 12.15 p.m. we gave a tremendous salvo from 6 batteries in honour of the King, who had come over to present decorations at Bailleul to-day. A draft of 200 men arrived in charge of Capt. T. M. Ellis, who had been a wounded prisoner at Mons and managed to escape. After about a fortnight wandering about in disguise, he managed to get to Boulogne and thence home, since then, after a little leave, he has been with a special Reserve Battalion. We put the draft in our reserve dug-outs.

"*Friday, 4th December.*—A certain amount of shelling, chiefly shrapnel, till 2 p.m. The new reinforcements relieved the supports at 5 p.m., and supports went into firing trenches, they going to reserve. Heavy rain started about 6 p.m., which made it very bad for making new trenches some 75 yards in rear of the firing trenches, but afterwards stopped. I went round the firing line and the digging party in the new support trenches we are making. As the moon is very bright, and a lot of sniping going on, it is a good way of blooding the new draft, and getting them used to being shot at. Fortunately no damage was done to any of them.

"*Saturday, 5th December.*—A very wet night. A certain amount of shelling at intervals all day but not many high explosives. The Manchester Regiment took over our trenches, starting at 5.30 p.m. and finishing everything completely at 7 p.m. We then marched 8 miles via Bailleul to St. Jean Capelle but stopping for three-quarters of an hour at Neuve Eglise, where we had our cookers waiting in a field with plenty of hot tea ready for each platoon as they marched up from Wulverghem independently. We afterwards marched at 9.15 p.m. and arrived just before midnight, where we got into our billets. The men marched better than I expected, $2\frac{1}{4}$ miles per hour in spite of the state of their feet after 3 days and nights in the trenches, which in places are nearly knee deep in mud.

"*Sunday, 6th December.*—A frosty morning. Our new Brigadier-General Cooper came round to see me about 11 a.m., and had a short chat about things in general. A new reinforcement of about 200 men and 3 officers, under Capt. C. H. Unwin, arrived at 10 a.m., which makes us up to 850 men and 14 officers. I rode round our billets, which are in scattered farms, about 3.30 p.m. Thackeray, Cox, Edwards, and 2 N.C.O.'s went home on 7 days' leave, departing by motor-bus from Bailleul, which is only about 1 mile from our Headquarters, at 4 a.m. They motored direct to Boulogne, about 60 kilometres, caught the boat there at 10.30 a.m. and should be home by 3 p.m.

"*Monday, 7th December.*—Did some parade to-day to smarten and shake the new drafts up. There are now 500 men and 14 new officers joined during the last 3 weeks, and the Regiment is now 850 strong. Most of the new draft are Special Reserves, and it will be difficult to keep the Battalion up to something like Regimental form. Met General Cooper 11 a.m., and rode with him back towards Headquarters. In the afternoon I had a long ride out towards Hazebrouck, nice undulating country, but it is difficult to get out of billeting areas, as the whole country is now full of troops for miles around.

"*Tuesday, 8th December.*—Parade 9.30 a.m. Rode round and saw the new drafts at their billets 10 a.m. Brigadier came round 11.30 a.m. Taylor and I had a good look round in the afternoon 2.30 p.m., and had a look round at the country due west. Fairly mild weather and no rain. Order came round re cancelling officers' leave, which looks like an advance shortly. Men to be inoculated to-morrow 40 at a time.

"*Wednesday, 9th December.*—A very wet night and muggy morning. Rode round billets 11 a.m. with Taylor. Saw A and C Companies on parade. Rode round to the Brigade Office and had a talk to the General re marching to-morrow to Dranoutre. In the afternoon rode by another road to St. Jean Capelle and called at King's Own Yorkshire Light Infantry billet to see Hodson, who I find has gone home on a week's leave.

"*Thursday, 10th December.*—Rode out 11 a.m. for an hour. Paraded 1 p.m. and marched to Dranoutre, about 4 miles, where we found ourselves in very poor billets, it turned out a wet afternoon. Arrived about 3 p.m. Met Eustace Archer with a company of Norfolks on the road. I was sent for to the Brigade Headquarters 4 p.m. and got orders to send one company at 10.30 p.m. to-night to dig new support trenches ready for an advance in a couple of days. Just what we have been expecting.

"*Friday, 11th December.*—Quite funny hearing guns again after being practically away from them for nearly a week. Our batteries were moving into position most of last night. There are also a lot of new batteries connecting here now. I saw 2 heavy batteries, 60-lbs, I think, passing to-day. Digging party 2 p.m. to work after dusk. Beastly day. Draft of 130 men under Lieut. W. E. Maynard arrived 11 a.m., he belongs to the Durham Light Infantry. Expect an advance soon. Left 2.30 p.m. to ride round Locre and back via Bailleul Road, but as all the roads are crowded with guns, waggons, and troops it is not particularly good exercise.

"*Saturday, 12th December.*—Another wet and foggy day, went to Brigade Office 10.30 a.m., and then on for a ride near Bailleul to get some exercise. Orders came re going into trenches to-morrow, and I sent down two digging parties, one at 2.30 p.m., and the other at 10.30 p.m., another company making fascines. Thackeray and the other officers who went home for a week returned late last night.

"*Sunday, 13th December.*—Rode round billets 10.30 a.m., and to Brigade Office at 3 p.m. for orders re attack to-morrow morning. Marched 3.15 p.m. to Wulverghem and arranged to take over trenches from the West Kent Regiment. Completed taking over at 9.30 p.m. Orders received re attack by French to Wytschaete to-morrow 6 a.m. The trenches are perfectly awful, but our Headquarters are in a nice farm, which has been untouched for some reason or other; not on map perhaps. The men in trenches are up to knees in mud and water, and all the reserve dug-outs near the Headquarters are full of water, almost impossible to bale out.

"*Monday, 14th December.*—Received orders late last night, 2 French Corps attacking in morning, and our 3rd Division also, on our left. We are also to advance when point 75 on map is reached by 3rd Division. Tremendous shelling started 7 a.m. We got shelled out of our Headquarters, and the farm set on fire, but we saved some outbuildings, where we remained in a pigsty until evening, when we made our bedding down in a shed full of potatoes and turnips. I had been afraid of this happening from the very moment we took over, as the farm, which had a thatched roof, is only 600 yards at the most from the German trenches, and I cannot imagine why they have not destroyed it long ago, they must know that it has always been occupied by us and used as a Headquarters. However, it has been done at last. My servant, Blake, was wounded 2 p.m. by a shrapnel in the right shoulder, but not dangerous. The trenches are perfectly dreadful, up to the waist in some places. German trenches are on our left within 25 yards, and constant sniping, and even throwing mud at each other. Lost 4 killed, 11 wounded. One officer, Croft, hit on funny-bone, but not damaged. This was rather curious. He was in the hay loft above our Headquarters, and was on the look-out to see if he could spot any movement in the German trenches about 600 yards away. Several shrapnel had burst just short of the farm, then one burst close in front, knocking some bricks and rafters out, one of which hit him on the elbow. He was a bit scared at first, but not damaged. This is his first day under fire, as he only came up with the last draft. It would have been bad luck if he had been knocked out first round.

"*Tuesday, 15th December.*—Quiet night, but shelling again. Artillery bombardment at 7 a.m., which went on all day incessantly. The 3rd Division could not advance further owing to enfilade fire, until the French Corps had got past West Château and secured their left flank. We remained same as yesterday with orders to wait for 3rd Division, who were to push back the enemy in conjunction with the French Corps on their left towards Messines and in which we were to join when they had pushed on as far as point 75 on map. Casualties 3 men wounded. Beastly day, lived in potato shed, which stinks, next door to old pigsty.

"*Wednesday, 16th December.*—Slept again in the potato shed, but the smell was so bad that we turned out of the place and made our Headquarters at a small cottage 500 yards north, which was still intact. Not quite so much shelling to-day. The West Kents relieved us at 5.30 p.m., but relief took 3¼ hours, the trenches being so wet and muddy, many men had to be pulled out with ropes, poor devils. Do not know how they will stand this for long. We marched to billets, a farm 1½ miles away. Major Tyndall[1] arrived. One casualty.

"*Thursday, 17th December.*—Marched 6.45 am. to our new trenches in support, about 1 mile from billet. Everything quiet all day as far as the enemy were concerned until 3 p.m., when about a dozen 11-inch high-explosive shells came over our heads. No news from the left flank, except slight advance at the cost of 400 men. I believe the French made no progress at Wytschaete. Looks very much like being hung up."

---

[1] Major W. E. M. Tyndall, D.S.O.

CHAPTER X

WINTER QUARTERS, 1914. HILL 60, APRIL 18TH–MAY 5TH, 1915.

TOWARDS the latter end of November, 1914, the British Army retired into winter quarters. Not, be it well understood, into the comparative comfort enjoyed by Marlborough's troops, when they, too, were campaigning in "the cock-pit of Europe." Of the conditions under which the British Army lived during the first winter in Flanders so much has been written since the war that detailed reference is unnecessary. It may be of wider interest, however, to soldiers to compare past campaigning methods with those now initiated by endeavouring to picture war conditions under our own "Iron Duke" in the Peninsula, or under John Churchill, Duke of Marlborough, in Flanders. If ever disease among troops at the front could be considered inevitable the situation in the trenches in 1914 might fairly be quoted. But thanks to the wonderful efficiency of the R.A.M.C. organization disease was almost entirely absent. Such scourges as typhoid, typhus, or even low fevers were practically unknown. "Trench-feet" and vermin were the main causes of trouble, but what were these compared to the terrible conditions at the front so late as even in the Crimean War?

On the other hand, latter-day methods for improving trench conditions are apt to cause those of the winter of 1914 to be almost forgotten. A man's first experience of the trenches in 1916 or 1917 may have seemed to him bad enough, but they were not the utter hell of those during the months of December–January–February of 1914–1915.

Although the incessant fighting of the preceding period slackened it never actually ceased. It was high time for a reorganization of the British line, and this was in full swing when the 5th Division became once again reunited. The line it was to occupy henceforth ran partly east of Wulverghem up the inclined ground to the Wulverghem–Messines Road, thence along the crest of Hill 75. On the 20th the Battalion was in billets at Locre. On the 27th it marched to Wulverghem and between these two places and Dranoutre, Neuve Eglise, and Bailleul it spent the winter until the middle of February. Though a cynic might say the weeks passed near Wulverghem were not worth living—no trenches were worth living in the first winter in France—life was at least an improvement upon what the Battalion had so far known.

Among other incidents, on December 16th Major W. E. M. Tyndall, D.S.O., rejoined and took over command from Major (now Colonel) E. G. Harrison, C.B., D.S.O., who on Christmas Day proceeded home on leave, and on January 12th took over command of the 12th Service Battalion the Manchester Regiment. On December 23rd, when in the trenches near Ravetsberg, Sergt. Hirst brought in a wounded man under heavy fire and was recommended for the V.C. Various drafts were received during this period but casualties were very light. On December 29th 2nd Lieuts. C. T. Young and C. L. Hart and 25 other ranks joined the Battalion.

During January and February, 1915, the following reinforcements arrived and were taken on the strength :—

January 4th : 2nd Lieuts. Wheatley and W. Inchley with 69 other ranks.
January 28th : 2nd Lieut. R. P. M. Hudson and 121 other ranks.
February 16th : Lieut. G. P. Sleigh with 63 other ranks.
February 24th : Lieut. R. H. Owen with 60 other ranks.

On February 19th the Battalion moved to Vlamertinge, where it arrived about 3.30 p.m. and was lodged in huts south of the village. The following day orders were issued for A and C Companies to move into dug-outs near Zillebeke in support of the West Kents. B and D Companies billeted in Ypres in the convent. Battalion Headquarters was established close to A and C dug-outs. The companies relieved one another and the West Kents up to February 26th, when the Battalion returned to Vlamertinge.

March, 1915, was an equally uneventful month, as months were reckoned in the trenches. On the 1st the Battalion relieved some of the 83rd Brigade in the trenches near Zillebeke. Ypres and Zillebeke were the trench " in and out " until March 10th, when the Battalion retired to hutments at Ouderdom. On the 12th Capt. B. J. Barton, D.S.O., Lieut. C. W. G. Ince, and 25 other ranks arrived. The latter took over the duties of Adjutant. The General Officer Commanding II Corps inspected the Battalion the following day. Sir Horace Smith-Dorrien thanked the Regiment for its splendid services since the beginning of the war. He added what in the light of the immediate though unknown future now sounds prophetic—" but the Duke of Wellington's could always be depended on to do whatever they were asked." Hill 60 was not long to wait for ! Kruisstraat, Rosental, and Lankhof Châteaux were in turn visited by the Battalion during March, until on the 27th it returned to hutments on the Vlamertinge–Ouderdom Road. During March the usual reinforcements joined up : on 17th 2nd Lieut. Gibson and 14 other ranks, and on 21st 2nd Lieut. H. Crisp with 50 other ranks. Major Tyndall, who had been three weeks on the sick list, rejoined on 25th and took over command.

The last days of March were passed in rest camp, but on March 31st orders came for the 13th Brigade to relieve the 15th in the trenches. The same evening, at 8 p.m., the " Duke's " took over a portion from the 1st Battalion the Bedfords. Every one who has been through the mill can recall if he will his feelings when it was time to go back into the trenches. "Out," it was usually pleasant enough though there might be shelling. " In," well, the thought of going " in " took different men in different ways. Few men would be prepared to say they *liked* the idea.

EASTER SUNDAY AT YPRES

For the "Duke's" April came in like the proverbial lamb, though it certainly went out like a lion. In the trenches at Zillebeke, the sector round Battalion Headquarters at Dormy House was quiet enough. Easter Day saw the Battalion attending Church service at Ypres, where the Lord Bishop of London had come on a visit.

The following lines had not long been written at the front, and at Easter, 1915, a distinguished officer in a letter home to England spoke of them thus: "It seems to me that such words as these should be made known to the public, for apart from their intrinsic beauty they are full of comfort to those who are sorely stricken in this terrible war."

ON A WELL-KNOWN WAY-SIDE SHRINE, NORTHERN FRANCE.

"O pallid Christ within this broken shrine,
Not those torn Hands and not that Heart of Thine
Have given the nations blood to drink like wine.

Through weary years and 'neath the changing skies,
Men turned their back on those appealing eyes
And scorned as vain Thine awful Sacrifice.

Kings with their armies, children in their play
Have passed unheeding down this shell-ploughed way,
The great world knew not where its true strength lay.

In pomp and luxury, in lust of gold,
In selfish ease, in pleasures manifold,
'Evil is good, good evil,' we were told.

Yet here, where nightly the great flare-lights gleam,
And murder stalks triumphant in their beam,
The world has awakened from its empty dream.

At last, O Christ, in this strange, darkened land,
Where ruined homes lie round on every hand,
Life's deeper truths men come to understand.

For lonely graves along the countryside,
Where sleep those brave hearts who for others died,
Tell of life's union with the Crucified.

And new light kindles in the mourner's eyes,
Like day-dawn breaking through the rifted skies,
For Life is born of life's self-sacrifice."

Holy Week, Northern France. By Canon
F. G. Scott of Quebec, serving with the
3rd Brigade, Canadian Division.

On April 5th Lieut.-Colonel P. A. Turner arrived and took over command of the Battalion. 2nd Lieut. Cunningham also joined up from the 3rd Reserve Battalion of the Regiment. On the 10th the "Duke's" were relieved in the trenches and went into reserve at Ypres. There they remained in comparative peace until April 17th. Then the storm broke.

There are certain incidents in war as opposed to actual battles which strike the imagination and seem to stand out in a sense peculiarly their own. Why this should be so it is not easy to say. Upon similar occasions the actual fighting may have been as severe, the numbers engaged as great, the losses even more heavy, yet there clings to such episodes as the taking of Hill 60 a special glamour, a glorious memory never likely to be obliterated. As an officer of the Regiment, present both at the taking and loss by poisoned gas of Hill 60, wrote :[1]—

"None of the Duke of Wellington's Regiment who survived the Great War and took part in the actions at Hill 60 on April 18th and May 5th will ever forget these fights."

"At 6 a.m. on April 18th, 1915," says the official Diary of Events, "the Battalion were called out of their dug-outs near Ypres." A strictly accurate if somewhat unimaginative preface to one of the most desperate hand-to-hand fights of the war. To quote again from Lieut. Ince's account already referred to : "Though only small affairs when compared to some of the greater battles which took place during the war, these two actions were very serious ones for the 2nd Battalion of the Regiment."

Hill 60, as it will be known to the British Army for all time, is in actual fact no hill at all. It rises barely 50 feet above the surrounding level. Like the Dump and the Caterpillar on the west side of the railway, Hill 60 owes its existence, for the most part, to the original excavations from the cutting through which runs the line from Ypres to Comines. This cutting is nowhere more than 20 feet deep where it crosses the Zwarteleen ridge. That its possession was so highly prized was due to the fact that it gave the Germans an observation post of surpassing value as well as complete command over the British position to the north and north-west.

"Early in April," wrote Lieut. Ince, "the Battalion, which with the sister ones of pre-war days in Ireland (2nd Battalion K.O.S. Borderers, 1st Battalion the Queen's Own Royal West Kent Regiment, and 2nd Battalion K.O.Y.L.I.) still constituted the 13th Brigade, 5th Division, under command of Sir Charles Fergusson, found itself in reserve, in billets in Ypres, busily preparing for the attack against Hill 60, timed to take place on the 17th.

"Hill 60, although only a small mound situated to the south-east of Ypres was 'a commanding hill which afforded the enemy excellent artillery observation towards the west and north-west, and lay opposite the northern extremity of the line held by the II Corps.' Sir John French decided it must be captured, and preparations for mining the locality had been going on for some days.

---

[1] Lieut. (now Major) C. W. G. Ince, M.C.

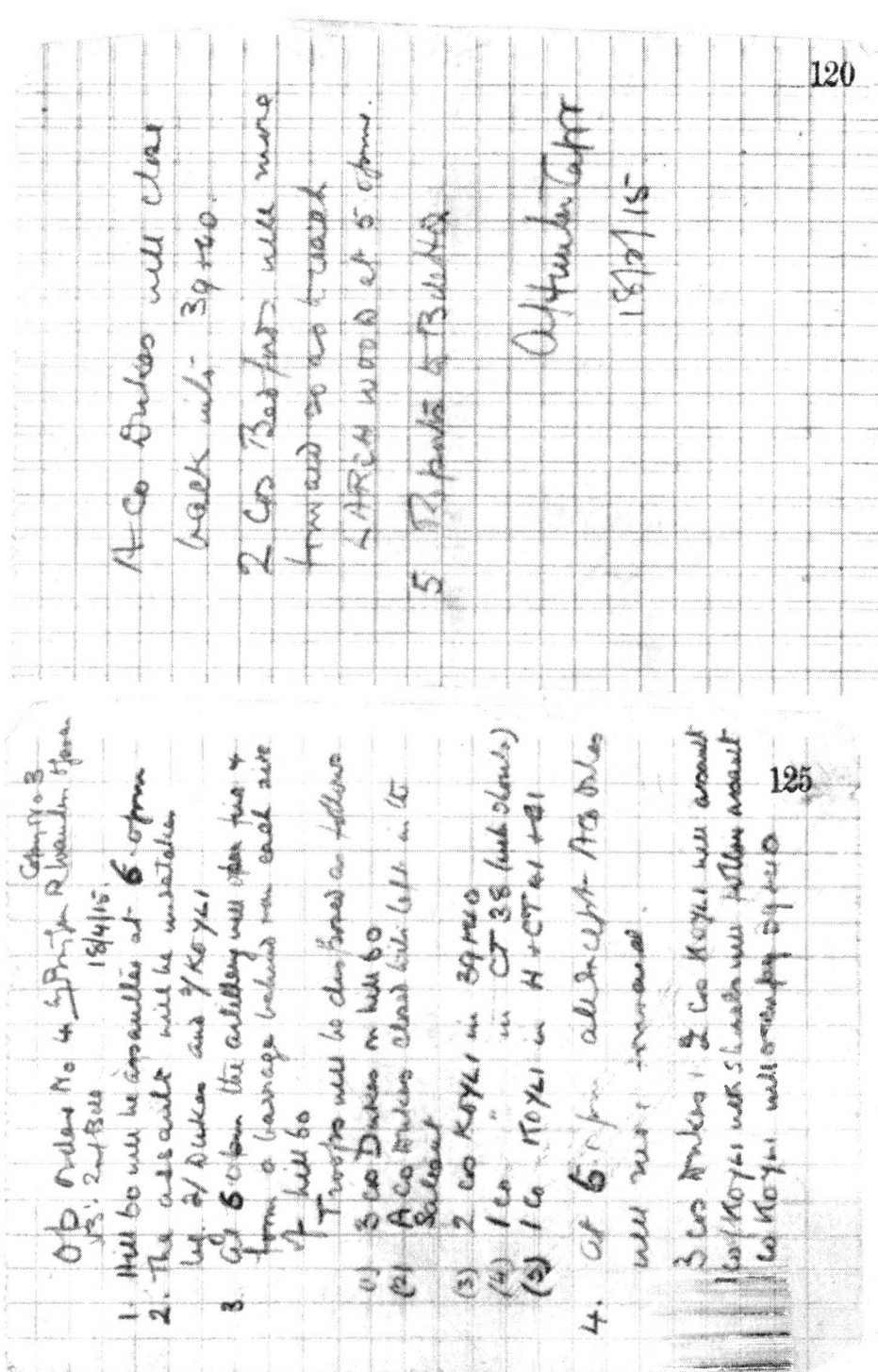

COPY OF THE ORIGINAL ORDER FOR THE ATTACK ON HILL 60, 18TH APRIL, 1915

HILL 60

"On Friday, April 16th, all day and night, also during the whole day of Saturday, 17th, the Battalion had been employed in supplying working parties for the 15th Brigade, and in making dug-outs near Zillebeke.

"At 7 p.m. on the 17th three mines were successfully fired and immediately afterwards the hill was attacked and carried without difficulty by the 1st Battalion the Royal West Kent Regiment, and the 2nd Battalion K.O.S.

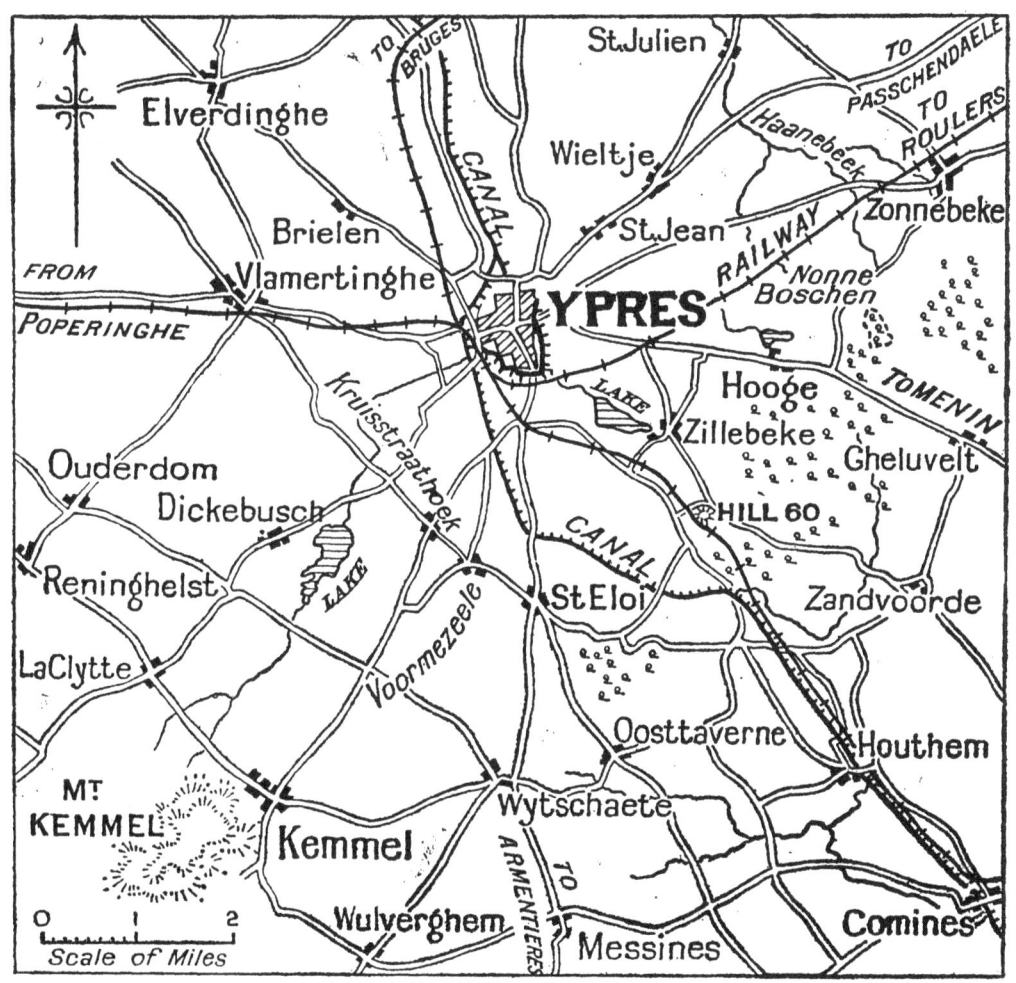

THE YPRES DISTRICT.

Borderers, who occupied the craters on the crest and what was left of the German trenches just south-east of it. On the 17th/18th desperate night-fighting took place in which both these battalions suffered large casualties in hand-to-hand combat. During the night the enemy succeeded in regaining one or two small trenches.

"From the moment the assault on Hill 60 took place, Ypres became an absolute inferno, and life there which till then (with the exception of the daily periodical shelling of the Cathedral and fine old Cloth Hall) had been comparatively normal, became impossible. Shells rained incessantly on the town day and night—all business was stopped, and after a few days the whole civilian population, except a few of the bravest who stayed on in their cellars, left the place. Ypres, as everybody knows, eventually became a heap of ruins, nothing more.

"At the time the mines were fired, the 2nd Battalion was in its billets in the town. Some of us were enjoying a well-earned and excellent dinner cooked by our soldier staff. It was not long, however, before we received orders to move up in support of the units of the 13th and 15th Brigades on Hill 60.

"Lieut.-Colonel P. A. Turner, who was in Command, Major W. E. M. Tyndall, D.S.O., 2nd in Command, and the Adjutant (Lieut. C. W. G. Ince) moved at once with Headquarters and two companies into dug-outs on the railway embankment near Zillebeke—A Company took over some old battery dug-outs in Zillebeke, and one company occupied others situated in rear of the railway embankment

"At 3 a.m. on April 18th A Company was ordered up into the line, and at 6 a.m. the remainder of the Battalion moved up in relief of the 1st Battalion Royal West Kent Regiment and the 2nd Battalion K.O.S.B.'s, taking over the trenches these regiments had captured the previous evening. A Company were already in the advanced craters.

"The dispositions of the Battalion at 9 a.m. were as shown in the sketch opposite.

"Poor old A Company in its advanced position suffered badly owing to the close proximity of the enemy. The latter, as already stated, had regained ground during the night prior to the Battalion taking over the hill. A Company was heavily bombed with hand grenades and early in the day had severe casualties, which included its Commander, Capt. Milbank, who was badly wounded, subsequently dying of his wounds. Things got hotter and hotter. Just before noon the Commanding Officer with the Adjutant and a couple of orderlies visited these advanced trenches. This was a most precarious journey, as the very shallow communication trench leading to them was almost blocked with dead and wounded. None of this small party were hit, however, either going or coming back, although at times in full view of the enemy.

"On his return about noon, Lieut.-Colonel Turner ordered B Company, augmented by one platoon from each of C and D Companies, to reinforce A Company, which for many hours had gallantly and grimly held its ground until nearly wiped out. It was whilst taking the men up to the craters that Capt. Ellis was killed.

"About 4.30 p.m. an order was received from Brigade Headquarters that the battalion was to attack and dislodge the Germans from that portion of the Hill they had regained during their counter-attacks made the previous night. Colonel Turner at once issued orders for the remainder of the Battalion (i.e. C and D Companies less one platoon each) to move up into the craters in

THE COUNTER-ATTACK AT HILL 60

readiness, whilst the 2nd Battalion K.O.Y.L.I. occupied the trenches they vacated in readiness, and joined in to support the attack as second wave.

"B Company (Capt. C. E. B. Hanson) was given the right section of the attack, C (Capt. B. J. Barton) the centre, and D (Capt. E. R Taylor) the left section, whilst A Company, which had suffered so heavily during the day, was held in reserve. Battalion Headquarters was in the centre crater.

"Under supporting artillery fire, with bayonets fixed, at 6 p.m. the

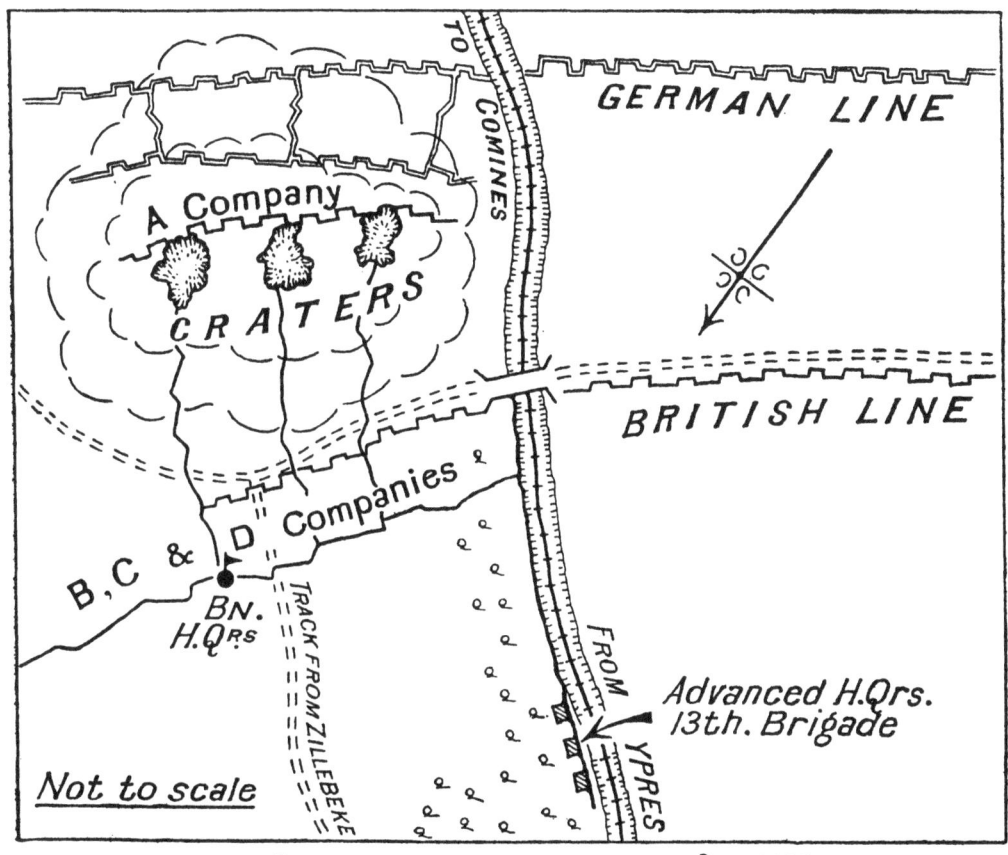

HILL 60. SITUATION AT 9.0 A.M., APRIL 18TH, 1915.

Battalion went over the top. B Company reached their objective without much difficulty, but lost Lieut. R. H. Owen, who was killed during the advance.

"C Company had to charge over some 50 yards of open ground and suffered very heavily, Capt. Barton and a few men only reaching the objective. They, however, captured the trenches allotted to them, killing and capturing a number of the enemy.

"Ptes. Behan and Dryden of this Company particularly distinguished themselves in this operation, and took charge after their platoon officers and sergeants had been killed or wounded. Both these brave fellows received the Distinguished Conduct Medal.

"D Company (Capt. Taylor) had some distance to charge over open ground and lost all their officers at the start, Capt. Taylor, Lieut. Thackeray, and 2nd Lieut. Croft being killed and 2nd Lieuts. Crisp and Cheetham being wounded. Ably supported by the 2nd Battalion the K.O.Y.L.I. this Company nevertheless captured the German trenches allotted as its objective. Not one inch of ground was lost.

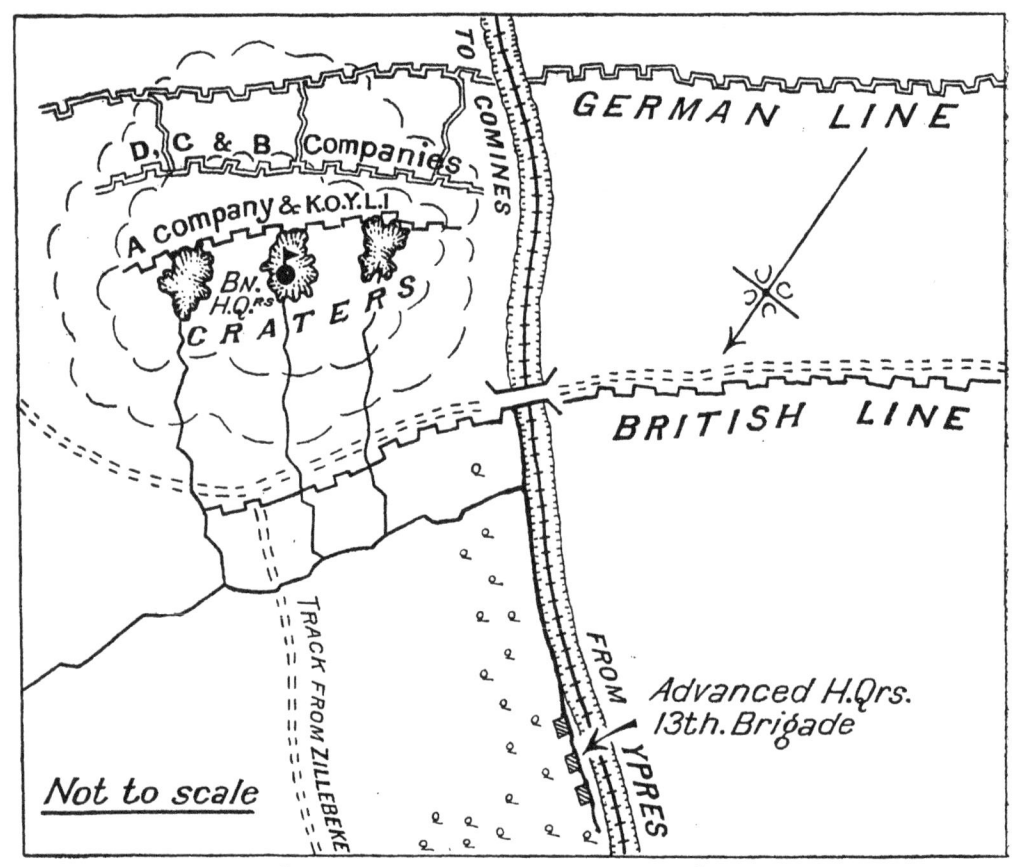

HILL 60. SITUATION AT DUSK ON APRIL 18TH, 1915.

"Dusk was now rapidly approaching, and under cover of darkness, the trenches won were consolidated, the German communicating trenches blocked and new communication trenches to our own reserves dug.

"The above sketch shows the position on April 18th at dusk.

"It was whilst superintending the attack, accompanied by the Adjutant, that Lieut.-Colonel Turner was unluckily hit first in the right leg and a quarter of of an hour later in the other leg, thus becoming a casualty. Major W. E. M. Tyndall, D.S.O., 2nd in Command, was also gravely wounded whilst directing operations in another part of the field. He subsequently died in England as a result of his wounds.

"Beyond some unsuccessful grenade throwing, sniping, and heavy shelling no counter-attack was made that night by the Germans on the captured trenches.

"The attack and defence of Hill 60, a mere episode in the British operations, and a very minor occurrence in the whole of the front held by the Allies, will nevertheless go down in history among the finest exploits performed by British troops during the war. Officers who experienced the bombardment prior to the attack of the Prussian Guard on November 11th, and also underwent that directed on Hill 60 state, indeed, that the latter was by far the worse of the two.

"What our troops withstood can to some degree be realized if it be remembered that the space fought over on the four and a half days between April 17th and 21st was only about 250 yards in length, about 200 in depth. On to that small area the enemy for hours on end hurled tons of metal and high explosive, and at times the hill-top was wreathed in clouds of poisonous fumes. And yet our gallant infantry did not give way. They stood firm under a fire which swept away whole sections at a time, filled the trenches with dead bodies, and so cumbered the approaches to the front line that reinforcements could not reach it without having to climb over the prostrate forms of their fallen comrades.

"In these circumstances the losses have naturally been heavy. Nevertheless, they have not depressed the men, who are all, including the wounded, extremely cheerful, for they know that the fight for Hill 60 has cost the Germans far more than it has us.[1]

"At 5 a.m. on the 19th April the Battalion was relieved by the Bedfords and East Surreys of the 15th Brigade and moved into dug-outs west of the Zillebeke Pond.

"The total casualties of the Battalion from the evening of the 17th until relieved at 5 a.m. on the 19th were :—

Officers killed, died of wounds	7	Other ranks killed	29
,, wounded	8	,, ,, wounded	334
,, missing	Nil	,, ,, missing, believed killed	43

"Roll of officers present with the Battalion in this action :—

Lieut.-Colonel P. A. Turner, C.M.G. (Commanding). Wounded.
Major W. E. M. Tyndall, D.S.O. (2nd in Command). Died of wounds.
Capt. E. R. Taylor. Killed.
 ,, B. J. Barton, D.S.O.
 ,, T. M. Ellis. Killed.
 ,, R. P. C. Milbank. Died of Wounds.

[1] "Eye-Witness at Headquarters in France," in *The Times* of April, 1915.

Capt. C. E. B. Hanson.
,, M. N. Cox, M.C. (Transport Officer).
Lieut. C. W. G. Ince, M.C. (Adjutant).
,, F. R. Thackeray, M.C. Killed.
,, R. H. Owen. Killed.
2nd Lieut. W. O. Edwards. Wounded.
,, A. H. Cheetham. Wounded.
,, T. Hutton. Wounded.
,, J. A. C. Croft (Royal Warwick Regiment). Killed.
,, W. O. Field. Wounded.
,, C. T. Young. Wounded.
,, G. H. Beyfus. Wounded.
,, H. Crisp. Wounded.
Lieut. W. O. Tobias, R.A.M.C.
Major A. Ellam, M.C.(Quartermaster).

" It is difficult so long afterwards to write fully about the details of this action; one can but feel everlastingly proud of the Battalion which once again has so greatly distinguished itself. Congratulations were received from the Commander-in-Chief and many other Generals, and in addition Field-Marshal Sir John French visited the 13th Brigade in person and officially complimented all Battalions at a special parade.

" At the time we sometimes wondered what it was all for, this attack on what was called a 'hill' but which to us at the time was merely a system of muddy trenches, shell-torn ground, and a haunt of death. The place was practically a cemetery, and hundreds must have been buried on the ground, it proving impossible, when digging trenches, not to disturb some poor fellow in his last long sleep.

" Yes, at the time we may have asked was it worth it? The answer, I think, is Yes, as I have since visited that battle-ground and stood on the very spot from which our attack was launched, when I was enabled to fully appreciate the commanding view to be got thence of the surrounding country, especially that portion of the ground in which used to be the British Lines. Without a doubt the Germans required Hill 60 as an observation point, and we required it for a similar purpose, hence Lord French's order that it was to be taken. It was a tough fight but the 13th Brigade, including the old 76th Regiment of Hindoostan and Peninsula fame, won it for the time being.

" On April 20th the Battalion returned to Zevecoten and went into rest billets. Two drafts of 20 and 88 other ranks joined it the same day from the Base.

" We were not, however, allowed to rest long, being quickly called out to assist in stopping the first German gas attack north of Ypres. The Battalion, however, took no great part in this operation, as usually it was either in support or reserve. Neither of these positions were, however, very enviable ones, as most of the time we were either in very poor trenches or lying behind hedgerows or behind any cover we could obtain."

GERMAN GAS ATTACK ON HILL 60

On April 24th the Battalion was at Hooge in reserve to the 15th Brigade, and on following days moved to Potijze, where it remained in the same capacity to the Lahore and 27th Divisions. During this time a large draft of officers joined the Battalion. Capts. C. H. Unwin and G. W. Robins, East Yorkshire Regiment attached. Lieuts. W. M. Ozanne, C. F. Whitaker, N. W. Hadwen, W. Inchley, and F. D. Chadwick. Lieut. H. J. Miller, East Yorks, ; 2nd Lieuts. C. A. Bailey, G. A. Chalcraft, E. B. Davis, West Yorks Regiment; 2nd Lieut. C. C. Covernton, 3rd Essex Regiment, with 14 other ranks. 2nd Lieut. Gunn, 2nd Lieuts. G. H. Beyfus and A. B. T. Simpson rejoined, also a draft of 230 other ranks. C.S.M. Metcalfe and Corpl. Siddle were awarded the D.C.M.

[1]" On May 1st, 1915, the Battalion found itself once more in reserve to the 5th Division in some woods near Kruistraat just south of Ypres. Several officers joined the Regiment that day, and on May 2nd a large draft of 230 other ranks joined.

"On May 4th we received orders to relieve the Devons on Hill 60 and took over trenches 38, 39, 40, 42, 43, 45. The relief was complete by 3.30 a.m. on the 5th. The trenches we took over were not the same as those we had captured on April 18th, some of these having in the interval been regained by the Germans, but still we were on the crest and we meant to hold it.

"Alas, what would have happened under natural circumstances was impossible under supernatural ones. At 8 a.m. the Germans, aided by a favourable wind, sent over asphyxiating gas (chlorine) with disastrous effects, a proceeding rightly described by the Commander-in-Chief in his despatch of June 15th as 'a cynical and barbarous disregard of the well-known usages of civilized war, and a flagrant defiance of the Hague Convention.' Gas had been first employed by the enemy on April 22nd at the commencement of the second Battle of Ypres and fully effective counter-measures had not yet been established. We had not received gas masks yet, only a piece of gauze soaked in a preparation prepared by the medical authorities. This solution after a few minutes required renewing, a procedure absolutely impossible, of course, in action. On came this terrible stream of death, and before anything could be done, all those occupying the front line over which it swept were completely overcome, the majority dying at their posts—true heroes. By this foul means the Germans quickly got possession of trenches 40, 43, 45, there being practically no one then left to hold them. Capt. G. W. Robins, East Yorkshire Regiment, attached to the Battalion was the last man to leave of the few who managed to crawl away, and he, poor fellow, died in agony that night from the effects of the gas.

"Our support trenches 38, 39, some 100 yards in rear, were held secure, also a small portion of the front line trench 40 on the lower slopes of the crest line was reoccupied. The few holders of these, assisted by strong reinforcements from the Dorset Regiment, counter-attacked and regained some of the lost trenches, but the actual crest of the hill remained in the enemy's hands.

[1] Diary of Lieut. (now Major) C. W. G. Ince, M.C.

"The Battalion suffered over 300 casualties that morning, large numbers dying as a result of this barbarous gas. The writer will never forget the sight of men writhing in agony and slowly dying from the asphyxiating effects of the chlorine, nor of the feeling of helplessness at being unable to do anything for them."

Some who had the privilege of knowing the late Capt. G. W. Robins may be unaware of the many-sided character of the man. That "the last to leave Hill 60" was a very gallant soldier all knew who served with him, but that he was also no mean poet and a first-class man to hounds may come as a surprise. In Capt. Robins' *Lays of the Hertfordshire Hunt and other Poems* he wrote in stirring verse of the sport he loved. His loss to the Hunt and to himself as a friend is feelingly described in the preface to that book by General, the Earl of Cavan, K.P., G.C.M.G., K.C.B., at one time Master of the Hertfordshire Hunt.

"He (Robins) was," wrote Lord Cavan, "the last to leave Hill 60. Only those members of the Hunt who have served and suffered in this war will perhaps fully appreciate what that short sentence means. To me it means absolute self-sacrifice, splendid courage, and an undying example. And history will not forget those who fought that great fight of May 5th, 1915. . . ."

Roll of officers present with the Battalion May 5th :—

Capt. B. J. Barton, D.S.O. (Commanding).
,, C. H. Unwin. Wounded.
,, G. W. Robins, East Yorkshire Regiment. Wounded, died later.
,, M. N. Cox, M.C. (Transport Officer).
Lieut. C. W. G. Ince, M.C. (Adjutant).
,, W. M. Ozanne, M.C. Wounded.
,, N. W. Hadwen. Wounded.
,, H. J. Miller, East Yorkshire Regiment. Wounded, died later.
,, G. H. Beyfus. Wounded and missing.
2nd Lieut. W. Inchley. Wounded.
,, C. F. Whitaker. Killed.
,, A. B. T. Simpson. Missing.
,, A. Gunn. Missing.
,, L. C. Adye. Wounded.
,, F. D. Chadwick. Wounded.
,, C. A. Bailey. West Yorkshire Regiment. Killed.
,, G. A. Chalcraft, West Yorkshire Regiment. Missing.
,, E. B. Davis, West Yorkshire Regiment. Missing.
Lieut. W. O. Tobias, M.B. (R.A.M.C.).
Major A. Ellam, M.C. (Quartermaster).

"At 2.30 a.m., May 6th, what was left of the Battalion was relieved and ordered to Ouderdom, south of Ypres. All that remained out of some 500 of all ranks after the second action on Hill 60 were: The Commanding Officer, Capt. Barton; the Adjutant, Lieut. Ince; Transport Officer, Capt.

PLATE 14

Cox; Medical Officer, Lieut. Tobias; the Quartermaster, Major Ellam, and some 150 other ranks.

"This ends a short story of the part played by the 2nd Battalion the Duke of Wellington's Regiment, the old 76th, at Hill 60. It is difficult for the writer, who took part in both actions, to find words to express his own admiration and pride at what those of the Regiment did during those days. They won the hill with the 13th Brigade on April 18th, foul means alone deprived them of it on May 5th when they held the trenches to the last man. All honour to those heroes who gave their all for their King, their country, and the honour of the Regiment they loved so well. Their names will live for all ages engraved in the Roll of Honour and may the memorial of their devotion to duty, 'Hill 60' borne on the Colours of the Regiment, cause April 18th and May 5th to be days never to be forgotten by the Duke of Wellington's Regiment."

From the Brigadier Commanding the 13th Brigade to the Commander-in-Chief of the British Armies many congratulations were received when the Battalion came back to Zevecoten in reserve.

"The old Duke of Wellington would, if he saw the Regiment now, be as proud of it as he was in his time," was the comment of Brig.-General R. Wanless O'Gowan.

Sir John French, addressing the "Duke's" and "Bedfords," said:—

"I have come here to-day as your Commander-in-Chief to say a few words to you in acknowledgment of the splendid work you have done throughout the last week in the capture of that very important position Hill 60 which was held in strength by the enemy. . . . The enemy's counter attacks with bombs and other means of attack which they employed so well were all to no purpose through the bravery shown by all concerned. The British soldier never seems to know what defeat is. . . . Officers, N.C.O.'s, and men, I tell you from the bottom of my heart that I am grateful to you for the work which has been done. The capture of that hill is of the utmost importance to us as it is one of the main positions round Ypres."

CHAPTER XI

MAY, 1915–JANUARY, 1917: ON THE SOMME. BATTLE OF ARRAS. ALBERT, BERTRANCOURT, BEAUMONT HAMEL. POPERINGHE. BACK TO THE SOMME. THE FLERS LINE, THE ATTACK AT LESBŒUFS.

DURING the remainder of May, 1915, what was left of the Battalion rested in huts at Zevecoten. By various drafts the strength was rapidly regained. Three officers, Capt. A. G. Adamson, 3rd North Staffords, 2nd Lieuts. H. M. Morris and G. R. Thomas, 4th Manchesters, and 394 other ranks, joined for duty on 10th. The new "sport" of bomb-throwing was assiduously practised, while a new pattern respirator was tried and added to the already overpowering number of gadgets the war had produced and men had to carry. Other officers, who joined up temporarily, posted to the Battalion were Lieut. H. J. Birch, 2nd York and Lancaster, Lieut. L. J. P. Green and 2nd Lieuts. E. W. Bowyer-Bower and Murrie, East Surreys, 2nd Lieut. Whittaker, 2nd Lieut. Smith of the Somersets, and Lieut. G. W. Wittington of the Norfolks, Lieut. Miller, 2nd Lieuts. D. C. H. Edwards, Locke, E. M. Cunningham, C. O. Daubeny, R. S. Thatcher, L. C. Sheppard, all of the Somersetshire Light Infantry, 2nd Lieut. G. L. S. Hawkins, 4th South Staffords, Lieut. B. E. Leader and 2nd Lieut. C. Robertson, 3rd Battalion Royal West Surrey Regiment, and a draft of 25 other ranks. Capt. R. J. A. Henniker rejoined his Battalion and 2nd Lieut. A. S. Lowe, 4th South Staffords, was posted for duty, while 200 other ranks helped to fill the Hill 60 vacancies. On May 29th Major R. N. Bray, Lieuts. W. H. Key-Jones, Davis, and W. R. Downey joined for duty, the former taking over command of the Battalion on June 3rd.

June and July found the 13th Brigade, under Brig.-General Wanless O'Gowan, in the trenches near St. Eloi. Throughout these two months the Battalion had a fairly quiet time. When not in the trenches, huts behind Dickebusch were no mean alternative. Mid-June found the Headquarters of the "Duke's" in dug-outs at Voermezeele. On Waterloo day General Sir T. Morland, commanding 5th Division, visited the trenches. 2nd Lieuts. W. S. Newroth, P. R. J. Henry, and A. W. Edwards joined for duty from the 3rd Battalion. On July 21st the 13th Brigade was relieved by the 7th Brigade, 3rd Division. The Battalion marched to Boeschepe via Reninghelst. There Lieut.-Colonel F. A. Hayden, D.S.O., and Capt. A. E. Miller, Adjutant, of the 9th Battalion of the "Duke's," had the pleasure of a very cheery meeting with their comrades of the 2nd Battalion. The 9th Battalion was in huts at Ouderdom

THE SUMMER OF 1915

at the time. The same night the 2nd Battalion was ordered to move to Steenworde, where it was quartered in farms west of that place.

The following week was one of real rest. Football competitions, a Battalion concert, and a mounted gymkhana in the transport lines almost made the "Duke's" forget the nightmare of the trenches. But on the 26th the peace of life at Steenworde was gently broken by a visit from General (now Lord) Plumer, commanding the Second Army. Visits from high commanders were already reckoned as presaging some unexpected and not entirely bloodless change in the daily life of battalions or brigades. In this case it was so, for Lord Plumer announced to the 13th Brigade that it was going south to form the nucleus of the new Third Army on the Somme. On July 30th the 2nd Battalion entrained for Corbie, near Amiens.

By the middle of August the 5th Division had taken up a new line just north of the River Somme in relief of French troops. That portion of the line occupied by the 13th Brigade stretched from the right of the 14th Brigade, north-west of Maricourt, to the summit of the ridge looking down towards Mametz. The new position north of the Somme had many advantages over the ground in which the Battalion had hitherto campaigned. That portion of Picardy, one of the oldest provinces of France, is open, undulating country sprinkled with isolated woods. For once in a way the British trench line had general command over that of the enemy. The actual trenches in the chalk soil were a revelation to troops whose main idea of trenches had hitherto been the water-logged, mud-filled channels of the low ground in Flanders. Under Lieut.-Colonel Bray life on the Somme became a distinct improvement upon that in the Ypres salient.

From August, 1915, until early January of 1916 the town of Bray and its vicinity, Carnoy, Billon Wood, Bronfay farm, remained the centre of the great struggle for the Duke of Wellington's Regiment. If things in the trenches are quiet, as they were in this sector, one day is much like another except to the man who stops a bullet.

While these weeks of early summer passed the Allied High Commands were engaged in studying the new conditions under which war was to be carried on. Neuve Chapelle, Festubert, and Loos were costly experiments. The French Commander-in-Chief, General Joffre, still hoped and intended to drive back the Germans and to clear the large portion of France they had overrun.

Near Noyon they were only 50 miles from Paris. On the Somme only 20 miles from Amiens, the main connecting link between British and French. Further north the Germans were only 40 miles from Calais. In general agreement with Joffre, though distinctly opposed to the latter's idea of a strong British thrust south of the La Bassée canal, Sir John French prepared to take his share in the main plan. A great attack in Champagne, together with the capture of Vimy Ridge by the Tenth French Army under Foch, was to be the allied *pièce de resistance* for 1916. All the attacks failed. But the Allied commanders were learning—at a cost—how to break through.

Towards the end of August, 1915, Brig.-General Maynard took over the 13th Brigade from Brig.-General Wanless O'Gowan, who had been promoted.

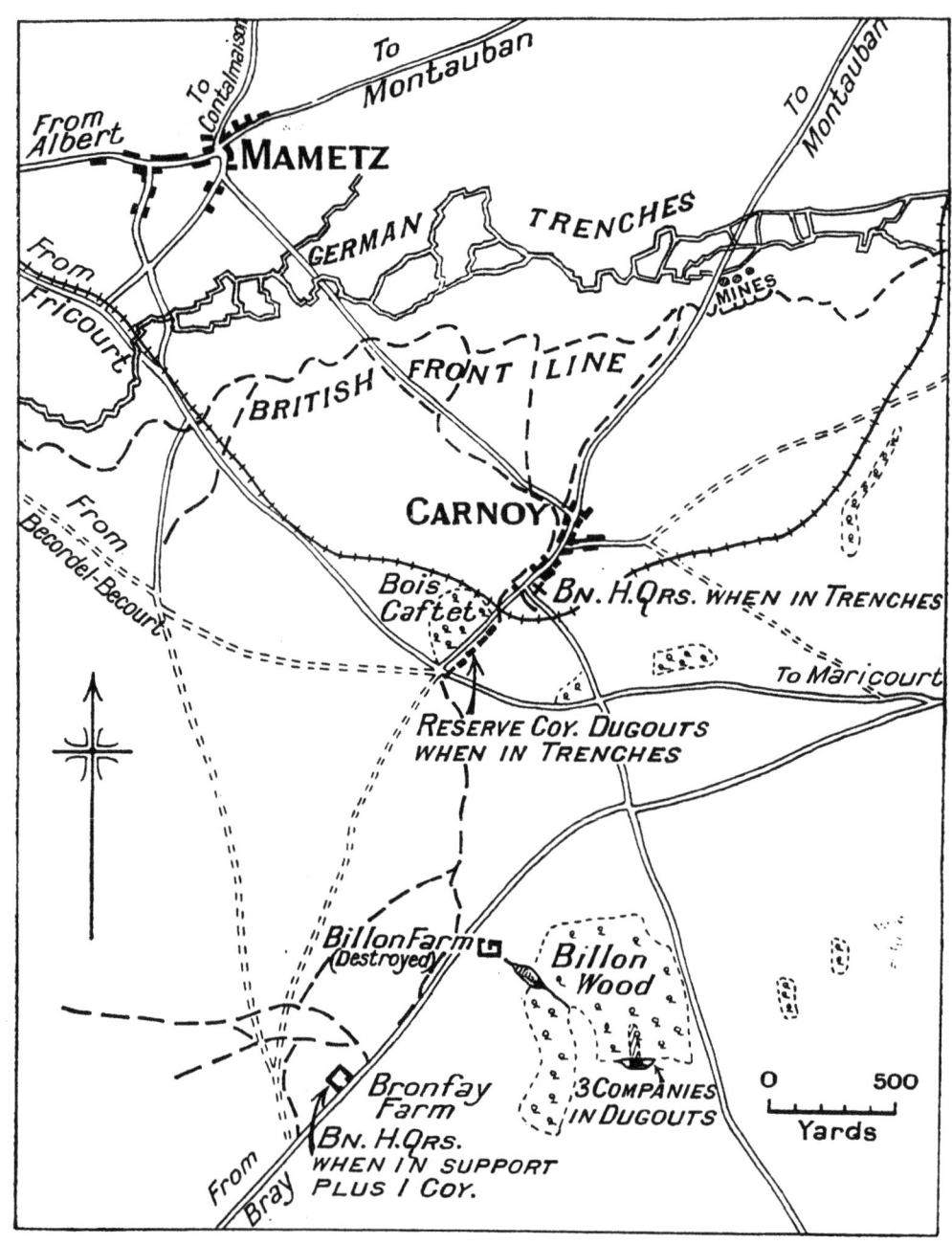

THE FRONT NEAR CARNOY, AUGUST, 1915, TO JANUARY, 1916.

Various drafts joined up. The officers were 2nd Lieut. C. C. Miller, 2nd Lieut. F. D. Chadwick, 2nd Lieut. P. S. Sainsbury, 2nd Lieut. J. W. Hodge and Capt. K. J. Milln, 3rd Somersets.

In order to coincide with the British attack at Loos in September, a projected feint had been arranged for the 5th Division against Pozières ridge. But as the Loos attack broke down chiefly from want of reinforcements in time, no move was made by the 5th Division. The curiously uneven lives led by troops in the front line could hardly be better indicated than by an entry for October 1st in the Battalion diary. While Rawlinson's Army Corps was fighting tooth and nail round Vermelles, Hulluch, and other places near Loos, the " Duke's " in billets at Etinhem were beating the 5th Division Cyclists at " footer " by six to nil. As autumn drew on new " man killers " were making their appearance. Catapults, trench mortars, and bomb-throwers had to be handled at first with due care, for they had the nasty habit of performing otherwise than " according to plan." The approach of winter found the chalk soil not quite so amenable to trenching as it was at first supposed to be. An incident which helped to break the routine of ordinary life occurred in the trenches north of Carnoy at the end of October. G.H.Q. required samples of German wire, so 2nd Lieut. P. Walsh and Pte. Marshall promptly procured it from across " No man's land." Among rewards received by officers of the Battalion this autumn were the D.S.O. to Capt. H. Gardiner attached to the 8th Battalion, and the Military Cross to Capts. M. N. Cox and C. W. G. Ince, while Sergt. G. W. Bazeley earned the *Croix de Guerre*. By November the Battalion had once more reached almost its full strength, there being 26 officers and 950 other ranks on the roll. It was not until January 9th, 1916, that a move was made away from Bray. It was a great blow to the " Duke's " to part from the intimate companionship of their many friends in both their own Brigade and the 5th Division. For eighteen months of almost perpetual fighting, and for four and a half years altogether, the Battalion had known a happy home among tried and trusted companions in arms whom it had learned to depend on in many a bloody fight. Mons, Le Cateau, the Aisne, and Hill 60 were fights which cemented closely the ties which already bound together those who had fought there side by side. The " Duke's " were given a great send off by the regiments of the 13th Brigade now under the command of Brig.-General Jones. Major-General—now Sir Charles—T. McM. Kavanagh, C.B., C.V.O., D.S.O., commanding 5th Division, met the Battalion at Corbie and expressed his appreciation of their splendid fighting qualities and his regret at losing them from his Division. It had been found necessary, he said, to send some of the old battalions to the new formations arriving from England, hence the change.

Via Sailly-Laurette and La Houssoye was the march in cold, fine weather. The Battalion now became part of the 12th Brigade temporarily attached to the 4th Division.

In the new Brigade the Battalion found itself alongside the 2nd Essex Regiment, the 1st Battalion The King's Own Royal Lancasters, and the 2nd Battalion the Lancashire Fusiliers. Their new Brigadier was Brig.-General

F. G. Anley, the Divisional Commander, Major-General Lambton, and the Corps Commander, Major-General (now Lieut.-General Sir A. G.) Hunter Weston. At Mailly Maillet and Mesnil, some 6 miles north of Albert, it found billets. Battalion Headquarters, No. 3 and No. 4 Companies at the former place attached to the 107th Ulster Brigade, No. 1 and No. 2 Companies at Mesnil attached to the 11th Brigade. It was here that all ranks lost with regret the services of their French interpreter, Sergt. Raymond Boutard, who had been with them since the very beginning of the war. Major K. J. Milln of the Somersets, Capt. E. G. Gatacre and Lieut. N. W. Hadwen joined up for duty, the first named as Second-in-Command.

January, 1916, when not detailed for working parties, was passed by all spare N.C.O.'s and men mainly at intensive training of all kinds. February saw little difference, though the Battalion moved to billets at Bertrancourt in reserve to the 12th Brigade, which rejoined the 4th Division from the (36th) Ulster Division. Fatigues on a railway line near Acheux in the snow kept all ranks fit until February 11th, when the "Duke's" took over trenches south-east of Hebuterne from the Essex Regiment. "In and out" from Bertrancourt was the order of the day for the rest of February. Unfortunately among the casualties was Capt. Gatacre, seriously wounded, who succumbed the following day, February 20th.

It was on February 21st, 1916, that the Germans opened their great attack on Verdun. All through March, April, and May it continued with ever increasing determination. Early in June, so serious had the situation become for the French, that Sir Douglas Haig prepared to launch the British offensive north of the Somme. During these months of desperate fighting round Verdun, Haig's armies had been preparing to take their share and as far as might be to draw off the German thrusts from General Pétain's sorely tried *poilus*. Up to mid-June the 12th Brigade, like others, were keeping their hands in raiding German trenches, sending bombing patrols to rouse the new German levies opposite to them, and generally improving their fighting efficiency: the coming attack was now known to be imminent. A move to Halloy, then to Barly, brought the "Duke's" to billets in the latter place, whence they returned to Halloy only to continue on to Bailleuval. "In and out" west of Ransart and billets at Bailleuval was the routine for April. Then at the end of that month a move was ordered to Warluzel by a very dusty night march. May and June slipped away while the German sledge-hammer battered down the various outer defences of Verdun. Warluzel, Brevillers, Le Suich are mere names now, though each in turn gave billets to the "Duke's" during May. From Bertrancourt, to which place it had returned, the Battalion in Brigade moved to Bernaville on the 23rd and into Yvrencheux, where it remained until June 8th. Various changes in *personnel* were constantly taking place. Lieut. P. Walsh and three others suffered at the hands of a refractory bomb during practice. Capt. C. W. G. Ince left the Battalion to be attached to 8th Corps Headquarters. Capt. F. H. Fraser took over the duties of Acting Adjutant, 2nd Lieut. F. W. Beard reported for duty from the R.F.C. on probation, and 2nd Lieuts. C. K. Homfray, N. I. Graham,

BATTLE OF THE SOMME, JUNE, 1916

G. D. Johnston, E. S. Plumb, A. V. Maunder from the 3rd Battalion, with Lieut. G. H. Sugden, 2nd Lieuts. J. S. Millican and Glover with a draft of 82 other ranks joined up. Early in June Brig.-General F. G. Anley was succeeded by Brig.-General J. D. Crosbie. June 9th saw a move to Bernaville and on to Beauval, thence to Bois de Marnimont and back to the old May camp at Bertrancourt.

In the summer of 1916 Ludendorff was frank as to the British attacks on the Somme:—

"When the battle of the Somme began," he wrote,[1] "the Entente had a tremendous superiority, both on land and in the air. G.H.Q. was surprised at first. Reinforcements were quickly thrown in, but it had never succeeded in wiping out the enemy's superiority in artillery, munitions and aircraft, even to a limited extent.

"The Entente troops had worked their way further and further into the German lines. We had heavy losses in men and material. At that time the front lines were still strongly held. The men took refuge in dug-outs and cellars from the enemy's artillery fire. The enemy infantry, coming up behind their barrage, got into the trenches and villages before our men could crawl out from their shelters. A continuous yield of prisoners to the enemy was the result. The strain on physical and moral strength was tremendous and divisions could only be kept in the line for a few days at a time. They had to be frequently relieved and sent to recuperate on quiet fronts."

On June 28th the Battalion should have assembled for the commencement of the great struggle on the Somme, but owing to weather the attack, so far as it was concerned, was postponed for forty-eight hours. On June 30th everything was ready. Late that night after a God-speed from Colonel Bray to each company, the "Duke's" under cover of the dark moved up to their assembly trenches east of Sucerie. By 2 a.m. on July 1st they were ready, and as men always were when the time came to go forward anxious for the "kick off."

That the particular doings of the 2nd Duke of Wellington's Regiment are the subject of these memoirs of the Great War has already been remarked, but what their part was can only be understood by knowing in a general way the main influences which brought about the Battle of the Somme.

The fighting known under that name in British official papers actually began by the preliminary bombardment on June 24th, 1916, the day on which the Crown Prince's armies almost broke through Pétain's splendid defence east of Verdun. During the last week in June German trenches, which were opposite the British line, were, in their turn, constantly raided and harried, gas being also sent over the German defences.

"These sanguinary prodigious struggles, extending over many months, are often loosely described as 'Battles.' Judging by the number of men who took

[1] *My War Memories.* Ludendorff.

148 HISTORY OF THE DUKE OF WELLINGTON'S REGIMENT

their turn in the fighting at different times, by the immense quantities of guns and shells employed, and by the hideous casualty totals, they certainly rank, taken each as a whole, among the largest events of military history. But we must not be misled by terminology. If to call them 'battles' were merely a method

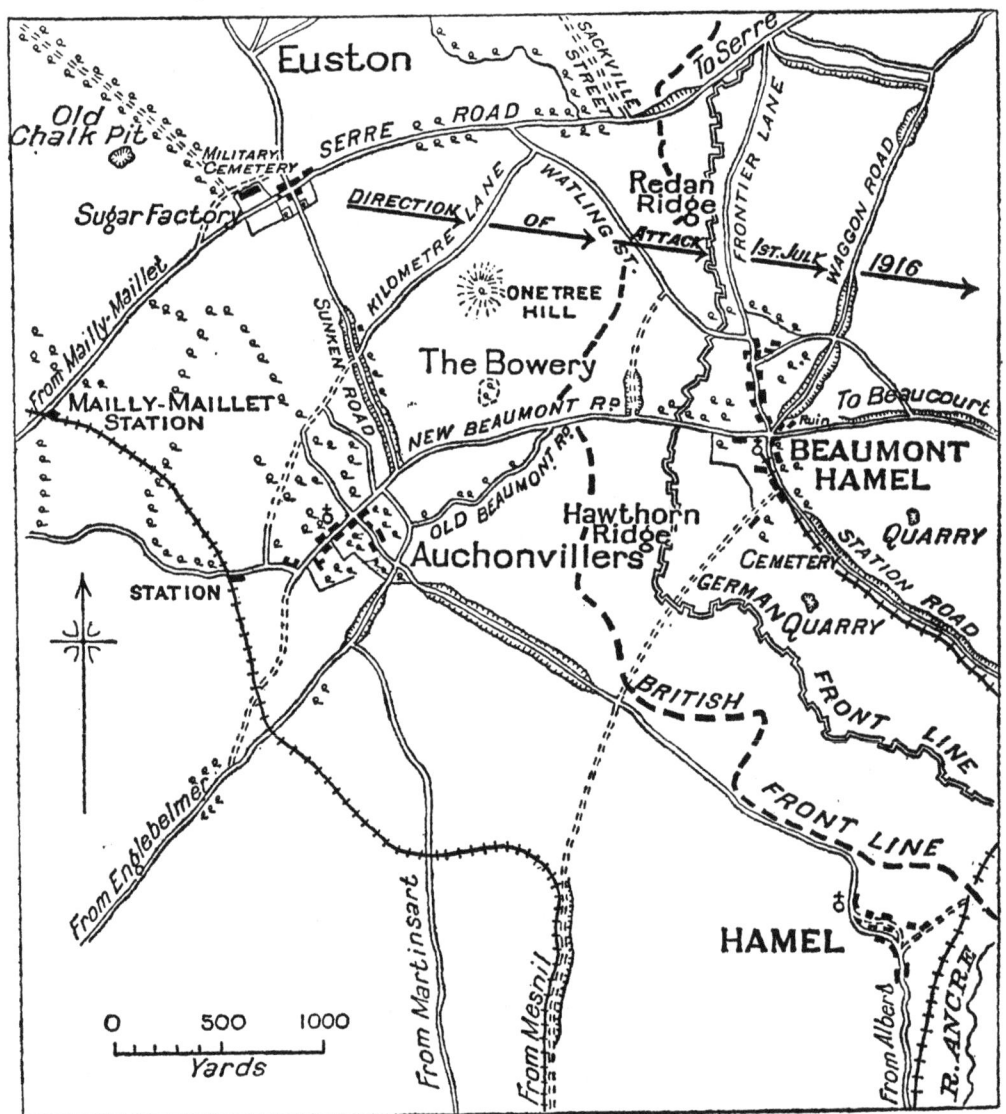

AREA OF ATTACK, JULY 1ST, 1916.

of presenting a general view of an otherwise confusing picture, it might well pass unchallenged. But an attempt has been made by military commanders and by a whole school of writers to represent these prolonged operations as events comparable with the decisive battles of the past, only larger and more important.

To yield to this specious argument is to be drawn into a wholly wrong impression, both of military science and of what actually took place in the Great War."[1]

It has been truly said that " the troops which were about to attack the German trenches from Gommécourt to the Somme included the flower of British manhood, and no more splendid body of men has ever gone forward to battle."[2]

The main attack was to be delivered by Rawlinson's Fourth Army, between the Ancre River and Maricourt, 2 miles north of the Somme, where it joined up with the Sixth French Army astride that river. A subsidiary attack of the Fourth Army was to be made north of the Ancre, and still another by the Third Army upon the Salient at Gommécourt. That both subsidiary attacks, that of the Fourth Army north of the Ancre, and that of the Third Army on Gommécourt, as well as the main attack of the British left failed and with heavy losses, is now past history. But so successful was the main British right attack, and that of the French troops astride the Somme, that it was considered by the High Commanders worth while to continue the battle. In doing so the British Commander-in-Chief, Sir Douglas, now Lord, Haig, made new plans to divide his battle front between two armies. The Fourth, Rawlinson's, was to endeavour to push the advantages already gained on the British right, while General Sir Hubert Gough with the Fifth Army was to keep the Germans busy on the left and to act as a pivot for the Fourth Army.

Let us now endeavour to follow the fortunes of the 2nd Battalion Duke of Wellington's Regiment. The VIII Corps, under Lieut.-General Sir A. G. Hunter Weston, to which the Duke's belonged, was ordered to attack the German trenches between Hamel and Serre. The divisions composing the Corps and their positions for attack were as follows: right division the 29th Division, centre division the 4th Division, left division the 31st Division. The reserve was composed of the 48th Division less two battalions. The 4th Division, to which as has been already said the " Duke's " belonged, was to attack between the villages of Beaumont Hamel and Serre, and to gain the Puisieux ridge. The dispositions of the 4th Division for attack were: the 11th Brigade with two battalions of the 48th Division were to make the first assault and to capture the first and second line German trenches. They were supported by the 10th Brigade on the right and by the 12th Brigade on the left. The supporting Brigade orders were to pass through the leading Brigade and to push on and capture the Puisieux ridge.

The " Duke's " formed the left support battalion of the 12th Brigade. The King's Own and the Essex were the leading battalions. The Lancashire Fusiliers formed the right support battalion. At first the chief rôle of the " Duke's " was to carry forward R.E. material to consolidate the captured position. Each battalion, besides this, had to provide 125 men to act as Brigade carriers of ammunition, rations, bombs, etc., a lesson learned from previous failures for want of such essentials.

[1] *The World Crisis*, 1916-1918, Part I. By the Rt. Hon. Winston Churchill, C.H., M.P.
[2] *Enc. Brit.*

The following officers went into action with the 2nd Battalion :—
B.H.Q. :
    Lieut.-Colonel R. N. Bray
    Act.-Adjutant : Capt. F. H. Fraser
    Signal Officer : Lieut. H. R. Holdsworth
                  2nd Lieut. F. C. Glover
    M.O. : Capt. C. Macleod, R.A.M.C.

No. 1 Company :
    Capt. K. J. Milln, S.L.I.   Lieut. L. C. Adye
    Lieut. A. F. Hemming   2nd Lieut. H. K. Homfray

No. 2 Company :
    Lieut. N. W. Hadwen   2nd Lieut. H. R. Thelwell
    Lieut. S. R. Lord   2nd Lieut. G. D. Johnston
    2nd Lieut. D. M. Brown

No. 3 Company :
    Capt. C. L. Hart   2nd Lieut. C. W. G. Grimley
    Lieut. G. H. Sugden   2nd Lieut. C. R. Sanderson
    Lieut. P. J. Sainsbury

No. 4 Company :
    Lieut. R. N. Davis   2nd Lieut. A. V. Maunder
    2nd Lieut. F. L. Harry   2nd Lieut. C. H. Bowes

Bombing Officer :   2nd Lieut. S. B. Kington
Scout Officer :   2nd Lieut. E. S. Plumb
Brigade Intelligence Officer :   2nd Lieut. J. S. Millican
Brigade Carriers :
    Lieut. A. W. H. Lawless   2nd Lieut. N. I. Graham.

At 5.30 a.m., July 1st, in the assembly trenches south of Sucerie, the "Duke's" took breakfast. Hot tea, vegetable, and meat rations. Thus do we moderns make war ! At 8.55 a.m., with breakfasts well digested, the leading companies moved out of the assembly trenches and commenced the advance ; but within half an hour unexpected orders came for the Battalion to halt. So far casualties had been light. Runners went forward to halt the companies, which No. 4 Company did, but in order to avoid an unpleasant barrage the 1st, 2nd, and 3rd Companies continued their advance and gained the German front lines, some men even reaching the German second line. For some time no information was received from any of the companies. Meanwhile Battalion Headquarters had been established in Taupin trench, from whence men could be seen retiring to what appeared to be the German second line. Here they were reorganized, and what remained of the 11th Brigade, with the leading Battalion of the 18th Brigade, pushed on again. They were eventually forced to retire owing to being enfiladed by machine-gun fire from Serre and Beaumont Hamel. A portion of the troops, made up from men of various units, remained in the quadrilateral till dusk and then retired to their own trenches. About 3.30 p.m.

Plate 15

R.Q.M.S. E. MOSELEY

R.S.M. C. E. METCALFE, D.C.M. & BAR, M.M.

C.S.M. R. GRADY

Lieut.-Colonel Bray was sent for by the Brigadier, who told him to reorganize and hold the Brigade's front line. The sector to be held reached from the junction of Trelawney and Wulf trenches to Cat Street. B.H.Q. was in Valade trench. Colonel Bray was placed in command of the King's Own, the Essex and the " Duke's " to hold this sector. The trenches held by the Battalion were Burrow, Wulf, and Legend; Lieuts. Davis and Sugden being in command, the other officers being 2nd Lieuts. Homfray, Harry, Johnston, and Maunder. Neither the King's Own nor the Essex had any officers with them.

The night was comparatively quiet and the Battalion took over a little more of the line from the 1st Rifle Brigade. The total casualties for the day were heavy in officers, being 3 killed and 11 wounded. Of N.C.O.'s and men 18 were killed, 251 wounded, and 40 missing. The officers killed were Capt. C. L. Hart, Lieut. N. W. Hadwen, and 2nd Lieut. C. H. Bowes. Wounded, Capt. K. J. Milln, Lieuts. A. F. Hemming, L. C. Adye, S. R. Lord, D. N. Brown, H. R. Thelwell, C. R. Sanderson, E. S. Plumb, S. B. Kington, C. W. G. Grimley, G. D. Johnston. The first reinforcements to reach the Battalion that night consisted of Lieut. C. N. Cheetham, 2nd Lieuts. S. G. Clifton, P. F. Lambert, F. B. Leece, D. A. Bennett, and about 95 other ranks under Major F. A. Armitage (Second-in-Command).

Early on the morning of July 2nd, Major Armitage took over command of the Battalion in the front line, while Colonel Bray was in charge of the whole sector. Artillery shelling was indulged in by both sides during the day, and the Battalion's trenches were blown in places, though few casualties occurred. Towards evening word came from Brigade Headquarters that the Germans had been seen from the direction of Beaumont Hamel carrying tins down to their front line. A *Flammenwerfer* attack was expected but failed to mature. The casualties included: officers, 5 wounded—2nd Lieuts. J. S. Millican, D. A. Bennett, F. L. Harry, S. G. Clifton, and N. I. Graham. Other ranks, 4 killed and 41 wounded.

From July 2nd to July 10th no further advance took place in this sector. Intermittent shell fire caused casualties, but only very slight ones. Upon rearrangement of trenches Colonel Bray remained in command of the Battalion, and on the 10th the " Duke's " were relieved in the trenches by the 1st Rifle Brigade. They marched to rest camp between Bertrancourt and Acheux after ten consecutive days and nights in the trenches. While in camp the Brigade paraded for inspection by the Corps Commander. Lieut.-General Sir A. Hunter Weston praised and thanked all ranks for the gallant manner in which they had fought on July 1st.

Until July 21st the time was spent " in and out " of the trenches east of Auchonvillers. On that date the Brigade was relieved by the 35th Infantry Brigade, the " Duke's " handing over to the Suffolks, and marched out to Louvencourt and on the following day to Authieule, the 23rd into Doullens. While at Bertrancourt Lieut. G. P. Sleigh, 2nd Lieuts. E. E. Arkless and G. W. M. Harpley joined for duty from the base.

Entraining at Doullens the Battalion reached Cassel the same afternoon, marching out to Houtrerque, where it went into billets just after midnight. Fate had swept the " Duke's " once into the Ypres salient, but not for long.

Midsummer of 1916 passed on the " Canal bank." During August the usual drafts to fill casualties took place. The following officers joined for duty: 2nd Lieuts. T. W. Robertson, L. G. Watson, Macnamara, J. S. Braine, and Simkins. Other ranks 65. Major C. J. Burke, D.S.O., Royal Irish, as Second-in-Command, Major W. E. Keates, Temporary Major T. H. J. Gillam and Lieut. F. H. King, West India Regiment. Decorations were distributed to Corpl. Burch, and to Ptes. Wooley and Chayter the Military Medal for gallantry at the fighting on the Somme. Capt. G. Macleod, R.A.M.C., Military Cross, R.S.M. C. Shepherd the D.C.M., C.S.M. Metcalf awarded a clasp to D.C.M., also for good work on the Somme in July. Poperinghe for a clean-up was a break in trench routine, then back to take over in the support line from 5th Canadian Mounted Rifles. Battalion Headquarters was at Swan Château. On September 16th at Poperinghe one of the usual "surprise packets" was handed out to the Division, which was ordered to move at once back to the Somme, Bertangles being the temporary billets of the 2nd Battalion. During the remainder of September and up to October 9th intensive training of all ranks went on uninterruptedly. By October 9th the Battalion had slowly worked its way across country from Corbie via Morlancourt and Carnoy, up to the new British line east of Bernafay Wood. So far had the attack which started on July 1st then progressed. As usual drafts were filtering in, some among them being old 2nd Battalion men wounded earlier and now recovered. Major A. G. Horsfall, who had come straight from the 1st Battalion in India, joined up on October 8th. Badly as both officers and other ranks were needed in the front line, their arrival was usually somewhat behind requirements. Nor is this to be wondered at, considering the extraordinary congestion there was bound to be in rear of the fighting line. Having reached Abbeville, Major Horsfall proceeded, he writes in his diary, " by very slow train to Méricourt L'Abbaye. Some idea of the rate of progress may be gained from the fact that men frequently got out to milk cows in the fields and caught up the train later."

On October 9th the " Duke's " moved up into what was commonly known as the Flers line, and by 2 a.m. on the 10th had " taken over " from the Queen's Westminster and 8th Middlesex. It has been said of the fighting on the Somme during the later autumn of 1916 that it " deserves to rank high in the records of British hardihood. The fighting had not the swift pace and the brilliant successes of the September battles. Our men had to strive for minor objectives, and such a task lacks the impetus and exhilaration of a great combined assault. On many occasions the battle resolved itself into isolated struggles, a handful of men in a mud hole holding out and consolidating their ground till their post was linked up with our main front. Rain, cold, slow reliefs, the absence of hot food, and sometimes of any food at all, made these episodes a severe test of endurance and devotion."[1]

Towards the end of September the line held by the British ran from what was well known as the Schwaben Redoubt, about half a mile north of Thiepval,

[1] *A History of the Great War.* John Buchan.

ATTACK AT LESBŒUFS ON GERMAN "BROWN LINE"

in an eastward and southward curve to Morval, where it was held by the French. The line passed north of Courcellete, north and east of Martinpuich, Flers, Gueudecourt, and Lesbœufs. On the left the line ran mainly along the ridge. As it bent south and linked with the French the trenches followed the lower slopes. Generally speaking, the fourth German line was the British objective, but to reach this very strong intermediate positions, spurs, buildings, sunken dug-outs, and concealed machine guns had to be taken, and mainly by infantry assault.

While the 4th Division had gone north the dogged, continuous attacks had never ceased on the Somme. The Germans had been driven back into their fourth line and there was no doubt that their morale had been badly shaken by this pressure. October opened with unduly wet and inclement weather, which sorely hampered offensive fighting as opposed to troops remaining on the defensive.

On first getting into the trenches to the right of Lesbœufs, the "Duke's" were chiefly occupied clearing wounded left by other regiments. Casualties from being shelled or from snipers began with 2nd Lieuts. Braine, Simkins, and Beard being killed and 2nd Lieut. F. C. Glover and 70 other ranks wounded. Preparations for the coming attack went on. Reinforcements and reserve N.C.O.'s were pushed forward to Bernafay Wood. The 4th Division had been ordered to attack what was known as the "Brown Line." On its right was the 6th British Division. On their right French troops. The 4th Division attacked with the 12th Brigade (2nd Duke of Wellington's) on the left, the 10th Brigade on the right. The 11th Brigade was in Divisional Reserve. The "Duke's" and 2nd Lancashire Fusiliers were the assaulting battalions of the 12th Brigade, the Essex and King's Own being in Brigade Reserve. The Battalion was under command of Major C. J. Burke, with Capt. F. H. Fraser as adjutant. No. 1 Company was commanded by Lieut. F. H. King with 2nd Lieut. G. E. Elliot: both these officers were killed during the attack. No. 2 Company was commanded by Capt. B. E. Leader, having as subaltern officers G. P. Sleigh and 2nd Lieut. F. B. Leece and 2nd Lieut. P. F. Lambert. Capt. Leader and 2nd Lieut. Leece were both killed. No. 3 Company lost its commander, Lieut. G. H. Sugden, while 2nd Lieut. J. W. Hodge was missing, believed also killed. No. 4 Company was in command of Capt. R. N. Davis, with 2nd Lieut. E. E. Arkless. Capt. Davis was killed and 2nd Lieut. Arkless seriously wounded.

Let us briefly follow the subsequent events of this typical day, for they were what British troops had been doing on the Somme for weeks on end. The assault was timed for 2.5 p.m., and the "Duke's," leaving their trenches to the second, charged forward with magnificent dash. It took three minutes for the enemy to open his barrage, and by that time the men were mostly clear of the assembly trenches, so consequently suffered few casualties in reaching their first objective. By 2.12 p.m., not bad going, the first report reached British Headquarters from No. 3 Company on the left. It said that the company had reached the German front line and that the Germans had surrendered freely. The next report came from No. 4 Company on the right, a verbal message which stated that the company was on the "Brown Line" at 2.40 p.m. and were commencing to consolidate. As no information had been received from either Nos. 1 or 2 Companies "runners" were sent out. Not until over an hour later was there any answer. By 3.35 messages came back from No. 1 Company, sent by Lce.-Corpl. Wilson, saying there were neither officers nor N.C.O.'s left, and that the company was in a bad way. From Lieut. Sleigh with No. 2 Company a message came back at 5.5 p.m. saying that he was at the first objective with some 50 men, but had seen nothing of his company commander, Capt. B. E. Leader, since the

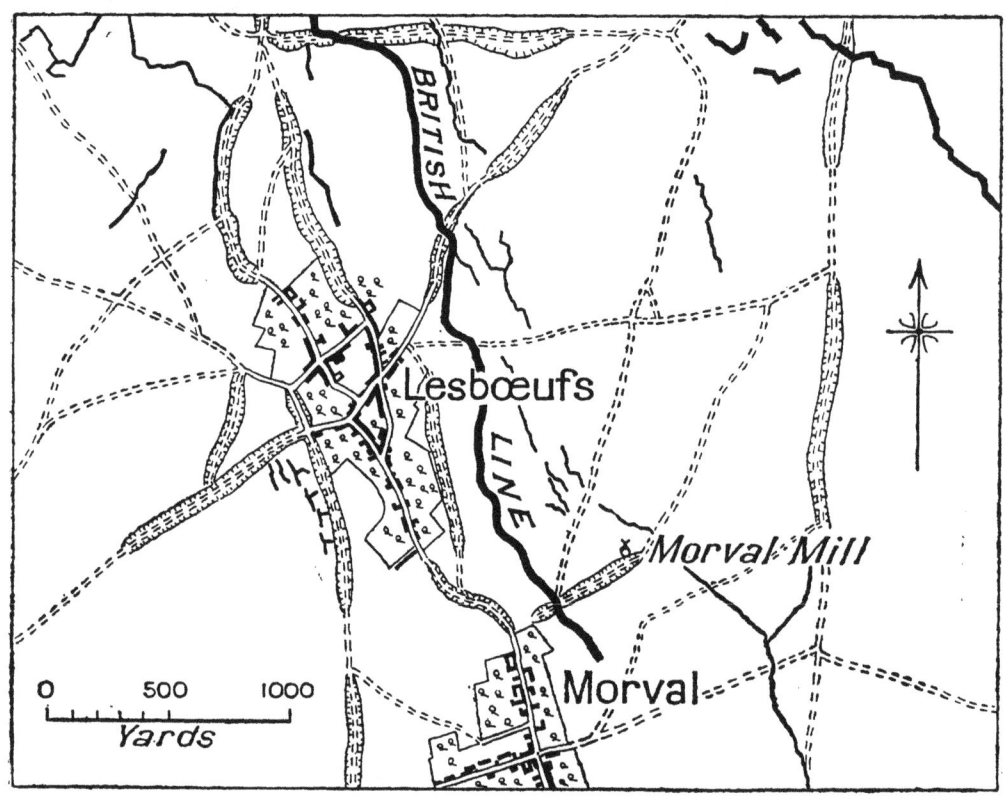

LESBŒUFS, OCTOBER, 1916.

start of the attack. At 4.43 p.m. C.S.M. Pearce sent back stating that he expected to be counter-attacked. This did not mature and he was ordered to keep touch with the Lancashire Fusiliers on the Battalion's left, to establish a firing-line and to get in touch with Lieut. Sleigh. By nightfall all these matters had been put right, and when the fighting died down the work of evacuating the wounded commenced. Rarely has Red Cross work been more vividly and more poignantly described than by a young American officer who fought in France.

"Between attacks," he wrote, "the stretcher bearers and the Red Cross men on both sides did their utmost for the wounded who were scattered through the wheat around the hill, and who now, under the torture of stiffening wounds and the hot sun, began to cry out. As the afternoon advanced, you heard pitiful voices! little and thin across the fields: 'Ach Himmel, Hilfe, Hilfe! Brandighe! . . . Liebe Gott, brandighe!' . . . 'First aid—this way. First aid, for the love of God!' . . . From most wounds men do not appear to suffer greatly at first. There is the hot impulse of the attack, and perhaps a certain shock from the missile, so that the nerves are numb. One has gone forward with the tide at the highest; life is a light thing to lay down, death a light thing to venture. Yonder is the enemy. One has come a long way to meet him, and now the affair can be taken up personally. Then something hits—the wheat cuts off all the world. An infernal racket goes on somewhere—Springfields and Mausers, Maxim guns and Hotchkiss—sometimes closer, sometimes receding. Bullets zip and drone around; there may be shells, shrapnel, and H.E., searching the ground, one can hear them coming. 'Is it gonna hit me—is it gonna hit me, O Lawd—Christ! that was close!'

"Presently pain, in recurring waves. Pride may lock a man's lips awhile . . . left long enough most men break, and no blame to them. A hundred brave dead, lying where the guns cut them down, are not so pitiful as one poor wailing fellow in a dressing station. . . ."[1]

The October 12th attack near Lesboeufs was a mere episode in this grim battle on the Somme. But it cost the "Duke's" 5 officers killed, 2 officers wounded, and 2 missing, believed dead. Of other ranks 43 were killed, 236 wounded, and 54 missing, mostly dead.

Back in reserve in the Flers line the Battalion was given a bare week to reorganize. On the 19th the Brigade was ordered to take over part of the line from the 11th Brigade. 2nd Lieut. Macnamara, who had been sent to make arrangements with the East Lancashires, was killed by a shell on the way. Having taken over, an order was received for the "Duke's" to provide one company 100 strong for a special mission in an attack the following day. Here we have still another type of very ordinary battalion job. Capt. R. J. A. Henniker, who had just rejoined from the Staff, was in command, with 2nd Lieut. K. A. Hellon as the only other officer. The Fourth Army and the French on the right of the Brigade were to resume the general attack the following day. The special mission of Capt. Henniker's company was to clear what was locally known as the Sunken Road, to mop up the dug-outs, and to consolidate and garrison the little position. Strong points were to be dug on each side of the Sunken Road. When the time came for this little force to start in there was some disorganization partly caused by British Artillery, which had been dropping shells short most of the morning. 2nd Lieut. Hellon and a small party got into the Sunken Road and proceeded to dig in. A party of bombers cleared the immediate trench and reinforcements, 1 sergeant and 10 men, were sent up to Capt. Henniker's party in Spectrum Trench. Dark coming on Lieut. Hellon proposed to rejoin the Battalion, as nothing more could be done and the enemy had regained a large portion of the Spectrum Trench. The main attacks by the Essex Regiment and Lancashire

---

[1] *Fix Bayonets.* By John W. Thomason, Junr., Captain U.S. Marine Corps, 1926.

Fusiliers not maturing, Capt. Henniker's company withdrew. Through artillery fire before the actual attack began, and by machine-gun fire during the advance, the company had lost somewhat out of proportion to the success achieved. The total casualties were, Lieut. Hellon and 23 other ranks wounded; 5 other ranks killed and 9 missing.

The end of October found the Battalion out of the trenches at Maricourt, where various drafts joined. Officers: 2nd Lieuts. F. B. Cooper, R. Anderton, G. Rodgers, E. Y. Yelland, H. E. Williams, J. H. Hill, E. Rawnsley, and J. D. V. Macintosh from the 4th Battalion, Capt. C. Bathurst, 2nd Lieuts. G. W. Goldsworthy and G. R. Crockett and P. F. Lambert from the Base. Other ranks 280. The following awards were received: Sergts. Liversidge and Griggs, and Ptes. O'Kelly and Culliton the Military Medal; 2nd Lieut. N. H. Rutherford and C.S.M. L. J. Pearce the Military Cross; Pte. Lawson the D.C.M., all three for gallantry in the fight of October 12th described above.

Mericourt to Arraines by train, then on to Fosceville and Neuville by march were the next moves. But a few days later the Battalion passed on to Vismes. December, 1916, found the "Duke's" still at Vismes, and the intervening period had been uneventful, except in matters of personal interest to them. Drafts arrived and strenuous training went on. Officers joining were Lieut. R. W. Edwards, 2nd Lieuts. N. M. Ward, W. E. Mitchell, J. F. Rhodes, N. Patchett, S. Baldwin, and J. Pullan, with 173 other ranks. Ptes. Stopps and Beirne received the Military Medal; C.S.M. Richards and Sergts. Hannah, Spriggs, Waller, and Dennison were also presented with this decoration by the General Officer Commanding the Division.

In the middle of November Lieut.-Colonel Bray went on hard-earned leave, handing over command to Major A. G. Horsfall.

Early in December the Brigade had finished its short breathing space at Vismes, and once more moved up into the front line near Maurepas. On December 16th, Lieut.-Colonel Bray received the reward he had so well earned, and was appointed Brig.-General to command 87th Infantry Brigade. He had led the "Duke's" for over a year of strenuous fighting, and what that means to a commanding officer always in the trenches only those know who have tried the experiment. His successor, Major A. G. Horsfall, had not the same experience, but he soon made up for this by the untiring and unselfish performance of his new duties as Commanding Officer.

Perhaps the greatest trial during these dreadful winter months on the Somme, far more so than any attentions from the enemy, was the mud. What the mud in the trenches was few can imagine who have not experienced it. In his diary, already quoted from, Major Horsfall wrote of this December: "Am mud from head to foot, hair, face, everything. One is just a moving mud clot. One can hardly tell where one's breeches end and boots begin. . . . I spent two hours digging a man out with my hands, he had been in twenty hours and was nearly a goner. They sniped us all the time, but were damned bad shots, and we got the man out."

Of another December day Major Horsfall wrote: " Still bitterly cold.

WINTER ON THE SOMME, 1916/17

This morning when we got up the Padre found his false teeth, which he had left in a tumbler last night, at the bottom of a solid block of ice, and had to thaw them out. This was in a hut where five of us are sleeping with a stove going all night and not a very big hut either. However, it will be warmer up in the line in dug-outs as these huts are always a bit draughty. Anyway, this cold is much better than mud."

About this time came the German peace offer of December 12th, met, as was obvious to anyone in the world but Germans, it would be, by a calm and dignified " No thank you " from the Allies. Peace on German terms was unthinkable. There could be no peace without retribution and reparation to Belgium and France, and guarantees for the future in Europe. Then came President Wilson's offer of mediation, politely declined this time, and 1917 broke with every intention on the part of British and French to " see it through " at all costs.

New Year's Day, 1917, found the Battalion in billets at Bray, where things were very quiet until February 1st. On that date it was ready to move into the trenches again and on February 10th was in the line near Bouchavesnes. Additions to the Battalion in officers during January and February were Capts. H. W. Glenn and K. E. Cunningham, Lieuts. S. G. Clifton, J. S. Braine, W. S. Newroth, and 2nd Lieuts. W. E. Horsley, A. H. Larcombe, and S. A. Belshaw.

Addressing the 12th Brigade on May 14th, Maj.-General Hon. W. Lambton, C.V.O., C.B., C.M.G., D.S.O., congratulated all ranks on their gallantry in the April attacks, and on the good work done during the fighting of the previous month.

The commencement of the Battle of Arras synchronised with the entry of the U.S.A. into the world war. It had taken President Wilson a long time to induce the " plain man " in the States to see the world situation as he and others saw it. But in April, 1917, the time had come. June found the 12th Brigade " resting " at Maiziere, and there it remained until on June 10th it passed through Arras to go into the trenches again, the " Duke's " at the chemical works in front of Fampoux they knew so well.

CHAPTER XII

FEBRUARY, 1917–MAY, 1917: BRAY. CORBIE. ARRAS. FAMPOUX. THE CHEMICAL WORKS. MAIZIERE. U.S.A. IN THE WAR. A BATTALION RAID. BACK TO YPRES, PILKEM. DEATH OF COMMANDING OFFICER LIEUT.-COLONEL A. G. HORSFALL, D.S.O.

IN February, 1917, Capt. W. G. Officer joined from the 1st Battalion in India. The end of February saw the Battalion out of the trenches and in billets at Bray, from whence it moved after a day's stay to Corbie. During March the " Duke's " were training hard while they were moving slowly northwards. Unknown to them the Battle of Arras lay just ahead. From Corbie to Caumont and Tollent via St. Pol to Bailleul took them most of the month, every hour filled with intensive training under specialist officers, themselves fresh from Haig's latest schools of instruction in " how to kill Germans." Thus were those same schools explained by the new type of rank and file.

As early as November 22nd, 1916, the new German command had decided that it must withdraw its fighting front and reconcentrate on what became famous later as the Hindenburg line. Curiously enough it was about the same date, November 16th, that Haig and Joffre met at the Chantilly Conference to arrange for a fresh attack in the spring of 1917, for choice in February. Owing to Joffre being superseded by General Nivelle in December, 1916, the original plan was altered, and Haig's difficulties thereby considerably increased. When the Battle of Arras began in April instead of in February, the 4th Division formed part of the XVII Corps of the Third Army. The primary object of the XVII Corps was to establish a line along the German third system of trenches (Brown Line). The objective allotted to the 4th Division was the capture of the German fourth system of trenches west of the village of Fampoux and the establishment of a line east of that village (Green Line). The 12th Brigade was to attack on the right; the 11th Brigade on the left; with the 10th Brigade in reserve. The battle order for the 12th Brigade was, on the right the King's Own, centre 2nd Lancashire Fusiliers, left 2nd Essex Regiment. The Duke of Wellington's in Brigade Reserve.

The share of the " Duke's " in the Battle of Arras is one more record of hard slogging, sticking it, and the determination not to be beat so characteristic of the New Armies. From April 9th to the end of that month thrust after thrust was made at the German line. What that line stood for in the matter

FAMPOUX AND THE BATTLE OF ARRAS

of fortifications the world now knows, but they were powerless to stem the inflowing British attacks. Vimy Ridge, that far-famed German view-point south of Lens, fell to the Canadians. The XVII Corps took Fampoux and the Hyderabad Redoubt, and later Gavrelle, while from as far north as Lens to as far south as Bullecourt British infantry and guns pushed east irresistibly. May saw yet another main attack from north of Arleux on a 12-mile front to Bullecourt. Frenoy, Roeux cemetery and the Chemical Works were in British hands by May 11th, the 4th Division being responsible for the capture of the

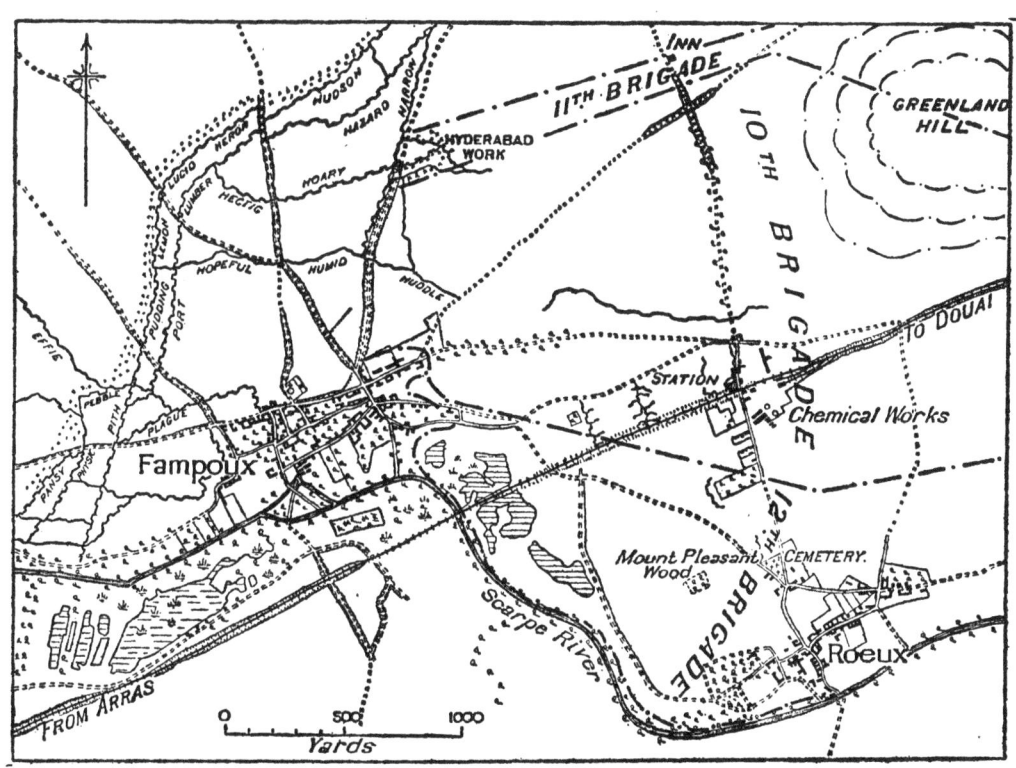

FAMPOUX AND CHEMICAL WORKS, APRIL–MAY, 1917.

latter after desperate fighting. As already related, the "Duke's" were ready for the fight, and 5.20 a.m., April 9th, saw them moving up to their assembly area.

"We took part in the big show on April 9th," wrote Lieut.-Colonel A. G. Horsfall, their C.O., and proceeds to tell the story in the restrained and unemotional manner so typical of his class and kind. "It was, I think, the most spectacular battle ever fought. Another Division was to take the first three German systems (Black, Blue, and Brown Lines), then our Division was to go through and capture the fourth German system, and then we were to go through and capture Fampoux, and dig in about 300 yards beyond it. We marched at

5.15 a.m. in a snowstorm to the assembly area about 5 miles away, where we had a hot meal and rum ration, and picks and shovels were drawn. The last mile or so up to this place we were passing through continuous heavy guns and howitzers, all firing hard; you never heard such a row. We passed streams of wounded, and dense columns of prisoners kept coming in. During our halt here we had one man hit by a stray bullet—Lord knows where it came from. We heard the Black Line was captured before we moved off: we then went up the Athies–Plouvain Road, gangs of sappers were already hard at work on it. The enemy barraged the road and the 1st K.O.'s[1] ahead of us lost heavily, but we kept a bit to the south and got to the Blue Line (which had been captured in the meantime) with only one other man hit.

"The Blue Line here was an enormous railway embankment, we sat on it and watched our heavies strafe Athies and the Highlanders take the place—just like a cinematograph—then moved on and got into our positions of readiness while our guns hammered the fourth German system. The advance from here was in artillery formation of section columns and was done just like a drill movement, every section in its proper position moving steadily on. The German position was just over a ridge, and we did not know we were so close to it when suddenly a hare got up and came dodging in and out of the columns. All the men cheered and watched it while the Boche with his hands up came streaming out to us; but no one cared a damn for them compared to the hare. It was lucky the Boche had the wind up, as their wire was hardly touched and their trenches intact.

"From here we pushed on to Fampoux. On our right, south of the Scarpe our attack had not got forward so well and the Boche M.G.'s kept going hard at us, but I don't think anyone was hit, thanks to the very long range they were firing at. We had to wait some time for our heavies to paste the place; (as a matter of fact they did very little damage, but the Boche guns during the next few days practically flattened the place out). During this halt a few Boche guns got on to us and a subaltern was killed close to me and several men wounded. We fairly rushed the village, which was a very big one: luckily for us the enemy was a bit on the run and it was not until we got near the far end that we had any real fighting; here we had to bomb them out of one or two houses. I don't think we lost many men from this fighting. The Boche made a stand beyond the village, holding a railway embankment on our right, several trenches, and a line of houses beyond, with M.G.'s. Trying to advance to the Green Line we lost about 80 men and 6 officers in two or three minutes; the survivors had to lie flat, any man showing himself the slightest bit being shot to pieces. I decided that without artillery support we could not push further, so we dug in along the forward edge of the village. It was rather an anxious time for a bit as south of the river on our right a heavy Boche counter-attack had gone clean past and about three-quarters of a mile behind us; and on our left, where we were warned an attack was expected, the rest of the Brigade had not come up into line. So, we were just holding the forward end of the village and a bit either

[1] King's Own Royal Lancaster Regt.

side of it with both flanks in the air. However, I managed to get a company of the L.F.'s to join up on our left, and the rest of the Brigade came up into line—or rather part of them did during the early hours of next day, and I got the K.O.'s who were in support to hold a bridge over the river for us (in our rear).

"The next day we were warned to attack the buildings in front without a barrage. Fortunately I told our Brigadier that it would be simply murder to take men out to do so, and they then said the Cavalry would charge the trenches between us and the buildings, and we go up in support. However, the Cavalry jibbed and nothing happened. Luckily our G.S.O.(I.) came up to see the situation and I took him round as much of our front line as it was prudent to get to; by an especial mercy the Hun was barraging every street with M.G.'s, and really pasting the village with H.E., and it rather impressed the G.S.O.(I.), who even told me he thought it foolhardy to move about the village, but I rubbed it in that the infantry had no choice.

"The next day we and the K.O.'s went over the top, but instead of attacking the buildings in front were to do a right incline, crossing the railway embankment diagonally and attacking buildings well south of it. The ground beyond the village was deep mud and swamp, and the barrage very thin and far too quick, the men could not keep up. They captured some German trenches held by Prussians of a fresh Division, and then, while they were climbing up a high embankment the barrage got a long way ahead. Only about 50 men of the two Battalions got across, with most of the officers; then had to get cover under a low bank and lie there all day; the enemy holding a very strongly fortified point beyond. Another Brigade was to have been on our left but must have misread its orders, as only one platoon of it ever came south of the Athies–Plouvain Road. The result of this was that a great part of the railway embankment, a lot of Boche trenches and all the buildings between the railway and Athies–Plouvain Road were never attacked and all were stiff with M.G.'s. Seeing the attack held up I went up into the line. We tried to turn the strong point along the river but were held up by swamps and lack of cover. Then the C.O. of the K.O.'s and I had a consultation. He thought the Brigade on our left had gone bang through, and wanted to attack the buildings north of the railway. I went forward a bit and did a reconnaisance and also got reports of one platoon of ours that had gone well forward and had to fall back, and from the platoon of the Brigade on our left, and thought we would have no earthly hope of getting in; and so said I would take my Battalion forward if he ordered it but was against doing so. He then asked what I suggested, so I said we must hold the captured trenches. They were not continuous and we had a lot of digging to do, but finally got a continuous line. It was now snowing like blazes. We held from the road to the railway and then back along the railway to a point where we joined the Corps south of the river. The L.F.'s had come into the line by now. Just then the enemy made a counter-attack and got clean round on our left flank, which merely rested on the road and was actually within bombing distance. We held the left, the L.F.'s[1] the right of the trench,

[1] Lancashire Fusiliers.

and the K.O.'s the embankment. The men were beat to the world and their rifles all clogged with clay and snow, and for some time a Company S.M. with a Lewis gun and myself with a rifle held the line. The men had not got the wind up, they were simply dead beat. I forgot to say we were counter-attacked twice the previous night, and since 5.15 a.m. on the 9th our men had practically had no rest and no sleep, had taken part in two attacks and dug in twice and been heavily shelled and fired at by M.G.'s all the time. Finally the men got going and we beat the Boche off. (The General was very good to me over it and I got the D.S.O. and the Company S.M. the M.C.) I then set out to look for the Brigade on our left and finally found they had taken a real knock and were back in our jumping-off trenches a long way behind us. I finally got one company of them into some trenches north of the road which the enemy had abandoned, and soon after dark the rest came into line and the 4th Battalion of our Brigade filled up the gap between us.

"The next day the Higher Command put in a fresh Brigade of another Division to attack the buildings north of the railway. They put in a whole Brigade and told them they had a soft job and gave them a really good barrage. Poor devils, they were absolutely wiped out, about 100 men surviving. The next night we were relieved and went into reserve for a week or more, and were told we would go over the top again but were suddenly taken out for a rest. Our casualties were, I think, 1 officer killed, 10 wounded, and about 185 other ranks killed and wounded. Our rest consisted in marching and counter-marching with 4 days' halt in one village. During those 4 days one had to train Lewis-gun teams, bombers, grenadiers, etc., besides generally reorganizing. Luckily we got some top-hole drafts.

"On the night of April 30th/May 1st we came back again into much the same area; during the interval two Divisions had been practically wiped out trying to take those buildings. We had two days in the trenches and then (on May 3rd) went over the top. This time we were just south of the railway and our final objective was a line about 2 miles beyond the buildings. The Battalion did magnificently. They went bang through together with some men of another Brigade and reached the second objective about 2000 yards away. There all the surviving officers were casualties and the remnants of the Battalion fell back to the Black Line, about 1000 yards ahead of our jumping-off trench, and about 30 of them, under a Company S.M., dug in there."

At this point, which was probably the Blue Line, the Battalion was heavily swept by machine-gun fire, both frontal and enfilade. All surviving officers became casualties and the remnants of the Battalion, some 30 men, under C.S.M. Bamborough, fell back to the Black Line, where in company with remnants of different units of the 10th and 12th Brigades, about 100 men in all, they dug in. A message from Sergt. Reid stated that they were "200 yards from the railway and 30 yards in front of the Black Line; that they had about 30 men and no officers, that there were only a few of the 10th Brigade over on the right, and that the Germans were on the left." Sergt. Reid's message also said that " they were cut off " and asked for reinforcements. Sergt. Thornton and Lce.-Corpl. Elbell had brought back Sergt. Reid's message and they reported that Sergt. Reid and a party of six men had during their advance captured two German machine guns, which they buried. This was subsequently confirmed. A message was sent to C.S.M. Bamborough ordering him, if possible, to withdraw fighting to the Chemical Works. Neither of the two N.C.O.'s sent with this message succeeded in delivering it. Various attempts made later to get the message forward all failed.

"Meanwhile on the left the attack had also failed completely. They even lost some of the front-line trench, and though some men of the Brigade on the right had gone on they had never mopped the Château and other buildings near it. I had detailed a very strong company to mop up the Chemical Works and had warned every man personally that his job was not to go forward beyond there but to hold those buildings. The result was we held these all day, but the enemy had the houses on either side chock full of M.G.'s and swept the gap. The men in the Chemical Works could only just hold on in shell holes, etc. : two messengers from the Battalion got back to H.Q., and I tried all morning and early afternoon to get to them but not a single man got forward to them alive all day, after the attack had once started. I begged for reinforcements to take up and do a fresh attack on the Château and the Brigadier tried hard to get them for me, but they did not come till late in the evening and meanwhile a heavy Boche counter-attack had gone clean over the Black Line.

"The rest of that day I was holding a Battalion front with my H.Q. party and one M.G., and about one-third of the H.Q. party or more were knocked out. They had the worst barrage on us I ever saw, and every time a man showed a hand about three M.G.'s were on to him.

"Well, the reinforcements came up and took over the line ; that night, exclusive of H.Q. signallers, runners, etc., the Battalion total was 16. However, more men got back from the Chemical Works after dark, and from shell holes, and were returned by other units, and we finally mustered 54, including 9 Brigade carriers who had not been over the top. The survivors were practically all moppers-up. We went back into support, then the fragments of the Battalion, 2 platoons, were attached to the L.F.'s and were finally in close support on May 11th, when the other 2 Brigades went up again. This time they only had to capture the buildings and were not given an objective miles beyond, so they got them and the next day pushed forward about 200 yards, and then we came out of the line. Our casualties this time were 1 officer killed, 5 wounded, 6 wounded and missing. We then went out on May 13th to rest at Maizieres." When Lieut.-Colonel Horsfall went on leave Major W. G. Officer assumed temporary command. While withdrawn from the trenches the following drafts joined up. Officers : 2nd Lieuts. R. A. McDowall, E. R. G. Willey, D. Harrison, and R. Wood from 3rd Reserve Battalion. Also Lieut. P. Walsh and 119 other ranks.

"On June 8th the Corps Commander presented Lt.-Colonel A. G. Horsfall's D.S.O. at a medal presentation parade. The following extract is from Army

Orders, Third Army, 12.5.17—' Lieut.-Colonel A. G. Horsfall, 2nd Battalion Duke of Wellington's Regiment. This officer displayed the greatest gallantry and energy throughout the operations about Fampoux from the 9th to the night 12th/13th April, 1917, and it was largely due to his personal example that the operations of his Battalion were so successfully carried out. The value of his services cannot be overestimated.'"

Officers who took part in the attack on April 9th, 1917:—

Headquarters:
    Lieut.-Colonel A. G. Horsfall, D.S.O.
    Capt. F. H. Fraser, M.C.
    2nd Lieut. R. Anderton (4th Battn.)
    Capt. A. Climie, R.A.M.C.

No. 1 Company:
    Capt. L. G. Watson
    2nd Lieut. P. F. Lambert, M.C.
    " G. M. Hill (4th Battn.)
    " A. H. Larcombe (2nd Bn. Scott. Rifles)
    " W. E. Horsley (6th Battn.)

No. 2 Company:
    2nd Lieut. R. G. Crockett
    " S. M. Goldsmith
    " J. S. Braine
    " H. P. Coates

No. 3 Company:
    2nd Lieut. S. Baldwin (4th Battn.)
    " N. Patchett (5th Battn.)
    " F. S. Laughton

No. 4 Company—Carriers:
    Capt. K. E. Cunningham
    2nd Lieut. W. Rees

Battalion Reserve: 2nd Lieut. A. E. Taylor

Officers' Casualties on April 9th, 1917:—

Killed:
    2nd Lieut. A. E. Taylor

Wounded:
    Capt. L. G. Watson
    2nd Lieut. S. M. Goldsmith
    " J. S. Braine
    " S. Baldwin (4th Bn.)
    " H. P. Coates

Wounded remained on duty:
    2nd Lieut. G. M. Hill

During the attacks on April 11th the following officers were wounded:—
    2nd Lieut. R. G. Crockett
    2nd Lieut. N. Patchett (5th Battn.)

Wounded remained on duty:
    2nd Lieut. F. S. Laughton

Officers with Battalion Headquarters and Companies on night of April 11th/12th and onwards:—

Battalion Headquarters:
    Lieut.-Colonel A. G. Horsfall, D.S.O.
    Major R. J. A. Henniker, M.C.
    Capt. F. H. Fraser, M.C.
    2nd Lieut. R. Anderton
    Capt. A. Climie, R.A.M.C.

PLATE 16

SPLINTER-PROOF SHELTER IN RESERVE LINE, HALIFAX TRENCH, JULY, 1917

THE MILL AT FEUCHY

AID POST AT FAMPOUX AFTER BOMBARDMENT ON 11TH APRIL, 1917

BATTALION H.Q., FAMPOUX, APRIL, 1917
Entrance to Hall and Stairway to Cellar—
The Dark Doorway in Centre

THE "DUKE'S" IN THE 4TH DIVISION AT FAMPOUX

No. 1 Company:
    2nd Lieut. G. M. Hill
       "   A H. Larcombe
       "   W. E. Horsley

No. 2 Company:
    2nd Lieut. P. F. Lambert, M.C.

No. 3 Company:
    2nd Lieut. F. S. Laughton

No. 4 Company—Carriers:
    Capt. K. E. Cunningham
    2nd Lieut. W. Rees

The 4th Division received the thanks of the Corps Commander in the following terms. It was not the first time that Sir Charles Fergusson had tested the fighting powers of the old 5th Division.

"To General Officer Commanding 4th Division,

"I wish to express to the Division through you my congratulations and thanks for the good work they have done and the fine spirit they have shown during the operations of the last fortnight.

"Quite apart from their great success on the first day, when they broke through the fourth German system of trenches, they have held the line for nearly a fortnight without relief under the worst possible conditions of weather. Their grit and endurance have been worthy of the best traditions of the old Army, of which they are still representatives. . . .

                "CHARLES FERGUSSON,
                "Lieut.-General,
                "Commdg. XVII Corps."

21.4.1917.

Officers who took part in the attack on May 3rd, 1917:—

Battalion Headquarters:
    Lieut.-Colonel A. G. Horsfall, D.S.O.
    Capt. A. Climie, R.A.M.C.
    2nd Lieut. J. P. Colson
       "   R. Anderton

No. 1 Company:
    2nd Lieut. P. F. Lambert, M.C.
       "   A. H. Larcombe
       "   A. Middlewood

No. 2 Company:
    Capt. G. R. C. Heale, M.C.
    2nd Lieut. E. W. Adolpho
       "   J. F. Rhodes

No. 3 Company:
    2nd Lieut. G. W. Goldsworthy
       "   S. A. Belshaw

No. 4 Company:
    Capt. K. E. Cunningham
    2nd Lieut. J. D. V. Macintosh
           (4th Battn.)
       "   W. Rees
       "   H. L. Vile

Battalion Reserve:
    2nd Lieut. G. D. Johnston
    2nd Lieut. C. C. Crowther

During the attack on May 3rd the following casualties occurred to officers:—

Killed:
  2nd Lieut. H. L. Vile
    „   A. Middlewood

Wounded and Missing:
  Capt. G. R. C. Heale, M.C.
    „   K. E. Cunningham
  2nd Lieut. P. F. Lambert, M.C.
    „   J. F. Rhodes
    „   J. D. V. Macintosh (4th Battn.)

Wounded:
  2nd Lieut. G. W. Goldsworthy
    „   E. W. Adolpho

Missing:
  2nd Lieut. A. H. Larcombe
    „   S. A. Belshaw
    „   W. Rees

Wounded remained on duty:
  2nd Lieut. R. Anderton

Other ranks killed, wounded, and missing 391.

Though the spring of 1917 saw the entry of the U.S.A. into the war, so far it was an entry merely in name. Against this new asset—and on the side of the Allies it was a great moral asset—must be set the disastrous revolutionary outbreak in Russia. In that ill-fated country disintegration had begun. As the dry-rot in the Russian armies ate deeper and deeper so lighter and lighter became the pressure against Germany's eastern frontier. There was no longer any serious question of fighting on two fronts. Germany could and did begin the transfer of more and more Divisions to the Western Front. To follow, came in May–June the mutinous outbreaks in the French armies in reserve and near Paris, outbreaks which only General Pétain's wonderful force of character served to check, and which, for the time being, threw an even greater strain upon the already battle-worn British troops. Nor had the French attack on the Aisne realized early expectations, so that in the early portion of 1917 it was hard indeed to be optimistic.

Whilst the 4th Division was holding the line east of Arras Haig's great Flanders attack began with the wonderful explosion of mines at Messines and the capture of that ridge.

The latter half of June at Barossa Camp was given up to training, with the last two days, quite quiet, in the trenches. By the end of July and throughout August until mid-September the Battalion was "in and out" near Pelves and Monchy, a little further south. Cloudless skies and hot days were a wonderful change from the eternal mud of the previous winter. A big farm with, of course, an equally big manure heap in the centre of the yard, was no bad billet. To quote Colonel Horsfall's diary: "The women do work hard here. There are two girls, daughters of the farmer, I think, about fifteen or sixteen years of age, and they never seem to rest from 6 a.m. to 8 p.m. Some of our men give them a help with the milking and working of the cream-separator, etc. They certainly seem to be the best of friends. Then there is a little boy about seven or eight, and our men have taught him to box and get him to challenge all the other

AN AUGUST RAID, SUMMER OF 1917

village boys; he is as keen as mustard. The other evening I saw our Corporal in charge of the shoe-maker's shop, on his knees, with gloves on, boxing this little boy and another boy about the same size: he had to kneel down to make himself the same height as the boys."

In a Divisional Horse Show the "Duke's" showed in the pack-pony class a pony captured from the Germans at the Battle of the Marne. Such a good pony was it that the judges, two "Gunner" Generals, would not place it first, giving the Yorkshiremen the credit of putting in a charger as a pack-pony. Such is the reputation of "the Tykes" in horse-dealing! Some recompense came, however, when the Battalion cleared the board at the 12th Brigade sports. As the late spring merged into early summer immediately behind the lines a wonderful transformation was seen. "Everything green, the trees in full leaf and quite a lot of flowers about. Very pretty. Corncockles, poppies, pimpernel, stretches of yellow mustard, and a sort of purple vetch. Campions, big knurwort, a big lavender flower I forget the name of, and several other flowers one does not see in England. In places the red clover is growing of itself, and great stretches of ground are deep crimson with it. The seeds must have lain dormant a long time in the ground. . . . Every shell-hole is becoming a little flower garden, I found some of those large blue wild geraniums to-day . . . there is some tall yellow toad-flax just like a yellow snap-dragon outside my hut. . . . Cuckoo-pint is pretty common, also a flower I have never seen in England almost like an ox-eye daisy, but on a slender stem and a beautiful deep blue mauve in colour."[1] But the grim contrast of life in the trenches was never long absent. Intermittent shelling was varied by an occasional raid of enemy trenches. And to reach these across no-man's-land, one's own wire entanglement, the German's, and a wilderness of shell-holes, was on a dark night not exactly a picnic. Nor was such a raid as the following.

Report on raid on night of August 9th, 1917, 2nd Duke of Wellington's Regiment:—

The raiding party consisted of 2nd Lieut. V. F. de W. W. Vredenberg in charge, 2nd Lieut. Wood, and 38 other ranks. Object: To raid and hold Arrow Trench and act as rearguard to 2nd Essex Regiment and 12th Division.

7.20 p.m.—Enemy commenced to heavily shell Monchy ridge and north-east outskirts of Monchy village.

7.40 p.m.—2nd Lieut. Vredenberg gave the order for the party to leave the trenches. No difficulty was experienced in getting out. Enemy fire, which consisted chiefly of M.G.'s from both flanks, commenced as soon as the men got over the top.

The raiding party then crawled forward clear of our wire, got into line, then doubled about 120 yards forward and again dropped and crawled forward to Arrow Trench and the shell-holes on our side of it, the extreme right of the party being 90 yards south of Bit Lane, while the left was 30 yards north of Bit Lane. During the final crawl towards the enemy 2nd Lieut. R. Wood, who was firing at the enemy who were on the parapet of Devil's Trench, was shot

[1] Diary, Lieut.-Colonel A. G. Horsfall, D.S.O.

through the head. The Lewis gunners were on the left flank throughout the operation and continued firing until they had exhausted all their ammunition. Shortly after this both the No. 1 and No. 2 on the gun were killed.

At 8.50 p.m. 2nd Lieut. Vredenberg gave the order for the party to withdraw, the men crawling back to our line. Lieut. Vredenberg saw the last man back into our line and then crawled out again to look for wounded, and in doing so reached a point about 50 yards north of Bit Lane. He lost his bearings and had to remain in a shell-hole till 2.30 a.m., when he was able by moonlight to find his way back. During the whole period that the party was out the enemy fire was so heavy that it was impossible for men to rise up. A certain number of the enemy were observed kneeling in groups of four and five on their own parapet firing at our men. No trench mortar shells were observed to burst and a few rifle grenades passed over our party.

Casualties: 1 officer 4 other ranks killed, 5 other ranks wounded. 2nd Lieut. Vredenberg was later awarded the Military Cross. Pte. J. Knight, Military Medal. During this turn in the trenches near Monchy enemy infantry were very active with sniping, Capt. E. M. Cunningham, M.C., at the time acting as Adjutant, was unfortunately shot dead by an enemy sniper. The following night the Battalion snipers crawled out and shot the man believed responsible for the death of Capt. Cunningham, also a German officer who was believed to be killed. Lieut. E. C. Coke took over the duties of Acting Adjutant.

Such was the steady but never-ceasing wear-and-tear even in the so-called " quiet " times. Speaking of the difficulty of carrying on regimentally with a constant stream of new officers replacing others who had been wounded, a Battalion Commanding Officer wrote: "All our best officers seem to have been hit, and then just as one began to despair and wonder how to carry on a young officer who was always an absolute rotter and good at nothing was suddenly left in command of a Company and proved as gallant as any man could be and did most valuable work. It has been the making of him. Another fellow, a sleepy lethargic Cambridge Don, did very well: led his men by 40 yards in a charge although wounded two days previously and did grand work while the show was on." Besides Capt. Cunningham, who had lately joined, other officers were Capt. R. E. Edwards and 7 subaltern officers from the 3rd Battalion, 2nd Lieut. J. Heskett, 2nd Lieut. S. K. Maddrell, 2nd Lieut. Vredenberg, 2nd Lieut. G. W. Hanna, Lieut. M. C. Hoole, Lieut. D. H. W. Thomson, and 350 other ranks.

It was on September 20th that the next change took place, when the 4th Division were withdrawn from the Arras line and sent north to the Ypres salient. Once again the "Duke's" were back in, to them, familiar ground, but this time they were to sample trenches north of Ypres, east of the canal bank, Pilckem way. Entraining at Baumetz they reached railhead at Peselhoek, when they marched to Suez Camp. A week later found the Battalion entrained again for Elverdinghe. By the end of September it was holding the front line east of Pilckem on the way, it was hoped, to Passchendaele. Through August the Fifth Army, Sir Hubert Gough's, had striven hard but had failed with very heavy

CAPT. K. E. CUNNINGHAM

Q.M. & CAPT. C. SHEPHERD, M.B.E., D.C.M.

CAPT. A. CLIMIE, M.C., R.A.M.C.

CAPT. W. O. TOBIAS, R.A.M.C.

casualties to make much way. General Sir Herbert Plumer took over and other plans were maturing. September was a month of preparation, but just about the time when the 4th Division went north the British attacks recommenced along the Zonnebeke front.

On October 8th at 11 p.m. the "Duke's" moved up to the line near Louis Farm, their jumping-off point, where they were ready by 4 a.m. on the 9th.

"The last stages of the so-called Third Battle of Ypres were probably the muddiest combats ever known in the history of war. It rained incessantly—

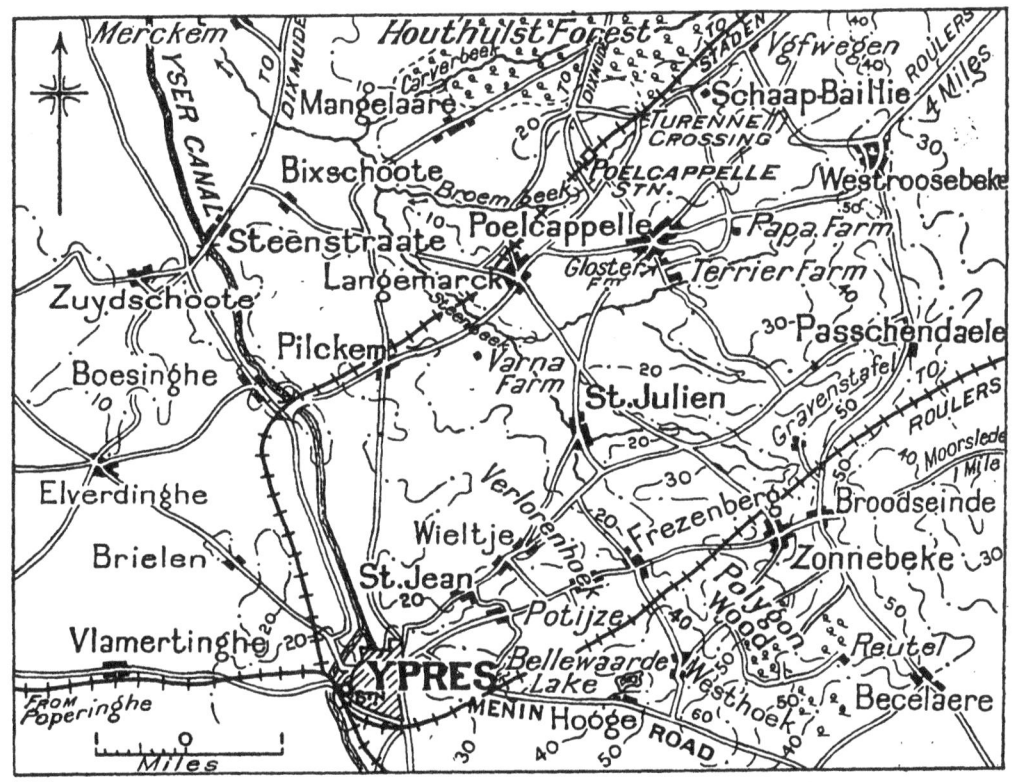

BATTLE AREA N.E. OF YPRES, SEPTEMBER–OCTOBER, 1917.

sometimes clearing to a drizzle or a Scots mist. . . . Tuesday, the 9th, was the day fixed for an advance on a broad front by both French and British, but all day on the 7th and 8th it rained and the night of the 8th was black darkness above and a melting earth beneath."[1]

The chief sector of attack so far as concerned the 4th Division was from a point east of Zonnebeke to just north-west of Langemarck. The actual objective, Poelcappelle, or what was left of it.

Zero time for the 12th Brigade was 5.20 a.m., the Duke of Wellington's being in close support when the Brigade advanced. The first objective was

[1] *A History of the Great War.* John Buchan.

captured almost at once, but the front line was held up at Landing Farm. Owing to this the "Duke's" moved up into the front line to fill a gap. Realizing the importance of the proper handling of the companies Lieut.-Colonel Horsfall was leading them up himself. Touch had been already established and the Company was moving from one shell-hole to another. Whilst giving orders to a runner Lieut.-Colonel Horsfall was picked off from the flank, a bullet passing through his heart. He only breathed a few moments. Capt. Coke and Lieut.-Colonel Horsfall's orderly, Pte. Ramsden, stayed by him all day, and this very gallant officer now lies buried in Bard Farm Cemetery, on the Yser Canal. After the death of the Commanding Officer, being the senior present, Capt. Browning assumed command of the Battalion, which moved to the support line the same evening, when Major Officer took over command. The following day Major Officer and the Adjutant, Capt. E. C. Coke, were both wounded, so Capt. J. S. Browning again took over with 2nd Lieut. Moody as Acting Adjutant. On the 11th at 1 a.m. the Battalion were withdrawn from the line and Major Henniker returned from the 1st King's Own to take over command of it.

Battalion casualties during the operations :—

Officers.—Killed : Lieut.-Colonel A. G. Horsfall, D.S.O.
  Wounded : Major W. G. Officer.
  Capt. E. C. Coke.
  Lieuts. H. N. Turner, F. S. White, P. Harrison, W. E. Horsley.
  Missing : Lieut. Johnson.

All ranks.—Killed . . . 22
  Wounded . . 99
  Missing . . . 49
  Total . . 170

Lieut.-Colonel A. G. Horsfall came straight from the 1st Battalion in India. No one could have been more overjoyed than he was at getting "out to France." Landing on October 7th, 1916, Major Horsfall fought with, and for ten months as its Lieut.-Colonel led, the 2nd Battalion in many a stirring fight, while more than one Battle Honour was being won for the Colours. Just a year "at the front," but what a year! The excitement and experience of a life-time crammed into twelve fleeting months of sublime existence. Horsfall had already won the D.S.O. As a sportsman in India the late Commanding Officer had made his mark. As a soldier in France he was rapidly making a reputation which would shortly have won him promotion and had already earned him offers of further advancement. A "soft" job behind the lines or at home had no attractions for Horsfall, though *someone* who had already been through the mill had to teach the new armies. "I said I did not think it was a man's job," was his reply to one offer. "They ought to take only fellows who are maimed or unfit for active work." He paid with his life for these refusals to leave the front, and to the

DEATH OF LIEUT.-COLONEL A. G. HORSFALL, D.S.O.

eternal honour and glory of his native land he was but one of an ever-increasing band of brothers like him. By October 23rd the Battalion was back at Arras, that town of a wonderful underworld of caves, galleries, and prospective catacombs where whole Divisions could assemble concealed even from air-craft. Schramm Barracks for " a wash and brush up " was a pleasant change, but the end of the month saw the " Duke's " into the trenches east of Wancourt. " In and out " from Arras during November saw the fourth winter approaching. The beginning of November saw also Major R. J. A. Henniker, M.C., promoted and in command of the 2nd Battalion. Throughout the cold, dreary months until spring came the " Duke's " endured the usual fighting routine. But the amenities of trench life which helped to make it possible were a wonderful change from the first winter in Flanders. Extra winter clothing consisting of fur waistcoats or leathern jerkins, woollen underclothing, gloves, waterproof cap-covers, etc., were an improvement on the not exactly wind or water-proof khaki great-coat of 1914!

Christmas Day was spent at Arras in Schramm Barracks where, thanks partly to the contributions of " old Duke's," both officers and men made up for lost time in the way of meals. " A splendid Christmas dinner " was the general verdict. Earlier in the month the 12th Brigade had paraded for a presentation of ribbons by Lieut.-General Sir Charles Fergusson, Bart. In the Battalion the following officer, N.C.O.'s, and men were decorated. With D.C.M.'s: Sergt. Dyson and Lce.-Corpl. Hood. Military Medals: Pte. Dockerty, Lce.-Corpl. Shenall, Pte. Field, Pte. Burke, Pte. Chaplin. Capt. E. C. Jervis was awarded the M.C.

Addressing the 12th Infantry Brigade at the presentation Sir Charles Fergusson said:—

" . . . I want to impress upon all ranks that there are two things necessary to win. The first is discipline and the second is determination. . . . This parade to-day is in order to give ribbons to officers, N.C.O.'s, and men of this Brigade which have been won by our comrades in the recent fighting. . . I might add that every one of these officers, N.C.O.'s and men have been decorated for some conspicuous act of gallantry in battle, either by holding on under most trying conditions, or by saving the lives of comrades by carrying them in when wounded. We feel proud of them and hold them in high esteem and are very grateful for what they have done. . . ."

CHAPTER XIII

JANUARY, 1918–NOVEMBER, 1918: GERMAN PLANS FOR 1918 OFFENSIVE. MARCH OFFENSIVE. TRANSFERRED TO 10TH BRIGADE. ARRAS. LA BASSEE CANAL, PACAUT WOOD. A "RUGGER" RAID. VIS EN ARTOIS. STIPE COPSE. ST. SERVIN'S FARM. SAULTZOIR, VERCHAIN, THE PIMPLE AND HERMAN STELLUNG. PRESEAU. BACK TO MONS. THE ARMISTICE.

NEW YEAR'S DAY of January, 1918, though few realized it, heralded the dawn of a new world to the millions of fighting men at that time in arms. The end of 1918 was to see the curtain fall on a drama which had wellnigh ruined Europe and had shaken the very foundations of civilization. "What made this war different from all others," wrote General Ludendorff, "was the manner in which the home populations supported and reinforced their armed forces with all the resources at their disposal. Only in France in 1870–1871 had anything of the kind been seen before."

Such had been the general trend of events on the Western Front in 1917 that the German Supreme Command—now Ludendorff and Hindenburg—elected for a decisive battle attack in the early spring of 1918. Writing to his Supreme War Lord—the late Kaiser—in February, 1918, to report, Ludendorff emphasized that "the battle in the west which the year 1918 will bring presents the biggest military problem ever set before an army."[1]

The well-nigh insuperable difficulties facing this extraordinary man prior to the great German attack in 1918 were sufficient to have disturbed the serenity of Napoleon or Wellington themselves. That they were manifold and of vital importance goes without saying, but from the first two main objects were clear to the master mind of Ludendorff. The first was that his best chance lay in making the main attack against the British armies, so he thought. The second, that a wedge must be inserted and the French and British armies separated entirely on this front of attack. Among subsidiary points to be considered were the necessity for having a strong natural feature like the River Somme on the immediate left of the German main advance in order to prevent a French thrust on its flank; the advisability of starting the attack at the tactically weakest point in the British 140-mile front; and the necessity for dealing once and for all with the British armies on French soil before turning to polish off their French allies. Such, baldly and inadequately summarized, were

[1] *My War Memories*, General Ludendorff, 1914–1918, Vol. I.

THE BEGINNING OF THE END

the guiding principles by which Ludendorff and his gigantic General Staff worked in the spring of 1918. March 10th saw the commencement of the bringing up of the German munitions. On March 21st this great German attack began. Already Ludendorff had been obliged to form special *Stoss-truppen*, picked battalions for attack. These *Stoss-truppen* consisted of:—

    1 Machine Gun Company with 6 machine guns.
    4 Infantry Companies, each of 100 men.
    1 Bombing Company.
    1 Flame-throwing Company.
    1 Battery of Assault Artillery.

But these were in themselves a confession of loss of morale. The attack was delivered on a front nearly 50 miles in breadth by three German armies, the Seventeenth, Second, and Eighteenth, between Croiselles, 8 miles south-east of Arras, southwards to La Fère, 15 miles north-west of Laon. It took both the Third and Fifth British Armies by surprise and until March 25th the Eighteenth and left of the Second German Armies continued to win their way west.

While Ludendorff's stupendous effort was making itself felt south of Arras, the "Duke's" lay just north of the immediate battle front. The 10th Brigade to which they now belonged held trenches in the Roeux sector. January had been passed still near Arras. Major P. L. E. Walker, 7th Hussars, was then in command of the Battalion. Their medical officer, Capt. A. Climie, who had been with them since February, 1917, had received promotion to command the Convalescent Base Camp at Etaples. He had also been mentioned in New Year Honours for conspicuous service. February, except for a successful raid and the cold, was almost monotonous. 2nd Lieuts. Caldwell and McDowall, with 60 N.C.O.'s and men and 4 stretcher-bearers, were the team for this raid. The object of the raid can have left no room for doubt in the minds of those concerned as to what was required of them. In the somewhat bald phraseology employed in Battalion Orders the object of the raid was stated as follows : " Object of raid is to take prisoners, secure identification, kill Germans, capture M.G.'s, and destroy dug-outs." That these instructions were to some extent at any rate carried out is to be gathered from the fact that the raiding party brought back 5 German prisoners of the 139 I.R. 24th Division (Saxon) and that 2nd Lieut. Caldwell was awarded the Military Cross.

During January and February the following officers and drafts joined up : 2nd Lieuts. H. G. Henderson and W. H. Roy, A. King, H. G. Card, E. C. Capon, and Wildbourne, with 250 other ranks. A further and welcome addition from the 8th Battalion of the "Duke's" consisted of Capt. L. Shaw, M.C., Lieut. H. Livsey, 2nd Lieuts. G. S. Lomax, W. Susman, F. Griggs, F. Charlesworth, R. W. Lee (3rd Battn.), and L. Morris, with 158 other ranks.

In the second week of February the Battalion left the 12th Infantry Brigade to join the 10th Brigade. The latter was composed of the 2nd Duke of Wellington's, 1st Royal Warwickshires, and 2nd Seaforth Highlanders.

The early portion of March was spent in steady training at Arras, Major

W. G. Officer taking over command from Lieut.-Colonel P. L. E. Walker. Then came the greatest effort in the history of war, Ludendorff's push for Amiens. The immediate effect, so far as concerned the " Duke's," was the formation of a defensive flank along the north bank of the River Scarpe, the Division on their right having withdrawn over a mile. At the end of the month the Battalion was holding what was known locally as the Army Line. On the 28th the Germans attacked in strength the front line Battalion and about 3 p.m. the troops from there commenced to fall slowly back on the Army Line. Later, part of the ground lost was retaken by No. 1, 2, and 3 Companies of the " Duke's," the West Yorks, and the K.O.S.B.'s. Barring M.G. fire not much opposition was encountered. Casualties included 2nd Lieut. R. A. McDowall and 47 other ranks wounded, 9 other ranks killed, and 8 missing. Capt. W. S. Newroth and 2nd Lieut. M. Banham were admitted to hospital suffering from poison by lethal gas.

April saw a change in position. On the 14th the 10th Infantry Brigade relieved the 76th Brigade on the bank of the La Bassée Canal, and the following day an attack was made with the Warwicks on Pacaut Wood. The " Duke's " attacked from the west, the Warwicks from the south-east (see map, p. 176). Heavy German attacks were being made against the 4th Division front, but these were repulsed after severe fighting. The operation at Pacaut Wood cost the " Duke's " the following casualties: Officers killed—2nd Lieut. Hughes and 2nd Lieut. Heskett. Died of wounds—2nd Lieut. J. Stocks (6th Battn.). Wounded—Capt. J. S. Browning, M.C., 2nd Lieuts. Caldwell, M.C., H. G. Card, W. H. Roy, Henderson, and A. King. Missing: Lieut. Walker. Other ranks—killed, 32; wounded, 179; missing, 7. Posthumous awards were made to 2nd Lieut. Hughes and Pte. Naylor of M.C. and M.M. For the next few days the Battalion was in trenches on the canal bank near Hinges, where, as Lieut.-Colonel Officer was twice wounded, Major Berkley took over command. Up to the end of August the vicinity of Pacaut Wood and the La Bassée Canal saw the Battalion " in and out," and in the West Front sense of the words hard at work in the fighting line. Daily shelling, German attacks, raids, and counter-attacks prevented any monotony. They also caused those steady yet never-ceasing casualties to officers, N.C.O.'s and men which some considered the only way to win the war—provided it was the enemy who suffered.

At the end of April Lieut.-Colonel F. Pawlett, Canadian Army, took over command of the Battalion and 14 new officers joined—Lieut. W. A. Croxson, 2nd Lieuts. G. T. M. McCulloch, T. A. Blackburn, S. Johnson, J. H. Law, H. H. Anson, G. E. Craven, H. Fillingham, B. Hebblethwaite, W. G. MacFarlane, H. W. Little, W. Butler, A. K. Morgan, W. Tunstall, and V. Biddle (5th Battn.).

All through the second quarter of the year the German attack continued with fierce determination. The Amiens thrust had just fallen short of its object, although Ludendorff persisted elsewhere all along the Western Front. But these various attempts to break through do not directly concern this narrative.

May, when " out," was spent for the most part at L'Ecleme. When " in," the usual toll was exacted from all ranks. Early in the month 2nd Lieuts. Lomax, Morgan, and McFarlane were wounded, 2nd Lieut. McCulloch knocked out by

PLATE 18

SERGT. J. BOURN, D.C.M.

SERGT. J. R. OGDEN, D.C.M.

SERGT. A. BUTTERWORTH

PRIVATE F. HARTE

shell fire, and 2nd Lieut. Wildbourne killed. A small raid in order to obtain enemy identification took place early one morning. The raid savoured somewhat of the dash of the "three-quarter line" in a Rugger final, and possibly for that reason appealed specially to C Company of the "Duke's." At 8 a.m. Corpl. Padley and six men dashed over and came upon an unoccupied enemy post. Still seeking, metaphorically, the adversary's goal line, the "three-quarters," pushing further ahead and slightly left, came across a post occupied by three of the enemy. One ran away—small blame to him—the other two were collared. In four minutes by the Referee's whistle the raiding party were back behind their own goal line. A model of a raid, it may fairly be said, covered, incidentally, by an intense concentration of Lewis gun fire on both flanks of the raided posts. The two prisoners were a German N.C.O. and a musketeer belonging to the 5th R.I.R.

During the month the following officers, N.C.O.'s, and men were awarded distinctions: Capt. D. G. R. Bilham, M.C.; Sergts. Bourne and Ogden, and Corpl. Tustin, the D.C.M.; Sergt. Howlett, Ptes. Gardner, R. Wood, J. Carrol, F. Tidswell, A. Rennison awarded M.M. Major R. N. Carr, M.C. (6th Service Battn.), Border Regiment, joined as Second-in-Command and 2nd Lieut. Huffam and 60 other ranks. That the home drafts were not of the physique or age they had been was already becoming apparent. The drain on the manhood of England had never ceased. But it was the same with both Allies and the enemy, the latter, unaided, having to find the fresh material, "cannon-fodder as the Germans called it," to replenish their terrible losses as their attacks continued.

June was very quiet on the Brigade front at La Bassée, as was July with the exception of a successful raid on Pacaut Wood. Five officers and 200 other ranks had been taken out of the line a week previously to prepare for this raid. The officers taking part were Capt. F. H. Hill in command, 2nd Lieuts. G. E. Craven, M. Banham, J. P. Huffam, and H. W. Little. Accompanying the party were three sappers from 526 (Durham) Field Company R.E. The raiders were divided into four platoons of 50 N.C.O.'s and men each, with 3 Lewis guns and 8 stretcher-bearers. As a sample of the effect of previous training in team work the raid was a complete success.

The details, insignificant as in one sense they were, show in what a high state of discipline the Battalion remained all through those long years of trench warfare.

"A detachment of the Battalion will carry out a raid on July 18th, 1918.
Intention: To clear a sector of Pacaut Wood in two phases, and capture the garrison, thus obtaining identifications and causing casualties.
Phase 1: Penetrating and clearing houses, orchards, and enemy positions immediately outside the north-east edge of Pacaut Wood.
Phase 2: To penetrate and clear from north to south-west so much of Pacaut Wood as lies within the limits named.
No titles, regimental patches, or other articles which might cause identification are to be worn by any of the party. Special raid identity discs are being issued. White bands will be worn on the left arm."

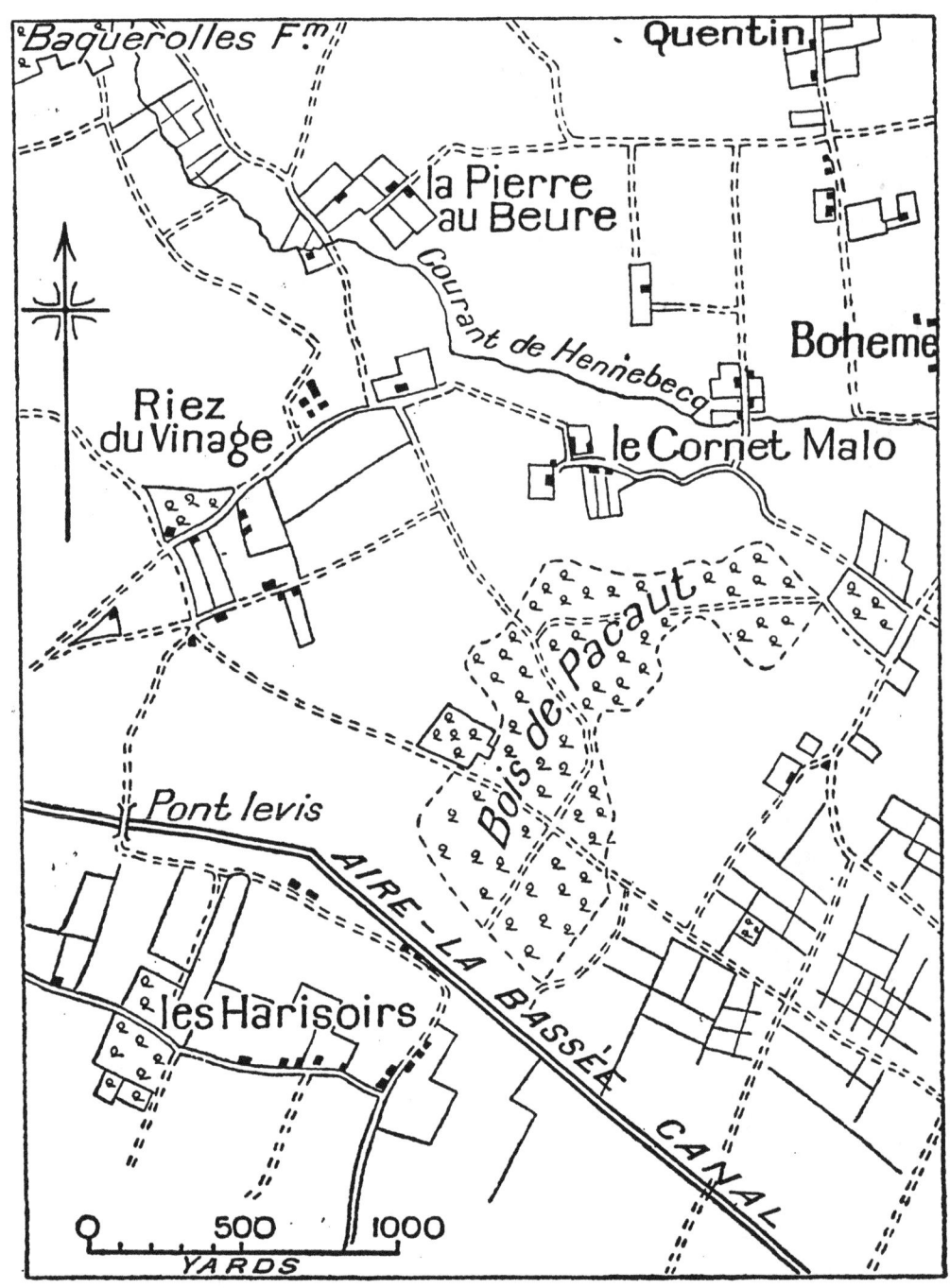

PACAUT WOOD.

COMMENCEMENT OF THE FINAL ADVANCE

Simultaneously with the coming down of the artillery barrage punctually at 2.30 p.m., zero time, the first wave mounted the parapet, followed at 25-yards' intervals by the other three waves (A, B, C, and D Platoons).

A Platoon advanced to within 50 to 60 yards of the barrage, halting, and on the latter lifting each party of 10 men rushed on its objectives, which included a known enemy M.G. post, which was taken, as also were prisoners. All other objectives were reached as per schedule without encountering the expected opposition from the orchard fence or having many casualties.

The second phase, the advance back to the Battalion lines through the sector of the wood, was begun by means of signals, the blowing of horns, first by the officer in command of the party, then it was taken up along the line. Owing to the thick bush the passage through the wood was in places extremely difficult.

The Battalion's own line in Wood Lane was reached approximately at Zero plus 20, the whole operation occupying twenty minutes.

Enemy casualties: Stokes barrage on their main line of resistance in the wood caused many enemy casualties. Evidence of dug-outs being blown in and occupants being killed was apparent in many places. Some refused to surrender and were shot or blown up with Mills grenades. In one case a M.G. and its crew were thus disposed of. The estimated enemy casualties in that sector of the wood were between 30 and 40. In addition to these, enemy were seen to run out from the wood, and they must have been caught in our protective barrage and casualties would certainly occur. The number of prisoners brought in was 29, these having been captured in parties of 2 to 8. One M.G. was captured and 3 destroyed.

Our casualties were 5 killed, 25 wounded, 2 missing, known to be killed. Messages of congratulation on the successful raid reached the " Duke's " from the Army Corps, Division, and Brigade Commanders.

Early in August resolute and systematic patrolling gave rise to the suspicion that the Germans were evacuating the section of the line opposed to that the Brigade was holding. A patrol of the " Duke's," 4 men under 2nd Lieut. L. A. Morris, located a listening-post of the enemy, took 1 prisoner and disposed of the rest. More patrols were sent forward and as no enemy was located the Brigade line was advanced until the village of Quentin was captured. A Company of the " Duke's," under Capt. M. C. Hoole, with the Warwicks and 2nd Seaforths, were responsible for this, the Company greatly distinguishing itself though it suffered somewhat, chiefly from enemy machine guns: 7 killed and 27 wounded was the bill it had to pay. Decorations for the last raid were awarded to the following officers, N.C.O.'s, and men: Capt. F. H. Hill, 2nd Lieut. M. Banham, and 2nd Lieut. G. E. Craven received the M.C.; Sergt. Denton and Pte. W. Marshall the D.C.M.

On August 24th the Brigade were taken out of the line and *via* Lozinghem and Pernes entrained for Pt. Hovvin, whence they marched to Villers au Bois. From Mont St. Eloi the Battalion entrained and finally reached St. Catherine, near Arras. A march to an assembly point at Feuchy Chapel took it with right flank resting on the Arras–Cambrai Road, to where the 4th Canadian Division was holding the line. Just in front of Vis en Artois this line ran, on August 28th, along the near banks of the River Sensee. Losing no time, patrols from the "Duke's" the following day pushed forward and captured Haucourt, occupying a line immediately east of that place. On the 30th and 31st forward attacks continued. The fighting was close, and though the men went forward magnificently and attained the final object allotted to them, they found both flanks in

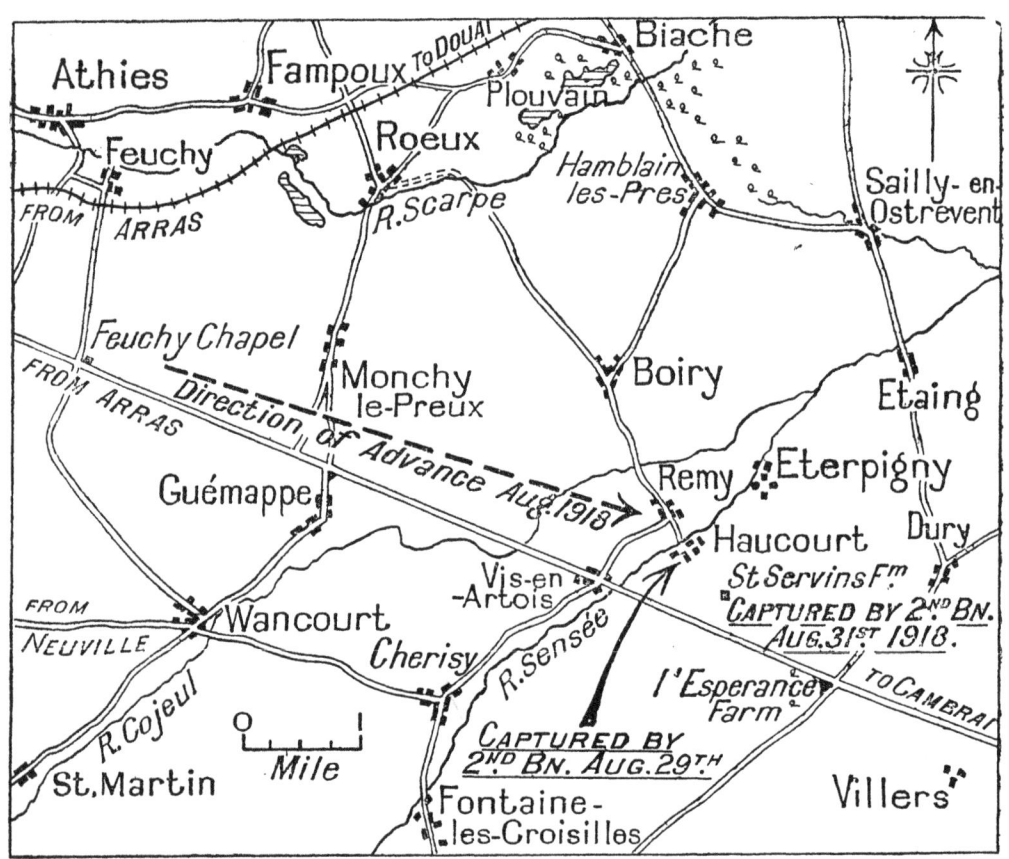

DIRECTION OF ADVANCE OF 2ND BATTALION, AUGUST, 1918.

the air. Throwing out protective flanks they fell back to the first objective, bringing in 43 prisoners and 1 officer. 2nd Lieuts. J. E. Ward and H. W. Little were killed, 2nd Lieuts. W. Tunstall, B. Hebblethwaite, L. Morris, M. Banham, M.C., and S. Johnson were wounded; 36 other ranks were killed, 162 wounded, and 7 missing. On the last day of August an unsuccessful attack, without any barrage, took place in the morning to capture a small copse. Unsuccessful in that owing to depleted numbers a heavy counter-attack, preceded by a violent bombardment, forced the "Duke's" out of the copse, having already gained possession of it.

PLATE 19

LIEUT. J. P. HUFFAM, V.C.

THE SITUATION IN SEPTEMBER, 1918

At dusk, however, the morning's failure was retrieved in style. In splendid form the "Duke's" recaptured Stipe Copse and St. Servin's Farm, taking 45 prisoners, including 2 officers. The Battalion's losses that day were: Killed—2nd Lieut. D. O. Watmough and 2nd Lieut. Anson. Died of wounds—2nd Lieut. S. Johnson. Gassed—2nd Lieut. T. A. Blackburn; Lieut. C. Skelton, M.C., was also admitted to hospital. Other ranks—14 killed, 36 wounded, 17 missing. During this operation the Battalion captured 9 enemy machine guns and 1 enemy field-gun.

On September 1st the following message appeared in orders:—

"4th Division, G.A. 86,
10th Brigade, No. B.M. 45.

"10th Infantry Brigade,

"The G.O.C. wishes you to convey to Lieut.-Colonel Pawlett and all ranks of the 2nd Duke of Wellington's Regiment his great appreciation of the magnificent way in which this Battalion has fought during the past days' heavy fighting east of Monchy.

"The Battalion has shown fighting spirit worthy of the best traditions.

"(Signed) LAWRENCE CARR,
"Lieut.-Colonel, General Staff, 4th Division.

"*1st September*, 1918."

All through July and August the British and French armies had been improving their positions. Byng's and Rawlinson's armies had cleared Amiens and the British line of communication, and had driven the enemy back first from Montdidier, then to Peronne. In early August Ludendorff commenced his withdrawal, and after his intention had been understood he got little peace. On September 2nd, with Rawlinson's army eastward of Peronne, Haig struck again, this time astride the Arras–Cambrai Road against what was known as the Drocourt–Quéant Switch. On September 1st the "Duke's" with the 1st Warwicks attacked and captured Pear Trench and then next day became the Battalion in Divisional Reserve. On the 4th the "Duke's" marched to Tilloy and there "embussed" for Averdoignt, some 5 miles east of St. Pol. Until September 18th the Battalion were right back resting and required it. Then came orders for a move back to the fighting line and there it took over the L'Eclase sector from the 8th Middlesex of the 56th Division. The end of the month found the "Duke's" on their old ground near St. Servin's Farm and conditions fairly quiet. While at rest at Averdoignt various details had joined up. Officers: 2nd Lieuts. R. C. Harvey, V. R. Shaw, W. Starkey, B. Houghton, L. Wolfenden, H. C. Kay, W. McHugh, and T. Walsh, with 180 other ranks.

The first ten days of October were passed at Arras (St. Catherine's), where the opportunity was taken for practising open warfare. The very name sounded strange when for four long years men had been accustomed to burrow like moles and never to show above a parapet unless they were " asking for it." It has been said, and with truth, once fighting above ground had become fashionable once more, that " trained soldiers fight best with rifles. Men get tired of carrying grenades and chaut-chaut clips ; the guns cannot, even under most favourable conditions, keep pace with the advancing infantry. Machine-gun crews have a way of getting killed at the start ; trench mortars and one-pounders are not always possible. But *the rifle and bayonet go anywhere a man can go, and the rifle and the bayonet win battles.*"[1] Machine-gun nests were the chief weapon of defence the now retiring Germans depended upon ; and manfully was this new type of rearguard handled. But they *had* to be captured or the advance was held up. On moving back into Arras the Battalion was played in by the brass band of the 4th Battalion the Duke of Wellington's Regiment.

On the 11th the 2nd Battalion was moved forward by busses to the outskirts of Cambrai and from there marched to St. Olle, thence to Naves, and on the 18th relieved one of its own sister battalions, the 1/6th, in the Saultzoir sector. The position at this time—midway between Cambrai and Valenciennes—meant advances which even a few weeks back were hardly considered possible. In Saultzoir the " Duke's " took over outposts which consisted of a line guarding the approaches to the river, all the bridges over which had been blown up. The rest of the Battalion were on the Main Line of Resistance on the hill in rear of the village. The task set before the 4th Division was as follows :—

It was to press forward by stages on the lines—
(1) Haspres–Saultzoir.
(2) Monchaux–Verchain–Sommaing.
(3) South of Maing–Querenaing–Artres.

The first phase was given to the 10th Brigade on the right, to the 11th Brigade on the left.

The second phase to the 10th Brigade on the right, to the 12th Brigade on the left.

The third phase to the 11th Brigade on the left, to the 12th Brigade on the right.

The two attacks affecting the 2nd Battalion covered a period of eight days, 18th to 25th October, and the operations were as follows :—

On the night of the 19th and morning of the 20th the " Duke's " took Saultzoir in advance of schedule time by crossing the stream and, mainly, by peaceful penetration. There was a little fighting for the railway. During the 20th the 2nd Seaforths passed through the " Duke's " and captured the high ground ; the latter assisting and taking up a position in support. On the 23rd further orders for attack were issued for phase 2 as above. This included Querenaing as a possible objective.

[1] From *Fix Bayonets!* By John W. Thomason, Junr., Captain U.S. Marine Corps, 1926.

PLATE 20

LIEUT.-COLONEL F. H. B. WELLESLEY

LIEUT.-COLONEL C. J. PICKERING, C.M.G., D.S.O.

CAPTURE OF THE PIMPLE AND THE SUNKEN ROAD 181

On the 23rd the 10th Brigade attacked, supported by a shrapnel barrage of 6 brigades of Field Artillery. Speaking of these artillery barrages General Ludendorff had ideas of his own not shared by most German infantry soldiers.

"The barrage had come to be regarded as a universal panacea," he wrote.[1] "The infantry insisted on it, but unfortunately it had come to confuse many sound theories. A barrage is all very well in theory, but in practice only too often it collapses under the storm of the enemy's 'Destruction Fire.' Our infantry, which had come to rely on the barrage alone for protection, were far too inclined to forget that they had to defend themselves by their personal efforts."

On the right of the attack were the "Duke's," on the left the 1st Warwicks. They captured Verchain, the line of the River Ecaillon, the high ground, and Mur Copse in one operation. The enemy were in force, first, on the line of railway, secondly, on the line of the river, thirdly, on the high ground, again at Mur Copse, and finally at the Sunken Road on the Pimple, and east of that point, where they had dug a system of trenches and put up wire entanglements. The country was extraordinarily difficult, and the enemy with numerous machine guns were strongly posted, but all these obstacles were overcome by the efficient leadership of the officers and N.C.O.'s, and by the fighting qualities of the men.

Dawn on the 24th found the Battalion a little short of its objectives, the Pimple, Sunken Road, and trenches in rear. Its right was in the air owing to the failure of the 51st Division to reach its objective "on time." There had been heavy casualties already. The Divisional Staff, whilst not insisting on its capture, intimated that it was a vital matter for future operations that the Division should be in possession of the Pimple and the trenches behind it. This led to a hastily organized attack in the afternoon under a shrapnel barrage. The attack was entirely successful with the Battalion organized into two companies: the right under the command of Capt. J. Cook, M.C., the left under Lieut. J. A. Lennon, M.C. The "Duke's" took all the high ground and the trenches already referred to with many prisoners and machine guns. This with slight casualties. The losses in the earlier phase when capturing the village, river, and Herman Stellung had been over 200 killed and wounded. So far as the Battalion was concerned this for the time being ended the operations of October 18th to 25th. Their value may be gathered from the fact that over 350 prisoners were captured, with 31 machine guns and 2 Minnenwerfers. The country operated over was most difficult, yet objectives were gained of great value to future operations. On the night of the 24th October alone the enemy was compelled to withdraw a distance of over 2,000 yards.

On the night of the 24th the 10th Brigade was relieved, though the "Duke's" were kept in the line until the next operation had started. On the morning of the 25th patrols discovered early the withdrawal of the enemy, so the Battalion established itself in its final objective, the 11th Brigade passing over to continue operations. The "Duke's" returned to their billets in Verchain. During the operations described the following casualties occurred: Officer killed—2nd Lieut. L. Wolfenden. Officers wounded—2nd Lieut. W. McHugh,

[1] *My War Memories.* Ludendorff.

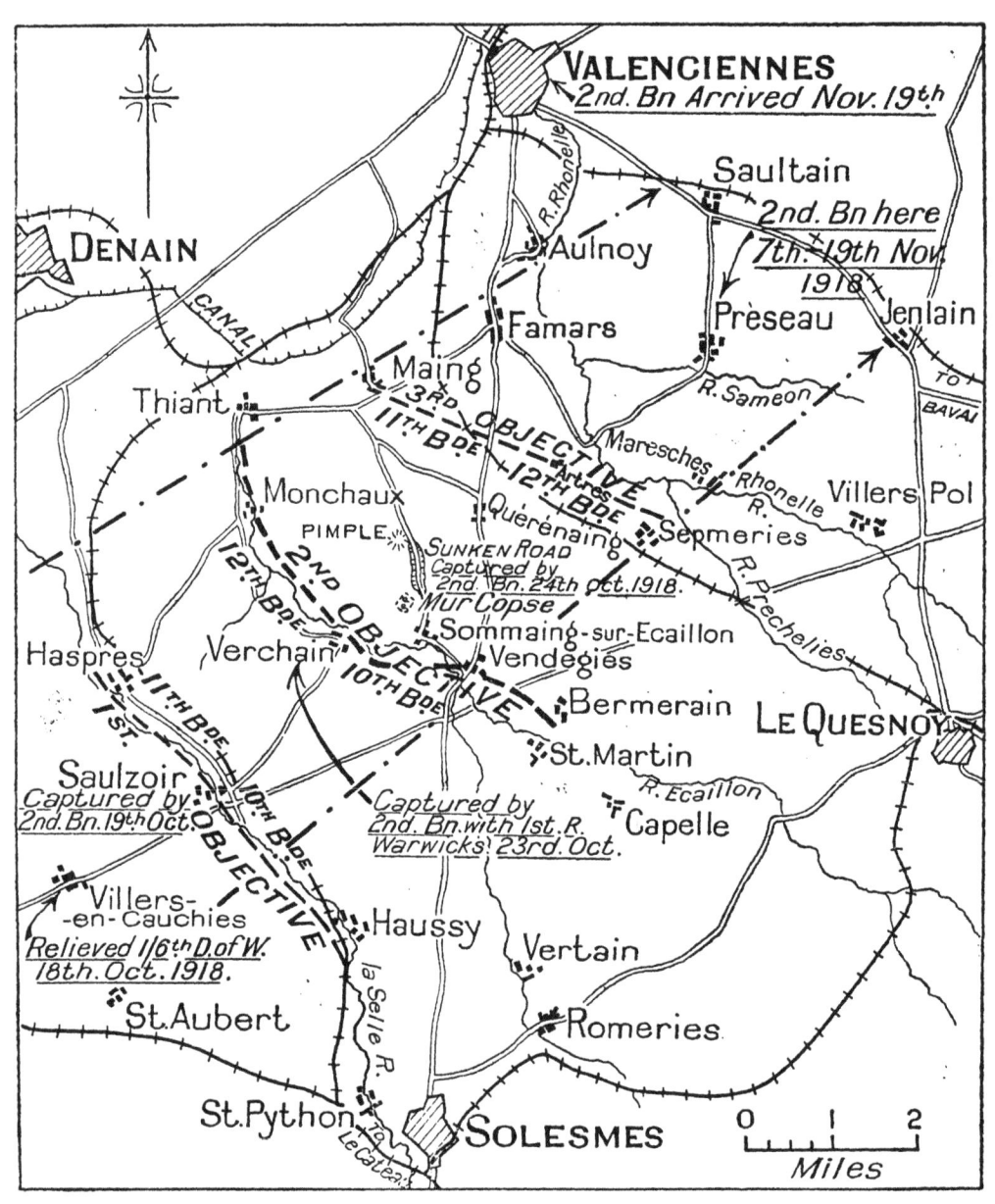

MOVEMENTS OF THE 2ND BATTALION, OCTOBER–NOVEMBER, 1918.

Lieut. G. Jackson, Lieut. H. Livsey, M.C., Lieut. F. E. C. Shearme, M.C., 2nd Lieut. H. C. Kay, 2nd Lieut. T. A. Blackburn, and Capt. F. H. Hill, M.C. Other ranks—killed 46, wounded 163. Awards published in Divisional Orders for gallantry at St. Servin's Farm were: Lieut.-Colonel F. Pawlett the D.S.O. Bar to the M.C., to Capt. M. C. Hoole, M.C. The M.C. to Capt. J. Cook and to Lieut. H. Livsey. The D.C.M. to Sergt. W. Reed and Corpl. J. R. Kliber.

To the end of October and on into early November the Battalion remained at Verchain, as usual training hard.

Meantime events of vast importance had been occurring elsewhere. As early as October 1st the German Supreme Command, exemplified in Hindenburg and Ludendorff, were confessing to their civil politicians and statesmen that there must be a peace at any price. That marvellous machine, the German Army, if it had not yet broken down, was almost worn out, refusing to work any longer. By October 5th President Wilson had been approached and asked to mediate a peace for Germany. The fighting which took place the ensuing week was perhaps the decisive factor in ending the war. By mid-October the British and French armies had reached, in places, comparatively open country. At long last fighting above ground took the place of trenching and mining. German defence on the West Front, if not already collapsed, was crumbling fast. Men thought in terms of Foch and Haig, no longer in those of Ludendorff and Hindenburg. On October 26th Ludendorff resigned, Germany's last hope. The man could do no more.

November 3rd saw the 2nd Battalion marching to Saultzoir, the end rapidly approaching. There it remained until November 7th. On the 4th Haig continued the offensive on a front of 30 miles from Valenciennes, in the north, to Oisy on Sambre, in the south. On the 7th the "Duke's" were at Preseau, barely 20 miles from Mons. They had almost completed the circle. On the same date, a day of final disillusion to every German born into the world, the Kaiser's peace delegates left Berlin. Their destination was a train in the Forest of Compiegne, where sat the Allied representative, Marshal Foch.

Terms were asked for, terms already decided upon given them. In seventy-two hours they must be accepted or refused. The mentality of the delegates being German, they proposed a provisional suspension of hostilities. The answer was, Fight on. Berlin, consulted, had perforce to accept unconditionally. 5 a.m. on November 11th saw the Armistice signed. By 11 a.m. peace reigned from Switzerland to the sea. The greatest war in history was over.

In the extraordinarily virile language of a consummate master of English prose, this for four long years is what happened:—

" For month after month the ceaseless cannonade continued at its utmost intensity, and month after month the gallant divisions of heroic human beings were torn to pieces in this terrible rotation. Then came the winter pouring down rain from the sky to clog the feet of men, and drawing veils of mist before the hawk-eyes of their artillery. . . . A vast sea of ensanguined mud, churned by thousands of vehicles, by hundreds of thousands of men and millions of shells replaced the blasted dust. Still the struggle continued. Still the remorseless wheels revolved. Still the auditorium of artillery roared. At last the legs of men could no longer move; they wallowed and floundered helplessly in the slime. Their food, their ammunition lagged behind them along the smashed and choked roadways. Unconquerable except by death, which they had conquered, they have set up a monument of native virtue which will command the wonder, the reverence, and the gratitude of our island people as long as we endure as a nation among men."[1]

. . . .

Though the Great War was over the vast military machine of which the 2nd Duke of Wellington's Regiment was a humble cog-wheel had to be kept running. During the remainder of the month of November, 1918, subsequent to the Armistice, training was carried on, officers and other ranks continued to join up, and honours already earned were distributed. Among the latter were the following: Bar to the M.M.—Lce.-Corpl. Hainsworth, M.M., Ptes. Bates and J. Spellman, M.M. M.M.—Sergt. T. Cooper; Corpls. H. Prior, A. Ball, S. Cockroft, E. Walker; Lce.-Corpls. Cunningham and G. W. Wormald; Ptes. Hills, W. Kirby, C. G. Brook (Acting Lce.-Corpl.), J. Carrol, D. Bates, H. Doyle, S. W. Bowers, C. Bates, J. Costello.

On November 19th the Battalion marched to Valenciennes, where it moved into billets. The time was spent partly in practising long-forgotten ceremonial drill and rifle-range shooting, in both of which almost unknown exercises military routine once more came into its own. On December 4th the Battalion had the honour of parading before His Majesty the King, and two days later a Colour-party left for England to bring back the Colours.

Boxing, football, and Divisional tug-of-war competitions helped to keep all ranks fit: but most men felt the change from hard and severe exercise to comparative inaction. Demobilization had already begun. During December the following decorations and awards already earned fell to the Battalion: The V.C.—2nd Lieut. J. P. Huffam. The D.S.O—Capt. J. A. Lennon, M.C., 2nd Lieut. (Acting Capt.) J. Cook, M.C. The M.C.—2nd Lieut. W. Starkey. Bar to M.C.—Temporary Capt. G. D. Watkins, D.S.O., M.C., R.A.M.C. The D.C.M.—Sergts. A. W. Harrison, M.M., and A. Frear.

"WAR OFFICE,
26th December, 1918.

His Majesty The King has been graciously pleased to approve of the award of the Victoria Cross to the undermentioned Officers, N.C.O's, and Men :—

. . . .

2nd Lt. James Palmer Huffam, 5th Battalion, W. Rid. R. (T.F.), attd. 2nd Battalion.

For most conspicuous bravery and devotion to duty on the 31st Aug., 1918. With three men, he rushed an enemy machine-gun post and put it out of action. His post was then heavily attacked and he withdrew fighting,

[1] *The World Crisis*, 1916-1918, Part I. By the Rt. Hon. Winston S. Churchill, C.H., M.P.

OFFICERS OF THE 2ND BATTALION CADRE WHO RETURNED FROM FRANCE IN 1919
Capt. D. G. R. Bilham, M.C. Q.M. & Lieut. C. Sheppard, M.B.E., D.C.M. Capt. J. Cook, D.S.O., M.C. Lieut. J. P. Colson, M.C., M.M. Major F. H. B. Wellesley.
Lieut.-Colonel F. Paulett, D.S.O.
(Saskatchewan Regt.)

CADRE OF 2ND BATTALION, HALIFAX, 16TH JUNE, 1919

Back row.—(1) Not known, (2) Corpl. A. Humphries, (3) Not known, (4) Pte. A. Huckleby, (5) Pte. F. Day, (6) Corpl. H. Beaumont, (7) Corpl. T. Beirne, M.M.

Third row.—(1) Pte. F. Finan, (2) Pte. S. Aveyard, (3) Pte. H. Smith, (4–7) Not known, (8) Pte. Costello, M.M., (9) Not known, (10) Pte. F. Townson, (11) Pte. G. Hawe, (12) Pte. F. Whitwam, (13) Not known.

Second row.—(1) Corpl. D. G. Houghton, (2) Not known, (3) C.Q.M. Sergt. A. Harvey, D.C.M., M.M., (4) Q.M. and Lieut. C. Shepherd, M.B.E., D.C.M., (5) Capt. J. Cook, D.S.O., M.C., (6) Major F. H. B. Wellesley, (7) Lieut.-Colonel F. Pawlet, D.S.O., (8) Capt. D. G. R. Bilham, M.C., (9) Lieut. J. P. Colson, M.M., (10) R.Q.M. Sergt. W. Nicholson, (11) Sergt. E. Moseley, (12) Pte. A. Butterworth, (13) No: known.

Front row (on ground).—(1 & 2) Not known, (3) Sergt. J. H. Shaw, D.C.M., (4) Sergt. H. Waller, M.M., (5 & 6) Not known, Sergt. F. Short, M.M.

PLATE 22

RETURN TO ENGLAND OF 2ND BATTALION CADRE

carrying back a wounded comrade. Again on the night of 31st Aug., 1918, at St. Servin's Farm, accompanied by two men only, he rushed an enemy machine gun, capturing eight prisoners and enabling the advance to continue. Throughout the whole of the fighting from Aug. 29th to Sept. 1st, 1918, he showed the utmost gallantry."

Christmas Day, 1918, was naturally an especial feature in such a year, and, like the New Year, was spent by the Battalion at Valenciennes. Among the New Year Honours was the grant to Lieut. and Q.M. C. Shepherd, D.C.M., of the M.B.E.

Early in January, 1919, the 10th Brigade moved to Binche and there Major F. H. B. Wellesley took over command of the Battalion. The Meritorious Service Medal was awarded to C.Q.M.S. A. J. Brown, Sergt. A. Halfacre, and Sergt. E. Pogson, D.C.M.

As time passed it was found that demobilization was so depleting the numbers of the Battalion that it had to be reduced to an organization of only two companies. But even so, representing the XXII Corps, it won the First Army Championship Cross-country Running, five of the Battalion team finishing in the first ten: Sergt. Garside first, Pte. Bastow second.

Until June 6th, 1919, the 2nd Duke of Wellington's remained at Binche, in Belgium. Almost the last ceremony connected with the 4th Division was the presentation by it of a Union Jack to the town. The presentation, in which representatives of the Battalion participated, was made by Lieut.-Colonel F. Pawlett, D.S.O., commanding temporarily the 4th Division.

On June 6th the Battalion cadre, consisting of 5 officers and 60 other ranks, entrained for Antwerp. The officers were: Major F. H. B. Wellesley (in command), Capt. D. G. R. Bilham, M.C. (Adjt.), Lieut. and Q.M. C. Shepherd, M.B.E., D.C.M., Capt. J. Cook, D.S.O., M.C., Capt. J. P. Colson, M.C., M.M.

On June 8th the cadre sailed from Antwerp and landed at Tilbury. Not for the first time in its history did a battalion of the Duke of Wellington's Regiment make this brief voyage. After the Seven Years' War and the Peace of Fontainbleau (1763) the 33rd, "battered and war-worn, with a record for bravery and distinguished service of which they might well be proud,"[1] returned to Gravesend from Germany. Again, after the disastrous Netherlands Campaign of 1795, the 33rd, led by Lieut.-Colonel Arthur Wellesley, landed at Harwich. They had taken part in the final terrible retreat under General Walmoden acting for the Duke of York. They "always presented a steady attitude when overtaken that averted attack or ended in the repulse of the assailants."[2]

Such were some of the memories which had sustained all ranks who served with the 2nd Battalion during the Great War.

May the glorious traditions they created with all their hallowed memories long remain to be the pride and support of future generations in the Duke of Wellington's Regiment.

---

[1] Albert Lee, *History of 33rd Regiment.*   [2] *Ibid.*

CHAPTER XIV

THE DEDICATION OF THE MEMORIAL CHAPEL IN YORK MINSTER.

THE REGIMENTAL WAR MEMORIAL

IT was not until late in 1921 that the form the Regimental Memorial should take was finally decided upon. The scheme was divided into two parts.

1. A Regimental Chapel in York Minster as a memorial to those of the 21 battalions whose names appeared on the Roll of Honour of the Great War, as well as to other past members of the Regiment.

2. A Memorial confined to the 1st, 2nd, and 3rd Battalions consisting of :—

(a) A Pension Fund for Warrant Officers, N.C.O.'s, and men of the three battalions to be administered in close connection with the Old Comrades' Association. This is referred to more fully in the Appendix.

(b) A Memorial Panel in the Sandhurst Chapel, especially subscribed for by the 1st and 2nd Battalions, on which the names of fallen officers of the Regiment who were cadets at the Royal Military College would be carved, the inscription to end " and to all officers and other ranks of the Regiment who died in the Great War."

THE MEMORIAL CHAPEL

The site selected lies at the east end of the south aisle of the choir, to the south side of the Lady Chapel. Originally dedicated as the " All Saints Chapel" by Archbishop Bowet of York in 1413, it, like others, was dismantled at the time of the Reformation (*circa* 1550), since when it was unused until restored in 1923 as the Regimental Memorial to our fallen.

The east window in the Chapel, which in its lights illustrates events connected with St. John the Evangelist, has been badly damaged (probably during the fire, 1829), but its colours are very beautiful. The window had just been cleaned and releaded prior to the opening dedicatory ceremony, the cost being defrayed, most appropriately, by brothers in arms as recorded in an inscription placed below. The inscription reads :—

" THE COST OF THE PRESERVATION OF THIS WINDOW WAS BORNE BY THE OFFICERS NONCOMMISSIONED OFFICERS AND MEN OF THE NORTHERN COMMAND AS A THANKSGIVING FOR VICTORY OVER OUR ENEMIES 1914

IVOR MAXSE.
G.O.C. IN C. NORTHERN COMMAND 1923."

PLATE 23

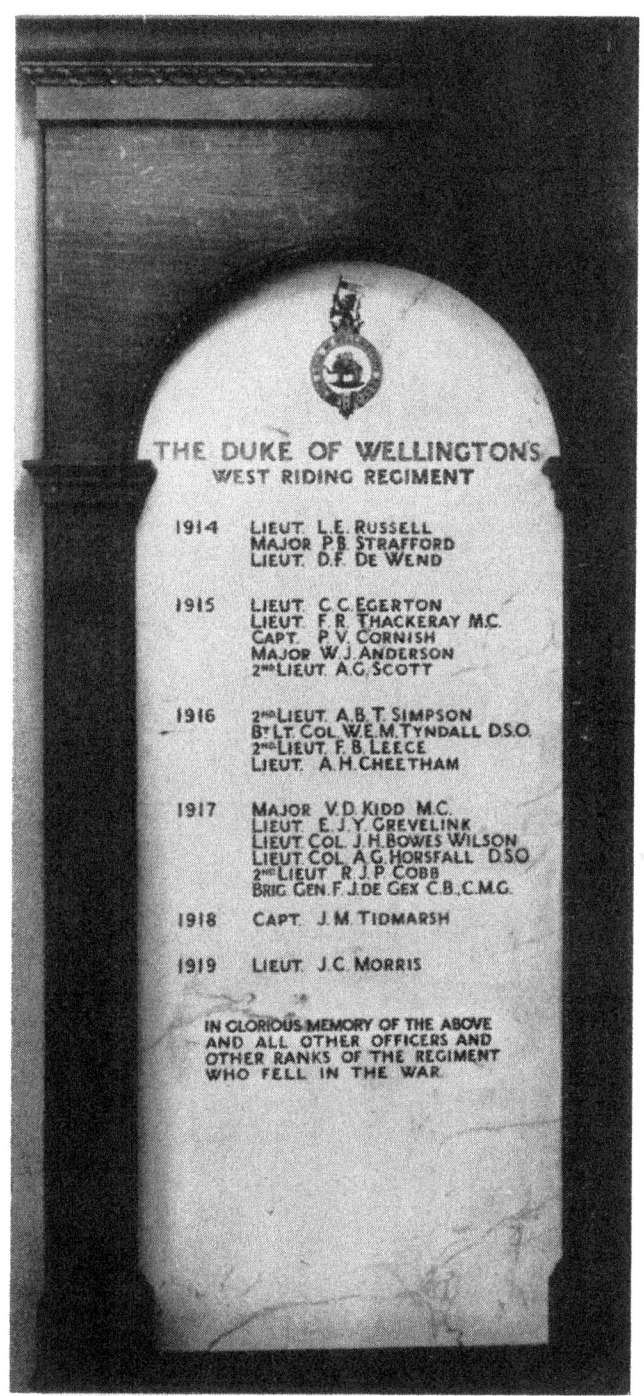

MEMORIAL TABLET IN THE CHAPEL OF THE ROYAL
MILITARY COLLEGE, SANDHURST

THE MEMORIAL CHAPEL AND THE ROLL OF HONOUR

There are two other windows in the Chapel, both on the south side. That nearer the east end was presented in 1804 by the Earl of Carlisle, who obtained it from St. Nicholas' Church, Rouen. The subject is the visit of the B.V. Mary to St. Elizabeth. The Carlisle arms are introduced into other lights of this window.

The second window dates from about 1400. Chief subjects: The Prophet Isaiah—The Descent from the Cross—King Edwin—The Vision of Ezekiel.

The area available for the Chapel, some 45 feet in length and 22 feet 6 inches in breadth, was cleared as far as possible of existing memorials, and enclosed with a temporary rail and gates until such time as the provision of permanent ones becomes feasible. The Crimean, Abyssinian, and South African Regimental War Memorials were moved from the south transept and fixed on the south wall, where also a stone was let in just above the Roll of Honour, bearing the inscription :—

> "THIS CHAPEL IS SET APART AS A MEMORIAL TO THOSE OF THE DUKE OF WELLINGTON'S REGIMENT (WEST RIDING) WHO FELL IN THE GREAT WAR, WHOSE NAMES ARE INSCRIBED IN A ROLL OF HONOUR, AND TO OTHER PAST MEMBERS OF THE REGIMENT."

The altar consists of a stone mensa resting on octagonal legs. At the back is a retable, standing on a stone substructure. Carved in wood, it has five panels containing representations of the emblems of the Evangelists with the Agnus Dei in the centre one. On the retable stand a cross and pair of candlesticks of bronze coated with pure gold, also a pair of vases 12 inches high of bronze heavily gilt. All are executed in the style of the Renaissance period and were presented by Mrs. John Trench in memory of her husband, Colonel S. J. Trench.

The altar frontal and superfrontal are of green brocade heavily embroidered in gold. It is hoped shortly to place a replica of some old master, suitably framed, behind the altar. Until such times, a red dossal has been hung there as a temporary measure. Immediately over the centre is the Regimental Crest carved in white alabaster and emblazoned in scarlet and gold.

On the south side of the Chapel, just outside the communion rail is kept the Roll of Honour Book which was subscribed for by all battalions of the Regiment in proportion to the number of names of each which are inscribed therein. The book is a superb work of art executed by Messrs. J. and E. Bumpus, bound in scarlet levant morocco, with the Regimental Badge superimposed in the centre. The title and dedication pages are richly illuminated. The wording of the latter reads :—

> "In this book are inscribed the Names of over 8,000 soldiers of all Ranks belonging to the 21 Battalions of THE DUKE OF WELLINGTON'S REGIMENT (WEST RIDING) who gave their lives for their Country.
>
> "The Altar in this Chapel in York Minster with this Roll of Honour were dedicated to the Glory of God and in memory of these Men, on the Twelfth day of May in the Fourteenth Year of the reign of His Majesty King George V."

On the next page are illuminated the Battle Honours of the Regiment as now borne on the Colours of all battalions. This page is followed by another on which the complete Battle Honours granted to the Regiment for the Great War appear in the order they are given in the Army List. The Roll of Fallen Officers comes next, followed by alphabetical lists for each battalion and the Depot. The names are engrossed in black, with the initial letter in red, and in sequence, conform to the official casualty lists of the fallen issued by the War Office.

The Roll of Honour is contained in a casket made of English walnut with carved and gilded panels. Down each side of the frame of the plate-glass lid are carved the Armorials of Great Britain, the Regimental Crest, the White Rose of York, and the Minster Badge, each painted in correct heraldic colours. The casket was given by Mrs. Watson and her daughters in memory of Lieut.-Colonel A. G. Horsfall, D.S.O.

The furniture of the Chapel further includes:

A chair of Mediæval design upholstered in red damask and a small reading desk in English oak with red damask book-rest, given by his relatives in memory of Pte. G. W. Vint.

A carpet for the sanctuary presented by Messrs. John Crossly and Sons, Ltd., of the Dean Clough Mills, Halifax.

A set of six books for the use of the officiating clergy printed on handmade paper and bound in red levant morocco leather with the Regimental Crest and Minster Arms stamped in gold on the covers, viz.:—

Altar Missal	given in memoriam,	Capt. John William Mowat, M.C., 4th Bn.
Bible	,,	,,	Capt. Cedric Fawsett Horsfall, 7th Bn.
Prayer Book	,,	,,	Deceased Comrades by the Old Comrades' Association of the 1st and 2nd Bns.
Prayer Book	,,	,,	Colonel C. Conor, late commanding 1st Bn.
Hymn Book	,,	,,	Deceased Comrades by the W.O.'s, N.C.O.'s, men 1st Bn.
Hymn Book	,,	,,	Deceased Comrades by the W.O.'s, N.C.O.'s, and men 2nd Bn.

Suitable inscriptions have in each case been engrossed on the inside cover of the books.

Thirty-six chairs (twenty-nine being individual and seven collective memorials), made of English oak with the Regimental Crest carved on the centre of the back. A small brass plate let in the top rail shows in whose memory each one was given, and, in each case of the individual memorials the date of death is given as well.

The inscriptions so recorded read:—

Brig.-General R. N. Bray, C.M.G., D.S.O. 23 Oct., 1921.
Colonel H. J. Johnston, D.S.O 7 Aug., 1915.
Lieut.-Colonel A. G. Horsfall, D.S.O. 9 Oct., 1917.

DEDICATION CEREMONY

Lieut.-Colonel W. E. Maples. 14 Dec., 1916.
    ,,   A. A. St. Hill, D.S.O. 27 Oct., 1918.
    ,,   W. E. M. Tyndall, D.S.O. 1 Aug., 1916.
    ,,   J. H. B. Wilson. 7 June, 1917.
Major V. N. Kidd, M.C. 21 Mar., 1917.
  ,, P. B. Strafford. 24 Aug., 1914.
  ,, H. P. Travers. 7 Aug., 1915.
Capt. C. O. Denman-Jubb. 24 Aug., 1914.
  ,, T. M. Ellis. 18 Apr., 1915.
  ,, E. G. Gatacre. 20 Feb., 1916.
  ,, R. C. A. P. E. Milbank. 10 May, 1915.
  ,, E. E. Sykes, M.C. (4th Bn.). 4 July, 1916.
  ,, E. R. Taylor. 18 Apr., 1915.
  ,, H. N. Waller (4th Bn.). 3 July, 1917.
  ,, H. E. Whitwam (7th Bn.). 9 Oct., 1917.
Lieut. D. F. de Wend. 11 Nov., 1914.
  ,, C. C. Egerton. 18 Apr., 1915.
  ,, E. J. Y. Grevelink. 6 June, 1917.
  ,, R. H. Owen. 18 Apr., 1915.
  ,, L. E. Russell. 24 Aug., 1914.
  ,, L. M. Tetlow (7th Bn.). 29 May, 1915.
  ,, F. R. Thackeray, M.C. 18 Apr., 1915.
  ,, J. H. L. Thompson. 17 Sept., 1914.
  ,, J. M. Tidmarsh. 3 Sept., 1918.
  ,, G. Williamson. 12 Nov., 1914.
2nd Lieut. F. W. Fleming (4th Bn.). 19 Dec., 1915.
In Memoriam, those of the 5th Battalion who fell 1914-1918.
       ,,   ,,   ,, 6th ,,   ,,   ,,
       ,,   ,,   ,, 7th ,,   ,,   ,,
       ,,   ,,   ,, 8th ,,   ,,   ,,
       ,,   ,,   ,, 9th ,,   ,,   ,,
       ,,   ,,   ,, 10th ,,   ,,   ,,
       ,,   ,,   ,, 12th ,,   ,,   ,,

.   .   .   .

THE DEDICATION OF THE MEMORIAL CHAPEL IN YORK MINSTER

> "If I should die, think only this of me:
> That there's some corner of a foreign field
> That is for ever England. There shall be
> In that earth a richer dust concealed;
> A dust whom England bore, shaped, made aware. . . ."
>
>   RUPERT BROOKE.

No ceremony could have been more impressive than that when the Memorial Chapel was dedicated to the memory of Our Glorious Dead. The dedication took place on Saturday, May 12th, 1923, in the presence of some 1500 persons interested in the Regiment. The guests included H.R.H. The Princess Mary, who, accompanied by her husband, Viscount Lascelles, honoured the Service with her presence.

The absence of both line battalions on foreign service, the 1st at Constantinople and the 2nd in Egypt, was much to be regretted, but they were well represented on the occasion by the Colonel of the Regiment, Lieut.-General Sir Herbert Belfield, those serving officers and men who happened to be in England, and a large number of past officers and of other ranks of the two Battalions. Detachments from the Depot representing the line and Special Reserve, from every Territorial battalion, as well as a formed body of ex-service officers and men in which were representatives of the whole twenty-one Battalions which had taken part in the Great War, were on parade under command of Bt.-Lieut.-Colonel C. J. Pickering, C.M.G., D.S.O. A large number of relatives of our fallen comrades had also journeyed from all parts of the country to be present at the dedication.

The service, truly beautiful in its simplicity, began with the hymn "Thy Kingdom Come, O God." The opening prayers intoned by the Rev. H. T. S. Gedge were followed by the chanting of Psalm 126, after which the Lesson, taken from Ecclesiasticus xliv. 1-15 : "Let us now praise famous men. . . . Their bodies are buried in peace : but their name liveth for evermore . . . and the congregation will show forth their praise," was read by the Chaplain-General to the Forces (Bishop Taylor-Smith).

The Duke of Wellington next stepped forward and drew aside the Union Jack which veiled the Altar, saying as he did so :—

> "Let us remember with thanksgiving and with all honour before God and men, the Officers, Warrant Officers, Non-Commissioned Officers, and Men of the Duke of Wellington's Regiment who gave their lives in the Great War."

A two-minute silence ensued, after which the Archbishop of York dedicated the Chapel and Memorials in the following words :—

"By virtue of our sacred office in the Church of God we do now consecrate and for ever set apart from all profane and common uses this Altar with its ornaments and fittings and the furniture of this Chapel dedicated many centuries ago in the name of All Saints; and we do devote them for all time to the Glory of the ever blessed Trinity, Father, Son, and Holy Ghost. Amen."

The dedication was followed by the singing of the Hymn of Sacrifice, "O valiant hearts," and by special prayers offered by the Vicar of Halifax (Bishop Frodsham).

The Archbishop, in his address, said :—

It was no time for words : it was a time for memories, regrets, and hopes, and to some of them for thoughts that were too deep even for tears, yet he asked them for a few moments to try and give voice to the united heart which

PLATE 24

MEMORIAL CHAPEL OF THE DUKE OF WELLINGTON'S REGIMENT
YORK MINSTER

was then beating in proud and thankful memory of those men of the Duke of Wellington's Regiment. Pathos was there, no doubt, deep and bitter in the thought that more than eight thousand men went and never returned. Most of them were in the prime of their manhood, swept in the full prime of their youth into the silent sea of death, and yet it would be wrong to lament for them. They went, they endured, they died, ungrieving and ungrudging. They would do those men dishonour if they were to grieve for them or grudge their sacrifice : for once in their lives their manhood was strengthened and uplifted by a great purpose to which they gave their body and their soul. We should not trouble ourselves with the question whether or not those men had died in vain. In our present confusion and disappointments and the sickness of heart which came from hopes long deferred we might sometimes be tempted to ask that question. Let them banish it from their minds that day. We had got to think what our lives would be now if in addition to all our burdens, difficulties, and trials we had to bear the yoke which our relentless enemy would have laid upon our necks.

MEN LIKE THOSE WEST RIDING LADS HAD GIVEN US A NEW FAITH IN HUMAN NATURE.

For his part he could never see those working men of the West Riding in their mines, their mills, and their factories without being able with a proud and thankful heart to say : "We who lived in the days of the Great War know the stuff of which these men are made." The memory of them would surely rebuke for ever, at least in our generation, the voice of the cynic and the pessimist, and would lift our faith in human nature to the level of the love which "believeth all things, hopeth all things, and endureth all things." And yet we should not be forgetful of the debt of honour which those men had left for us to pay. They had given to our trust the common life of England. We could never forget that but five years ago we were a community for whom the youngest, the best, and the bravest of our men were dying, and dying every day, and the common life had been redeemed by all that precious blood. It was and must be true of all of us that their sacrifice should kindle within each of us a resolve that we should do our best by our example and by our service to make the common life of England sane and strong, high-toned and true to God, nourished by the bread of faithful work and the wine of brotherly goodwill. To every man and woman of this generation a bond had been given that he should henceforth be a dedicated spirit : the bond had been sealed by the red blood of sacrifice, and it was for each of us to honour it. The names of those eight thousand men—mostly of their own Yorkshire blood—were enrolled in that noble book of remembrance, and he was sure that their comrades of the old and famous Regiment would feel a thrill of pride when they opened the book and remembered all those—young working men for the most part—who poured out their gallant lives in the service of the old Regiment in the time of its greatest trial. The Archbishop said he would like to think that the old Duke—model of all soldiers—might himself be pleased and honoured if to his name should be added the names of those West Riding lads.

Following the address the Nunc Dimittis was sung by the Minster choir and the concluding prayers were said by the Dean of York. The Blessing was pronounced by the Archbishop and after a pause the Last Post, followed by the Reveillé, was sounded by the buglers. The singing of the National Anthem brought this never-to-be-forgotten dedication to an end.

The first service to be held in the Memorial Chapel took place the following day. On Sunday, May 13th, at 8 a.m. the Dean of York celebrated the Holy Communion, at which many of those who had journeyed to York for the Dedication were present.

. . . .

In perfect weather and bright sunshine, Wednesday, February 24th, 1926, witnessed the first occasion of old Regimental Colours being deposited in the Chapel, viz. :—

1. Those presented to the 33rd Regiment in 1879, and replaced on July 30th, 1925.

2. Those presented to the 76th Regiment in 1830, which, since retirement in 1863 had hung in All Saints, Royal Garrison Church, Aldershot, until quite recently, when permission was given for their transfer to York.

3. The framed Regimental Colour of the renovated original Hon. East India Company's Stand, granted to the 76th Regiment in 1803.

The special train arrived from Halifax at noon, bringing the Colour Guards; the band of the 1st Battalion, which had come up specially from Gosport, and a large contingent of present and past members of the Regiment. The troops fell in on the York Station Square at 1.30 p.m., under the command of Capt. R. H. W. Owen, in the following order :—

No. 1 Guard (33rd Colours), Commander—Capt. M. E. Crane; Colour Officers—Lieuts. C. I. E. Haslock and L. E. Bishop, M.C.

No. 2 Guard (76th Colours): Commander—Capt. D. Paton; Colour Officers—Lieuts. W. A. Marshman and S. Naylor, M.C.

A detachment of the Territorial battalions, under command of 2nd Lieut. J. Mc.D. Slater, 4th Battalion.

Headed by the band, the parade marched to the west entrance of the Minster, where the Colonel of the Regiment and a large gathering of officers and guests were assembled on the steps. The troops formed three sides of a square, with the Colour Parties in line, in the centre, facing the west door.

At 1.55 p.m. the farewell general salute was given to the Colours, after which, to the strains of "Auld Lang Syne," with the Guards still at the "Present," they were marched in slow time into the Minster. Halting, the Colours were uncased, whilst the spectators and troops moved to their places in the Chapel to the playing of a voluntary on the great organ.

All being ready, the Dean of York, Dr. Lionel Ford, D.D., accompanied by Canon C. C. Bell (Precentor), and the Rev. H. T. S. Gedge (Vicar Choral),

STAND (d), 33RD REGIMENT, NOW IN POSSESSION OF LORD WHARTON

PLATE 25

PLATE 26

FRAMED REMNANTS OF THE ORIGINAL HONOURABLE EAST INDIA COMPANY'S REGIMENTAL COLOUR, NOW IN YORK MINSTER

THE ORIGINAL SPEARHEAD ON THE HONOURABLE EAST INDIA COMPANY'S COLOUR POLES

COLOURS DEPOSITED IN MEMORIAL CHAPEL

entered the Chapel, and took their places in front of the Altar. During the recital of the opening sentences of the special service by the Dean, the Colour Officers moved up the aisle and halted in line at the Altar rails. Lieut.-General Sir Herbert Belfield, who was standing just inside the rails, next pulled a silken cord, and disclosed the East India Colour, which, owing to its weight, had been placed in position that morning on the centre pillar on the north side of the Chapel screened by the Union Jack. He then requested the Dean to accept the custody of the Colours, addressing him as follows :—

"Very Reverend Sir,—I have to ask you to accept the custody of these two stands of Colours, and the framed remains of an old Colour, and to place them in this our Memorial Chapel. I desire to emphasize the peculiar significance which they have for us, in that they bear the regimental numbers of our two regular Battalions which were extinguished at the amalgamation of the historically numbered regiments in 1881. Those which bear the number of the 33rd were carried so lately as July last by the 1st Battalion of the Regiment when I had the honour of presenting new Colours to that Battalion. Those of the 76th have hung, since 1869, in All Saints' Church, at Aldershot, and we are grateful to the authorities for having raised no objection to their removal.

"But it is to the framed Colour that I specially desire to draw attention. In 1803 the Honourable East India Company awarded a set of Colours to the 76th, in recognition of distinguished services rendered in India, under Lord Lake. These Colours were additional to those ordinarily carried and that Regiment, now our 2nd Battalion, has since then had the distinction of being the only one in the Army entitled to carry four Colours. The original Colours were carried by the 76th, during the Peninsular War. When, in 1830, these special, or, as we have always called them, Honorary Colours, became much dilapidated, the embroidered centre and the Battle Honours were transferred to a new groundwork. The India Office granted an entirely new set of Colours in 1888, and the remains of the old ones were framed. One only of these is now left, as the King's Colour was destroyed in a disastrous fire in Burma in 1900, and the framed Regimental Colour I now hand over to you. I hope I have made it clear that this Colour is quite unique, both in the circumstances of its presentation, and as being, in its essentials, the original presented to the 76th Regiment nearly a century and a quarter ago.

"All these Colours, as I have said, mean a lot to us, and we can confide them to no better or fitter keeping than yours, to be displayed in our Memorial Chapel in this great Minster."

The Dean of York in reply on behalf of the Dean and Chapter said they were glad and happy to receive the Colours for safe custody, and they accepted charge, adding : "We know these Colours mean much to you, and all whom you represent here to-day, and we hope we shall be found worthy custodians of them."

Lieut.-General Sir Herbert Belfield next took the Colours in turn from the Colour Officers and handed them to the Dean, who laid them on the Altar.

A moment of silence ensued, and then the Dean offered up the following special prayer for the Regiment:—

"We pray Thee, most merciful Father, to bless the widows and orphans of those who, under the British Flag, have fallen in the course of duty and in the service of their King and country, and we commend to Thy gracious care and protection the Officers and Men of the Duke of Wellington's Regiment wheresoever they may be serving. And, as we place their honoured banners here in this Thy Holy House, beside many similar tokens of gallant deeds and patriotic lives—we pray Thee to give peace in our time, O Lord; to make wars to cease throughout the world and to control and subdue the unruly wills and angry passions of men. Enable them to live in harmony one with another, and ever to fight together the true fight of faith, as good soldiers of the Cross, against sin, the world, and the devil, under the great Captain of our Salvation, Jesus Christ our Lord. Amen."

After the Blessing, the singing of the National Anthem by the vast congregation, who had remained standing during the whole of the service, to the accompaniment of the Regimental Band, brought this short but very impressive ceremony to an end.

. . . .

In the Regimental Memorial Chapel in York Minster are now to be seen some of the past "Colours" of both battalions. Nor could any more honoured or more suitable resting-place be found for the proud relics of former glorious days.

From almost prehistoric times we find some sort of insignia (ensign) used as a rallying-point or as a chief's distinctive mark in battle. From tribal fights in the days of Boadicea and the Druids to the Great War is a far cry, but battle insignia, "Colours" we now call them, have survived. It has always been the custom for the higher leaders—who, it should be remembered, in earlier days fought hand-to-hand, alongside their men—to have some kind of banner to indicate their presence, and to serve as a rallying-point when the fortune of war was going against them. The Eagles of Rome were a historic example of such usage. Her legions had tramped and fought under these revered symbols throughout the world as then known, just as did the regiments and divisions of the British Empire during the Great War.

It was not until the sixteenth century[1] that the application of the word "colour" to such insignia first became the regular custom. Since that period all great military leaders, like Napoleon, have attached the highest importance to retaining regimental Colours.

Although Colours have ceased to be carried in the fighting-line in the British Army since the Battle of Isandhlwana (1879), both the Russian and Japanese Armies adhered to the practice in the war of 1904–1905. There are, and always will be, leaders whose imagination lacks the compelling power of

---

[1] *Encyclopædia Britannica*, XI Edition.

that of a Napoleon or of a Nelson. But it is for such leaders as these that men will die willingly. They alone realize the fighting value of a mere flag or phrase.

It is to be regretted that in olden days correct records of regimental stands of Colours were not kept, as is now done, in a central Record Office. But this is no doubt due to there having been no official instructions regulating their issue before 1743. Up to that date Colours were provided regimentally, frequently by the Colonel at his own will and pleasure, and made according to his own designing. It was not until September, 1743, that a Royal Warrant was issued regulating the Colours of the Army. It reads as follows :—

"The Union Colour is the first Stand of Colours in all Regiments, royal or not, except the Foot Guards. With them, the King's Standard is the first as a particular distinction.

"No Colonel to put his arms, crest, device, or livery, in any part of the appointments of his Regiment.

"The first Colour of every marching Regiment of Foot is to be the Great Union ; the second Colour is to be the colour of the regiment, with the Union in the upper canton, except those regiments faced with white or red, whose second Colour is to be the Red Cross of St. George in a white field, and a Union in the upper canton. In the centre of each Colour is to be painted in gold Roman figures, the number of the rank of the regiments, within a wreath of roses and thistles on one stalk, except those regiments which are allowed to wear royal devices or ancient badges ; the number of their rank is to be painted towards the upper corner ; the length of the pike and Colours to be the same size as those of the Foot Guards ; the cord and tassels of all the Colours to be crimson and gold."

Then follows a list of regiments[1] distinguished " by particular devices, and therefore not subject to the preceding articles for Colours " ; also regulations for the Cavalry.

The red cross on a white field, with the Union in the upper corner, was regulation for those regiments having red facings, as had the 76th, 33rd, and 53rd Regiments.

All these regiments wore red facings from the period of their formation, chosen usually by their founders simply for the sake of variety or distinction.

A further general Warrant was issued July 1st, 1751, which, whilst it embodied all the points of that of the 1747 one, gave fuller details describing special patterns, etc.

On the Union with Ireland in 1801 an Order in Council was issued, laying down that the cross of St. Patrick was to be added to the Union flag.

"The Union flag shall be azure, the crosses saltire of St. Andrew and St. Patrick quarterly per saltire counterchanged argent and gules, the latter fimbriated of the second surmounted by the cross of St. George of

---

[1] "Royal Regiments," "Fusilier," and "Marine Regiments," "The Old Buffs," 5th, 6th, 8th, 27th and 41st Regiments.

the third, fimbriated as the saltire. It is further ordered that the shamrock should be introduced into the Union wreath wherever that ornament or badge be used."

In 1820 the "Vellum Colour Book" was drawn up consisting of hand-paintings of stands of Colours for all infantry units of the Army. The approved design, colouring, and Battle Honours were painted in detail. (Plate 29).

The Colours of line battalions are renewable by regulations every twenty years. Those of the Guards once in every ten years.

. . . .

COLOURS OF THE 33RD REGIMENT

Definite records of the earlier Colours of the 33rd Regiment are, as in most cases where regimental Colours are concerned, incomplete. From such information as has been collated, thanks chiefly to the careful research and industry of Colonel J. A. C. Gibbs, it may be assumed that the 33rd Regiment had in all eight stands of Colours. These were:—

(a) The Colours carried at Dettingen in 1743, reported to be deposited at Halifax (Nova Scotia).
(b) The Colours carried in the American War of Independence and at the time of Lord Cornwallis' surrender at York Town in 1782. These were deposited at Taunton in the Church of St. Mary Magdelene, to which town the 33rd Regiment was sent on return from America.
(c) A new set of Colours presented to the Regiment at Taunton in 1783.
(d) A stand of Colours, the property of Major Richard Dansey, belonging to the 33rd Regiment. This officer's father and grandfather both served in the 33rd Regiment.[1] (Plate 25).
(e) "A set carried by the 33rd at Waterloo (new in 1813) were in use until 1830 when they were reported on at Spanish Town as being very old and scarcely to be described as Colours."[2] The whereabouts of these Colours was unknown until quite lately when the regimental Colour was discovered to be at the Royal United Service Institution.

A glass shade in one of the showcases containing relics of "The Iron Duke" has the following label attached to it :—

"3373—Remnants of the Regimental Colour of the 33rd Regt. (The Duke of Wellington's), together with the Tassels, Poleheads and Shoes, which were carried at the Battles of Quatre-Bras and Waterloo in 1815. They became the property of Lieut.-Colonel J. M. Harty, K.H. Deposited by Miss Vickers."

The records of the Institution show they were lent in 1912, when Miss Vickers lived in Chelsea. Later she wrote and said she was leaving that locality but gave no new address. It is to be hoped that some day this lady may be traced as it might then be possible to find out what became of the King's Colour belonging to this historic stand.

[1] Reference to the above sets of Colours is made in *The History of the 33rd Duke of Wellington's Regiment*. By Albert Lee.
[2] The late Mr. Milne in *Standards and Colours of the Army*.

THE HONOURABLE EAST INDIA COMPANY'S COLOURS, NOW IN USE IN THE 2ND BATTALION

PLATE 28

REGIMENTAL COLOUR 33RD REGIMENT, 1832–1854

REGIMENTAL COLOUR 76TH REGIMENT, 1830–1863

THE KING'S COLOURS OF THE ABOVE CARRY THE SAME BADGES AND HONOURS. BOTH STANDS ARE IN YORK MINSTER

(f) A stand presented at Weedon in 1832 by General Sir Charles Whale, K.C.B., then Colonel of the Regiment. The Colours were made in strict accordance with Royal Warrant, 1743. The regimental one with the Red Cross of St. George on a white field has the two Honours " Peninsula " and " Seringapatam " emblazoned on it. These Colours were never in action, but they are associated with two interesting events. Whilst stationed at Gibraltar, 1838 to 1840, the late Duke of Cambridge, then Prince George of Cambridge, was attached to the Regiment on joining the Army. Again, at the Duke of Wellington's funeral on November 18th, 1852, the Regiment was brought to London from Glasgow to take part in the procession and these Colours proved a conspicuous mark.

They were retired from service at Dublin in 1854 prior to the 33rd proceeding to the Crimea and were deposited at Danesbury, Welwyn, Herts., with the Commanding Officer. At his death they were presented by his widow to the Royal United Service Museum, on April 13th, 1861. They remained there until August, 1926, when by the kindness of the Council they were returned to the Regiment to be deposited in the Memorial Chapel in York Minster. (Plate 28).

(g) A stand concerning which the following appears in the 33rd Digest of Service :—

"On the 28th February, 1851, at the Royal Barracks, Dublin, new Colours were presented by the Colonel, Maj.-General D'Oyley." These Colours were replicas of the 1832 stand. They went with the 33rd to the Crimea, earning the Battle Honours " Alma," " Sevastopol," and " Inkerman," which were added to the Regimental Colour, and later " Abyssinia," for services in that campaign. On retirement in 1879 they were deposited in Halifax Parish Church.

(h) The stand presented by Maj.-General Mark Walker, V.C., C.B., at Kamptee on March 3rd, 1879. In make these resembled the previous Colours. They remained in service until July, 1925, when they were replaced, and are now in the Memorial Chapel in York Minster. During their forty-four years' service the Battle Honours of the former 76th Regiment were placed on the Regimental Colour, in 1881. After the South African War, the Honours " Relief of Kimberley," " Paardeberg," and " South Africa 1900–02 " were also added.

.   .   .   .

COLOURS OF THE 76TH REGIMENT

Three regulation stands are known to have existed :—

(a) The Colours presented soon after the Regiment was raised in 1787 which were taken by it to India in 1788. After some twenty years of constant campaigning these Colours were eventually handed over to the then Commanding Officer by Lieut.-General Don, following the presentation of the original

Honorary Colours. In thus handing them over General Don said: "Major Covell, I now deposit in your custody as Commanding Officer of the Regiment these banners reduced to their poles by the shot of the enemy."[1]

The honorary stand of Colours just referred to were, according to the records, the only Colours carried by the Regiment for the next twenty-three years.[2] It was not until April, 1829, that when sending an application to the Court of Directors of the Hon. East India Company for the renewal of the Honorary Colours that the then Commanding Officer, Lieut.-Colonel Moberly, applied to the Colonel of the Regiment for new Regulation Colours, it being his duty in those days to provide them.

(b) This latter application was evidently complied with without delay. The new Regulation Colours were taken into use in 1830 when the Regiment was stationed at Templemore. Unfortunately, the records give no account of any presentation ceremony. On being retired in 1863 these Colours were deposited in All Saints' Royal Garrison Church, Aldershot. They were afterwards moved to the Memorial Chapel in York Minster in 1926, as already related. (Plate 28).

(c) A stand of Colours consecrated at Aldershot, which was presented by General Sir John Pennyfather on April 29th, 1863. These Colours were still in use at the date of the amalgamation of the 33rd and 76th Regiments into The Duke of Wellington's Regiment in 1881. They then became entitled to bear the Battle Honours of the 33rd Regiment. They were deposited in the Parish Church at Halifax, Yorkshire, and replaced in 1888 by the first stand of Colours issued to the Duke of Wellington's Regiment under the Army Order of 1881. These were lost by fire in 1901, and replaced in October, 1906.

. . . .

THE HONORARY COLOURS AND THEIR ORIGIN

As most military readers are aware, the old 76th Regiment carried an Honorary stand of Colours granted by the Governor-General of India in Council, with the subsequent approval of His Majesty King George III, to commemorate its achievements in the Maharatta Campaign, under General Lord Lake. The distinction was unique in the annals of British Infantry. The final token of appreciation of the Regiment's distinguished services made by the Court of Directors of the H.E.I.C. on its leaving India in 1807 was a representation submitted to H.M. King George III

"that the 76th was the Regiment which rescued the Great Mogul and captured Delhi and Agra, the Capitals of Hindoostan."

In consequence of this representation the 76th Regiment was permitted to place the word "Hindoostan" on its Colours and appointments.

A further honour was sanctioned in the *London Gazette* of February 7th, 1807. The *Gazette* reads:—

"In consequence of the earnest recommendation of General Lord

---

[1] *Historical Records, 76th Hindoostan Regt.* Lieut.-Colonel Hayden, D.S.O.
[2] This stand was carried by the 76th through the Peninsular War.

PLATE 29

FROM PAINTINGS IN THE VELLUM BOOK

2ND BATTALION COLOURS (1906) NOW IN USE

1st BATTALION COLOUR (1925) NOW IN USE

THE HONORARY COLOURS

Lake, Commander-in-Chief of His Majesty's Forces in India, His Majesty has been pleased to signify his most gracious pleasure that, in addition to the permission recently granted to the 76th Regiment to place the word 'Hindoostan' on its Colours and appointments, as an honorary badge, the Regiment should be allowed to place the 'Elephant' on its Colours and appointments, inscribing the word 'Hindoostan' around it, as a distinguishing testimony of its good conduct and exemplary valour during the period of its services in India."

Up to the present time four stands—or it would perhaps be more correct to write three stands and one entirely renovated one—have been issued of the Honorary Colours.

(*a*) The original Colours granted in 1803 were actually not made until after the return of the 76th from India in 1807. The date of presentation was January 27th, 1808. The ceremony took place at Jersey where, after consecration by Dr. Dupré, the Dean, they were presented by General Don.

(*b*) In 1829 Lieut.-Colonel W. L. Moberly, M.P., commanding 76th Regiment, petitioned the Court of Directors H.E.I.C. that the Colours might be renovated. This was granted, but as they were in tatters a practically new stand was made by mounting the old embroidery, including centre badges, Battle Honours, etc., on new silk grounds. New poles with spear-heads similar to the original ones were issued, and the additional Battle Honours, " Peninsula " and " Nive," were added. This renovated stand was presented to the Regiment at Templemore on July 3rd, 1830, by Lieut.-Colonel Moberly, M.P., " in the name and on behalf of the Court of Directors."

The regulation stand of 1830 was taken into use about the same time, since when the Regiment has always carried four Colours.

On being replaced in 1886, the remnants of this stand were mounted and framed, the King's Colour being hung in the Officers' Mess and the Regimental Colour in the Sergeants' Mess. The former, as stated in a previous chapter, was, unfortunately, destroyed by fire at Rangoon in December, 1901, but the latter, happily, escaped destruction, and in May, 1925, the Warrant Officers and Sergeants of the 2nd Battalion unanimously expressed a wish that it might be placed in the Memorial Chapel, at York, where it now is. The reproduction of this Colour is in its original frame, but before being hung in the Chapel the 2nd Battalion had a handsome scarlet and gold moulding fitted over the front of the frame, which has done much to enhance the beauty of and to show up this fine old Colour. A brass plate at the foot reads :—

" This Colour replaced in 1829 one of the original Stands of Honorary Colours represented to the 76th (Hindoostan) Regiment by the Hon. East India Company in 1807, for deeds performed in the Campaign of 1803–04 under Lord Lake, and which was later carried by the Regiment during the Peninsula War. In 1886 it was itself replaced by a new Colour by the

Secretary of State for India in Council. The King's Colour of this Stand was destroyed by fire in Burma in 1901." (Plate 26).

The original spearheads found at Aldershot have been mounted on top of the frame. (Plate 26).

(c) In 1886, the Colours having become quite unserviceable, Colonel Hodges, then commanding 2nd Battalion, petitioned the Secretary of State for India in Council to again renovate them. Records in the India Office show that when considering the petition a close examination of the remnants was made, when it was found impossible to use any of the old embroideries again : consequently it was decided to present the Regiment with entirely new Colours, replicas of the original 1807 stand. The poles and spearheads issued in 1830 were, however, used again, small silver plates being fixed on the former engraved : " These Colours were renewed by the Court of Directors of the East India Company in 1829 and again by the Secretary of State for India in Council in 1886." The new stand arrived in Bermuda in 1888 and was trooped with great ceremony.

(d) Early in 1902, the Secretary of State for India in Council, on receiving the official notification of the loss (by fire), at once sanctioned the Colours being replaced, subject to the approval of the Secretary of State for War, which was readily given. The new stand reached India late in 1905, but as the Battalion was shortly due to return to England it was decided, as in the case of the regulation stand which had also perished in the fire, to defer the presentation ceremony until after the Regiment arrived home. The ceremony took place at Lichfield on October 20th, 1906, when after consecration by the Lord Bishop of Lichfield (Dr. Legge) the two new stands were presented by His Grace the Duke of Wellington. Plate 27 shows the present Colours in detail complete with all the Battle Honours won by the old 76th Regiment, including " Mysore," granted by Army Order March, 1889, and " Corunna," by Army Order 58 of 1908.

. . . .

BATTLE HONOURS OF THE REGIMENT

By an Army Order of November, 1920, the full title of the Regiment was altered to " The Duke of Wellington's Regiment (West Riding)," whilst " The Duke of Wellington's Regiment " was alone to be used for official correspondence, etc.

An Army Order of September, 1922, set up Regimental Committees under the chairmanship of their respective Colonels, to select Honours from the official list of " engagements " of the Great War, the guiding principle in the selection being that Headquarters and a minimum of 50 per cent of at least one Battalion of the Regiment must have been present at the engagement for which the Honour was claimed. Further instructions issued to Colonels of regiments directed that each battalion be represented on the Committee.

PLATE 31

1st BATTALION COLOUR (1925) NOW IN USE

PLATE 32

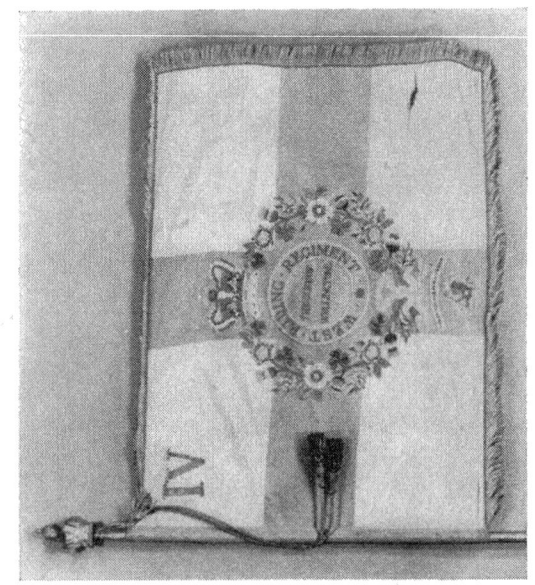

3RD (MILITIA) COLOURS (1864–1889), NOW IN YORK MINSTER

BATTLE HONOURS OF THE REGIMENT

The following officers represented their respective Battalions on the Committee under the chairmanship of the Colonel of the Regiment, Lieut.-General Sir H. Belfield, at the final meeting held on March 1, 1924.

>   1st Battn. Bt. Lieut.-Colonel C. J. Pickering.
>   2nd „   Capt. R. O'D. Carey.
>   4th „   Lieut.-Colonel A. L. Mowatt.
>   4th „   Capt. P. G. Bales.
>   5th „   Capt. K. Sykes.
>   6th „   Lieut.-Colonel C. M. Bateman (unavoidably absent).
>   7th „   Major B. C. Lupton.
>   8th „   Major C. M. Durrant (unavoidably absent).
>   9th „   Lieut.-Colonel P. R. Simner.
>   10th „   Major W. N. Town.
>   12th „   Lieut.-Colonel R. B. Clifton.
>
>   *Hon. Sec.* Major C. W. G. Ince.

An Army Order of December, 1922, decreed that Battalions of Infantry, Regular, Militia (Special Reserve), and Territorial will have emblazoned on their King's Colour Battle Honours up to a maximum of ten to commemorate their services in the Great War, such Honours to be selected by Regimental Committees from the list of " Great War " Honours to be shown in the Army List. The Honours emblazoned on the King's and Regimental Colours will be the same for all units comprising the regiment concerned, and will be shown in the Army List in thick type.

The following is the list of those Honours finally approved for the Regiment, as they appear in the Army List of to-day :—

The Great War—21 *Battalions*—"**Mons**", "Le Cateau", "Retreat from Mons," "**Marne, 1914, '18**", "Aisne, 1914", "La Bassée, 1914", "**Ypres, 1914, '15 '17**", "Nonne Bosschen", "**Hill 60**", "Gravenstafel", "St. Julien", "Aubers", "**Somme, 1916, '18**", "Albert, 1916, '18", "Bazentin", "Delville Wood", "Pozières", "Flers-Courcelette", "Morval", "Thiepval", "Le Transloy", "Ancre Heights", "**Arras, 1917, '18**", "Scarpe, 1917, '18", "Arleux", "Bullecourt", "Messines, 1917, '18", "Langemarck, 1917", "Menin Road", "Polygon Wood", "Broodseinde", "Poelcappelle", "Passchendaele", "**Cambrai, 1917, '18**", "St. Quentin", "Ancre, 1918", "**Lys**", "Estaires", "Hazebrouck", "Bailleul", "Kemmel", "Béthune", "Scherpenberg", "Tardenois", "Amiens", "Bapaume, 1918", "Drocourt-Quéant", "Hindenburg Line", "Havrincourt", "Epéhy", "Canal du Nord", "Selle", "Valenciennes", "Sambre", "France and Flanders, 1914–18". "**Piave**", "Vittorio Veneto", "Italy, 1917–18". "Suvla", "**Landing at Suvla**", "Scimitar Hill", "Gallipoli, 1915". "Egypt, 1916".

A stand to replace the old 33rd Colours was presented to the 1st Battalion at Gosport on July 30th, 1925, by Lieut.-General Sir Herbert Belfield, K.C.B., K.C.M.G., K.B.E., D.S.O., Colonel of the Regiment. Plates 30 and 31, give these Colours in detail. The chief differences in pattern to those issued in 1906 to the 2nd Battalion are as follows:—

(a) The new centre badge in which "WEST RIDING" is circumscribed "THE DUKE OF WELLINGTON'S REGIMENT."
(b) The re-arrangement of the Battle Honours, and—
(c) The transposition of the two crests in the lower corners.

This pattern will in future be the standard one for all battalions of the Regiment, save only as regards the battalion number in the upper corner nearest the poles.

. . . .

MILITIA AND SPECIAL RESERVE

On the introduction of the Territorial System Gen. Order 41 of May 1st, 1881, provided for two Militia Battalions to be called the 3rd and 4th Battalions of The Duke of Wellington's (West Riding) Regiment. These were formed from the 1st and 2nd Battalions of the 6th West York Militia.

3rd Battalion.

This Battalion has had two stands of Colours:—

1. Those of the 6th West York Militia (originally consecrated and presented at Halifax on April 29th, 1864), which on July 1st, 1881, became those of the senior Militia battalion, and so continued until July 30th, 1889, when a new stand of regulation Army pattern was presented by H.R.H. the late Duke of Clarence. The old Colours were presented to H.R.H. as a memento, and were escorted to Marlborough House on September 9th, 1889. The following year they were moved to Sandringham, where they hung until June, 1926, when His Majesty King George V most graciously had them returned to the Regiment so that they might be placed in the Memorial Chapel, York Minster, where they have now been deposited. (Plate 32).

2. The 1889 regulation stand mentioned above, when the Battalion was embodied the following year for active service during the South African War, earned the Battle Honour granted under a special Army Order dated December 21st, 1904, "South Africa, 1900-1902."

In 1907, on the formation of the Special Reserve, the Battalion became the 3rd (Reserve) Battalion the Duke of Wellington's (West Riding) Regiment, serving as such during the Great War. Under Army Order 470 of 1922 the Colours have now been emblazoned with the full Regimental Honours as ordered for all battalions.

In 1924 the Battalion was once more changed into Militia.

4th Battalion.

This Battalion had only the one stand of Colours during its existence—namely, the regulation pattern ones presented by H.R.H. the late Duke of Clarence at Halifax on the same occasion that the 3rd Battalion received theirs. In 1890 the Battalion was amalgamated with the 3rd Battalion. In 1895 the Colours were given with the sanction of the War Office to the Commanding Officer, Lieut.-Colonel G. Stovell, in whose house they have hung till June, 1926, when he most kindly handed them back to the Regiment for the Memorial Chapel, where they have now been deposited. (Plate 32).

CONCLUSION

THE REGIMENT DURING THE GREAT WAR

By THE COLONEL OF THE REGIMENT

WHEREAS this history, which covers forty-two years, is largely concerned with the Great War, it deals with only two of the seven battalions of which the Regiment was composed at the outbreak of hostilities, viz.—one Special Reserve and four Territorial in addition to the two Regular battalions. Before the war was over fourteen additional battalions had been raised. Of these some were dispersed while the war was still in progress, and the remainder were disbanded shortly after its close, thus reducing the Regiment to the original number of battalions. A history covering the war period only, and dealing with all battalions of the Regiment, might have been undertaken, but for various reasons this was not attempted. There is now no chance that such a comprehensive history will be written, and it is improbable that any battalion which has not already done so will record the part it played in the great events of those four years.

The issue of this history offers an opportunity to chronicle very briefly (for space will not admit of more), and indeed mainly in tabular form, the war-story of the various battalions of the Regiment other than the 1st and 2nd, which are dealt with fully in this volume.

Appendix I shows when the additional battalions were raised, or in the case of existing Territorial battalions embodied in war-numbered brigades, the date on which each battalion proceeded overseas and the front on which it fought or the duties on which it was employed in this country. A few notes are added.

Appendix II gives the Battle Honours of the Regiment (the Colour Honours being distinguished by capitals) and the battalion or battalions which gained them.

I especially desire to direct attention to the services of the fourteen battalions —eight Territorial and six " Service "—which were raised only for the period of the war. In most cases the sole record of such a battalion consists in its Colour, hung in a church or elsewhere, and in the Regimental Roll of Honour, deposited in our Memorial Chapel in York Minster, wherein are inscribed the names of its members who gave their lives in the service of their country. Reference to Appendix II shows how much we of the existing Regiment owe to these specially raised battalions.

CONCLUSION

To be explicit—During the time that the 2nd line units of the 4th, 5th, 6th, and 7th Battalions fought as the 186th Brigade they added "BULLECOURT" and the Colour Honour of "CAMBRAI, 1917," to our record.

Without the 8th Battalion we could not have claimed the Battle Honours of "THIEPVAL," "LANGEMARCK," "SUVLA," "SCIMITAR HILL," "GALLIPOLI, 1915," "EGYPT, 1916," or the Colour Honour of "LANDING AT SUVLA." Together with the 10th Battalion they gave us "MESSINES, 1917."

To the 9th Battalion we owe the Battle Honours of "ST. QUENTIN," "AMIENS" and "EPEHY," and with the 13th and 12th Battalions respectively they allowed us to claim "ALBERT, 1918" and "DELVILLE WOOD."

We are indebted to our 10th Battalion for the Battle Honours of "MORVAL," "MENIN ROAD," "POLYGON WOOD," "VITTORIO VENETO," "ITALY, 1917–18" and the Colour Honour of "PIAVE." To it together with the 8th, as mentioned above, we owe "MESSINES, 1917."

As a Labour Corps the opportunities of distinction by the 12th Battalion were limited, for it was ordinarily employed in detachments of less than half its strength—the official minimum on which to base a claim for an Honour. But without it and the 9th we should not have acquired "DELVILLE WOOD."

The 13th Battalion was overseas for a very short time towards the close of the war. To it, conjointly with the 9th Battalion, we owe "ALBERT, 1918."

I hope that these few words, quite inadequate though they are, together with the accompanying tables, may serve as a constant reminder of the debt the Regiment owes to those who served for only a short time in its ranks, but who added to its distinction and proved themselves well worthy of its great traditions.

HERBERT E. BELFIELD

June, 1927.

APPENDICES

APPENDIX I

THE GREAT WAR

Services of Individual Battalions

No.	Title of Battalion.	Date of Formation.	Date of proceeding overseas.	Front on which employed.
1	1st		August, 1914	Western
2	2nd			
	Depot			
3	3rd (Sp. Res.)			
4	1/4th (Terr.)	The 4th, 5th, 6th, and 7th, renamed 1st line Terr. Bns., formed 147th Bde., 49th W. Rid. Divn.	April, 1915	Western
5	1/5th ,,			
6	1/6th ,,			
7	1/7th ,,			
8	2/4th ,,	August, 1914. Formed 186th Bde., 62nd W. Rid. Div.	January, 1917	Western
9	2/5th ,,			
10	2/6th ,,			
11	2/7th ,,			
12	3/4th ,,	April, 1915, as W. Rid. Bde., T.F.		
13	3/5th ,,			
14	3/6th ,,			
15	3/7th ,,			
16	8th (Service)	August, 1914	July, 1915, in 32nd Bde., 11th Div.	Gallipoli Egypt, Jan., 1916 Western, July, 1916
17	9th ,,	September, 1914	July, 1915, in 52nd Bde., 17th Div.	Western
18	10th ,,	September, 1914	September, 1915, in 69th Bde., 23rd. Div.	Western Italy, Nov., 1917
19	11th ,,	November, 1914		
20	12th ,,	March, 1916	April, 1916	Western
21	13th ,,	May, 1918	July, 1918	Western

APPENDIX I

THE GREAT WAR

Services of Individual Battalions

Remarks.

Retained for service in India.

Home Service. Training and drafting.
    Do.

On the reorganisation of the infantry brigades in three battalions early in 1918, the 147th Brigade was composed of the 1/4th, 1/6th, and 1/7th. The 1/5th was transferred to the 186th Brigade, and absorbed the 2/5th. This Brigade then consisted of the 2/4th, 5th, and 2/7th, and the 2/6th was distributed among them.

The 2/7th was disbanded in June, 1918, its place in the Brigade being taken by another Territorial battalion. The 1/4th, 2/4th, 5th, 6th, and 7th Battalions remained in France until 1919, returning to England on various dates between May and September of that year.

Home service. Training and drafting. These Battalions lost their brigade formation in 1916 and 1917; but they continued to train recruits and despatch reinforcements to overseas battalions until their services were no longer required.

Disbanded in February, 1918, on the reduction of the brigades to three battalions.

Disbanded in April, 1919.

Disbanded in April, 1919.

Although originally intended for service overseas, this Battalion, like others raised about the same time, was turned into a training and drafting unit early in 1915. It was disbanded in August, 1916.

Raised as a "Labour" battalion, the 12th, owing to reduction in numbers, eventually became the 24th and 25th "Labour" companies. No formal disbandment seems to have taken place.

Raised as a "Garrison" battalion with men of inferior physique, it dropped the title of "garrison" in June, 1918, when it was attached to the 178th Brigade and took part in the general advance of September, 1918. It was in the front line on Armistice day. It then proceeded to Dunkirk, where it had charge of a demobilisation camp, and was not disbanded until November, 1919.

APPENDIX II

THE GREAT WAR

Battle Honours of the Duke of Wellington's Regiment
(Colour Honours distinguished by **Capitals**)

BATTLE HONOUR	2nd	1/4th	2/4th	5th	1/5th	2/5th	1/6th	2/6th	1/7th	2/7th	8th	9th	10th	12th	13th
MONS	×														
Le Cateau	×														
Retreat from Mons	×														
MARNE, 1914	×														
MARNE, 1918		×			×										
Aisne, 1914.	×														
La Bassée, 1914	×														
YPRES, 1914	×														
YPRES, 1915	×														
YPRES, 1917	×	×			×		×		×		×	×	×		
Nonne Bosschen	×														
HILL 60	×														
Gravenstafel	×														
St. Julien	×														
Aubers		×			×		×		×						
SOMME, 1916	×	×			×		×		×		×	×	×	×	
SOMME, 1918	×		×	×								×			
Albert, 1916	×	×			×		×		×			×	×	×	
Albert, 1918												×			×
Bazentin		×					×							×	
Delville Wood												×		×	
Pozières		×					×		×						
Flers-Courcelette		×					×		×						
Morval														×	
Thiepval											×				
Le Transloy	×														
Ancre Heights	×										×		×		
ARRAS, 1917	×		×		×		×					×		×	
ARRAS, 1918	×														
Scarpe, 1917	×											×			
Scarpe, 1918	×														
Arleux	×														
Bullecourt			×		×		×		×						
Messines, 1917											×		×		
Messines, 1918		×					×		×						
Langemarck, 1917											×				

APPENDIX II

BATTLE HONOURS—*continued*.

BATTLE HONOUR	NUMBER OF BATTALIONS														
	2nd	1/4th	2/4th	5th	1/5th	2/5th	1/6th	2/6th	1/7th	2/7th	8th	9th	10th	12th	13th
Menin Road													×		
Polygon Wood													×		
Broodseinde		×					×								
Poelcappelle	×	×			×		×		×		×				
Passchendaele		×					×		×		×	×			
CAMBRAI, 1917			×			×		×		×					
CAMBRAI, 1918		×	×				×					×			
St. Quentin												×			
Ancre, 1918				×											
LYS	×	×					×		×						
Estaires		×					×								
Hazebrouck	×														
Bailleul		×					×								
Kemmel		×					×		×						
Béthune	×														
Scherpenberg		×					×		×						
Tardenois			×	×											
Amiens													×		
Bapaume, 1918	×		×	×									×		
Drocourt-Quéant	×														
Hindenburg Line	×		×	×					×		×				
Havrincourt			×	×											
Epéhy												×			
Canal du Nord			×	×											
Selle	×		×	×											
Valenciennes	×	×					×		×						
Sambre			×	×								×			
France and Flanders, 1914–18	×	×	×	×	×	×	×	×	×	×	×	×	×	×	×
PIAVE													×		
Vittorio Veneto													×		
Italy, 1917–18													×		
Suvla											×				
LANDING AT SUVLA											×				
Scimitar Hill											×				
Gallipoli, 1915											×				
Egypt, 1916											×				

APPENDIX III

THE ROLL OF HONOUR

OFFICERS

Battn.	Rank	Name	Date of death
1st and 2nd	Major	Anderson, William James	19th October, 1915
1st and 2nd	2nd Lieut.	Babb, Royland Nettleton (Attached 9th Battalion)	15th October, 1918
2nd	Capt.	Baird, David	2nd December, 1917
2nd	2nd Lieut.	Beard, Frederick Whiteley	10th October, 1916
1st and 2nd	2nd Lieut.	Bouchier, Charles Arthur (Attached 9th Battalion)	4th November, 1918
2nd	2nd Lieut.	Bowes, Cyril Hulme	1st July, 1916
3rd attd. 2nd	2nd Lieut.	Braine, William Thomas Coker	9th October, 1916
2nd	Brig.-General	Bray, Robert Napier, C.M.G., D.S.O.	23rd October, 1921
1st and 2nd	2nd Lieut.	Cameron, William George (Attached Lancashire Fusiliers)	4th September, 1918
1st	2nd Lieut.	Carruthers, Gordon (Attached 5th Battalion)	27th November, 1918
2nd	Lieut.	Cheetham, Alan Humphrey	16th November, 1916
2nd	2nd Lieut.	Cobb, Reginald John Preston (Attached Royal Air Force)	11th October, 1917
2nd	2nd Lieut.	Coldwell, Norman Goodman, M.C.	16th May, 1918
2nd	Capt.	Cunningham, Edward Malcolm (Attached 9th Battalion)	4th August, 1917
2nd	Capt.	Cunningham, Kenneth Edward	3rd May, 1917
3rd attd. 2nd	Capt.	Davis, Reginald Noel	12th October, 1916
1st and 2nd	Brig.-General	De Gex, Francis John, C.B., C.M.G. (Staff)	2nd April, 1917
2nd	Capt.	Denman-Jubb, Cyril Oswald	24th August, 1914
2nd	Lieut.	de Wend, Douglas Fenton	11th November, 1914
1st and 2nd	2nd Lieut.	Dunshee, Ernest Rowland (Attached 5th Battalion)	11th August, 1918
2nd	Lieut.	Egerton, Charles Caledon	18th April, 1915
3rd attd. 2nd	2nd Lieut.	Elliott, Geoffrey Edmund	12th October, 1916
2nd	Capt.	Ellis, Thomas Martin	18th April, 1915
2nd	2nd Lieut.	Elmitt-Browne Austin	15th June, 1916
2nd	Capt.	Gatacre, Edward George	20th February, 1916
2nd	Lieut.	Grevelink, Edward James Yzenhoed	6th June, 1917
2nd	2nd Lieut.	Gunn, Arthur	5th May, 1915
2nd	Capt.	Hadwen, Noel Waugh	1st July, 1916
1st and 2nd	2nd Lieut.	Harper, Harold Raymond (Attached 4th Battalion)	4th November, 1918
2nd	2nd Lieut.	Henderson, Patric Gordon	2nd May, 1918
3rd attd. 2nd	2nd Lieut.	Heskett, John	15th April, 1918

Battn.	Rank	Name	Date of death
2nd	Lieut.	Hodge, Jack Wheaton	12th October, 1916
2nd	Lieut.-Colonel	Horsfall, Alfred Garnett, D.S.O.	9th October, 1917
2nd	Lieut.	Hughes, John William, M.C.	15th April, 1918
1st and 2nd	2nd Lieut.	Jones, Rowland (Attached 9th Battalion)	13th October, 1918
1st and 2nd	Major	Kidd, Vivian Norval, M.C. (Staff)	21st March, 1917
2nd	2nd Lieut.	Lambert, Philip Felix	3rd May, 1917
2nd	2nd Lieut.	Larcombe, Archibald Herbert	26th October, 1918
2nd	2nd Lieut.	Leece, Francis Ballantyne	12th October, 1916
1st and 2nd	2nd Lieut.	Lyon, Eric (Attached Lancashire Fusiliers)	4th November, 1918
3rd attd. 2nd	2nd Lieut.	MacNamara, Joseph Bernard	19th October, 1916
1st and 2nd	Lieut.-Colonel	Maples, William Evelyn (Attached North Lancs.)	14th December, 1916
1st and 2nd	Lieut.	Marriott, Kenneth Melbourne Hugh (Attached Royal Air Force)	28th September, 1918
2nd	2nd Lieut.	Middlewood, Albert	3rd May, 1917
3rd attd. 2nd	Capt.	Milbank, Robert Charles Alfred Paslo Edmund	10th May, 1915
2nd	2nd Lieut.	Millican, John Stamper	3rd July, 1916
3rd attd. 2nd	Lieut.	Owen, Rowland Hely	18th April, 1915
1st and 2nd	2nd Lieut.	Phripp, Arthur Thornton	19 October, 1917
3rd attd. 2nd	Lieut.	Plumb, Edward Stephen	8th September, 1917
1st and 2nd	2nd Lieut.	Potts, Richard Harold Urwin (Attached Lancashire Fusiliers)	2nd December, 1918
1st and 2nd	Lieut.	Roch-Austin, Sidney Leslie (Attached 4th Battalion)	4th November, 1918
2nd	Lieut.	Russell, Lawrence Edward	24th August, 1914
1st and 2nd	Lieut.-Colonel	St. Hill, Ashton Alexander, D.S.O. (Attached Northumberland Fusiliers)	27th October, 1918
1st	2nd Lieut.	Scaife, Joseph	21st March, 1918
2nd	2nd Lieut.	Scott, Arthur George	23rd December, 1915
3rd attd. 2nd	2nd Lieut.	Simkins, Walter Francis	9th October, 1916
2nd	2nd Lieut.	Simpson, Anthony Bean Tracey	6th May, 1915
1st and 2nd	2nd Lieut.	Stent, Harold Rudolph	20th July, 1918
2nd	Major	Strafford, Percy Belcher	24th August, 1915
3rd attd. 2nd	Lieut.	Sugden, Guy Hatton	12th October, 1916
1st and 2nd	2nd Lieut.	Sugden, John (Attached 5th Battalion)	29th March, 1918
2nd	2nd Lieut.	Taylor, Albert Edward	9th April, 1917
2nd	Capt.	Taylor, Ernle Rumbold	18th April, 1915
2nd	Lieut.	Thackeray, Frederick Rennel, M.C.	18th April, 1915
3rd attd. 2nd	2nd Lieut.	Thelwell, Harry Rowland	8th July, 1916
2nd	2nd Lieut.	Thomas, Eric Hand	18th January, 1918
2nd	Lieut.	Thompson, John Henry Louis	17th September, 1914
1st and 2nd	2nd Lieut.	Thomson, James Stein (Attached Lancashire Fusiliers)	22nd July, 1918
1st and 2nd	Capt.	Tidmarsh, John Moriarty (Attached Royal Air Force)	3rd September, 1918
1st and 2nd	Major	Travers, Hugh Price (Attached 8th Division)	7th August, 1915
2nd	Bvt. Lieut.-Colonel	Tyndall, William Ernest Marriott	1st August, 1916

APPENDIX III

Battn.	Rank	Name	Date of death
3rd attd. 2nd	2nd Lieut.	Vicat, Frederick Hollod	8th December, 1917
2nd	2nd Lieut.	Ville, Hubert Leslie	3rd May, 1917
1st and 2nd	2nd Lieut.	Walker, Adolphus (Attached 5th Battalion)	15th April, 1918
1st	Lieut.	Walker, Arthur (Attached Machine Gun Corps)	10th August, 1918
1st	Lieut.	Watkin, Harry	21st October, 1918
2nd	2nd Lieut.	Watmough, Oscar Oswald	1st September, 1918
3rd attd. 2nd	Lieut.	Whitaker, Charles Frederick	5th May, 1915
3rd attd. 2nd	Lieut.	Williamson, George	12th November, 1914
1st and 2nd	Lieut.-Colonel	Wilson, John Hutton Bowes (Attached Yorks and Lancs.)	7th June, 1917
2nd	2nd Lieut.	Wolfenden, Laurence	24th October, 1918
1st and 2nd	2nd Lieut.	Woodhouse, Henry (Attached 9th Battalion)	4th November, 1918

APPENDIX IV

THE ROLL OF HONOUR

WARRANT OFFICERS, NON-COMMISSIONED OFFICERS AND MEN

1st BATTALION

20259 Sgt.	Akers, William	15.7.18	
18444 Pte.	Allen, Oliver Charles	16.12.17	
10067 Pte.	Alvey, Patrick	19.12.18	
9823 A/Cpl.	Atkinson, William	27.5.19	
9467 Pte.	Best, Ben	1.7.15	
10006 Pte.	Brennan, Iohn	28.8.14	
8326 L/Cpl.	Carter, John	9.7.15	
9056 L/Cpl.	Clayton, Herbert	12.12.15	
14106 Pte.	Connely, Joseph	1.1.18	
9343 Pte.	Cusick, James	15.2.19	
29749 Pte.	Denning, Frederick	11.3.17	
9985 Pte.	Dews, Frank	2.11.18	
8853 Pte.	Goring, Harry	31.5.16	
9211 Pte.	Green, Percy	18.8.18	
30729 Pte.	Griswell, Ernest	9.9.17	
31114 Pte.	Harrison, Thomas Henry	27.8.17	
8849 Pte.	Haskins, Archibald James	31.12.16	
29552 Pte.	Hurley, Martin	28.3.16	
5210 Pte.	Hyland, James Ernest	23.12.17	
39929 A/Sgt.	Ince, Douglas Gordon Wayne	7.8.18	
17474 L/Cpl.	Line, Cecil	13.7.17	
10090 Cpl.	Lister, Arthur	6.9.15	
10202 Pte.	Long, Richard George	29.10.17	
9713 Pte.	Marples, George	4.12.14	
9029 Pte.	Martin, John	6.11.18	
8615 Pte.	Mawe, George	28.8.14	
10189 Pte.	McKenna, Daniel	31.10.14	
9592 Pte.	Moore, Albert Charles	31.12.16	
8243 Bdmn.	Mullen, Thomas	22.8.18	
10209 Pte.	Pilgrim, Alfred	16.9.17	
8836 Pte.	Pledge, George Henry	27.5.17	
9772 Pte.	Portsmouth, George	14.10.16	
31067 Pte.	Rayner, Ernest	27.5.19	
10085 Pte.	Regan, Harold	12.10.15	
9043 Pte.	Rose, Frederick Arthur	17.10.14	
9014 Pte.	Rumney, Arthur John	14.8.15	
9033 Pte.	Ryan, Herbert Edward	27.8.14	
9583 Pte.	Senior, Thomas	28.7.18	
17465 Pte.	Taylor, William E.	1.6.16	
9232 Pte.	Thomas, James	1.7.15	
9551 Pte.	Thompson, George Arthur	27.5.19	
9888 Pte.	Thorn, William Henry	25.6.16	
11674 Pte.	Todd, Edward Percival	7.11.18	
3748 Sgt.	Wilson, John	13.10.17	
7606 L/Sgt.	Woollard, Richard	29.12.15	

2nd BATTALION

16461 Cpl.	Ackrill, William Frederick	24.10.18	
3/10970 Pte.	Ackroyd, Arthur	5.5.15	
13553 Pte.	Ackroyd, William	1.5.17	
16165 Pte.	Acland, Ralph	1.9.18	
3/9395 Pte.	Acton, Stephen	8.11.14	
265304 Pte.	Adams, Joseph	9.8.17	
25357 Pte.	Adams, Percy Guy	10.10.17	
7752 L/Sgt.	Addison, Alfred	4.7.16	
3/16060 Pte.	Addison, Reginald Francis	12.10.16	
12011 Pte.	Adey, Frank	5.5.15	
12168 Pte.	Aharne, John	5.5.15	
3/10586 Pte.	Ainley, Ellery	11.4.17	

HISTORY OF THE DUKE OF WELLINGTON'S REGIMENT

18063 Pte.	Ainley, Fred	12.10.16	10500 Pte.	Banks, James Henry 23.8.14
19667 Pte.	Akeroyd, Arthur Helliwell	11.10.16	23775 Pte.	Banks, John Henry 12.10.16
			265311 Pte.	Banks, Joseph 3.5.17
34765 Pte.	Alcock, Henry	30.8.18	24210 Pte.	Bankhead, John 24.10.18
31775 Pte.	Allan, Edgar	30.8.18	25358 Pte.	Barker, Alfred Edmund 2.2.18
24369 Pte.	Allan, Henry Eustace	3.5.17	10710 Pte.	Barker, Fred 1.7.16
14587 Pte.	Allen, Ernest	6.5.15	24283 Pte.	Barker, George 19.12.16
5004 C.S.M.	Allen, William	24.8.14	3/10275 Pte.	Barker, John 11.11.14
24852 Pte.	Allison, Ernest	27.4.18	22608 Pte.	Barlow, Albert Edward 10.11.18
267165 Pte.	Alton, George Herbert	14.8.18	306716 Pte.	Barnes, Charles William 10.10.17
8310 Pte.	Amon, Edward	25.11.15	26041 Pte.	Barnes, Frank 11.10.17
265305 Pte.	Anniford, John	23.9.17	3/9751 Pte.	Barnes, James Henry 24.11.14
9943 Pte.	Archer, Charles John	11.11.14	11923 Pte.	Barraclough, Ina 30.8.18
268759 Pte.	Arnold, Arthur	10.10.17	204152 Pte.	Barrett, John 31.8.18
20219 Pte.	Ardill, Albert William	3.2.17	3/12888 Pte.	Barrett, Thomas 12.10.16
18048 Pte.	Armitage, Albert	28.3.18	26111 Pte.	Barrett, William Tatlock 31.8.18
267480 Pte.	Armitage, Willie Hick	2.2.18		
23978 Pte.	Armstrong, Frank	11.5.18	35470 Pte.	Barron, Gilbert James 24.10.18
24957 Pte.	Armstrong, John Willie	8.4.17	23321 Pte.	Barry, William 3.5.17
23777 Pte.	Armstrong, Robert	12.10.16	15515 Sgt.	Bates, George 13.5.17
8685 Sgt.	Arrah, Henry Horace	12.10.16	10778 Pte.	Bates, James 18.10.16
			7754 Pte.	Bates, Joseph Alfred 11.11.14
6617 Pte.	Arrowsmith, Walter	28.11.14	10763 Pte.	Batty, Harold 24.2.15
6213 Pte.	Ashbey, John	31.10.14	19416 Pte.	Battye, John 12.10.16
3/10590 Pte.	Ashurst, Leonard	18.4.15	202181 Pte.	Baxter, Clement 31.10.17
30102 Pte.	Ashworth, Charles Ellis	2.6.17	19491 Pte.	Baxter, John Alfred 12.10.16
			8583 Pte.	Bazeley, John Ernest 8.11.14
12130 Pte.	Ashworth, Thomas Roger	18.4.15	9686 Pte.	Beardsworth, Arthur Gibson 8.11.14
22416 Pte.	Askey, James	30.8.18		
10842 Pte.	Asling, Edgar	7.5.15	235241 Pte.	Beaumont, Edgar Hanley 28.3.18
306507 L/Cpl.	Aspinall, Harry	24.10.18	17793 Pte.	Beaumont, Henry 12.10.16
25535 Pte.	Atkinson, Tom	15.4.18	6680 L/Cpl.	Beaumont, Henry 11.11.14
24206 Pte.	Atkinson, William	3.5.17	6816 Pte.	Bebee, Harold 18.4.15
8204 Pte.	Austin, William Joseph	7.8.15	15756 Pte.	Bedford, Thomas 7.5.18
29615 Pte.	Avery, Edgar	31.8.18	34881 Pte.	Beeby, Alfred 24.10.18
10803 Pte.	Ayres, Alfred Ernest	12.10.16	6710 Pte.	Beech, Frank Walter 13.4.15
26110 Pte.	Bailey, George William	24.10.18	18864 Pte.	Belford, Arthur 5.7.16
14451 Pte.	Bailey, Joshua	1.7.16	14159 Pte.	Bell, Harold 5.5.15
25603 Pte.	Baker, Frank Burgoyne	30.8.18	25343 Pte.	Bell, John Henry 9.10.17
			10685 Pte.	Bell, John William 7.3.15
19884 Pte.	Balderstone, Herbert	3.5.17	23778 Pte.	Bell, William 12.10.16
20406 Pte.	Baldwin, Harold Evers	9.10.17	17697 Pte.	Bellas, George Schorah 12.2.17
267218 Pte.	Baldwin, Thomas	4.5.17	305700 Pte.	Bennett, Charles Reuben 8.11.18
3/12505 Pte.	Ball, William	1.7.16		
24963 Pte.	Balmford, Arnold	3.5.17	202876 Pte.	Bennison, William 15.4.18

APPENDIX IV

18702	Pte.	Benson, Harry	3.5.17	3/10754 Pte.	Bowen, Leonard	24.2.15
240423	Pte.	Benson, Percy	30.8.18	201109 A/Cpl.	Bower, Charles Henry	3.5.17
14940	Pte.	Bentham, William	12.10.16	6714 Pte.	Bower, Herbert	11.11.14
11228	Pte.	Bentley, Edward	5.5.15	3/10910 Pte.	Boyle, Thomas	5.5.15
10674	Pte.	Berriman, James	4.3.15	24490 Pte.	Bradley, Edward	11.4.17
23344	Pte.	Berry, Harry	10.4.17	235746 Pte.	Bradley, Francis George	30.8.18
8217	Pte.	Betts, Charles	12.10.16	7702 Pte.	Bradley, Henry Bernard	11.11.14
25539	Pte.	Bevan, George Albert	28.3.18	204245 Pte.	Bradley, Joe	8.8.18
14024	Pte.	Beverley, Arthur	5.5.15	3/10458 Pte.	Bradley, Walter	5.5.15
242707	Pte.	Bickley, Ernest Edward	28.3.18	17238 Pte.	Bradley, William	12.10.16
3/10835	Pte.	Binks, George	19.10.16	3/10977 Pte.	Brady, Thomas	17.7.15
6832	Pte.	Binns, Harry	11.11.14	29463 Pte.	Brady, Thomas	3.5.17
13990	Pte.	Binns, Joseph	5.5.15	3/10163 Pte.	Brammer, Thomas	5.5.15
12401	Pte.	Binns, William	8.9.15	13736 Pte.	Branston, Charles	12.10.16
3/10692	Pte.	Birch, Evan	6.4.15	11831 L/Sgt.	Brazey, Lewis	8.8.18
8180	L/Cpl.	Birch, Thomas	11.11.14	35320 Pte.	Brazewell, William	24.10.18
5598	A/Sgt.	Bird, Albert Thomas	12.10.16	16010 Pte.	Brazier, Herbert	15.11.17
6895	A/Sgt.	Bird, William	18.5.18	7870 L/Sgt.	Brier, Charles	11.11.14
19773	Pte.	Birk, Joseph	12.10.16	24109 Pte.	Brierley, Harold	3.5.18
8325	Pte.	Bishop, Edward	1.5.19	26104 Pte.	Brightmore, Edgar	10.10.17
24487	Pte.	Blackburn, Henry	6.3.17	235189 Pte.	Brighton, Walter	3.5.17
11785	Pte.	Blades, Richard Henry	5.5.15	24409 Pte.	Brinham, Charles Henry	10.10.17
34882	Pte.	Blakeway, Edwin	31.8.18	19701 Pte.	Broadbent, Harold	12.10.16
23703	Pte.	Blamires, Harold	11.4.17	10772 Pte.	Broadbent, Harry	16.4.18
235243	Pte.	Bland, Horace Arthur	3.5.17	11966 Pte.	Brook, Arthur	5.5.15
				10601 Pte.	Brook, Hildred	1.7.16
14610	Pte.	Bland, John	5.5.15	14408 Pte.	Brook, Tom	12.10.16
3/12472	L/Cpl.	Blezard, James Edward	31.1.16	10617 Pte.	Brooke, Herbert	28.3.15
				10580 Pte.	Brooke, James Edward	6.5.15
15519	Pte.	Blyth, Charles Henry	3.5.17			
24293	Pte.	Boak, Henry	4.2.17	22331 Pte.	Brookes, John Richard	30.8.18
14149	Pte.	Bolton, James	18.4.15			
22129	Pte.	Bone, Edward Arthur	25.10.18	8300 L/Cpl.	Broomfield, Charles Edward	25.9.18
3/10364	Pte.	Boocock, John Hiram	2.12.14	10458 Pte.	Brown, Alfred	11.11.14
				6967 Pte.	Brown, Alfred	24.8.14
7700	Pte.	Booth, George	18.4.15	8116 Pte.	Brown, Charles	11.11.14
3/9889	Pte.	Booth, Harry	22.10.16	7973 Pte.	Brown, Harry	26.1.15
7751	Cpl.	Booth, James	12.10.16	7481 Pte.	Brown, Herbert John	19.9.14
5863	L/Cpl.	Booth, Tom	8.11.14			
7553	Pte.	Booth, William	4.6.16	6875 L/Sgt.	Brown, John Frederick	27.4.17
17772	Pte.	Boothroyd, Denis Allen	12.10.16	15332 Cpl.	Brown, John	24.10.18
28792	L/Cpl.	Boothroyd, George Clement	9.2.17	8165 Pte.	Brown, Percy	24.8.14
				235225 Sgt.	Bruce, Robert Vernon	9.4.17
10643	Pte.	Bostock, Willie	3.5.17			
28814	Pte.	Bottomley, Ernest	3.5.17	8055 Pte.	Bryan, Frederick John	2.7.16
32372	Pte.	Bottomley, Fred	31.8.18			
3/10877	A/Sgt.	Bottomley, Joe Leonard	18.4.15	11394 Pte.	Buttler, Samuel	3.5.17
				35322 Pte.	Buckley, James	24.10.18

10542	A/L/Cpl.	Buckley, James William	4.5.17	16301	Pte.	Carter, William Henry	27.6.15
54837	Pte.	Buckley, Percy	9.8.18	6504	Pte.	Carvley, Richard	7.12.15
16278	A/L/Cpl.	Buffey, John	20.1.16	7601	Pte.	Cassidy, Patrick	11.11.14
204347	Pte.	Bullas, Sam Schofield	10.10.17	8011	Pte.	Casswell, William	1.9.14
8483	Pte.	Bullen, Ernest	27.10.16	24967	Pte.	Castle, Herbert	9.4.17
16578	Cpl.	Burch, Harry	13.10.16	8902	A/Sgt.	Caulfield, Patrick James	8.11.14
12318	Pte.	Burn, Charles	15.4.18	268764	Pte.	Causer, Joseph	10.10.17
10323	Pte.	Burnett, John	12.10.16	8419	Pte.	Chadwick, Percy	11.11.14
8197	Pte.	Burrows, Thomas Sampson	31.8.14	8206	Pte.	Chalkley, Sydney Thomas	11.11.14
25342	Pte.	Burt, William Owen	15.11.17	14889	Pte.	Challenger, Joseph Leonard	1.7.16
268911	Pte.	Burton, Albert William	30.8.18	14603	Pte.	Chambers, Harry	5.5.15
				3/10663	Pte.	Chambers, Reginald	12.10.16
24488	Pte.	Burton, Wallace	14.12.16	23226	Pte.	Chapelow, Joseph	7.5.18
3833	Pte.	Burton, Walter	20.4.15	11193	Pte.	Chapman, Henry Arthur	5.5.15
16589	A/Sgt.	Bushnell, Thomas	20.7.16	33862	Pte.	Chappell, Ernest	31.8.18
26054	Pte.	Butler, William Charles	8.8.18	3/10732	Pte.	Charlesworth, John	2.7.16
10808	Pte.	Butson, John	12.10.16	19669	Pte.	Charlesworth, Sam	24.10.16
23785	Pte.	Butterfield, Isaac	12.10.16	10571	L/Cpl.	Charlton, George	17.8.16
8664	L/Cpl.	Butterworth, Edgar	11.11.14	8046	Pte.	Charlton, George Edward	11.11.14
20048	Pte.	Butterworth, John	17.8.16	11431	Pte.	Chatburn, Thomas	5.5.15
24493	Pte.	Butterworth, William Brook	3.5.17	6624	Pte.	Chaytor, Joseph	3.5.17
6676	Pte.	Button, Thomas	15.11.14	13516	Pte.	Childs, Thomas	5.5.15
3/11133	A/Cpl.	Byrne, James	5.5.15	7557	Pte.	Chippendale, Theophilus	8.5.15
3/10107	Pte.	Bywood, Henry	12.8.15				
39071	Pte.	Caister, Leonard John	24.6.18	3/12452	Pte.	Chippendale, William Henry	10.10.16
3/10430	Pte.	Callaghan, Austin	12.10.16	10586	Pte.	Christie, Clarence	18.4.15
24211	Pte.	Callender, James	10.12.16	13043	Pte.	Christy, James	3.2.18
23859	Cpl.	Calvert, Arthur Irvin	16.4.18	5910	Sgt.	Church, Ernest William	23.10.14
15848	Pte.	Calvert, Harry	3.5.17	300178	Pte.	Churchman, Walter	15.4.18
24496	Pte.	Canavan, Francis	3.5.17	11338	Pte.	Clapham, Fred Louis	1.7.16
7943	Pte.	Cane, George Arthur	24.8.14	29448	Pte.	Clapham, James Ernest	13.4.17
3/11619	Cpl.	Cannon, James	10.10.17	7997	L/Sgt.	Clapp, Albert Edward	5.5.15
12090	Pte.	Capps, Benson Atkinson	5.5.15	3/9671	Pte.	Clarey, Fred	1.7.16
28978	Pte.	Carney, James	9.8.17	28774	Pte.	Clark, Frank	11.4.17
3/10649	Pte.	Carney, John	5.5.15	8289	Pte.	Clark, Frederick Frank	28.11.14
9679	Pte.	Carr, Thomas	3.5.17				
24498	Pte.	Carr, William Herbert	10.12.16	12170	Pte.	Clark, Thomas Henry	19.7.17
6735	A/Sgt.	Carrington, Frank, D.C.M.	18.4.15	7994	Pte.	Clarke, Albert	18.4.15
				7915	Pte.	Clarke, George Benjamin Kearsley	11.11.14
3/10796	Pte.	Carroll, George	22.12.15				
13416	Pte.	Carroll, Joseph	8.5.18	10558	L/Cpl.	Clarke, Walter	25.4.18
9019	A/Sgt.	Carter, Frederick George	11.11.14	3/10697	Pte.	Clarkson, Ernest	29.10.14
				3/10575	Pte.	Claxton, Max	18.4.15

APPENDIX IV

10277	Pte.	Clay, Samuel	24.9.14	23546	Pte.	Corley, James William	18.4.18
9284	Pte.	Clegg, Arthur	11.11.14				
3/10157	Pte.	Clegg, Ernest	23.2.15	6508	Pte.	Cornwell, Herbert	11.11.14
15997	Pte.	Clegg, Whittaker	11.10.16	25354	Pte.	Corrigan, Horace	27.9.17
10575	Pte.	Clements, William George	8.11.14	235277	Pte.	Corry, Norbert Cyril	3.5.17
				7723	Pte.	Covill, Edward	5.5.15
24385	Pte.	Clennell, Thomas	10.10.17	28803	Pte.	Coulson, William	14.4.17
24970	Pte.	Cliffe, James	24.10.18	8009	Sgt.	Cowdery, Andrew	12.10.16
269251	Pte.	Clough, Henry	31.3.18	6211	Pte.	Coward, John	15.11.14
35471	Pte.	Clough, John William	22.9.18	8829	Sgt.	Cox, William John	11.11.14
				6613	Pte.	Coxon, Alfred George	17.9.14
12106	Pte.	Clow, John	18.4.15				
3/12036	Pte.	Clues, Sidney	1.7.16	10813	L/Cpl.	Coyne, Allan	1.8.18
24499	Pte.	Coates, Fred	5.9.17	18337	Pte.	Crabtree, Fred	3.5.17
8267	Pte.	Coates, George Edward	8.11.14	13858	Pte.	Crabtree, George	5.5.15
				200289	Pte.	Cracknell, Robert	8.8.18
24466	Pte.	Cockroft, Edgar	11.4.17	35335	Pte.	Craddock, Edwin	24.10.18
29674	Cpl.	Cockroft, Sam	30.8.18	8125	Pte.	Craigan, Michael	5.5.15
3/10702	Pte.	Cockroft, Tom	7.3.15	3/10665	Pte.	Crampton, Peter	26.12.17
24008	Pte.	Cohen, Jack	30.8.18	35278	Pte.	Crawford, James	9.4.17
20191	Pte.	Coldwell, Lewis	9.11.16	204749	L/Cpl.	Crawshaw, Phillip	15.4.18
18595	Pte.	Coleman, Tommy	3.5.17	16469	Pte.	Credie, Frederick	3.5.17
3/11143	Pte.	Collett, Charles Edwin	3.3.16	269001	Pte.	Creighton, George	15.4.18
				23776	Pte.	Crisp, William	12.10.16
7946	L/Cpl.	Collett, Ernest	11.11.14	8919	Sgt.	Croft, George	12.10.16
10776	Pte.	Collier, James	8.11.14	3/9303	Pte.	Crone, John William	17.11.14
10735	Pte.	Collinson, Alfred	5.5.15				
6594	Pte.	Comber, James	10.2.15	33004	Pte.	Crookes, Charles	31.8.18
10139	Cpl.	Comper, George Edward	24.8.14	18053	Pte.	Crosland, Ernest	1.7.16
				202562	Pte.	Crossland, Harry	31.8.18
24391	Pte.	Conkerton, Clarence	3.5.17	18058	Pte.	Crossland, Thomas	1.7.16
11864	L/Sgt.	Conolly, Peter	10.10.17	24436	Pte.	Crossland, Walker	9.4.17
8291	Pte.	Connor, John	11.11.14	7964	Pte.	Crow, Frederick	24.8.14
307701	Pte.	Connor, Thomas	31.8.18	5911	Pte.	Crowther, Charles	24.11.14
7546	Drmr.	Constantine, Albert	11.11.14	18633	Pte.	Crowther, Stanley	12.10.16
266961	Cpl.	Constantine, Tom	20.10.18	6925	L/Cpl.	Cruse, Charles	11.11.14
3/9260	Sgt.	Conway, William	16.11.14	10810	Pte.	Cryer, James Albert Greenwood	20.3.15
14213	Pte.	Conway, William	5.5.15				
3/12381	Pte.	Conwell, John	10.10.16	8384	Cpl.	Cudworth, John	1.11.16
8697	Pte.	Cook, Charles Frederick	11.11.14	29055	Pte.	Cull, Joseph	10.4.17
				8266	Pte.	Cullen, Frederick Walter	15.4.15
3/10476	L/Cpl.	Cook, John William	1.7.16				
33518	Pte.	Cook, Robert	6.4.18	26107	Pte.	Cummings, Charles Edward	10.10.17
25517	Pte.	Coope, Thomas Henry	2.9.18	3/11831	Pte.	Cunningham, Thomas	18.4.15
22276	Pte.	Cooper, Andrew	16.4.18				
308111	Pte.	Cooper, Arthur	28.4.18	28981	L/Cpl.	Cunliffe, Ellis	25.11.17
35327	Pte.	Cooper, James Stephen	24.10.18	17867	Pte.	Currie, Joseph	3.5.17
				3/9446	Pte.	Curry, Owen	28.11.14
16315	Pte.	Cope, Arthur	20.10.18	10696	Pte.	Curtis, Samuel	8.11.14
6705	Sgt.	Corbett, Fred	12.10.16	3/10385	Pte.	Cutforth, Albert Arthur	12.10.16
12265	Pte.	Corcoran, Thomas	18.4.15				
9563	Pte.	Cordwell, Herbert	11.11.14	16400	Pte.	Dale, Christopher	16.9.16
18243	Pte.	Cork, John	9.8.17	267386	Pte.	Daley, Felix	2.4.18

17511	Pte.	Dalton, James	12.10.16	9646 Pte.	Doel, Ernest	6.5.15
18720	Pte.	Darby, Herbert Charles	12.5.17	24212 Pte.	Dolan, Nicholson	30.9.17
6007	Sgt.	Davey, John	6.5.15	305427 Pte.	Donbavand, John	30.8.18
23788	Pte.	Davidson, Francis	18.7.18	3/10624 Pte.	Donley, Thomas	5.5.15
7305	Pte.	Davies, Enoch	11.11.14	23808 Pte.	Doolan, Patrick	10.10.17
7928	Pte.	Davies, John Henry	16.11.14	3/10254 Pte.	Dougherty, John Thomas	23.12.14
10304	Pte.	Davies, Robert William	1.7.16	11389 Pte.	Dowd, John	17.5.15
14649	Pte.	Davill, Harry	9.10.16	11284 Pte.	Dowd, Willie	6.5.15
6444	Pte.	Davis, Henry George	15.9.14	11361 Pte.	Dowden, George William	5.5.15
12513	Pte.	Davis, William Alfred	6.5.15	3/10849 Pte.	Downes, John	5.5.15
9802	Sgt.	Davison, Frederick	24.8.14	265765 Pte.	Downes, Tom	28.10.18
8399	Pte.	Davison, Harry	7.5.15	3/10173 Pte.	Drabble, Harry	12.10.16
16401	Pte.	Davoll, John William	23.10.16	10671 Pte.	Drake, Ernest	6.1.15
3/16394	Pte.	Dawes, Frederick	21.10.16	7792 L/Cpl.	Drake, Walter	1.2.15
24213	Pte.	Dawson, Bright Francis	12.4.17	3/10621 Pte.	Drake, Randall	5.5.15
16193	Pte.	Dawson, Charles	3.5.17	10682 Pte.	Dransfield, Norman	18.4.15
14907	Pte.	Dawson, George Willie	1.7.16	14026 Pte.	Draper, Alfred Edward Frost	5.5.15
23789	Pte.	Dawson, Henry	12.10.16	3/10560 Pte.	Dray, John	14.10.16
18387	Pte.	Dawson, Herbert	13.4.17	16839 Pte.	Drinkwater, John	3.5.17
18609	Pte.	Dawson, John William	11.4.17	15719 Pte.	Drury, John	6.4.18
29205	L/Cpl.	Dawson, William	10.10.17	9075 Pte.	Drury, William	24.3.15
10438	Pte.	Dayle, Bertrand	20.4.15	11116 Pte.	Dryden, Charles, D.C.M.	5.5.15
5267	C.S.M.	Deacon, George	5.5.15	235196 Pte.	Duckworth, Fred	15.4.18
19467	Pte.	Dean, Willie	12.10.16	9653 L/Cpl.	Dubery, Sidney Thompson	24.8.14
10781	L/Cpl.	Degnan, Michael	5.5.15	3/10423 Pte.	Duddy, Charles	5.5.15
10670	Pte.	Demain, Alfred	16.7.15	28743 Pte.	Duerdon, Percy	17.12.17
268073	Pte.	Denby, Samuel	6.5.18	8696 Pte.	Duffy, John	20.5.15
24015	L/Cpl.	Dennis, Henry Joseph	30.8.18	13499 A/Cpl.	Duffy, John	18.4.15
12147	Pte.	Dennison, Arthur	18.4.15	7456 Pte.	Duffy, John	12.10.16
3/11051	Sgt.	Denton, Harold Ellis, D.C.M.	8.8.18	23768 Pte.	Dungait, Robert	12.10.16
16251	Sgt.	Devine, Noah	9.7.16	10899 Pte.	Dunn, Henry	5.5.15
12392	Pte.	Dewhirst, George	28.6.15	3/11068 Pte.	Dunn, Leonard	5.5.15
9204	Pte.	Dewhirst, Harry	13.11.14	12173 Pte.	Dunn, William	5.5.15
18804	Pte.	Dewhirst, Lewis	3.5.17	16677 Pte.	Dunning, George	18.7.18
3/10817	L/Cpl.	Dewhurst, John	18.4.15	26081 Pte.	Dunning, Thomas Edwin	10.10.17
9370	Pte.	Dibbins, Fred William	2.7.16	3/9717 Pte.	Durkin, James	5.5.15
3/10289	Pte.	Dickinson, George	18.4.15	32454 Pte.	Dyer, Tom	2.4.18
3/9390	Pte.	Dickinson, James	5.5.15	3/10435 Pte.	Dyson, Arnold	5.5.15
9355	Pte.	Dillon, Dennis	11.11.14	24467 Pte.	Dyson, Arthur	10.10.17
10753	Cpl.	Dobbyn, Thomas	26.10.16	18054 Pte.	Dyson, George Donald	11.4.17
3/10124	Pte.	Dobson, Norman	24.2.15	23744 Pte.	Dyson, John Woodhouse	17.2.17
8076	Pte.	Dodd, William Edward	8.11.14	9509 Pte.	Dyson, John Joseph	7.3.15
				3/8942 Pte.	Eade, Walter	11.11.14
				7462 Pte.	Earnshaw, John	8.11.14
				8635 Sgt.	East, George	10.3.15
				14949 Pte.	Eastwood, Robert	8.5.17

APPENDIX IV

16702	L/Cpl.	Eccles, William	12.10.16	10483 Pte.	Firth, Bentley	5.5.15
5827	Pte.	Edmondson, George Henry	24.8.14	235200 Pte.	Firth, Richard Jacob	3.5.17
17621	Pte.	Edmunds, Frederick	6.5.15	19374 Pte.	Firth, George Handell	2.4.18
6998	L/Cpl.	Edmunds, Leslie Charles	9.11.15	235284 Pte.	Fisher, Arthur	20.5.18
3/8725	Pte.	Egan, James	9.11.14	3/10818 Pte.	Fisher, Lockburn	1.4.15
8213	L/Cpl.	Eggleton, Frederick Thomas	5.5.15	26232 Pte.	Fisher, Thomas	30.8.18
7379	Pte.	Elgin, George	6.5.15	3/10765 Pte.	Fitzpatrick, John	5.5.15
16680	Pte.	Eland, Skelton	1.7.16	4826 Pte.	Flaherty, Patrick	21.4.17
8059	Cpl.	Elbell, William Thomas	10.10.17	3/10190 Pte.	Fleming, Edward	7.3.15
16404	Cpl.	Elkington, Edward	29.8.18	24019 Pte.	Fletcher, Ephraim	15.4.18
7315	Pte.	Elliott, William	18.4.15	18716 Pte.	Fletcher, George	12.10.16
18285	Pte.	Ellis, Harry	31.1.17	12393 Pte.	Fletcher, Thomas Campbell	18.4.15
17648	Pte.	Ellis, Levi	3.5.17	204760 Pte.	Fletcher, Thomas Edward	15.4.18
3/9406	L/Cpl.	Emmott, Walter	20.3.15	15708 Pte.	Flint, Herbert	3.7.16
8379	Pte.	Emmott, John Edward	5.5.15	11584 Pte.	Flinton, Frederick William	5.5.15
29041	Pte.	England, Fred Watson	15.4.18	3/11637 Pte.	Foley, Michael	12.10.16
8136	L/Sgt.	Estall, Alexander George	24.8.14	7348 Pte.	Ford, Benjamin	24.8.14
24971	Pte.	Evans, David Ferdinand	11.4.17	7264 Pte.	Ford, James	13.9.14
10329	Pte.	Evans, Walter	5.5.15	7409 Pte.	Ford, Thomas, D.C.M.	23.10.14
10365	Pte.	Eves, Reginald Charles	28.6.15	12401 Pte.	Fort, Joseph William	18.4.15
18857	Pte.	Evitt, Fred	3.5.17	31787 Pte.	Foster, Albert	18.7.18
12008	L/Cpl.	Fallon, Edgar	24.2.15	29227 Pte.	Foster, Frank	10.10.17
305985	Pte.	Farrand, William	31.8.18	19449 Pte.	Foster, Fred	10.12.16
12786	Pte.	Farrar, Harry	30.8.18	9745 Sgt.	Foster, Frederick	30.3.18
6788	Sgt.	Farrar, Nelson	24.2.15	3/11007 Pte.	Foster, James	15.10.15
16295	Pte.	Farrell, James	28.9.17	24742 Pte.	Foster, James	13.11.18
307706	Pte.	Faulkes, John	28.3.18	14038 Pte.	Foster, John Willie	5.5.15
26225	Pte.	Favell, Herbert	22.10.18	9776 Pte.	Foster, Lawrence Richard	24.8.14
3/10614	Pte.	Fawbert, Harold	5.5.15	3/11257 Pte.	Foster, Ralph	2.8.16
266382	Pte.	Fawcett, George	1.9.18	28830 Pte.	Foster, Stanley	16.9.17
268947	Pte.	Fell, George	15.4.18	23884 Pte.	Fothergill, John William	7.5.18
10042	Pte.	Fells, William	8.11.14	14622 Pte.	Fox, Norman	5.5.15
3/16407	Pte.	Fenton, George	31.1.16	11759 Pte.	Foye, Thomas	3.5.17
3/9951	Pte.	Ferguson, Joseph	12.10.16	12653 Pte.	France, Edward	3.5.17
18293	Pte.	Fernsides, Frank Dudley	23.10.16	16540 Pte.	Francis, Samuel	3.11.16
204573	L/Cpl.	Field, Harry, M.M.	15.4.18	25531 Pte.	Fraser, James	1.9.18
10620	Pte.	Fieldhouse, Ernest	21.5.15	26070 Pte.	Fraser, Alexander	10.10.17
24955	Cpl.	Fielding, Harold	1.9.18	7766 Pte.	Freeman, George Henry	11.10.16
25598	Cpl.	Fielding, Sidney Hunter	31.3.18	9883 Pte.	Fryer, Albert	1.6.18
14244	Pte.	Fielding, Thomas	15.3.15	35676 Pte.	Fullalove, John Thomas	22.10.18
3/10346	Pte.	Filby, Thomas	5.5.15	7770 Pte.	Futter, Ernest William	6.9.14
8095	Pte.	Finch, George William	11.11.14	17457 Pte.	Galloway, Albert Edward	30.8.18

3/9691	Pte.	Gannon, Anthony	11.11.14	10860	Pte.	Gray, Horace	8.11.14
24314	Pte.	Gardam, James	5.2.17	10795	Pte.	Grayston, Roy	1.7.16
14036	Pte.	Garforth, George	6.5.15	202221	Pte.	Green, Arthur	31.8.18
268974	Pte.	Garland, George Walls	15.4.18	24938	Pte.	Green, John Israel	3.5.17
26280	Pte.	Garner, Frederick Charles	24.10.18	10718	Pte.	Green, George Stanley	2.7.16
24936	Pte.	Garrett, Henry	3.5.17	17615	Pte.	Green, Harry	23.6.18
201739	Pte.	Garside, Harry	10.10.17	19632	Pte.	Green, William	10.9.16
3/10761	Cpl.	Gartside, William	2.9.17	20009	Pte.	Greenfield, Wilfred	12.10.16
9108	L/Cpl.	Gates, James	5.5.15	35480	Pte.	Greensides, James	24.10.18
24937	Pte.	Gaukroger, Arthur	2.5.17	20123	Pte.	Greenwood Frederick	12.10.16
10559	Pte.	Gee, George Arthur	11.11.14	24236	Pte.	Greenwood, Harold	22.5.17
11244	Pte.	Gee, Lewis George	5.5.15	23794	Pte.	Greenwood, Herbert	21.10.16
7470	Pte.	Geldard, Walter Hall	11.11.14	8072	Pte.	Greenwood, John William	24.8.14
14857	Pte.	Gibbons, Thomas	21.9.16	32077	Pte.	Greenwood, Sam	31.8.18
3/9637	Pte.	Gibson, George	5.5.15	6513	Pte.	Greenwood, Thomas	24.8.14
22435	Pte.	Giles, Arthur	30.8.18	15527	Pte.	Greenwood, William	1.5.17
19702	Pte.	Gill, Arthur	3.5.17	24939	Pte.	Greenwood, Willie Victor	11.4.17
7294	L/Cpl.	Gilligan, Charles	7.4.15				
7647	Pte.	Gilligan, James	11.11.14	14022	Pte.	Gregson, Ernest	5.5.15
8416	Pte.	Gillespie, James	11.11.14	6726	Pte.	Gresswell, Fred	5.5.15
7757	Pte.	Gipp, Frederick Charles	11.11.14	3/11090	Pte.	Grey, Martin Conley	5.5.15
				12395	Pte.	Grimwood, Bertie	5.5.15
8255	Pte.	Glanfield, John Lester	22.10.14	10752	Pte.	Grout, Harry	14.12.14
				7563	Pte.	Guest, Harry	24.8.14
204953	Cpl.	Glassbrook, Harry	18.7.18	14928	Pte.	Guilfoyle, Stephen	22.12.15
18805	Pte.	Gledhill, Harry Wells	1.7.16	17399	Pte.	Haigh, Archie	31.3.18
				24975	Pte.	Haigh, Ernest	19.2.18
23890	Cpl.	Gledhill, Ernest	24.10.18	3/10599	Pte.	Haigh, George	3.7.16
10153	Pte.	Gledhill, Joseph	11.11.14	6873	L/Cpl.	Haigh, Joseph Garside	16.9.14
16580	Pte.	Glen, Alexander	1.7.16				
10794	Pte.	Glover, Joseph	12.10.16	13444	L/Cpl.	Haigh, Wilfred	27.3.18
242611	Pte.	Goddard, Herbert	15.4.18	28870	Pte.	Haigh, Wilfred	15.4.18
24319	Pte.	Goforth, George Albert	3.5.17	11273	Pte.	Haigh, William Herbert	18.4.15
9253	Pte.	Goggin, William	10.10.17	31247	Cpl.	Hainsworth Harold	22.4.18
3/10007	Pte.	Golding, Solly	5.5.15				
19961	Pte.	Goldsbrough, Fred	12.10.16	8989	Pte.	Hales, Horace Roderick	24.8.14
7277	Pte.	Goodall, Ernest	23.8.14				
235201	Pte.	Goodall, Granville	9.4.17	3/10693	Pte.	Haley, James	5.5.15
35445	Pte.	Goodall, Percy	24.10.18	24977	Pte.	Haley, Fred	11.4.17
24316	Pte.	Goodwill, Dennis	14.3.18	3/11490	Pte.	Hall, Herbert	2.7.16
28736	Pte.	Gorell, Austin	11.4.17	24382	Pte.	Hall, Tom	14.6.17
12214	Pte.	Gorman, Francis	2.3.15	23695	Pte.	Hall, William	31.8.18
3/11211	Pte.	Gorman, Patrick	28.7.16	10654	L/Cpl.	Hall, Walter Bloye	19.9.14
11491	Pte.	Gorman, Patrick	19.4.15	24940	Pte.	Hallas, Charles	3.5.17
7570	Pte.	Gott, John William	18.4.15	24243	Pte.	Halmshaw, Ernest	3.5.17
10788	Pte.	Grady, Harold	14.12.14	24511	Pte.	Halpine, Walter	3.5.17
11498	Pte.	Granger, John	3.5.17	18410	Pte.	Halstead, John William	1.7.16
9948	Pte.	Gray, George Edward	8.11.14	3/10742	Pte.	Hamer, William	6.5.15

APPENDIX IV

7860	L/Cpl.	Hamilton, Alexander George	23.12.14	31878	Pte.	Hatley, William	28.3.18
16656	L/Cpl.	Hamilton, Charles Frederick	12.12.15	3/10497	Pte.	Hatton, Edward Arthur	18.4.15
24282	Pte.	Hamm, John Henry	11.12.16	12377	Pte.	Harvey, John William	5.5.15
7949	Pte.	Hammond, Albert	5.5.15	34844	Pte.	Hawkins, George Henry Charles	30.8.18
16419	Pte.	Hammond, Richard	26.5.15	16085	Pte.	Hawkins, Horace	1.7.16
3/10709	Pte.	Hamnett, Arthur	7.3.15	29096	Pte.	Hawley, Alfred	24.10.18
3/10278	Pte.	Hampton, Frederick	26.3.15	8345	Pte.	Haynes, Alfred	11.11.14
15867	Pte.	Hancock, Thomas	14.7.15	9672	Pte.	Head, Arthur	11.11.14
20409	Pte.	Hanley, Joseph	12.10.16	15364	Pte.	Healey, Albert	3.5.17
6900	C.S.M.	Hanson, Albert	11.11.14	12182	Pte.	Heaton, Fred	6.5.15
17756	Pte.	Hardaker, Edgar	18.12.16	3/12584	Pte.	Heaton, Thomas	11.10.16
28749	Pte.	Hardcastle, Hermann	9.4.17	3/10111	Pte.	Hegney, Christopher Stephen	14.12.14
3/10507	Pte.	Hardwick, Samuel	3.7.17	3/9603	Sgt.	Helliwell, Harry	20.10.16
7408	Pte.	Hardy, William	10.4.15	5925	A/Sgt.	Hemmingway, Johnson	15.11.14
7448	Pte.	Hare, Arthur	24.8.14	8184	Pte.	Henderson, George	24.10.14
24266	Pte.	Harland, Cecil	9.4.17	3/9866	Sgt.	Henderson, Harold	18.4.15
16108	Pte.	Harper, Herbert	1.7.16	17566	Pte.	Hepworth, Leslie	18.4.15
306708	Pte.	Harris, Frank	29.9.18	8015	Pte.	Herd, Edward	5.5.15
8956	Pte.	Harris, Frederick George	11.11.14	35481	Pte.	Heslod, Matthew	24.10.18
26037	Pte.	Harris, Robert William	10.10.17	268989	Pte.	Hesseldon, Job	15.4.18
14904	Pte.	Harris, Tom	7.11.16	12395	Cpl.	Hewitt, William Henry	3.7.17
11511	Pte.	Harris, William	5.5.15	23446	Pte.	Hewson, Arthur	31.3.18
9472	Pte.	Harrison, Arthur	3.5.17	10751	Pte.	Hey, Harold	6.5.15
10971	Pte.	Harrison, Benjamin	23.2.15	19658	Pte.	Heywood, John	3.5.17
3/10290	Pte.	Harrison, Charles	9.11.14	11325	Pte.	Hibbert, Francis	19.4.15
3/12500	Cpl.	Harrison, James	12.10.16	10657	Pte.	Hickey, James	23.8.14
35347	Pte.	Harrison, George	20.10.18	3/10141	Pte.	Higgins, Samuel	7.5.15
3/10505	Pte.	Harrison, James Richard	7.7.16	6988	Sgt.	Higgins, Alfred William	11.11.14
11235	L/Cpl.	Harrison, John William	3.5.17	268944	Pte.	Higgins, Lawrence	26.9.18
10790	Pte.	Harrison, Peter	9.4.17	3/10804	Sgt.	Higson, John North	12.10.16
7370	Pte.	Hartley, Charles	25.6.16	17249	Pte.	Hiley, Harold	30.8.16
17926	Pte.	Hartley, Frank	3.5.17	6945	Pte.	Hill, Arthur	11.11.14
24244	Pte.	Hartley, Herbert	3.5.17	20120	Pte.	Hill, Arnold	9.4.17
24941	Pte.	Hartley, John	3.5.17	3/10749	Pte.	Hill, Henry	5.5.15
19552	Pte.	Hartley, John James	23.11.17	7796	Pte.	Hill, Thomas	23.7.16
267988	Pte.	Hartley, Lewis	31.8.18	16655	Sgt.	Hind, Harold	3.5.17
265645	Pte.	Hartley, Walter	2.10.17	14520	Pte.	Hind, John	5.5.15
33790	Pte.	Harvey, James	1.11.18	6841	Pte.	Hindle, Joshua	8.11.14
16657	L/Cpl.	Harvey, Arthur Edward	3.5.17	14627	Pte.	Hinchcliffe, Harry	10.4.17
15986	Pte.	Haslam, John William	12.10.16	15553	Pte.	Hingley, Arthur	19.10.17
8231	Pte.	Haste, George Henry	11.11.14	3/9540	Pte.	Hingley, Fred	26.7.16
7187	Pte.	Hastings, Arthur	1.9.14	20320	Pte.	Hirst, Fred	10.4.17
10274	Pte.	Haswell, Harry Horace	12.10.16	31245	Pte.	Hirst, Frederick George	31.8.18
				13004	Pte.	Hirst, Joe	24.2.15
				14908	Pte.	Hirst, John	9.10.16
				7491	L/Sgt.	Hirst, Tom, D.C.M.	20.4.15

14648	L/Cpl.	Hitchin, Charlie	1.7.16	7463	Pte.	Hughes, John	24.8.14
10768	Pte.	Hobson, Albert	24.12.15	14085	Pte.	Hughill, George	5.5.15
28786	Pte.	Hobson, Edward	3.5.17	24268	Pte.	Humble, Charles Richard	7.5.17
14235	L/Cpl.	Hobson, Hubert	2.7.16	8080	Pte.	Hummell, James	24.8.14
12488	Pte.	Hobson, Richard Baxter	5.5.15	8690	Sgt.	Humphreys, Ernest Vernon	17.5.17
11893	Pte.	Hodge, John Thomas	31.8.18	12138	Pte.	Humphreys, Josiah	7.5.15
9387	A/Sgt.	Hodgson, Harold	29.11.14	16320	Pte.	Humphreys, Robert	3.9.15
14034	L/Cpl.	Hodgson, Herbert	5.5.15	16257	Pte.	Humphries, Frank	15.4.18
3/11999	Pte.	Hodgson, Thomas	5.5.15	8669	Cpl.	Huppler, Lawrence	22.4.15
7655	Pte.	Hoggarth, John	26.10.14	268982	Pte.	Hunter, Dennis	15.4.18
29304	Pte.	Hogley, Herbert Farrand	23.6.18	12279	Pte.	Hurfard, Samuel	5.1.15
18154	L/Cpl.	Holder, Harry	18.7.18	24370	Pte.	Hutchfield, William	12.4.17
14131	Pte.	Holdroyd, George	11.4.17	8775	Pte.	Hutchings, George	5.5.15
266877	Pte.	Holdsworth, Alfred	30.8.18	235440	Sgt.	Hutchinson, John George	15.4.18
242166	Pte.	Hollings, Rennie	1.8.18	10611	Sgt.	Hutchinson, Michael	10.10.17
267288	Pte.	Hollingsworth, Duke	10.10.17	10014	Cpl.	Hyde, William	2.12.14
18521	Pte.	Hollows, Arthur Purcell	30.7.16	3/11740	Pte.	Illingworth, John	14.12.14
				3/7969	Pte.	Ince, Harry	11.11.14
10028	L/Cpl.	Holmes, Edward	1.7.16	29486	Pte.	Ingham, James William	9.4.17
6022	Pte.	Holmes, James Arthur	20.10.14	1/10547	Pte.	Irvin, Tom	5.5.15
235805	Pte.	Hood, Alfred	24.10.18	6704	Pte.	Jackman, Robert	18.4.15
3/10645	Pte.	Hoonan, Robert	1.7.16	3/10050	Cpl.	Jackson, Alfred	19.6.15
9941	Pte.	Hopkins, Ernest	11.11.14	33573	Pte.	Jackson, Herbert	15.4.18
7930	Pte.	Hopper, William	11.11.14	16376	L/Cpl.	Jackson, Joseph	7.8.15
200382	Pte.	Horner, Harold	30.8.18	10178	Pte.	Jackson, Stanley Bertram	11.11.14
3/10557	Pte.	Horner, Richard	23.2.15				
3/10001	Pte.	Horner, Samuel	10.4.17	34771	Pte.	Jackson, William Sharp	30.8.18
3/9059	Pte.	Horner, William	5.5.15				
3/8790	Pte.	Horridge, James	26.10.14	12391	Pte.	Jagger, John Herbert	1.7.16
24895	Pte.	Horsfall, Harry	15.4.18				
24245	Pte.	Horsfall, James Hervey	3.5.17	204043	Pte.	Jagger, Wilfred	10.10.17
				24325	Pte.	Javerley, George William	3.5.17
7476	Pte.	Horsfall, Thomas	11.11.14				
24747	Pte.	Horton, Harry	15.4.18	10276	Pte.	Jenkins, William John	5.5.15
9867	Pte.	Houchin, Arthur Cecil	11.11.14	8482	Pte.	Jennings, William Henry	11.11.14
14006	Pte.	Howarth, Albert	7.5.15				
24512	Pte.	Howgate, William Henry	18.12.16	24327	Pte.	Jessop, William Henry	9.4.17
7547	A/Sgt.	Howie, Harry	23.2.15	11203	Pte.	Johnson, James	6.5.15
14145	Pte.	Howley, Thomas	9.3.15	23796	Pte.	Johnson, John George	12.10.16
24324	Pte.	Hudson, Albert	3.5.17				
19461	Pte.	Hudson, Charles	10.9.17	11730	Pte.	Johnson, Joseph	5.5.15
12329	Pte.	Hudson, John Rawlinson	18.4.15	35438	Pte.	Johnstone, Wesley	22.9.18
				3/10334	Pte.	Jones, George	11.11.14
3/9280	Pte.	Hudson, Robinson	11.11.14	8053	Pte.	Jones, Henry Albert	11.11.14
22390	Pte.	Hudson, Vernon	1.8.18				
24239	Pte.	Hudson, William Ernest	19.12.16	22841	Pte.	Jones, Jack	29.3.18
				8123	Pte.	Jones, Joseph	3.9.14

APPENDIX IV

3/10841	Pte.	Jones, William	7.5.15	266341	Pte.	Lambert, Richard	30.8.18
3/11221	Pte.	Jowett, Asa	5.5.15	19257	Pte.	Lamb, John William	12.10.16
10557	Pte.	Jowett, Lawrence	2.4.15			
3/11114	Pte.	Joy, John	5.5.15	35453	Pte.	Langhorn, Thomas Henry	22.10.18
3/10579	Pte.	Jubb, John	7.5.15			
23797	Pte.	Kaye, Davis	12.10.16	11274	Pte.	Langman, Thomas	5.5.15
7993	Pte.	Keeble, Walter	8.11.14	18906	A/Sgt.	Larrington, Frederick	11.5.17
3/8743	Pte.	Keen, Thomas	18.4.15			
15866	Pte.	Keene, Oswald Rees	5.5.15	8041	Pte.	Latham, Joseph Robert	24.8.14
35355	Pte.	Keeton, John	20.10.18			
3/10529	Pte.	Kellett, John	23.2.15	11422	Pte.	Lavin, Joseph	3.5.17
9127	L/Cpl.	Kelly, Arthur	23.10.14	8422	A/Cpl.	Law, George	8.11.14
265849	Pte.	Kelly, Andrew	24.10.18	35707	Pte.	Lawson, Herbert	24.10.18
11883	Pte.	Kelly, Lawrence	6.5.15	14650	A/Cpl.	Lawson, John Henry	24.10.18
11967	Pte.	Kelly, Daniel	5.5.15			
9096	Pte.	Kemp, Joseph Ernest	24.8.14	35704	Pte.	Lawson, Matthew	20.10.18
				3/10583	Pte.	Lawson, Sam Bancroft	11.11.14
8369	Pte.	Kenchatt, Charles Reading	10.11.14			
				10736	Pte.	Lawton, Frank Walter	12.10.16
3/9569	Pte.	Kennedy, David	5.4.15			
24371	Pte.	Kenny, James	24.10.18	15783	Pte.	Laycock, Lawrence	1.7.16
12427	A/Sgt.	Kent, Bertie	5.5.15	22354	Pte.	Leach, Walter	10.8.18
11366	Pte.	Kershaw, Fred	18.4.15	35482	Pte.	Leader, William	24.10.18
12539	Pte.	Kershaw, James	14.9.15	8274	Pte.	Leading, John William	11.11.14
3/9310	Pte.	Kershaw, John	18.4.15			
10889	Pte.	Kerwin, Patrick	28.7.16	11722	Pte.	Leake, Harold	29.8.18
235292	Pte.	Kewley, Fred	10.10.17	8716	L/Cpl.	Learner, Arthur	12.10.16
3/10901	Pte.	Killeen, James	5.5.15	9715	Pte.	Learner, Frederick Henry	11.11.14
14078	Pte.	Kilmister, Robert William	5.5.15			
				6237	Pte.	Leary, John	11.11.14
25293	Pte.	Kilty, James	1.9.18	3/10419	Pte.	Leather, Ernest	21.3.16
19622	Pte.	Kinder, James	12.10.16	268756	Pte.	Leaver, Frederick Percy	15.4.18
11299	Pte.	Kinder, Samuel	26.4.15			
11559	Pte.	King, Albert	3.3.15	3/10501	Pte.	Lee, Albert	29.5.15
6776	Pte.	King, Thomas Hurran	26.8.14	24979	Pte.	Lee, Frank	2.9.18
				11268	Pte.	Leech, John	9.4.15
21942	Pte.	Kirk, Charles William	18.10.18	16331	Pte.	Leedham, William	8.7.15
				12506	Pte.	Lester, Reginald	6.5.15
6411	Pte.	Kirk, William	11.11.14	33771	Pte.	Lewis, William James	29.7.18
12412	Pte.	Kiernan, Thomas	23.4.17			
28818	Pte.	Kitchin, William	16.4.17	28761	Pte.	Light, John Charles	3.2.17
3/10600	Pte.	Kitson, David	5.5.15	20253	L/Cpl.	Lilley, Fred	10.10.17
28873	Pte.	Knapton, Harold	11.4.17	23828	Pte.	Lillie, James	12.10.16
29465	Pte.	Knight, James	13.10.17	20158	Pte.	Limb, Allan	3.2.17
11552	Pte.	Kniveton, George	18.4.15	25522	Pte.	Liniham, James	15.4.18
7808	Pte.	Knowles, Thomas	11.5.15	13052	Pte.	Lister, Arthur	3.5.17
29868	Pte.	Knowles, Willie	3.5.17	13909	Pte.	Lister, Francis	16.7.15
23829	Pte.	Lacey, Geroge Wilson	12.10.16	9877	Dmr.	Lister, George Bertram	9.4.15
6565	Pte.	Lake, Arthur	5.5.15	12191	Pte.	Lister, Joseph William	10.10.16
11854	Pte.	Lally, Andrew	5.5.15			
10792	Pte.	Lally, Frank	8.11.14	6951	Pte.	Livesey, John	8.11.14
20222	Pte.	Lambert, John William	8.2.17	235206	Pte.	Loader, Arthur	3.5.17
				8432	Sgt.	Lockwood, Harold	12.10.16

10570	Pte.	Lockwood, Harry	24.8.14	6212	Pte.	Martin, James	26.10.14
14324	Pte.	Lockwood, Norman	15.4.18	10732	Pte.	Martin, Joseph	18.4.15
7394	Pte.	Lockwood, Ralph	20.4.15	35714	Pte.	Martin, John	24.10.18
8922	Pte.	Lodge, Ernest Henry	14.9.14	9273	Pte.	Martin, William Frank	18.4.15
268766	Pte.	Lodge, George	27.3.18	7697	L/Cpl.	Maslen, Arthur John William	18.4.15
16358	Pte.	Loftus, Bertram	29.6.15	16353	Pte.	Massey, Ernest	12.10.16
3/10389	Pte.	Long, John	5.5.15	11353	L/Sgt.	Matthews, Fred, M.M.	31.8.18
24765	Pte.	Long, William Arthur	23.3.18	26093	Pte.	Matthews, Frederick Richard	10.10.17
3/10531	Pte.	Longstaff, James	11.11.14	3/11368	Cpl.	Maude, William	12.10.16
7712	Pte.	Lonie, David	11.11.14	24904	Pte.	Maudsley, Harry	16.4.18
7990	Pte.	Lord, James Edward	31.1.16	10980	Pte.	Maunder, William Thomas	5.5.15
23826	Pte.	Lorimer, Andrew Wilson	12.10.16	8702	Pte.	May, Charles	17.11.14
11517	Cpl.	Lorimer, Horace	23.2.15	14461	Pte.	McAnaney, James	10.4.15
24247	Pte.	Lottey, Harold Edwin	21.12.17	7871	L/Cpl.	McCarthy, George Edward	5.5.15
3/9187	Pte.	Louis, Brown	18.4.15	6625	Pte.	McCarthy, Patrick	24.8.14
15903	Pte.	Lovett, Israel	17.9.16	23830	Pte.	McCaughey, David	8.11.16
10388	L/Sgt.	Lovett, Thomas	11.11.14	12257	Sgt.	McCavan, Brian	3.5.17
8914	Pte.	Lucas, Edward	5.5.15	10475	C.S.M.	McClelland, George	24.10.18
10573	Pte.	Lunn, George	9.5.15	11470	A/Sgt.	McDonald, William	18.4.15
235233	L/Cpl.	Lunn, James A.	3.5.17	23833	Pte.	McEvoy, Joseph Patrick	12.10.16
5987	Pte.	Lunn, James Edwin	23.8.14	3/10696	Pte.	McGeghin, Herbert	24.4.16
35363	Pte.	Lunn, Joseph Ernest Unwin	24.10.18	14460	Pte.	McGinley, William	21.2.17
11719	Pte.	Lutill, Richard James	12.12.17	3/10463	Pte.	McGovern, Bernard	8.9.15
9867	Sgt.	Lyons, John	9.10.17	4752	L/Cpl.	McGovern, Joseph Ambrose, D.C.M.	17.11.14
15359	Pte.	Lyons, Robert	3.5.17	6993	Pte.	McGowan, Charlie	25.10.14
14100	Pte.	Lyth, John	7.5.15	21639	Pte.	McGrath, James	3.5.17
3/8359	Pte.	MacDonald, John	11.11.14	5892	Pte.	McHugh, James	20.1.15
3/10659	Pte.	McIntosh, Samuel, M.M.	1.7.16	3/9640	Pte.	McIntyre, John	10.5.15
9876	Pte.	Mahoney, John	8.11.14	12005	Pte.	McKean, Arthur	12.8.15
33452	Pte.	Mains, John Robert	12.8.18	3/9910	L/Cpl.	McMahon, Thomas	11.11.14
17427	Pte.	Major, John Edward	3.5.17	3/10647	Pte.	McManus, Francis	26.10.16
3/10406	Pte.	Malcolm, Ernest	11.11.14	3/10349	Pte.	McMaster, Arthur	11.3.15
8223	L/Cpl.	Mallin, David	5.5.15	14237	Pte.	McMath, James	18.4.15
3/11053	Pte.	Mallinson, Victor	15.4.18	12415	Pte.	McMea, Bernard	5.5.15
7511	Pte.	Mallyon, James	10.11.14	16827	Pte.	McQuillan, James	24.10.18
18400	Pte.	Mamwell, John Edwin	3.5.17	3/10905	A/Sgt.	McQullen, John	13.6.15
10699	Pte.	Mansell, Joseph	5.5.15	6525	Pte.	McVeagh, Charles	8.11.14
265219	Pte.	Marcham, Ernest	10.10.17	16438	L/Cpl.	Medley, Benjamin	5.5.15
3/9530	Pte.	Maris, James	11.11.14	8962	Pte.	Mee, Frederick	30.4.18
29070	Pte.	Marshall, Charles Edward	10.10.17	14644	Pte.	Meeghan, James	10.7.15
7541	L/Sgt.	Marshall, William Stuart	11.11.14	35716	Pte.	Meek, Abraham	20.10.18
				20377	Pte.	Mellor, George	30.8.18
				20125	Pte.	Mellor, Irving	19.10.16
				31268	A/Cpl.	Mellor, Lewis	31.3.18
				7844	Pte.	Metcalfe, Alfred	11.11.14

APPENDIX IV

9827	R.S.M.	Metcalfe, Cecil Edward D.C.M. & Bar, M.M.	18.7.18	28780	Pte.	Moran, William	3.2.17
204330	Pte.	Metcalfe, James Parker	19.4.18	241761	Pte.	Morley, Frank	31.8.18
14896	Pte.	Metcalfe, Joseph	1.7.16	8152	A/L/Sgt.	Morris, Frank	1.7.16
3/9252	Pte.	Metcalfe, William	11.11.14	14045	Pte.	Morris, Harold	5.5.15
13086	Pte.	Metcalfe, William	5.5.15	3/9738	Pte.	Morris, James William	12.10.16
235211	Pte.	Mettrick, Ernest	28.3.18	1251	Pte.	Morris, James William	5.5.15
8403	Pte.	Middlehurst, Emanuel Thomas	8.11.14	34938	Pte.	Morrison, Angus	1.9.18
3/9438	Pte.	Middow, Albert	23.4.15	9735	Pte.	Morton, Thomas Henry	10.10.17
24392	Cpl.	Midgley, Godfrey Scott	1.5.17	35485	Pte.	Moss, Frederick	23.10.18
3/12808	Pte.	Midgley, Willie	12.10.16	242301	Pte.	Mossman, William Ferguson	1.9.18
23686	Pte.	Midwood, Henry	3.5.17	23024	L/Cpl.	Moule, Arthur	1.11.17
25526	Pte.	Miles, Charles Edwin	30.8.18	8378	Pte.	Moule, Frank Luke	11.11.14
14017	Pte.	Millar, Cyril	5.5.15	8144	Pte.	Mowbray, Richard	11.11.14
23834	Pte.	Miller, Robert John	12.10.16	7985	Pte.	Moye, Albert Edward	11.11.14
23837	Pte.	Millican, William	10.10.16	10675	Pte.	Mudd, Fred	5.5.15
23836	Pte.	Millne, Fred	17.12.16	10574	Pte.	Muir, Herbert	6.5.15
10726	Pte.	Mills, Clarence James	23.2.15	3/10672	Pte.	Mullen, John	5.5.15
7240	Pte.	Mills, William	27.11.14	11595	Pte.	Munro, Archie	12.10.16
3/9714	Pte.	Milner, John William	5.5.15	11372	Pte.	Murfett, John Henry	27.4.15
14096	Pte.	Mitchell, George	15.10.15	29595	Pte.	Murgatroyd, David	15.4.18
6948	Pte.	Mitchell, George	18.4.15	14037	Pte.	Murgatroyd, Ernest	5.5.15
3/10587	Pte.	Mitchell, George	6.5.15	11073	Pte.	Murphy, Cornelius	1.7.16
38528	Pte.	Mitchell, George Albert	31.8.18	17542	Pte.	Murphy, Nicholas Michael	4.9.16
20127	Pte.	Mitchell, Herbert	11.4.17	266168	Pte.	Myers, Frank	30.5.18
12436	Pte.	Mitchell, Michael George	18.4.15	24330	Pte.	Naggs, Cecil George	21.2.17
15470	Pte.	Mitchell, Richard	7.5.18	9930	Pte.	Narey, Luke	13.11.18
7596	Pte.	Mitchell, Thomas	5.5.15	308056	Pte.	Naylor, Horace	15.4.18
7719	Pte.	Mollan, Robert	10.11.14	15375	Pte.	Naylor, James	31.8.18
10799	Cpl.	Molloy, Thomas John	11.4.17	201689	Pte.	Naylor, James Harold, M.M.	29.7.18
9165	A/Cpl.	Moodycliffe, Herbert	1.7.16	235213	Pte.	Naylor, William	3.5.17
265327	Pte.	Moorhouse, Herbert	3.5.17	3/12890	Pte.	Naylor, Willie	1.7.16
3/9582	Pte.	Moorhouse, George	18.4.15	19903	Pte.	Neil, Herbert	8.9.16
14924	Pte.	Moore, Arthur	10.4.17	19645	Pte.	Nelson, John	28.8.16
24249	Pte.	Moore, Fred	10.2.17	24338	Pte.	Nendick, John	19.2.17
11774	Pte.	Moore, James	16.7.15	3/10588	Pte.	Nestor, Patrick	11.11.14
16349	Pte.	Moore, John	7.12.15	6621	L/Cpl.	Newton, Joseph	24.8.14
3/10800	A/Sgt.	Moore, Joseph Edmond	24.12.15	16321	Pte.	Newton, Thomas	3.6.15
204284	Pte.	Moore, Walter	15.4.18	11406	Pte.	Nichols, Thomas	18.4.15
3/9475	L/Cpl.	Moran, James	12.10.16	6046	Pte.	Nicholson, Richard	7.7.16
3/8947	Pte.	Moran, Michael	21.12.14	7434	Cpl.	Nicholson, Walter	8.4.15
3/9535	Pte.	Moran, Thomas	24.10.14	3/10286	Pte.	Nixon, John	5.5.15
				10683	Pte.	Nixon, Oscar	5.5.15
				20225	Pte.	Nollar, James	13.10.16
				7303	L/Cpl.	North, Fred	5.5.15
				28845	Pte.	North, George Arthur	9.4.17

242870	Pte.	North, James	28.3.18	23844	Pte.	Pickering, Matthew Henry	12.10.16
10680	Pte.	North, Tom	5.5.15	11453	Pte.	Pickles, Lionel	9.1.18
7727	Pte.	Norton, John	12.10.16	13182	Pte.	Pickles, William	15.11.18
35365	Pte.	Nussey, Joe Middlebrooke	20.10.18	3/10435	Pte.	Pickles, William	10.10.17
11438	Pte.	Nutting, George Arthur	18.4.15	3/10955	Pte.	Pickover, Walton	18.4.15
17544	Pte.	Odell, Percy	2.7.16	10599	Pte.	Pilgrim, Thomas Clarkson	31.5.15
16437	Pte.	Ogden, Herbert	5.5.15	8679	Pte.	Pimblett, Charles John Walter	24.8.14
3/12354	L/Cpl.	Ogden, Herbert Alexander	12.10.16	16203	Pte.	Place, Harry	21.4.18
10762	Pte.	Oldfield, Thomas Edgar	12.10.16	3/11052	Pte.	Plaiteer, Willie	5.5.15
				14021	Pte.	Platts, Tom	5.5.15
3/9605	L/Cpl.	Oliver, Harry	6.5.15	3/9378	Pte.	Playford, Albert	27.10.14
11473	Pte.	Oliver, William	18.4.15	10804	Pte.	Plews, Bernard Riley	5.5.15
3/10550	Pte.	O'Rourke, Thomas	3.5.17				
9308	Sgt.	Outram, Arthur	10.10.17	8087	Pte.	Plumb, William	9.11.14
267092	Pte.	Overend, Percy	31.8.18	12353	Pte.	Plumbley, Joseph Albert	12.10.16
8186	Pte.	Oxley, Albert John	14.9.14				
23841	Pte.	Oxley, George	12.10.16	11547	A/Cpl.	Pluright, George Dyson	18.4.15
15499	Pte.	Padgett, Sam	23.3.18				
24773	Pte.	Parker, Felix	3.5.18	11376	Pte.	Pluright, Joe	19.2.17
16284	Pte.	Parker, Harold	16.6.15	7710	Pte.	Pollard, Walter	19.3.15
3/10407	Pte.	Parker, James	11.11.14	32730	Pte.	Poole, Henry James	30.8.18
202954	Pte.	Parker, Robert	3.5.17	16253	Cpl.	Poole, James	1.7.16
3/12071	Pte.	Parker, Walter	16.12.14	8349	L/Cpl.	Poole, William	12.4.15
35371	Pte.	Parkin, Ward	24.10.18	306311	Pte.	Porter, Leonard	8.7.18
28939	Pte.	Parkinson, Christopher	3.5.17	19685	Pte.	Porter, Thomas William	16.4.18
23716	Pte.	Parkinson, Dawson	22.12.17	8640	Sgt.	Potter, George Henry	24.8.14
8071	Pte.	Paten, John	11.11.14				
24341	Pte.	Patrick, John William	3.5.17	10445	Pte.	Power, Francis Henry	18.12.14
3/10106	Pte.	Patterson, Peter	5.5.15	3/10223	Pte.	Pogson, Benjamin	11.11.14
203824	Pte.	Patterson, William James	1.9.18	23717	Pte.	Priestley, Edmund James	21.2.17
235816	Pte.	Pattin, Albert	24.10.18	26087	Pte.	Pringle, Charles	10.10.17
12737	Pte.	Payne, Ernest	2.2.18	24280	Pte.	Proctor, Edward	3.5.17
202677	Pte.	Payne, Albert Joseph	17.4.18	13910	A/L/Cpl.	Proctor, William	12.10.16
				12429	Pte.	Purcell, Harry	18.4.15
8118	Pte.	Peacock, Thomas	5.5.15	23845	Pte.	Pyle, John George	3.5.17
3/11024	Pte.	Peacock, Walter	5.5.15	8158	Sgt.	Quait, John Arthur	13.7.16
35375	Pte.	Peace, Fred	25.10.18	24256	Pte.	Quarmby, George	11.4.17
8006	Pte.	Pearce, Alfred	11.11.14	10603	Pte.	Quarton, Carl	12.10.16
12368	Pte.	Peckover, Herbert	5.5.15	8017	Pte.	Queinliven, James Edward	26.8.14
11177	Pte.	Percival, John	24.3.15				
8480	Pte.	Percy, Sydney	8.11.14	16455	Pte.	Quigley, Christopher	12.10.16
8283	Pte.	Perfect, Arthur Gordon	11.11.14	23846	Pte.	Quinn, William Henry	12.10.16
9546	A/Sgt.	Perigo, David, D.C.M.	11.11.14	3/10523	Pte.	Quinn, John Arthur	5.5.15
3/12593	Pte.	Pickard, Albert	12.10.16				
10556	Pte.	Pickard, Fred	23.10.16	24342	Pte.	Railton, John	30.8.18
15408	Pte.	Pickard, Henry	2.7.16	12518	Pte.	Raistrick, Ernest	1.7.16

APPENDIX IV

3/10603	Pte.	Raistrick, Frederick	12.10.16	26996	Pte.	Robinson, John	20.7.18
3/11131	Pte.	Raistrick, George	18.3.15	18145	L/Sgt.	Robinson, Albert Victor	30.3.18
26028	Pte.	Ramage, William Brown	11.10.17	16232	Pte.	Robinson, William	18.7.15
26066	Pte.	Raper, Charles	13.10.17	3/10499	Pte.	Robinson, Peter	19.1.15
13844	Pte.	Rattigan, Patrick	12.10.16	3/9677	Pte.	Robinson, Charles	23.2.15
11789	Pte.	Rawling, Ellis	18.4.15	23848	Cpl.	Robson, Frederick Simpson	18.7.18
6897	Pte.	Rawson, Reginald	16.11.14				
240309	Pte.	Rayner, Friend	18.7.18	23683	Pte.	Rodgers, Bert Ernest	9.5.17
8191	A/Cpl.	Raynor, John	11.11.14				
10613	Pte.	Raynor, Victor	18.4.15	24260	Pte.	Rodgers, Henry	11.4.17
11502	Pte.	Read, David	5.5.15	7178	Pte.	Rogers, Peter	11.11.14
16622	Pte.	Read, George Arthur	1.4.18	10731	Pte.	Roker, Leonard	18.4.15
23847	L/Cpl.	Readhead, Anthony	15.4.18	25604	Pte.	Rollason, James	7.10.18
12154	Pte.	Redman, Arthur	7.5.15	13468	Pte.	Rollin, Walter	3.2.17
7473	Pte.	Redgrave, Harry	8.11.14	13966	L/Cpl.	Rollins, Edgar	6.5.15
22245	Pte.	Reed, William	10.6.18	13029	Cpl.	Ross, John	30.8.18
9820	Sgt.	Reid, John	3.5.17	3/10640	Pte.	Ross, Harry	1.7.16
11098	L/Cpl.	Rennard, Norris	29.6.15	6408	Pte.	Rosendale, Arthur	8.11.14
10398	Pte.	Reynolds, Ernest	22.10.14	3/7658	Dmr.	Rosendale, John McGowan	24.8.14
3/9023	Pte.	Rhodes, Harry	14.1.14				
3/8454	Sgt.	Rhodes, William Ward	25.9.14	14113	Cpl.	Rotherforth, Joseph Bottomley	15.4.18
9369	Pte.	Richardson, Archibald Charles	12.10.16	201585	Pte.	Rothery, Arthur	11.9.18
				3/10230	Pte.	Rothery, John Edward	5.5.15
12205	Pte.	Richardson, Ernest	18.4.15				
4364	Pte.	Richards, Alfred	21.3.15	14473	Pte.	Rowan, William	5.5.15
16609	Pte.	Richards, James Meredith	19.12.16	3/12186	Pte.	Rowbottom, Samuel	12.10.16
16291	Pte.	Richards, Mark	7.7.15	12247	Pte.	Rowell, George	6.5.15
10284	L/Cpl.	Richards, William Frederick	11.11.14	8103	Pte.	Rowley, Frederick James	8.5.15
20194	Pte.	Ridley, Sam	12.10.16	16309	Pte.	Rugman, Henry	12.10.16
6537	Pte.	Riley, George	9.7.17	22451	Pte.	Rushby, Harold	28.3.18
15416	Pte.	Riley, James	19.5.17	28893	Cpl.	Rushforth, Reginald Arthur	24.10.18
202285	Pte.	Riley, Joe	9.8.17				
12258	Pte.	Riley, Joseph	3.5.17	8676	Pte.	Russell, William Henry	5.5.15
14791	Pte.	Riley, Samuel Edwin	7.5.16				
235215	Pte.	Riley, William	3.5.17	7840	Pte.	Rushworth, Andrew	5.9.14
205549	Pte.	Riley, Willie	1.9.18	12571	L/Cpl.	Ryall, Walter	5.5.15
269324	Pte.	Riley, Wilson	29.4.18	6944	Sgt.	Ryan, James	6.5.15
10795	Pte.	Roach, John Edward	6.4.18	10524	Pte.	Ryder, Arthur Preshous	24.8.14
7568	Pte.	Roberts, Alfred	5.5.15				
6422	Pte.	Roberts, George Ernest	24.10.14	7972	Pte.	Ryder, Edward	18.4.15
				7661	Pte.	Ryder, Harry	5.5.15
11533	Pte.	Roberts, Frank	23.10.16	8948	Sgt.	Ryder, Oliver	13.11.14
7400	Pte.	Robertshaw, John	16.11.14	7632	Pte.	Ryder, William	18.4.15
3/10512	Pte.	Robertshaw, George Wilfred	24.2.15	12705	Pte.	Ryecroft, George Henry	28.3.18
3/11248	Pte.	Robertson, Andrew	14.12.14	265945	Pte.	Saxton, Arthur	30.8.18
24456	Pte.	Robinson, Arthur	1.10.17	7405	Pte.	Saxton, Maurice	12.11.14
3/10886	Pte.	Robinson, Joshua	7.5.15	8008	L/Cpl.	Sams, Phillip	5.5.15
14837	Pte.	Robinson, Ernest	28.5.18	8188	Pte.	Sampson, Harry Samuel	11.11.14
3/11566	Pte.	Robinson, Sam	1.7.16				

3/10092	Pte.	Scanlon, James William	15.7.16	7452	Pte.	Simpson, Frederick	18.4.15
7649	Pte.	Schofield, Sam	10.11.14	7513	Pte.	Sinclair, Samuel	20.10.16
26027	Pte.	Schofield, Sydney	10.10.17	25564	Pte.	Skeath, John Robert	30.8.18
29443	Pte.	Schofield, Joseph	2.1.18	20043	Pte.	Skitmore, John William	12.10.16
23163	Pte.	Scott, Robert	31.8.18	3/10700	Pte.	Slater, Ernest	21.1.15
23763	Pte.	Scott, Robert	12.10.16	24346	Pte.	Slater, Hartley	7.10.17
24359	Pte.	Scott, Raymond	3.6.17	305351	Pte.	Slater, Clifford	30.8.18
3/10783	Pte.	Scott, John	5.1.16	3/16234	Pte.	Smart, Joseph	12.10.16
10491	Pte.	Screeney, Patrick	5.5.15	10604	Pte.	Smith, Arthur	24.8.14
5986	Pte	Seanor, Joseph	21.11.14	235218	Pte.	Smith, Arthur	3.5.17
3/9485	Pte.	Searle, Frank	11.11.14	16740	L/Cpl.	Smith, Charles	12.10.16
25510	Pte.	Sarson, John	24.10.18	10882	Cpl.	Smith, Daniel	3.5.17
9639	A/C.S.M.	Seccombe, James Alfred	2.3.15	16242	Pte.	Smith, Edward Arthur	24.6.15
28862	L/Cpl.	Seed, Oliver Harewood	15.4.18	10539	Pte.	Smith, Edwin Thomas	6.5.15
15628	Pte.	Senior, Albert	23.10.16	10838	L/Cpl.	Smith, Fred	12.10.16
9755	Cpl.	Senior, Sam	7.1.15	13127	Pte.	Smith, George	18.8.15
23721	Pte.	Settle, Herbert	3.5.17	3/10488	Pte.	Smith, Harry	7.5.15
241494	Pte.	Sewell, Arnold	31.8.18	32346	Pte.	Smith, John William	31.8.18
17529	Pte.	Shackleton, Harry	12.10.16	6666	Pte.	Smith, Joseph	19.9.14
15826	Pte.	Shallcross, William Henry	5.5.15	19683	Pte.	Smith, Lawrence	12.10.16
15963	Pte.	Sharp, Adrian	7.7.17	3/10491	Pte.	Smith, Norman	5.5.15
26724	Pte.	Sharp, Ben	11.4.17	203060	Pte.	Smith, Norman	3.5.17
3/10881	Sgt.	Sharp, Calvert	9.8.15	25139	Pte.	Smith, Reginald, M.M.	10.9.18
3/9469	Pte.	Sharp, Ernest	18.4.15	5458	Sgt.	Smith, Richard Daniel	31.10.14
17831	Pte.	Sharp, William	17.10.16				
26079	Pte.	Sharp, William	30.3.18	3/10477	Pte.	Smith, Richard Parker	18.4.15
201419	Pte.	Shaw, Herbert Andrew	15.4.18	12059	Sgt.	Smith, Sydney	10.10.17
242084	Pte.	Shaw, Thomas	4.4.18	11197	Pte.	Smith, Thomas	5.5.15
17902	Pte.	Shaw, Harold	12.10.16	24985	Pte.	Smith, William	3.5.17
18704	Pte.	Shaw, Kelita	12.10.16	17979	L/Cpl.	Smith, Willie	12.10.16
9111	L/Cpl.	Shaw, Joseph Henry	15.11.14	8159	Pte.	Smithies, Herbert	8.11.14
10517	Pte.	Shaw, Walter	24.8.14	39557	Pte.	Snape, James Albert	18.7.18
14628	Cpl.	Shaw, Harold	1.7.16	24402	Pte.	Snowley, Arthur Albert	9.10.17
242819	Pte.	Sheard, Percy	1.3.19				
10206	Pte.	Shellabear, Thomas	24.8.14	28824	Pte.	Southerin, George William	11.4.17
24779	Pte.	Shells, Herbert	15.4.18	23101	Pte.	Sowden, George	10.4.17
7775	Pte.	Shinn, Arthur	8.11.14	11404	L/Cpl.	Sowden, James	8.4.15
8598	A/L/Cpl.	Shipley, Bertram Frederick Septimus	9.7.16	201382	Pte.	Spence, Walter	15.4.18
35380	Pte.	Shore, Cyril	24.10.18	5833	Sgt.	Spence, William	3.9.14
9969	L/Cpl.	Silk, Fred	23.10.14	22497	Pte.	Speight, David	8.8.18
9483	Pte.	Silvers, Walter	11.11.14	240910	Pte.	Speight, Thomas	21.7.18
3/9104	Pte.	Simister, Thomas	25.10.14	8636	Pte.	Speight, Willie	18.4.15
7793	Pte.	Simmons, Edward	6.12.14	13994	Pte.	Spencer, Edward	1.7.16
3/10460	Pte.	Simon, Edward	12.5.15	12070	Pte.	Spencer, Ernest	10.10.17
8500	Pte.	Simpson, James	11.11.14	23633	Pte.	Spencer, Fletcher	3.5.17
28750	Pte.	Simpson, Clement	9.5.17	14838	Pte.	Spencer, Francis Robert	13.8.15
24458	Pte.	Simpson, William	2.5.18				

APPENDIX IV

8023	Pte.	Spiller, Walter Andrew	25.10.14	6880	Pte.	Sweet, Tom	12.10.14
23807	Pte.	Spink, Charlie	15.11.16	20028	Pte.	Sykes, Arthur	8.12.16
3/9836	Pte.	Spivey, William Henry	5.5.15	20387	Cpl.	Sykes, Edward	30.8.18
12431	Pte.	Spriggs, Albert	8.3.15	200205	Pte.	Sykes, Frank	3.5.17
12510	Pte.	Sreeve, William	12.10.16	11630	Pte.	Sykes, Joseph William	18.4.15
3/9706	Pte.	Stacey, Vincent	3.4.15	20246	Pte.	Sykes, Herbert Wadsworth	9.8.17
23805	Pte.	Stockhouse, Eli	12.10.16	7510	Pte.	Sykes, Richard	6.5.15
3/11188	Pte.	Stanbrey, William	1.7.16	11342	Pte.	Sykes, Tom	22.4.17
202418	Pte.	Stansfield, William Ingham	30.8.18	9312	Pte.	Talbot, Bernard	8.11.14
17237	Pte.	Stansfield, William	12.10.16	9294	A/Sgt.	Tappenden, Albert	29.4.15
7257	Pte.	Stansfield, Richard	5.5.15	24414	Pte.	Taylor, Arthur John	3.5.17
3/9148	Pte.	Stansfield, Fred	5.5.15	23761	Pte.	Taylor, Francis	12.10.16
7401	Pte.	Stanton, John	18.4.15	24986	Cpl.	Taylor, Fred	3.5.17
205075	Pte.	Start, Thomas Edward	18.4.18	10569	Pte.	Taylor, George	8.11.14
205456	Pte.	Stead, James Arthur	9.8.18	3/9629	Pte.	Taylor, Harry	13.10.14
16239	Pte.	Steele, Ernest	1.7.16	6493	A/Cpl.	Taylor, Harry	18.4.15
8833	Pte.	Steggall, Albert	13.10.14	14012	Pte.	Taylor, Percy	5.5.15
14620	Pte.	Stephens, William Norton	5.5.15	8175	Pte.	Taylor, Percy Harry	24.8.14
18298	Pte.	Stephenson, Ernest	11.9.16	3/9465	L/Cpl.	Tell, Charles	7.12.14
7446	Pte.	Stephenson, Samuel	24.8.14	9554	Pte.	Tennant, John Henry	11.11.14
28745	Pte.	Stimpson, John Robert	3.5.17	8386	Pte.	Tewkesbury, Frederick Robert	12.10.16
11602	Pte.	Stoker, William Clifford	5.5.15	3/10022	Pte.	Thackeray, Harry	11.11.14
202439	Pte.	Stoker, Albert	22.4.18	14922	Pte.	Theodore, Thomas Frederick	1.7.16
6834	Pte.	Stokes, Bertie	23.10.14	10048	Pte.	Thirkill, George	28.3.18
24434	L/Cpl.	Stone, Fred	3.5.17	8622	Sgt.	Thickett, Fred	29.10.14
10699	Pte.	Stones, John	3.5.17	3/10674	Pte.	Thomas, Aaron	5.5.15
238034	Pte.	Storey, Albert	18.7.18	24949	Pte.	Thomas, George Willie	3.5.17
24397	Pte.	Storr, William	3.5.17	14005	Pte.	Thomas, William Albert	5.5.15
19935	Pte.	Stott, Frank	11.4.17	13979	Pte.	Thomason, Frank	9.4.17
11755	Pte.	Stowell, Henry	9.4.15	13028	Pte.	Thompson, Charles Francis	12.10.16
17556	Pte.	Street, George Freak	12.10.16	266492	Pte.	Thompson, Herbert	30.8.18
9337	Pte.	Stripling, George Charles	19.2.17	29461	Pte.	Thompson, Robert	3.5.17
12380	Pte.	Stubbs, James	5.5.17	35493	Pte.	Thompson, Robert	24.10.18
26012	Pte.	Stubbs, George	15.4.18	11978	Pte.	Thompson, Maurice	18.4.15
8025	Pte.	Stumm, Arthur	11.11.14	3/10896	Pte.	Thompson, Edwin	12.10.16
11510	Pte.	Styring, John	6.5.15	16834	Pte.	Thornburn, Frank	24.10.18
11358	Pte.	Sullivan, William	18.4.15	23687	Pte.	Thornton, Bramwell	21.8.18
8016	Pte.	Sullivan, George	24.8.14	10748	Pte.	Thornton, Edmund	16.3.15
23710	Pte.	Sunderland, Alfred	22.5.17	19475	Pte.	Thornton, John	12.10.16
15582	Pte.	Sunderland, Giles	12.10.16	19439	Pte.	Thoseby, Arthur	23.10.16
30640	L/Cpl.	Sunderland, John Leslie	10.10.17	31838	Pte.	Thwaite, Frank	9.3.18
3/10530	Pte.	Sutcliffe, Irvin	11.11.14	20131	Pte.	Tillotson, Ben Harold	15.10.16
24984	Pte.	Sutcliffe, Tom	3.5.17	14025	Pte.	Tinker, Lewis Francis	5.5.15
6491	Pte.	Sutcliffe, Willie	11.11.14	35389	Pte.	Tinsley, Clarence	24.10.18
3/9644	Pte.	Swales, Alexander	18.4.15	3/12600	Pte.	Toal, John	1.7.16

3/10845	Pte.	Toft, Cornelius	5.5.15	20156	Pte.	Wailes, George Leslie	4.11.16
7803	Pte.	Toll, William Thomas	11.11.14	14645	Pte.	Wakefield, Benjamin	11.10.16
6949	Pte.	Tombs, Bernard	18.11.18	24224	Pte.	Walker, Arthur	3.5.17
19308	Pte.	Toney, Joseph	3.5.17	11503	Pte.	Walker, Clarence	31.5.15
3/7559	Pte.	Tordoff, Benjamin	11.11.14	30314	Pte.	Walker, Edward	30.8.18
6840	Sgt.	Town, Fred	8.11.14	16431	Pte.	Walker, Fred	4.7.16
10609	Pte.	Towey, Martin	5.5.15	156626	Pte.	Walker, Harry	3.5.17
204526	Pte.	Townend, Harold	15.4.18	18832	Pte.	Walker, Reginald	1.7.16
242924	Pte.	Townsend, Benjamin	2.4.18	204429	Pte.	Walker, Thomas Victor	16.4.18
16246	Pte.	Townsend, George	5.1.16				
8168	Pte.	Townsend, Arthur	24.8.14	3/12791	Pte.	Walker, William Edwin	21.2.16
11230	Pte.	Townsley, Arthur	5.5.15				
24951	Pte.	Townsley, Walter	11.4.17	10719	Pte.	Wallace, James	12.10.16
9124	Cpl.	Traynor, William	21.8.15	10780	Pte.	Wallace, John Joseph	15.4.18
14718	Pte.	Traynor, James Albert	10.10.17				
				13943	Pte.	Waller, Arthur	12.10.16
11061	Pte.	Trett, Alfred	7.5.17	24989	L/Cpl.	Waller, Denis, D.C.M., M.M.	22.10.18
7905	Pte.	Trevan, Fred	5.5.15				
12012	Col/Sgt.	Trivet, Frederick	26.9.16	268005	Pte.	Wallis, Harry	3.5.17
267906	Pte.	Truelove, Fred	3.5.17	14594	Pte.	Wallis, John William	1.7.16
10666	Pte.	Tuck, Victor	9.11.14	7234	Pte.	Walsh, Joseph	12.10.16
13006	Pte.	Tucker, William	12.10.16	9687	Sgt.	Walsh, Charles Edward	17.10.16
24365	Pte.	Tulley, Fred	3.5.17				
10300	L/Cpl.	Tulley, John William	6.5.15	11995	L/Sgt.	Walsh, Walter	5.5.15
14046	Pte.	Tullis, Alexander	5.5.15	305845	Pte.	Walton, Joe	10.5.18
22109	Pte.	Tunmore, David	17.11.18	12842	Pte.	Ward, James	10.10.17
10530	Pte.	Turnbull, James	8.11.14	14452	Pte.	Ward, William Henry	1.7.16
8496	Pte.	Turner, Albert	24.8.14	3/11439	A/Sgt.	Ward, James William	18.4.15
3/9220	L/Cpl.	Turner, Jonathan	12.5.15	6954	Cpl.	Wardle, Richard	5.5.15
3/12418	Pte.	Turner, Henry	12.10.16	12192	Pte.	Warton (?), Ernest	5.5.15
3/10545	Pte.	Turpin, John William	5.5.15	10812	Pte.	Waterhouse, Norman	1.7.16
15983	Pte.	Tuttle, Harry	1.7.16	3/10444	Pte.	Waterhouse, Willie	12.10.16
16245	Pte.	Tyman, John	6.2.16	26050	Pte.	Waterman, William Alfred	30.8.18
13848	L/Cpl.	Upton, Edward	10.10.17				
31558	Pte.	Valerio, Sylvester	24.6.18	28932	Pte.	Watson, Ernest	9.4.17
3/11025	Pte.	Varey, Thomas	7.5.15	10801	Pte.	Waud, Leslie Alvert William	18.4.15
26750	Pte.	Varley, Wood	11.4.17				
3/12787	Pte.	Venrbles, John	13.6.16	35400	Pte.	Wealthall, Richard Ward	24.10.18
11149	Pte.	Venning, Benjamin	2.5.15				
11716	Pte.	Verity, William	5.5.15	20269	Pte.	Weatherall, Harold	14.10.16
8477	Pte.	Vesty, Thomas	25.3.15	202858	Pte.	Weatherill, John	29.7.18
7982	Sgt.	Vincent, Ronald Harry	10.3.15	242374	Pte.	Weatherill, John	31.3.18
				25507	Pte.	Webb, Walter Bernard	8.8.18
3/9126	Pte.	Waddington, William	14.11.14				
				8373	Pte.	Webb, Thomas	23.10.16
3/10051	Pte.	Wade, Herbert	18.4.15	266457	Pte.	Webster, Harold Ernest	31.7.18
13931	Pte.	Wade, Isaac	5.5.15				
3/12601	Pte.	Wade, George William	12.10.16	9110	Pte.	Webster, Francis	8.11.14
				14134	Pte.	Weedon, Thomas	5.5.15
3/10103	Pte.	Waite, Charles Julian	18.4.15	10386	Pte.	Wells, George Arthur	11.11.14
3/11506	Pte.	Waite, William Herbert	1.7.16	5985	Pte.	West, Harry	8.11.14
				16269	Pte.	Wheat, Edward	10.10.16

APPENDIX IV

17541	Pte.	Wheatcroft, Willie	5.5.15	19681 Pte.	Wilson, Hubert	2.9.16
3/10510	Pte.	White, Bernard	5.1.15	3/10516 Pte.	Wilson, Fred	5.6.15
23690	Pte.	White, James Arthur	11.4.17	3/10743 Pte.	Wilson, John	30.12.15
7610	Sgt.	Whitehead, Percy	18.4.15	13143 Pte.	Wimpenny, John	3.5.17
28729	Pte.	Whiteley, James Gordon	3.5.17	8587 Pte.	Wimpenny, Fred	8.11.15
3/12795	Pte.	Whiteley, Harold	12.10.16	31251 L/Cpl.	Wimpenny, Sam	10.10.17
39344	Pte.	Whiteley, Arthur Hindle	31.8.18	12800 Pte.	Windross, William	12.10.16
3/9658	Pte.	Whitell, James	24.10.16	26652 Pte.	Winfield, Enoch Lawrence	31.8.18
10743	Pte.	Witham, Colin William	5.5.15	14563 Pte.	Winn, Charles	1.9.18
204350	Pte.	Whittaker, Fred	30.10.17	28837 Pte.	Winn, Richard	3.5.17
17933	Pte.	Whittaker, Harold	3.5.17	308176 Pte.	Winterbottom, Albert	30.8.18
22319	Pte.	Whittaker, Harry	13.5.18	19907 Pte.	Wolverson, Wilfred Saunders	3.9.16
300185	Pte.	Whittaker, Joe	3.5.17	307685 Pte.	Womack, Joe	9.8.18
6662	Pte.	Whittaker, William	11.11.14	7244 Pte.	Wood, John	28.10.14
14625	Pte.	Whitwam, Herbert	13.6.15	3/10285 L/Cpl.	Wood, William	12.10.16
	L/Cpl.	Whyte, Gordon	24.8.14	24164 Pte.	Wood, Ben	24.10.18
8663	Pte.	Widdop, Charlie	6.3.15	18604 A/Cpl.	Wood, Arnold	10.10.17
10965	Pte.	Widdup, Arthur	23.10.16	12536 Pte.	Wood, Ralph, M.M.	2.10.18
25607	Pte.	Wiggins, Heber	24.4.18	19178 Pte.	Wood, George	3.5.17
7435	Pte.	Wigglesworth, Clarence	8.11.14	14832 Pte.	Wood, Verdi	12.10.16
22266	Pte.	Wignall, Frederick	15.4.18	16087 Pte.	Wood, Henry James	12.10.16
14387	A/L/Cpl.	Wilcock, Thomas	23.10.16	20121 Pte.	Wood, William Lees	18.4.18
3/11274	Pte.	Wild, Thomas William	16.7.16	6839 Cpl.	Wood, William	24.8.14
11742	Pte.	Wild, William	5.5.15	24226 Pte.	Woods, John	9.4.17
7911	Pte.	Wilkinson, George	11.3.18	20390 Pte.	Woodhead, Hubert	12.10.16
15865	Pte.	Wilkinson, Isaac	5.5.15	11583 Pte.	Woodhead, John William	18.4.15
8121	Pte.	Wilkinson, Frank	11.11.14	307420 Pte.	Woodhead, Harold	10.10.17
26751	Pte.	Wilkinson, Tom Barker	11.4.17	14242 L/Cpl.	Woodhead, Norman	1.7.16
32759	Pte.	Williams, William John	19.4.18	3/10070 Pte.	Woodhead, Albert	18.4.15
22857	Pte.	Williams, Joseph	16.11.17	26756 Pte.	Woodruff, Willie	29.8.18
10625	Pte.	Williams, Albert	12.5.17	8288 Pte.	Woolbar, Thomas	5.5.15
16268	Pte.	Williams, John Thomas	12.10.16	8036 Pte.	Woolhouse, George	23.10.14
7177	Pte.	Williamson, Frederick	23.10.14	16265 Pte.	Woolley, Bertie	1.7.16
7841	Cpl.	Willis, Coates Henry	1.7.16	6586 Pte.	Worth, Robert	8.11.15
22267	Pte.	Willshaw, Joseph	3.6.18	25600 Pte.	Wyatt, Frank	25.10.18
10393	Pte.	Wilson, John James	2.11.14	205443 Pte.	Wright, Fred	15.4.18
17856	Pte.	Wilson, Frank	8.8.16	8689 Pte.	Wright, Herbert	11.11.14
10951	Pte.	Wilson, James	7.5.18	16267 Pte.	Wright, John Ernest	19.10.16
15687	Pte.	Wilson, Albert	3.5.17	10771 Pte.	Wright, Walter	23.10.16
24278	Pte.	Wilson, Robert	4.11.17	11356 Pte.	Wrigley, Wright	18.4.15
24953	L/Sgt.	Wilson, Evelyn Edmond	11.4.17	18883 Pte.	Yeadon, John	17.4.17
				267308 Pte.	Yeadon, Joseph	15.9.18
				26065 Pte.	Yellowlees, Alexander	10.10.17
12788	Pte.	Wilson, George Spencer	3.5.17	235747 Pte.	Youll, George	30.8.18
				33455 Pte.	Young, Robert	30.9.17
				7999 L/Cpl.	Zeppenfield, Phillip	8.4.15

DEPOT WEST RIDING REGIMENT

12517 Pte.	Dobb, Edward	5.8.18	200416 Pte.	Hey, Joss	11.11.18
15454 Pte.	Earnshaw, William Henry	5.3.15	11519 Pte.	McMahon, Stephen	23.5.16
203657 Pte.	Eccles, James	14.3.18	7942 Pte.	Palmer, Alfred Albert	4.8.17
8588 Pte.	Harris, Arthur Leonard	5.7.16	12886 Pte.	Robinson, George Henry	7.1.17

APPENDIX V

ARMY UNIFORMS 1702–1927

"TO see ourselves as others see us" was evidently impossible to the fighting men of two hundred years ago. To us, whose uniform stripped of the weighty pack we now carry, the bombs, gas-masks, and other trifles, is the acme of comfort, the wigs, flapped hats, feathers, and pigtails of two centuries ago sound utterly incomprehensible. Yet our civilian ancestors were equally content to disport themselves in silks and satins of all the colours of the rainbow where we now don " Oxford " bags or " plus-fours " and wear no hat at all.

Like not a few royal personages Queen Anne, by whose order the old 33rd was raised, was very strict in matters of detail concerning the dress of her courtiers. It is told of her that she once sent for Lord Bolingbroke in haste, who unwisely appeared in what was known as a Ramillies " Tie " wig when custom enjoined a " full-bottomed " wig. At this Queen Anne was greatly offended. During previous reigns, that is during those of Charles I, the Commonwealth, Charles II, James, and William III, " very wide brims and Flemish hats with curling feathers had been worn by Officers of the Army. As time passed the great inconvenience of these brims was strongly resented and first one flap, and then two flaps were turned up. About the time of Queen Anne the third flap was turned up, so the regular cocked hat of the eighteenth century came into existence."

During Queen Anne's reign the so-called chivalric costume can be said to have died out, though curassier gorgets and breast-pieces continued to be worn by officers of the Cavalry and Artillery. " People of fashion wore cocked hats, though some officers still tenacious of old custom adhered to the wide-brimmed hat turned up on two sides and trimmed with feathers as worn in previous reigns. The hair was worn, by some, tied behind, but generally very large perukes were the fashion. The following composed the ordinary habit of the nobleman or gentleman of that day: Square-cut coats and long-flapped waistcoats with large pockets in both; the stockings drawn up over the knee so high as to hide the breeches, but gartered below it. Large hanging cuffs and lace ruffles, the skirts of the coats stiffened out with wire or buckram from behind which peeped the hilt of the sword deprived of the broad and splendid belt in which it hung in preceding reigns. Blue or scarlet stockings with gold or silver clocks; lace neck-cloths, square-toed short-quartered shoes with high heels and small buckles. Very long and formally curled perukes, black riding-wigs, long wigs, and night-cap wigs, small three-cornered hats laced with gold or silver galloon and sometimes trimmed with feathers."

After Queen Anne's reign, about 1714, " perukes had fallen entirely out of fashion though the character of the uniform remained very much the same. Perukes were succeeded by the ' Tie ' wig and the ' Bob ' wig, and these again by the Ramillies tail and the pig-tail." What were known as " Clubs " were also worn. " ' Clubbing ' was done by having the head well pomateumed or larded and powdered. The thick tail of the long hair was turned up leaving a large knob below. The knob was secured by a strap. This was termed wearing the hair ' Clubbed.'

"Pigtails were adopted about 1745 (George II, 1727–1760). This was a period of heaviness and slowness in military movement and the uniform and accoutrements were cumbersome in the extreme. Particular attention seems to have been paid to the dressing of the hair and the 'cock of the hat.'" Halberts were taken away from the corporals and bombardiers. They fell in with carbines.

An instance of these somewhat hide-bound methods is afforded by an order of August, 1755, which reads: "It is ordered that no non-commissioned officer or soldier shall for the future go out of the barrack gate without their hats being 'cocked,' their hair well combed, tied, and dressed in a regimental manner, their shoes blacked, and clean in every respect." And a few years later, in 1756, an order appears to the effect that "Officers are desired not to appear on parade for the future with hats cocked otherwise than in the 'Cumberland' ('the Butcher' of Culloden) manner."

In 1786 we find an order issued that, "the non-commissioned officers and men are on all occasions, for the future, to wear their hair 'clubbed.'" During the long reign of George III (1760–1820) enormous changes took place in the uniforms of the British Army. About the year 1800 these commenced to emerge from the mediæval style that had characterized them up to date. "In the early part of this reign hats and wigs were perhaps the most striking and varied features. Wigs had been diminishing in size since the reign previous to George III, and in this reign the practice of frizzing, curling, plastering, and powdering the hair came into fashion. The common soldiers were perfect slaves to this practice and were compelled to appear on parade with curled and plastered hair and long tails hanging down behind. The officers wore pomatum, but the privates used the end of a tallow candle to keep their hair in order."

In the year 1804 pigtails grew to an enormous length and an order was issued to the Army to reduce them to 7 inches. In 1808 queues in the Army were ordered to be dispensed with. This order was obeyed, it was said with the most prompt alacrity, but the day after the order was given a counter-order came out. By this time, however, the queues were all gone.

As another instance of the tenacious folly of the authorities in adhering to old and useless customs the following may be quoted: "To such an excess was this practise carried (the wearing and powdering of queues) during the command of the late Duke of Kent at Gibraltar that when a field-day was ordered there were not enough barbers in the garrison to attend all the officers in the morning. The senior officers claimed the privilege of their rank. The juniors consequently were obliged to have their heads dressed the night before, and to preserve the beauty of this artistic arrangement, pomateumed, powdered, curled, and clubbed these poor fellows were obliged to sleep on their faces." In the office of the Adjutant of each Regiment was kept a pattern of the correct curls, to which the barber could refer.

During the reign of George IV (1820–1830) considerable changes in uniform took place. As far as the King's personal taste had any influence in such matters it seems to have expressed itself in a peculiarity for tightness. "In military dress a wrinkle was unpardonable, but a seam was advisable." In 1827 the Shako came in.

As a sailor, William IV (1830–1837) did not bother much about the details of Army dress, though towards the end of his brief reign he did. By his orders—scarlet being, he considered, the national colour—the whole British Army with the exception of Artillery and Rifles was clothed in red.

With Queen Victoria changes came in the dress of the British Army, but, at first, not by any means rapidly. So far as these changes concern uniform they may be roughly classed in three separate epochs: 1837 to 1854; 1855 to 1899, and from 1900 to the commencement

APPENDIX V

of the Great War. " Prior to 1854, military taste, or rather the taste of those in office (not necessarily the same thing) was still greatly influenced by the Georgian period. Large and unwieldly head-dresses with enormous plumes and high collars with stiff leather stocks were worn. Jackets and coatees were very tight and short-waisted with long tight sleeves. Loose trousers and overalls were also worn. The dress was more ornate and less serviceable.

" At the time of the Crimean War all this was changed and the very opposite extreme was reached. Loose tunics with long skirts, very low collars, very wide full sleeves, and diminution in lace and a certain slackness and appearance of ease, came into fashion." Never was the British Army more handicapped by its uniform than when it fought the Indian Mutiny.

With the second epoch of Queen Victoria's reign common-sense and the power of practical soldiers at the head of their profession brought about many changes for the better. During the third epoch referred to the whole world began to understand the benefits of hygienic clothing as well as of hygienic living. That the one is as important as the other may not, even now, be universally understood. But no section of the community has benefited more by the adoption of modern ideas of suitable clothing than all ranks of the British Army.

Books

1. *A Representation of the clothing of His Majesty's Household and of all the Forces upon the Establishments of Great Britain and Ireland.*
2. *History of the Dress of the British Soldier.* Luard.
3. *The Clothing of His Majesty's Forces.*
4. *Armies of Europe in 1812.* Goddard.
5. *The Picturesque Representation of the Dress and Manners of the English.* 1814.
6. *Military Costumes of the British Empire.* Hamilton Smith.

APPENDIX VI

PENSION FUND

The Duke of Wellington's Regiment

At present this consists of a Trust Fund specially subscribed by the 1st, 2nd, and 3rd Battalions. From the income derived from investments annual pensions are made available for ex-warrant officers, N.C.O.'s, and men of the three Battalions, or the wives and orphans of either of these ranks. As the income now stands the following pensions are available: one of £25 per annum and two each of £20 per annum, but if the capital of the Pension Fund could be increased by further donations or legacies, additional pensions, which are badly required, could be awarded.

Full control of the Pension Fund is in the hands of a Regimental Committee which consists of the Colonel of the Regiment, the officers commanding the 1st, 2nd, and 3rd Battalions or officers nominated by them, the officer commanding the Depot, Halifax, Yorks, with an Honorary Secretary.

The Committee have power to select pensioners from recommendations made to them as vacancies occur by the Committee of the Old Comrades' Association. The latter is the channel for the actual payment of the pensions.

The trustees of the fund are the Colonel of the Regiment and the officer commanding the Depot, Halifax, Yorks.

Here if anywhere is the chance of reminding ourselves that—

> "The best things any mortal hath
> Are those which every mortal shares."

APPENDIX VII

THE DEATH OF "THE CAMEL"

Many hundreds of those who have served in the 2nd Battalion will learn with regret of the death of that fine old war veteran, the "Camel," which took place from heart failure on Thursday, May 27th, 1926, at Carter's Hill Farm, Arborfield, where he had enjoyed well-earned retirement and comfort since September, 1922.

Joining the 2nd Battalion from the Remounts at Dublin as C.O.'s second charger in July, 1912, at the age of nineteen years according to his official medical history sheet, the horse was strongly recommended by the O.C. Remounts as having "in spite of his age, the heart of a colt." He was a tall, upstanding weight carrier of 17·2 hands, but decidedly skinny (photo is in book). He soon picked up under the care of Shaw, his groom, and was a delightful horse either to ride or drive.

At the outbreak of the war "the Camel" sailed to France with the Battalion on August 13th, 1914, and, in spite of being wounded four times, he never left it for four and a half years, during which period Mons, Ypres, Hill 60, the heavy fighting of 1916, Arras and Passchendaele Ridge in 1917, and the 1918 campaign, culminating in sweeping the Germans back through Belgium, were all actions in which he played his part, carrying some fourteen different C.O.'s. He was sent home early in May, 1919, with other "picked" horses for sale in London, thereby mercifully escaping falling into strange hands in Belgium. A wire from the Battalion reached Colonel Gibbs in time to buy him in for the Regiment, and for the next three months he enjoyed a comfortable stable and free range in both the Crystal Palace and grounds, where Colonel Gibbs was then in command. Proudly wearing his medal ribbons, five chevrons and four wound stripes on a leather shield attached to his brow-band, he might be seen daily about tea time walking through the main building to the A.T.A., where the men delighted in feeding him on buns, of which on one occasion he is credited with having consumed over a hundred. On another occasion Colonel Gibbs received an urgent telephone call in his private office saying one of the tobacco kiosk attendants wished him to "remove my horse," as she had given him nearly all her tea, but he still refused to move and would keep his head over the counter!

After the Battalion had re-formed at Sheffield, "the Camel" "rejoined" on August 5th and went with it to Ireland and then to Aldershot, performing light duties under the watchful eye of his old groom, Regt. Transport Sgt. H. Shaw, D.C.M. Just before the Battalion sailed for Egypt in September, 1922, Sergt. Shaw took him by road to Carter's Hill and handed him over to Mr. Dimond who had offered him an asylum in the evening of his days.

Early in August, 1919, the Secretary of "Our Dumb Friends' League" wrote that he had heard about the old horse's record, and sent a form to fill up, which resulted in the award of the special Blue Cross Fund Medals. These consisted of brass bosses to be worn on the brow-band, on which were blue enamel crosses with the inscription, "Treat me well, I've done my bit." Truly few horses ever did better!

APPENDIX VIII

BIRTH OF FIRST DUKE

As regards the actual birthplace of Arthur Wellesley or Wesley, the first Duke of Wellington, accounts vary. It was not until 1790 that the change in name was made from Wesley to Wellesley. The traditional one is that he was born either at 24 Upper Merrion Street, Dublin, or at Dangan Castle, Meath, either on April 29th or May 1st, 1769.

There has lately been some correspondence on the subject. One account quotes the *Freeman's Journal* of May 6th, 1769, as follows :

"[4th birth] Merrion Street, the Right Hon. the Countess of Mornington, of a son."

The actual house, says the writer, was probably that used for offices in connexion with the Irish Commission—Courts, Mornington House. The prescription compounded by Mr. Evans, of Dawson Street, for the mother on this interesting occasion is, or was quite recently, still to be seen framed in the shop and bears the address "24 Upper Merrion Street."

The writer goes on to say : "I am not aware in which of the Dublin Churches the child was 'baptized on April 30th, 1769,' but if such a record exists, as I quote, the child would appear to have been 'prematurely' baptized."

Brig.-General A. R. Burrowes (late Royal Irish Fusiliers), on the other hand, writes that there is "a tradition in my family that the Duke of Wellington was born at Dangan Castle, Co. Meath. My great-grandfather, Colonel Thomas Burrowes, purchased Dangan Castle from the Earl of Mornington."

A third account is that given by Capt. J. Russell, who writes : "When a Company of my Regiment (2nd Royal Welch Fusiliers) were stationed at Trim, Co. Meath, in 1872, an elderly lady—between 90 and 100 years, I believe—resided at Trim. She used to relate to us that she sometimes, when a little girl, nursed for her mother the first Duke. The old lady used to tell us that the first Duke of Wellington was born just before his mother landed at Dublin. I presume it may be assumed that child and mother were detained in Dublin for a little while pending being able to travel to Trim."

LIST OF SUBSCRIBERS

The Regimental History Committee wish to record their thanks to the following who have kindly subscribed towards the production of this Regimental History.

Lieut. F. R. Armitage

Col. N. B. Bainbridge
Major W. T. McG. Bate
Lieut.-Colonel H. W. Becher
Lieut.-General Sir Herbert Belfield
Capt. L. E. Bishop
Capt. R. H. D. Bolton
Major E. C. Boutflower
Lieut. W. F. Browne
Brig.-General C. D. Bruce
Major J. C. Burnett

Miss E. Caldecott
Capt. R. O'D. Carey
Lieut. T. St. G. Carroll
Lieut. J. Chatterton
G. W. Chibnall, Esq.
Major R. S. Cholmley
Capt. R. C. Coode
Corporals' Mess, 1st Battalion
Corporals' Mess, 2nd Battalion
Major M. N. Cox
Capt. M. E. Crane
Lieut. H. A. Crommelin
Lieut. G. R. T. Cumberlege
Col. A. R. Curran

Lieut. J. H. Dalrymple

Lieut. N. H. Everard
Lieut. K. G. Exham
Lieut. R. K. Exham

Lieut. C. K. T. Faithfull
Capt. V. C. Farrell
Capt. G. T. Fleming
Lieut. J. E. Frankis
Capt. F. H. Fraser
Lieut. A. J. Frith

Colonel J. A. C. Gibbs
Capt. J. V. Gibson
Major T. H. J. Gillam
Capt. V. C. Green
Capt. C. W. G. Grimley

Colonel E. G. Harrison
Lieut. H. Harvey
Lieut. C. I. E. Haslock
Lieut.-Colonel F. A. Hayden
Lieut.-Colonel R. K. Healing
Capt. Sir R. J. A. Henniker, Bart.
Lieut.-Colonel L. H. Herapath
Major C. R. Hetley
Lieut. A. G. Hiddingh
Lieut. W. Hodgson
Major E. R. Houghton
Lieut. J. P. Huffam
Brig.-General C. V. Humphrys
Capt. C. Hyde

Mrs. Ince
Major C. W. G. Ince

Lieut. R. L. J. Jones

LIST OF SUBSCRIBERS

Capt. H. R. Kavanagh
Mrs. Keely
Capt. H. G. Keet
Mr. J. J. Kelly
Lieut. S. B. Kington
Capt. J. V. Kirkland

W. J. L'Aimee, Esq.
Lieut. J. H. C. Lawlor
Colonel B. St. J. Le Marchant
Lieut. J. A. Lennon
Lieut. J. G. Lepper
Library, 1st Battalion
Library, 2nd Battalion
Library, Depot
Capt. C. H. E. Lowther

Major S. F. Marriner
Lieut. W. A. Marshman
Lieut. H. G. P. Miles
Major N. H. Moore
Capt. P. A. Mulholland

Lieut. L. P. Norman

Lieut. C. A. O'Connor
Officer Commanding, 1st Battalion
Officer Commanding, 2nd Battalion
Officers' Mess, 1st Battalion
Officers' Mess, 2nd Battalion
Officers' Mess, Depot
Major W. G. Officer
Old Wellingtonian Society
Lieut. C. W. B. Orr
Capt. R. H. W. Owen
Lieut. H. B. Owen
Capt. W. M. Ozanne

Mr. J. Paling
Lieut.-Colonel E. M. K. Parsons
Capt. D. Paton
Lieut.-Colonel F. G. Peake
Lieut.-Colonel C. J. Pickering

President Regimental Institutes, 1st Battalion
President Regimental Institutes, 2nd Battalion
Major A. J. Preston
Capt. O. Price

Mr. H. Rawson
Lieut. J. T. Rivett-Carnac
Lieut. T. W. Robertson
Lieut. E. W. Rogers
Lieut. C. Rowland
Major G. S. W. Rusbridger

Capt. A. E. H. Sayers
Lieut. J. W. Scott
Sergeants' Mess, 1st Battalion
Sergeants' Mess, 2nd Battalion
Sergeants' Mess, Depot
Capt. A. G. Smith
Lieut. Sydney Smith
Lieut.-Colonel F. W. Snell
Lieut. E. W. Stevens
Lieut. H. C. M. Stone
Mrs. P. B. Strafford

Lieut. H. C. H. Taylor
Capt. O. A. Taylor
Mrs. Trench
Lieut.-Colonel M. V. le P. Trench
Lieut. R. G. Turner
Brig.-General P. A. Turner

Brig.-General W. M. Watson
Mrs. W. M. Watson
Lieut. A. H. G. Wathen
Lieut. B. W. Webb-Carter
Lieut.-Colonel F. H. B. Wellesley
The Duke of Wellington
Capt. N. R. Whitaker
Mr. T. White
Lieut.-Colonel W. E. White
Major W. C. Wilson
Lieut. F. P. A. Woods
Lieut. W. A. Woods

INDEX

The roman numeral (I) after the entry indicates that the reference is to the First Battalion

ABBASSIA, 22 (I)
Abbeville, 112, 152
Abyssinian War, 8, 197 (I)
Acadie, 33
Acheux, 146, 151
Actions and Operations
  1st Bn., 5 *sqq.*, 8, 9 *sqq.*, 19–20, 21, 22–3
  2nd Bn., 36 *sqq.*, 48, 51 *sqq.*
  76th Regt., 3, 4, 31
Adamson, Capt. A. G. (3rd W. Staffs.), 142
Adolpho, 2nd Lt. E. W., 165, 166
Adye, Lt. L. C., 140, 150, 151
Afghanistan, 55
Afghanistan Campaign (1919), 19, 20 (I)
Agadir Incident, the, 45, 49
Agra, 198
Ahmadabad riots, 18
Ailette River, 100, 104
Aisne, Battle of the, 103 *sqq.*, 111
Aisne River, 100, 103, 104
  French attack on (1917), 166
  Rafting across, 105, 106
Alamanza, Battle of, 3 (I)
Albert, H.M., King of the Belgians, 57
Albert, 146
Alexander, Lt. (Royal Scots), 120
Alexander, Major E. W., V.C. (L Battery, R.H.A.), 84
Alexander, Sir William, 33
Aligarh, Storming of, 28, 29 *sqq.* (I)
Aliwal North, 12 (I)
Aliwal North district, 42 (I)
Alland River, 102
Allen, Sgt., 42, 43 (I)
Allenby, Major-Gen. Sir E., 83, 84, 86, 87–8, 94

Allied Positions, 1914
  Aug. 20, a.m., 59
  Aug. 21, 61
  Oct., extent of Battle-line, 112
All Saints' Church, Aldershot, 192, 193, 198
Alma, Battle of the, 8, 46, 197 (I)
Alsace, 58
  French Army of, 59
Amalgamated Regts., Honours and Distinctions of, 24
Amalgamation of 1881, the, 24 *sqq.*
Ambala, polo at, 15 (I)
American War of Independence, 4, 26, 196 (I)
Amfroipret, 85
Amiens, 66, 143
  Ludendorff's push for, 174, 179
Amritzar, 16 (I)
  Outbreak, the, 19 (I)
Ancre River, 149
Andaman Islands, 44
Anderson, Gen., 117
Anderton, 2nd Lt., 156, 164, 165, 166
Anglo-Russian Agreement of 1907, 55
Anjou, Philip, Duke of, 1
Anley, Brig.-Gen., 12th Bde., 145–6, 147
Anne, Queen, 1, 2–3 (I)
Annequin, 114
Annual Training, 45
Anson, 2nd Lt. H. H., 174, 179
Antwerp, 57, 60, 185
Archer, Capt. F. J. E. (Norfolks), 127
Ardennes, the, 60
Argyll and Sutherland Highlanders, 89

Arkless, 2nd Lt. E. E., 151, 153
Arleux, 158
Armies
  British
    Second, 143
    Third, 143, 149, 158, 163, 173
    Fourth, 149, 155, 168–9
    Fifth, 168
    Canadian, 174
Armistice, the, 183
Armitage, Major F. A., 151
Army Corps, 1914, *see also* Corps, *and* Rawlinson's
  I, 61
  II, 61
Army Council, the, 55
Army in India, Committee of 1912–13, 55
Army Line, the, 174
Army Reorganization, at home, 52 *sqq.*; in India, 55
Arraines, 156
Arras, 59, 114, 157, 171, 173, 177, 180
  Battle of, 158 *sqq.*
  Horsfall's account of, 159 *sqq.*
  Line E. of, 166, 168
Arras-Cambrai Road, 178, 179
Arrow Trench, raid on, 167–8
Artillery, *see also* Royal Artillery
  Divisional, 5th, 84
  Militia Garrison, 53
  Territorial, Coast, 53
  Field, 53
Artillery Barrages, Ludendorff on, 181
Asquith and Oxford, Rt. Hon. the Earl of, 18
Athies, 160
Athies-Plouvain Road, 160, 161
Atkinson, Pte. J., 43

INDEX

Auchonvillers, 151
Audregnies, 82
Austrian Succession, War of the, 4 (1)
Austro-Prussian War (1866), 8
Authieule, 151
Averdoignt, 179

BADEN-POWELL, Lt.-Gen. Sir R. S. S., G.C.M.G., G.C.V.O., K.C.B., 38
Bailey, 2nd Lt. C. A. (W. Yorks), 139, 140
Bailleul, 117, 118, 124, 126, 129, 158
— Road, 127
Bailleuval, 146
Baird, Major-Gen. David, 6
Baku, 20 (1)
Baldwin, 2nd Lt. S., 156, 164
Bales, Capt. P. G., M.C., 201
Balfour, Rt. Hon. Earl, 55
Ball, Col. (76th Regt.), 30
Ball, Cpl. A., M.M., 184
Ballard, Lt.-Col. C. R. (Norfolks), 84
Bamborough, C.S.M., 162, 163
Bangalore, taking of, 20
— Plague duty at, 40
Banham, Lt. M., 174, 175; M.C., 177, 178
Barbados, 32, 35
Barbary Coast, the 76th (86th) wrecked on, 26
Barbier, Madame, a Belgian heroine, 79
Bard Farm Cemetery, 170
Barly, 146
Baroda, the Gaekwar of, 7 (1)
Barossa Camp, 166
Barrackpore, 45
Barton, Capt. B. J., 111; D.S.O., 130, 135, 137, 140
Bassein, Treaty of, 7
Basseville-Hondevillers-Boitrun line, 101
Bastow, Pte., 185
Basutoland, 42
Bateman, Lt.-Col. C. M., D.S.O. (T.D.), 201
Bates, ——, 123

Bates, Pte., M.M., bar to, 184
Bates, Pte. C., M.M., 184
Bates, Pte. D., M.M., 184
Bath, 12
Bathurst, Capt. C., 156
Battle Honours, Selection of, regulations for, 200
— Committee of Selection 201
Battle Honours 4, 7, 8, 12, 15, 29, 31, 40, 41, 46, 179, 197, 198–9, 200, 202, 205; list of, for the Great War, 201; in the Roll of Honour Book, 188
Baumetz, 168
Bavai, 61, 80, 83, 84, 86
Bavai–St. Waast line, 85
Bavai–Valenciennes line, Von Kluck's attack on, 85 *sqq.*
Bazeley, Sgt. G. W., *Croix de Guerre*, 145
Beard, 2nd Lt. F. W. (R.F.C.), 146, 153
Beaumont Hamel, 149, 150, 151
Beauval, 147
Beauvois, 89
Becher, Capt. H. W., 41; Bt.-Major, 43
Bechuanaland Mounted Police, 36, 37 (1)
Bedford Regt., 1st Bn., 73, 76, 83, 90, 115, 116, 118, 130, 137, 141
Beirne, Pte., M.M., 156
Belfield, Lt.-Gen. Sir H. E., K.C.B., K.C.M.G., K.B.E., D.S.O., Colonel of the Regt., 16, 40, 41, 43, 46–7, 190, 192, 201
— Colours presented by, to 1st Bn., 1925, 202
— Speech by, on handing the Colours to the Dean of York, 193
— On the Regt. in the Great War, with special reference to the Territorial and Service Bns., 204–5

Belgian devotion to British wounded and temporarily missing, 79–80
— Stand in Aug., 1914, 57
Belgium, German advance through, 58
Bell, Canon C. C., 192
Belle Isle, Siege of, 26
Bellignies, 86
Belshard, 2nd Lt. S. A, 157, 165, 166
Benares, 45
Bengal, partition of, 17 (1)
Bennett, 2nd Lt. D. A., 151
Bennett, Lt. J., 114, 115, 120, 121, 125
Berar, Rajah of, 7
Berkeley, Lt.-Col., 174
Berlin, 112
Bermeries, 85
Bernafay Wood, 152, 153
Bernaville, 146, 147
Bertangles, 152
Bertrancourt, 146, 147, 151
Bethancourt, 95
Bermuda, 31 *sqq.*, 200 (1)
— Yachting at, 32–3
Bethulie, 42
Béthune and district, 112, 113, 114
Bevan, Pte. A., 43 (1)
Beyfus, 2nd Lt. G. H., 138, 139, 140
Biddle, 2nd Lt. V., 174
Bilham, Capt. D. G. R., M.C., 175; Adjt., 185
Billon Wood, 143
Binche, 61, 185
— Union Jack presented to, by 2nd Bn. "Duke's," 185
Pir Salem, 21 (1)
Birch, Lt. H. J., 142
Birkett, Pte. W., 43
Bishop, Lt. L. E., M.C., 192
Bismarck, Prince, 8
Bit Lane, 167, 168
Blackburn, 2nd Lt. T. A., 174, 179, 183
Black Watch, the, 116
Blake, Pte., 128
Blaugies, 83, 84
Bleville rest-camp, 51
Bligh's 20th Regt., 4

INDEX

Bloemfontein, 11 (1), 42
Bloemhof, O.R.C., 43
"Blue Noses," as sportsmen, 34 (1)
Boeschepe, 142
Bois de Boussu, 71
Bois de Marnimont, 147
Bomb-throwing, 142
Bombay, 12 (1)
    Riots at, 19 (1)
Bombay Cup won, 15 (1)
Bond, Lt.-Col. R.C.(K.O.Y.L.I.), 73–4, 90
Boonga, Chief, 38
Border Regt., 6th Service Bn., 175
Boshof, 12 (1)
Bostandjik, 23 (1)
Bouchavesnes, 157
Bougnies, 82
Boulogne, 126
Bourg-Venizel section, 104
Bourne, Sgt., D.C.M., 175
Boussu, 61
Boussu-Quiévrain Road, 84
Boussu-Wasmes-Paturages-Frameries line, 82
Boutard, Cpl., D.C.M., interpreter, 56; Sgt., 146
Boutflower, E.C. Capt., a/Major, temp. Lt.-Col., 18, 19; O.B.E., 21, 22 (1)
Bowyer-Bowyer, 2nd Lt. E. W., 142
Bowers, Pte. S. W., M.M., 184
Bowes, 2nd Lt. C. H., 150, 151
Bowet, Archbishop of York, 186
Boyce, Capt., 31
Braine, 2nd Lt. J. S., 152, 153, 157, 164
Braisne, 103
Brandfort, 43
Bray, Lt.-Col. R. N., C.M.G., D.S.O., 22, 142, 143, 147, 150, 151; Brig.-Gen., 87th Inf. Bde., 156, 188
Bray (town), 143, 145, 158
Brenelle, 103
Brenez, Alexandre, heroism of, 80
Brevillers, 146

Brigades
British
    Cavalry, composition of, 53
    1st, 95, 122
    3rd, 100, 101, 103
    4th, 100, 101
    5th, 85, 100, 101, 103
    Infantry, composition of, 53
    4th, 192
    Guards', 118
    6th, 146
    7th, 122, 142
    9th, 119
    10th, 153, 158, 162, 173, 174, 177, 180–1, 185
    11th, 153, 155, 180, 181
    12th, 145, 146, 149, 153, 155, 157, 158 sqq., 171, 173, 180
    13th, 60 sqq., 83, 105, 107, 112, 113 sqq., 124, 132, 133, 138, 141, 142, 143, 145; Nucleus of new Third Army, 143
    14th, 106, 107, 124, 143
    15th, 102, 106, 107, 137
    22nd, 118
    33rd, 151
    76th, 176
    83rd, 130
    107th Ulster, 146
    186th, 4th, 5th, 6th, and 7th Bns., "Duties" as, 205
Indian
    Infantry
    Presidency, 45
    Rawalpindi, 18
British Air Force, Oct., 1914, 110, see also R.F.C.
British Expeditionary Force, 1914, 59; inception of, 52, 53, see also Army Corps, under numbers
    Divisional System of, 53
    In France, 60 sqq.
    Line of, reorganization of, winter, 1914–15, 129
    Position on and after Sept., 1916, 152–3
British front, length of, in Jan., 1918, 172

British Infantry on Indian establishment, reorganization of, 18
Bronfay Farm, 143
Brook, Pte. (a/L./Cpl.) C. G., M.M., 184
Brooke, Rupert, lines by ("If I should die . . ."), 189
Brown, C.Q.M.S., A. J., M.S.M., 185
Browne, 2nd Lt. D. M., 150, 151
Browning, Capt. J. S., temp. C.O., 170; M.C., 174
Bruce, Capt. (76th), 26
Brussels, 58
Bruyeres–N.W. through Cugny–St. Remy line, 102
Buchan, J., on the autumn fighting on the Somme, 1916, 152, and on the last stages of the Third Battle of Ypres, 169
Buchanan-Dunlop, Capt. H. D. (R.W. Kents), 63
Buckingham, Duke of, Lord-Lieutenant of Ireland, 28 (1)
Buckley, Sgt. O., 41
Bucy le Long, 105
Bullecourt, 159
Buller, Rt. Hon. Gen. Sir Redvers, 37
Bullfontein, 43
Buluwayo, 36
Burch, Cpl., M.M., 152
Burhan Camp, near Attock, 18 (1)
Burke, Major C. J., D.S.O., 152, 153
Burke, Pte., M.M., 171
Burke, Pte. D., 43 (1)
Burma, 40, 41, 44
Burma Mounted Infantry Regiment, 12, War Service of, 40 sqq.
    Become 29th M.I., 43
    Casualties, South African War, 43
    Two Years' (War) Wastage in, 42
Burnand, Major (Lt.-Col.) N. G., D.S.O., 23 (1)

Burnett, Major J. C., D.S.O., 101
Burrow, Wulf, and Legend trenches, 151
Burton, Pte. W., 43
'Bus transport, 60, 112, 117, 179, 180
Bush fighting, 38
Bussigny, 86
Butler, 2nd Lt. W., 174
Butterworth, C.Sgt., D.C.M., 43
Buzancy, 103

CABOTS, the, 33
Cadiz, attack on, 1 (1)
Cadman, Sgt. J., 11 (1)
Cadmore, Sgt. W., 11 (1)
Cairo, 22 (1)
Calais, 143
Calcutta, 5 (1), 44
  Minto Centenary Fête at, 15 (1)
Calcutta Cup Record, 1903-13, 14-15
Calcutta Tournament, winning of, 14
Caldwell, 2nd Lt., M.C., 173, 174
Camberley Staff College, 52
Cambrai, 83, 180
Cambridge, F.M. H.R.H., the Duke of, attached 33rd Regt., 197
Cameron, Major (temp. Lt.-Col.) A. R., 75
Camerons of Callart, 26
Canadian Army, 174
Canadian Mounted Rifles, 5th, 152
Canadian success at Vimy Ridge, 158-9
Cape Colony, medal clasp, 41
Cape Mounted Rifles, 36
Cape Town Highlanders, 37
Capiau, Monsieur Hermann, 75, 79
Capon, 2nd Lt. E. C., 173
Capper, Brig.-Gen., later Maj.-Gen., C.B., D.S.O., 49, 50
Card, 2nd Lt. H. G., 173, 174

Cardwell, Lord, Army System of, 53
Carey, Lt. R. O'D., 120, 121, 125; Capt., 201
Carlisle, Earl of, 187
Carnoy, 143, 145, 152
Carr, Lt.-Col. L., Lt.-Col. Gen. Staff, 4th Div., 170
Carr, Major R. N., M.C., 175
Carrington, Major-Gen. C., 38
Carrol, Pte. J., M.M., 175, 184
Carter, Capt., 65, 66, 69, 72, 78
Casement, Sir Roger, 17
Cassel, 151
Castlereagh, Viscount, 53
Casualties, all ranks
  1st Bn.
    Fontenoy, 4
    South African War, 9, 11, 12
    Among officers from, who fought in the Great War, list of, 21
  2nd Bn.
    South African War, 43
    World War
      At the Battle of Mons, 78-9
      Retreat from Mons, 99, 111
      La Bassée, 114, 115, 116
      Ypres, 1st Battle of, 119, 121, 122, 125, 128
      Hill 60, 133 sqq., 137-8, 139-40, 141
      On the Somme, 145, 151, 152, 153, 155, 164, 166, 167-8, 170
      In 1918, in the push on Amiens, 174-5, 177, 178-9, 181-2, 183
Caterpillar, the, 132
Cavalry, see under Brigades, see also Gough's
Caumont, 158
Cavan, Lt.-Gen. the Earl of, on Capt. Robins, 140
Ceremonial Parades, 12 (1)
Chadwick, 2nd Lt. F. D., 139, 140, 145
Chalcraft, 2nd Lt. G. A. (W. Yorks), 139, 140
Chaman, 19, 20 (1)
Champagne, 143

Chanak, 23 (1)
Changis-Coulommiers front, 100
Channel Ports, German menace to, 86, 99, 110, 111, 114
Chantilly Conference, 158
Chaplin, Pte. M.M., 171
Charleroi, 59
Charlesworth, 2nd Lt. F., 173
Charly bridge, 101
Chartered Company of South Africa, the, 36
Chassemy, 103
Château-Signy Signets, 101
Château-Thierry, 98
Chayter, Pte., M.M., 152
Cheetham, 2nd Lt. A. H., 124, 136, 138
Cheetham, Lt. C. N., 151
Chelmsford, Major-Gen. Lord, 37
Chemical Works, the, 159, 163
Chemin des Dames (1914), 103, 104, 105
Cheshire Regt., 1st Bn., 72, 73, 84, 90, 114, 115, 118
Chezy, 102
Chiers River, 59
Chirol, Sir Valentine, cited on India and the Great War, 17-18
Chivres spur and valley, 105-6, 107, 108
Churchill, Rt. Hon. W., C.H., M.P., cited on the first three months of the Great War, 110, on the Battles on the Somme, 146 sqq., and the events of the four years of war, 183-4
Churchward, Rev. M. W., Chaplain to the Troops, Lichfield, 46 (1)
Ciry Salsogne, 103, 105
Clarence, H.R.H. the Duke of, Colours presented by, to 3rd Bn., 202, 203
Clements, Gen., 41
Clifton, Lt.-Col. R. B., 201
Clifton, 2nd Lt. S. G., 151; Lt., 157

INDEX

Climie, Capt., R.A.M.C., 164, 165; O.C. Convalescent Base Camp, Étaples, 173
Coates, 2nd Lt., 164
Coates, Sgt. B., M.S.M., 22 (1)
Code Message, an error in, 44
Cockroft, Pte. S., M.M., 184
Coke, Lt. E. C., a/Adjt., 168; Capt., Adjt., 170
Coldstream Guards, 122
Colenso, 37
Colley, Major-Gen. Sir G. P., 37
Colours of the Army, Royal Warrants on, 195
  Carried in the Russo-Japanese War (1904-5), 194
  Regimental, fighting value of, 194-5
  Regulations for renewal of, 196
Colours of the Regt., 4, 31, 33, 44, 45-6, 184, 196, 197
  Burnt at Rangoon, 33, 44, 46, 193, 199, 200
  Deposition of, in the Memorial Chapel, 192 *sqq.*
  Details of, 196 *sqq.*
  Honorary, 33, 44, 198 *sqq.*
  Present, 200
Colson, 2nd Lt. J. P., 165; Capt., M.C., M.M., 185
Combined Training (Henderson), 54
Commendations and Thanks
  1st Bn., 16, 20
  2nd Bn., 45, 47, 48, 50, 130, 138, 140, 141, 157, 165, 177, 179
Compiègne, Forest of, Peace terms discussed in, 183
Conchy-Hesdin Road, 112
Condé, 83, 84, 103, 104
Condé-Mons line, 60, 61
Condé Road, 106
Constantinople, 22, 23, 190 (1)
Coode, 2nd Lt. P., 38; Capt., D.S.O., 12, 43
Cook, Sgt. R., 11 (1)
Cooke, 2nd Lt. (a/Capt.) J., M.C., 181, 183; D.S.O. 184, 185

Cooper, Brig.-Gen., 126, 127
Cooper, 2nd Lt. F. B., 156
Cooper, Sgt. T., M.M., 184
Corbie, 143, 145, 152, 158
Cork, 5
Cornwallis, Lord, and the American Campaign, 4, 26-7, 28, 196; Colonel-in-Chief, "Duke's," 8 (1)
Coronation Durbar, Delhi, 16, 17 (1)
Corps
  British
    I, 82 *sqq.*, 100, 102, 105, 118
    I and II, reunion of, 97
    II, 82 *sqq.*, 86, 96, 99, 100, 101, 104, 132
    III, 94, 99, 100, 101, 102, 103, 105
    VIII, 146, 149
    Royal Flying, 146
    XVII, 158, 159, 163, 165
    XXII, 185
  German, XV, 7th Army, Retreat of, 102
Corunna, 15, 46, 200
Costello, Pte. J., M.M., 184
Courcelles, 103
Courcellette, 153
Covell, Major, C.O. (76th Regt.), 197, 198
Covernton, 2nd Lt. C. C. (3rd Essex), 139
Cox, Lt. M. N., 21, 125, 126; Capt., M.C. (Trspt. Off.), 138, 140-1, 145
Coyolles, 94
Crabb, Pte. W., 42, 43
Crane, Capt. M. E., 192
Craven, 2nd Lt. G. E., 174, 175; M.C., 177
Crawshay, Capt. O. T. R., 114
Crécy, 100
  Battle of, 88
Crépy en Valois, 94, 95, 97
Crimean War, the, 5, 8, 46, 129, 197 (1)
Crisp, 2nd Lt. H., 130, 136, 138
Crockett, 2nd Lt. R. G., 156, 164
Crocodile River, 43
Croft, 2nd Lt. J. A. C. (R. Warwicks), 128, 136, 138

Croisselles-La Fère line of German attack, March, 1918, 173
Croissiaux, Monsieur, 72-3
Crosbie, Brig.-Gen. J. D., 147, 151, 156, 161, 162, 165
Crossly, Messrs. J., & Sons, 188
Crowther, 2nd Lt. C. C., 165
Croxon, Lt. W. A., 174
Culliton, Pte., M.M., 156
Cunningham of Craigend, Capt., 26
Cunningham, Capt. K. E., 157, 164, 165, 166
Cunningham, Cpl. J., 11 (1)
Cunningham, L./Cpl., M.M., 184
Cunningham, 2nd Lt. E. M., 132, 142; Capt., M.C., a/Adjt., 168
Curragh, the, 22 (1), 25
Currie, Capt. R. A. M., Bde.-Major, 13th Bde., 73, 74
"Currie" Tournament of 1895, 38
Curzon of Kedleston, Marquis, Viceroy of India, 17
Cuthbert, Lt.-Col. (temp. Brig.-Gen.) G. T. C., 13th Bde., 75

D'AMADE, General, 59
Dammartin, G.H.Q., B.E.F., 97
Danesbury, Welwyn, Herts., 197
Dansey, Major R., 196
Dardanelles Committee, the, 56
Darjeeling, the Soldier's views on (verse), 13 (1)
Daubeny, 2nd Lt. C. O., 142
Davis, Lt., 142
Davis, Lt. E. B. (W. Yorks), 139, 140
Davis, Lt. R. N., 150, 151; Capt., 153
Day, ——, of the Salisbury Rifles, 40
De Aar, 41
Deccan Campaign, 28 (1)
Deeg, Siege of, 28, 30-1 (1)
Defence Committee of the Cabinet, the, 55

INDEX

Delhi, capture of, 198 (1)
   Coronation Durbar at, 16, 17 (1)
   Military Tournament at, 16 (1)
   Riots at, 18–20 (1)
Delhi Manœuvres, 1902, 44
Demerara, 35
Denman-Jubb, Capt., Adjt., 70, 72–3, 75, 78, 79, 189
Dennison, Sgt., 156
Denton, Sgt., D.C.M., 177
De Sausmarez, Brig.-Gen., C., C.B., C.M.G., D.S.O., G.O.C. R.G.A., on the Battle of Le Cateau, 93
Designations of Regiments of Infantry of the Line on amalgamation, 24, 25
   of the 33rd Regt. at different times, 4, 8, 10, 24, 25
Destruction Fire, Ludendorff on, 181
Dettingen, Battle of, 4, 196 (1)
Devil's Trench, 167
Devonshire Regt., 116, 139
de Wend, Lt. D. E., 111, 120, 121, 189
de Wet, Gen., 41, 42
Diamond Hill, medal clasp, 41 (1)
Dickebusch, 142
Diest, 57
Dieval, 112
Dinant, 58, 59
Dinapore, 45
Divisions
  British
    Cavalry, with B.E.F., 53, 98, 100, 101
    4th, 178
    Infantry
      1st, 101
      2nd, 103
      3rd, 100, 127, 128, 142
      4th, 86, 94, 98, 106, 145, 146, 153, 158, 159 *sqq.*, 165, 166, 168, 169, 174, 180–1 *sqq.*, 185
      5th, 90, 92–3, 96, 98, 100, 102, 106, 112, 113 *sqq.*, 129, 132, 142, 145; Losses of, on Aug. 23–4, 1914, 84–5; Cycling Coy., 62, 101, 145

Divisions, British Inf. (*contd.*)
      6th, 153
      12th, 167
      27th, 139
      51st, 181
      56th, 179
  Indian
    4th (Quetta), 20
    Lahore, 139
Dockerty, Pte., M.M., 171
Don, Lt.-Gen., 197, 198
Donoughue, Pte. D., D.C.M., 43 (1)
Doornkraal Farm, 41 (1)
Dormy House, 131
Dorsetshire Regt., 1st Bn., 68, 73, 74, 80, 90, 115, 139
Douai, 59
Doullens, 151
Dour, 61, 84
Downey, Q.M.Sgt. A. P., M.S.M., 22 (1)
Downey, Lt. W. R., 111, 142
Doyle, Pte. H., M.M., 184
D'Oyley, Major-Gen., Colonel, 33rd Regt., Colours presented by, 197
Drake, Pte. (a/Sgt.) R., M.S.M., 22 (1)
Dranoutre, 118, 124, 127, 129
Driefontein, Battle of, 43
   Medal clasp for, 41
Drocourt-Quéant Switch, 179
Drummond, Brig.-Gen. L., C.B., M.V.O., 48
Dryden, Pte., 135; D.C.M., 136
Dublin, 49, 197
   Labour unrest in, 50
Dufferin, R.I.M.S., 45
Duizel, 103
Duke of Cornwall's L.I., 89, 145
Duke of Edinburgh's Own Volunteer Corps, the, Cape Town, 37
Duke of Wellington's Regt. (West Riding), formerly 33rd Duke of Wellington's Regt., Early History of, 1 *sqq.*
   Amalgamation with, of the 76th Regt. (*q.v.*), 8, 25, 198

D. of Wellington's Regt. (*contd.*)
   Battalions composing, H.Q., and uniform of, 24, 25, 45
   1st, Raising of, and early history, 1 *sqq.*; Triple Command of, 3–4; Wellington's association with, 5 *sqq.*; Services from Waterloo onwards, 8 *sqq.*; Post-war, 23, 190; Reduced to a Cadre, 20; New Colours presented to, 1925, 202; Officers and Troops from, on other Fronts in the Great War (*see also under* Names), 21, 55, 152, 158, 170
   1st and 2nd passing on the voyage to and from India, 12, 45
   2nd, 4; passing the 1st on the voyage from India, 12, 45; Early Years of, History of, 24 *sqq.*; Service from 1893 to 1913, 36 *sqq.*; Armed with Lee-Enfield rifle, 44, with short magazine *do.*, 45, and re-armed with S.L.E. rifle, 49; Adjudged best in the Presidency Bde., 1905, 45; Pre-war training of, in Ireland, 49–50
   With B.E.F. in France and Belgium, 51 *sqq.*, 103, 145, 149, 158 *sqq.*, 173, 179, the first shots fired, 63–4; in the Battle of Mons and in the Retreat, 60 *sqq.*; six German Bns. driven back by, 84; at Goebin Wood, 111–12; in the first Battle of Ypres, 117 *sqq.*; Winter Quarters, 1914, 129; at Hill 60, 132 *sqq.*, Roll of Officers present at, 137–8, those left after, 140–1, congratulations,

INDEX

D. of Wellington's Regt. (*contd.*)
2nd Batt. with B.E.F. (*contd.*)
141; in the Battle of the Somme, 147, 149 *sqq.*, Officers in action there, 150; in the Battle of Arras, 158 *sqq.*, Officers taking part in the attacks on April 9 and May 3, 1917, 164–6; Officers with Bn. H.Q. and Coys., night of April 11/12 and onwards, 164–5; Horse Show, success of, 167; Raid on Arrow Trench, 167–8; in the Third Battle of Ypres, 169–70; in the March fighting, 1918, 173 *sqq.*; Parade before H.M. the King, 184; Raids by, 173, 174, 175–7, 179; Attacks by, on Oct. 18–25, 1918, 180 *sqq.*; in Nov., 1918, 183; at Binche, 1919, 185; after the Armistice, 184; Demobilization, 185; in Egypt, 1923, 190
Militia, 25, 202–3
Special Reserve, 190
Territorial and Service, 190 Honours gained by, 184, 205
3rd, 6th W. Yorks Militia, 25, 142, 147, 163, 168, 173, 202; Battle Honours gained by, 202; Changed back into Militia, 202; Colours presented to, by H.R.H. the Duke of Clarence, 202, 203
4th, 6th W. Yorks Militia, 25, 156, 164, 165, 180, 189, 202; Battle Honours won by, 205; Colours of, 203
5th, 164, 174, 189, Battle Honours gained by, 205; V.C. gained by, Officer of, 184
6th, 174, 189, Battle Honours gained by, 205

D. of Wellington's Regt. (*contd.*)
Battalion (*contd.*)
7th, 164, 189, Battle Honours gained by, 205
8th, 145, 173, 189, Battle Honours gained by, 205
9th, 142, 198, Battle Honours gained by, 205
10th, 189, Battle and Colour Honours gained by, 205
12th and 13th, Battle Honours gained by, 205
Territorial and Service (*see also under Numbers above*), 25, 190, 202–3; Services of, Col. Sir H. E. Belfield on, 204–5
Twenty-one, altogether, in the Great War, 190
Colours of (*see also* Colours), sole Regt. entitled to carry four, 193
Designations at successive Periods, 4, 8, 10, 24, 25, 200
in the Great War, with special reference to the Territorial and Service Bns., Col. Sir H. G. Belfield on, 204–5
Recruiting area of, 4, 9, 191
Reputation of, 32, maintained, 47–8, 84, 191
Sporting Prowess of, 14–15, 32, *see also* Football
"Dukes and the Highlanders," the, 37
Dum Dum, 45
Dump, the, 132
Duncanson, Lt.-Col. R., 3 (1)
Dunkirk, 114
Durban, 38
Durham L.I., 112, 127
Durrant, Major C. M., 201
Dyer, Gen., 19
Dyson, Sgt., D.C.M., 171

EAST INDIA Declaratory Act, the, 27
East Indies, the, 5 (1)
East London, 38
East Lancashire Regt., 155

East Surrey Regt., 1st Bn., 62, 137, 142
East Yorkshire Regt., 111, 140
Ecaillon River, 181
Edward VII, H.M., death and funeral of, 48
Edwards, Capt. R. E., 168
Edwards, Lt. R. W., 156
Edwards, 2nd Lt. A. W., 142
Edwards, 2nd Lt. D. C. H., 142
Edwards, 2nd Lt. W. O., 121, 126, 132, 138
Egerton, Lt. C. C., 71, 189
Egypt, 22 (1), 190
86th Foot Regiment, 26
Elbell, L./Cpl., 163
Elephant Badge of the 33rd Regt., 25, 199
Elephant Snuff-box, presented by the "Iron Duke," 44
Elgin, 9th Earl of, 33
Ellam, Q.M. and Major A., 67, 138, 140–1
Elliot, 2nd Lt. G. E., 153
Ellis, Capt. T. M., 134, 137, 189 Escape of, 79, 80, 81, 126
Elouges, 82, 83
Elrington, Lt. M.M. (Essex Regt.), 111, 166
Elverdinghe, 168
England, 22, 45 (1)
Escapes, 79–80, 81, 126
Esshowe, 37
Essex Regt., 111
2nd Bn., 145, 146, 149, 151, 153, 156
3rd Bn., 139
Estairs, 117
Estrées, 93
Etaples, Convalescent Base Camp at, 173
Eth, 84
Etinhem, 145

FACINGS, changes in, 25, 45
Red, Colours prescribed for, 195 & *n.*
Fairfax, ——, 123
Fampoux, 157, 159, 160, 164
Faremoutiers, 100
Farrer, Cpl. G., 11 (1)
Feather, Sgt. J., M.S.M., 22 (1)
Feignies, 85
Feignies–La Longueville line, 85

INDEX

Feigneux-Crépy en Valois area, 94
Fenn, Lt.-Col. E. G., 33
Fergusson, Major-Gen. Sir C., Bt., M.V.O., D.S.O., G.O.C., 13th Bde., 60–1; G.O.C., 5th Div., 83, 84, 90, 132; G.O.C. XVII Corps, 163, 165, 171
Ferozepore, 16 (1)
Festubert, 115, 116, 117, 143
Feuchy Chapel, 177
Field, Pte., M.M., 171
Field, 2nd Lt. W. O., 138
Fillingham, 2nd Lt. H., 174
Finigan, Cpl. I., 11 (1)
Finnigan, Cpl. E., 11 (1)
"First Yorkshire West Riding Regt.," 4 (1)
Flanders, attack in, 1917, 166
  Earlier campaigns in, 4–5, 185
  Trenches in, 143
  Winters in, 1914 and 1917, 129, 171
Fleming, Lt. G. T. (Adjt. T. Bde., Mesopotamia), 21 (1)
Fleming, 2nd Lt. F. W., 189
Flers line, 152, 153, 155
Flint, Lt. R. B., R.E., D.S.O., 105
Floyd, General, 6
Foch, Marshal, 143, 183
Fog of War, in Aug., 1914, 56 *sqq.*, 61
Fontainebleau, Peace of, 185
Fontenoy, Battle of, 4 (1)
Football, 13, 14, 15, 38, 45, 143, 145
Football Record of the Regiment from 1903 to 1913, 14–15
Foot Guards, 1st Regt. of, 3 (1)
Forbes, Lord George, of the 2nd Queen's Regt., the 76th Foot raised by, 26
Forest of Villers Cottérêts, 94
Forêt de Mormal, 61, 86, 87, 89
Fort de Condé, 111
Fort Spin Baldack, 19 (1)
41st Regt., Wellington's service with, 28

Fosceville, 156
Foster, Lt. F. L., 19 (1), 42
Frameries, 82, 83
France, 20, 21 (1)
  B.E.F. in, 51 *sqq.*
  War with, in 1793–4, 5
Franco-Prussian War of 1870, 8
Fraser, Lt. N. W., 38; D.S.O., 40, 121
Fraser, Capt. F. H., a/Adjt., 146, 150, 153; M.C., 164
Frasers of Culduthel, 26
Frear, Sgt. A., D.C.M., 184
French, F.M. (Viscount Ypres), G.C.B., K.C.M.G., C.-in-C. B.E.F., 53, 60, 82, 85, 86, 87, 88, 93, 94, 96–7, 98, 100, 101, 102, 104, 105, 124 (2), 132, 138 (2), 141 (2), 143
Fresnoy, 112, 159
Frodsham, Bishop, Vicar of Halifax, 190
Frozen music, 34

GALLIÉNI, Gen., 97, 98; on the Allied effort, 117
Gallway, H. E., Lt.-Gen. T.L., R.E., Governor and C.-in-C. Bermuda, 33
Gandhi, "Mahatma," 18
Gardiner, Capt. H., D.S.O., 145
Gardner, Pte., M.M., 175
Garney, Sgt. W., 11 (1)
Garrison Battalions in India in the Great War, 21
Garrison life
  Abroad, 32
  in England, 47–8
Garside, Sgt., 185
Gas attacks at Ypres and at Hill 60, etc., 138, 139–40, 147, 174
Gatacre, Lt. E. G., 21 (1); Capt., 146, 189
Gavrelle, 159
Gedge, Rev. H. T. S., 190, 192
General Staff, formed, 52
George III, 198, 199

George V, H.M. King, 12, 15, 16, 17, 34, 46, 48 (1), 79, 126 (2), 184 (2)
  Colours returned by, 1926, 202
German military organization and methods, study of forbidden, 55
Ghazi Mustapha Kemal Pasha, 23
Ghent, 80
Gibbs, Lt. J. A. C., 33, 38; Capt., 40, 41, 42; Bt. Major and mentioned in Despatches, 43 (1); Lt.-Col., 16, 49; C.O. 2nd Bn., 62, 65; C.B., 70, 77, 78, 79, 111, 196
  On the Battle of Mons, 70 *sqq.*, and on the Retreat, 78, 83
Gibraltar, 22 (1), 32, 197
Gibraltar (France), 101
Gibson, Cpl. W., 43
Gibson, 2nd Lt., 130
Gillam, Temp. Major T. H. J., 152
Givenchy, 114, 115
Givenchy-Noyelles Road, 114
Givet, 58
Givry, 82
Glasgow, 197
Gleichen, General Count (now Major-Gen. Lord), 76, 105, 124
Glenn, Capt. H. W., 157; Major (a/Lt.-Col.), 21 (1)
Gloucester, H.M.T., 51
Glover, 2nd Lt. F. C., 147, 150, 153
Goebin Wood, 111, 112
Godsell, Capt. K. B., R.E., on the Battle of the Aisne, 107 *sqq.*
Goldsmith, 2nd Lt. S. M., 164
Goldsworthy, 2nd Lt. G. W., 156, 165, 166
Gommécourt to the Somme, German trenches along, British attack on, 149
Gordon, ———, 122

INDEX

Gore, Major C. W., 35; Lt.-Col., 37
Goree, 26
Gosport, 202
Gosset, Lt. R. F. (E. Yorks), 111
Gough's Cavalry, 104
Gough, Major-Gen. Sir Hugh, G.O.C. 5th Army, 149, 168
Gould, Capt. J., 35
Gourkas, the, 116
Grady, C.S.M. R., War Service of, 20 (1)
Graham, Lt., 26, 72 (1)
Graham, 2nd Lt. N. I., 146, 150, 151
Grand Glairet-Venteuil line, 101
Grand Morin River, 98, 100, 101
   Line parallel to, 100
Grand Reng, 82
Gravesend, 185
Great Mogul, the, 198
Great War, 1914-18, origins and indications of, 8, 42, 45, 48, 49; military events before, general trend of, 52 sqq.; military training before, landmarks in, 49-50; outbreak of, 15, 16 (1); the four years of, described by Winston Churchill, 183-4
Green, Lt. L. J. P., 142
Greenhalgh, Sgt., 68
Grenadier Guards, 3 (1)
Grenfell, Capt. O., V.C., 84
Grey, Major R. (Inniskillings), 36
Grevelink, Lt. E. J. Y., 189
Griffiths, Sgt., 19 (1)
Griggs, 2nd Lt. F., 173
Griggs, Sgt., M.M., 156
Grimley, 2nd Lt. C. W. G., 150, 151
Guérin, Pte., interpreter, 56
Guescart, 112
Gueudecourt, 153
Gunn, 2nd Lt. A., 139, 140
Guzée-Thuin line, 59
Gwalior, storming of, 7 (1)
Gwelo, 38

HADWEN, Lt. N. W., 139, 140, 146, 150, 151
Haelen, 57
Hague Convention, violation of, 139
Haig, Lt.-Gen. Sir Douglas (F.M. Earl Haig), K.C.B., K.C.I.E., K.C.V.O., 61; G.O.C. I Army Corps, B.E.F., 61, 86, 88, 146; C.-in-C., 149, 158, 166, 179 (2), 183
Hainsworth, L./Cpl., M.M., bar to, 184
Haldane, Col., 30
Haldane, Rt. Hon. Viscount, Secretary of State for War, and Army Reorganization, 52-4
Halfacre, Sgt. A., M.S.M., 185
Halifax (Nova Scotia), 31, 33, 34, 196 (1)
   Sport at, 34 (1)
Halifax, Yorks, 10 (1)
   Parish Church, Colours of the 33rd Regt. placed in, 33, 197, 198, 200, 203
Halifax Regt. (Duke of Wellington's), 8 (1)
   T.F., 25
Hall, Cpl. B., 11 (1)
Hall, L./Sgt. F., 11 (1)
Halloy, 146
Ham, 94
Hamilton, Gen. Sir Ian, 37
Hamilton, Major-Gen. H. I. W., C.B., C.V.O., D.S.O., 88
Hanna, 2nd Lt. G. W., 166
Hannah, Sgt., M.M., 156
Hanson, Capt. C. E. B., 135, 138
Harden, Maximilian, on German anticipation of victory in Oct. 1914, 112
Hardinge, Viscount, Viceroy of India, attack on, 17
Hardinge, R.I.M.S., 12
Harpley, 2nd Lt. G. W. M., 151
Harravesnes, 112
Harris, General, 6
Harris, Major O., 11 (1)

Harrison, Lt. P., 170
Harrison, Major E. G., C.B. D.S.O., later Lt.-Col., 114, 129-30; on the fighting at La Bassée, 114 sqq., and on the First Battle of Ypres, 117 sqq.
Harrison, Pte. E., 43
Harrison, Pte. J., 42, 43
Harrison, 2nd Lt. D., 163
Harrison, Sgt. A. W., D.C.M., 184
Harry, 2nd Lt. F. L., 150, 151
Hart, L./Cpl., 86
Hart, 2nd Lt. C. L., 130; Capt., 150, 151
Hartal, the, in India, 18, 19, 198
Hartennes, 102, 112
Harty, Lt.-Col. J. M., K.H., 196
Harvey, 2nd Lt. R. C., 179
Harwich, 185
Haslock, Lt. C. I. E., 192
Haspres-Saultzoir line, 180
Hasselt, 57
Hasselt-Liège line, 61
Hastings, Major P. (R.W. Kents), 62, and his company, "wash-out" of, 71
Haucourt, 178
Hautrage Cemetery, 75
"Havercake Lads," 4, 9-10 (1)
Havre, 56, 58 (1), 99
Hawkins, 2nd Lt. G. L. S., 142
Hay, Capt. (R.A.), 31
Hayden, Lt.-Col. F. A., D.S.O., 16, 46, 49, 142
   Letter to, from the Mayor of Lichfield, 48
Hazebrouck, 59, 112, 126
Headlam, Lt.-Col. (temp. Brig.-Gen.) J. E. W., C.B., D.S.O. C.R.A. 5th Div., 75
Heale, Capt. G. R. C., M.C., 165, 166
Healing, Capt. R. K., 78; Lt.-Col., 22, 23 (1)
Hebblethwaite, 2nd Lt. B., 174, 178
Hebuterne, 146
Hellon, 2nd Lt. K. A., 155, 156

INDEX

Hely-Hutchinson, Sir Walter, Governor of Natal, 37
Hemming, Lt. A. F., 150, 151
Henderson, Col. G. F. R., 54
Henderson, Lt. H. G., 111, 119
Henderson, 2nd Lt., 174
Henniker, Lt. R. J. A., 117, 121; Capt., 142, 155; Major, M.C., 156, 164; temp. Lt.-Col., 170; Lt.-Col., 171
Henry, 2nd Lt. P. R. J., 142
Hermann Stellung, 181
Hermitage Château, 119, 120, 122
Heskett, 2nd Lt. J., 168, 173, 174
Highlanders in the 76th Regt., 26
Hill, 2nd Lt. F. H., 156; Capt., 175; M.C., 177, 183
Hill, 2nd Lt., G.M., 164, 165
Hill, Sgt. W., 11 (1)
Hill 60, 47, 72, 78, 80, 130, 145
  Casualties of the 2nd Bn. at, 142
  Gas attack on, 139-40
  Officers of the 2nd Bn. "Duke's," present at, on April 19, 1915, 137-8, and on May 5, 140-1
  Taking of, accounts of by "Eye-witness," 137
  by Ince, 132 sqq.
  Official, 132
Hill 75, 129
Hills, Pte., M.M., 184
Hindenburg, F.M., 172, 183
Hindenburg Line, the, 158
"Hindoostan" Battle Honour, 198, 199
"Hindoostan Regt." (76th), 46 (1)
Hinges, 174
Hirst, Sgt., recommended for V.C., 130
Hodge, 2nd Lt. J. W., 145, 153
Hodges, Lt.-Col., 200
Hodson, —— (R. Fusiliers & K.O.Y.L.I.), 121, 127
Holdsworth, Lt. H. R., Signal Officer, 150
Holkar, Maharajah of Indore, 7

Homfray, 2nd Lt. C. K., 146 150, 151
Hongkong, 32
Honourable East India Company, 27
  Colours given by, 44, 46, 192, 193, 198 sqq.
Honours and Awards
  1st Bn., 9, 16, 22
  2nd Bn., 40, 43, 126, 145, 152, 156, 171, 175, 183;
  V.C., 184-5
Honours and Distinctions of Amalgamated Regiments, 24
Hood, L/Cpl., D.C.M., 171
Hooge, 122, 139
Hooge Château, 121
Hoole, Lt. M. C., 168; Capt., 177, 183
Hornu, 62, 63, 67, 69, 71, 72, 73, 80, 83
  Chaussée near, 71
Hornu et Wasmes Colliery, slag dump of, 75
Horse-sickness, 37
Horsfall, Capt. A. G., 41; Major, 152; a/Lt.-Col., 156, 157 (1); Lt.-Col., 2nd Bn., 21, 159; D.S.O., 162, 163-4, 165, 170, 188
  On the Battle of Arras, 159 sqq., and on Life at Monchy, etc., 167
Horsfall, Capt. C. F., 7th Bn., 188
Horsley, 2nd Lt. W. E., 157, 164, 165; Lt., 170
Houdain, 61
Houghton, 2nd Lt. B., 179
Houtrerque, 152
Howlett, Sgt., M.M., 175
Hudson, 2nd Lt., 130
Huffam, 2nd Lt. J. P., 175; V.C., 184-5
Hughes, 2nd Lt., M.C. (posthumous), 174
Hulluch, 145
Humphrys, Major C. V., 12; Lt.-Col., 15, 16; Commandant, Central School of Musketry, Pachmari, 16 (1)

Hunter, Gen. Sir Archibald, 41
Hunter Weston, Major-Gen. (later Lt.-Gen.) Sir A. G., 146, 149, 151
Huntingdon, George, Earl of, 2-3 (1)
Hussars
  7th, 38
  8th, 41, 42
  11th, 121, 122
  15th, 121
  19th, 121
  20th, 120
Hutton, 2nd Lt. T., 124, 138
Hyder Ali, 5, 27
Hyderabad, Nizam of, 5, 6, 7
Hyderabad Contingent, the, 6 (1)

"If I Should Die . . ." (Rupert Brooke), 189
Îles les Villenoy, 97
Imperial Defence, Committee of, 55-6
Ince, Lt. C. W. G., Adjt., 111, 114, 130, 133, 138, 140; Capt., M.C., 145, 146; Major, 201
  On the Battle of Mons, 67 sqq., and on the end of the Retreat, 98-9
  On the Battle of Le Cateau, 88 sqq., 90
  On the Battle of the Marne, 101-2
  On Food at Missy, 109
  On the Bivouac in Goebin Wood, 111
  On the Taking of Hill 60, 132 sqq.
Inchley, 2nd Lt. W., 130; Lt., 139, 140
India, 44
  Army Reorganization in, 55
  British troops in, during the Great War, 21 (1)
  Military and political situation in, prior to, during, and after the Great War, 16 sqq. (1)
  Troops from, on various Fronts, 55, 116, 117, 150
  Voyage to, the two Battalions passing during, 12, 45

INDEX

India A.O. 726 of 1904, tests under, 45 (1)
Indian Hill Stations, Life at, lines on, 13 (1)
Indian response to the call of the Great War, 17–18
Indian Staff College, Quetta, 52
Infantry Battalions, all kinds, Battle Honours of, selection and display of, 201
"In Flanders fields," lines by Col. John McCrae, 116–17
Inkerman, Battle of, 46, 197 (1)
Inniskilling Fusiliers, 103
Inverness, 26
Invicta (Molony), *cited* on the crossing of the Aisne, 105
Ireland, 22 (1), 48
Irish Guards, 12
Isandhlwana, Battle of, 37, 195
Italy, 21 (1)

JACKSON, Lt. G., 183
Jalapahar, 44
Jamaica, 32
James I, 32, 33
Jenkins, 2nd Lt., 41
Jenkins, Capt. E. V., D.S.O., 70, 71, 72, 79, 80
Jenlain, 85
Jervis, Capt. E. C., M.C., 171
Joffre, Gen. (now Marshal), C.-in-C. French Armies, 57, 58, 59, 87, 94, 97 *sqq.*, 104–5, 106, 107, 143, 158
Johannesburg, medal clasp for, 41
Johnson, Pte. J., 43
Johnson, 2nd Lt. S., 174, 178, 179
Johnston, Capt. W. H., R.E., V.C., 105
Johnston, Col. H. J., D.S.O., 188
Johnston, 2nd Lt. G. D., 146–7, 150, 151, 165
Jones, Brig.-Gen., 145
Jouarre–Nogent line, 97
Jouy le Chatel, 100

Jubb, *see* Denman-Jubb

KAMPTEE, 197
Kandahar, 19
Kandahar Barracks, Tidsworth, 46
Kantara Rest Camp, 21 (1)
Karachi, 20 (1)
Karroo, the, 42
Kavanagh, Major-Gen. Sir C. T. McM., C.B., D.S.O., 145
Kay, 2nd Lt. H. C., 179; Lt., 183
Keates, Capt. W. E., 111, 114; Major, 152
Kelly-Kenny, Lt.-Gen. Sir Thomas, K.C.B., 9, 10 (1)
Kennedy, Pringle, wife and daughter of, murder of, 17
Kerman, Cpl. H. E., 80
Key-Jones, Lt. W. H., 142
Kimberley, Relief of, 12, 197 (1)
King, Lt. F. H., 152, 153
King, 2nd Lt. A., 173, 174
King's African Rifles, 122
King's Medal for the South African War, with two clasps, 41
King's Own Loyal Lancaster Regt., 1st Bn., 145, 149, 151, 153, 158, 160, 161, 162
King's Own Scottish Borderers, 2nd Bn., 51, 61, 62, 63, 71, 105, 106, 123, 125, 132, 133, 153, 174
King's Own Yorkshire Light Infantry, 2nd Bn., 63, 71, 73, 74, 75, 83, 105, 106, 121, 123, 127, 132, 133, 136
Kingsford, Mr., murder of, 17
Kington, 2nd Lt. S. B., 150, 151
Kirby, Pte. W., M.M., 184
Kitchener, F.M., Earl, K.G., 15 (1), 37, 41, 52, 55, 96–7
Kliber, Cpl. J. R., D.C.M., 183
Kluck, Gen. Von, 85–6, 92, 97, 98, 102
Knight, Pte. J., M.M., 168

Knox, Gen., 41, 42
"Kruger" telegram, the, 9
Kruistraat, 139
Kruistraat Château, 130
Kurseong, 13 (1)

LA BASSÉE, 114, 175
  Battle of, 113 *sqq.*
La Bassée Canal, 114, 143, 174
La Boiserette, 83
La Bosquet, 73, 75, 78
Ladysmith, 37
La Fère, 173
La Ferté sous Jouarre–Montmirail Road, 101
Lagny, G.H.Q., B.E.F., Sept. 1, 1914, 97
Lahore, 16, 18, 19 (1)
Lahore Division, *see under* Divisions
La Houssaye, 100, 145
Laing's Nek, 37
Lake, Lord, 28, 29, 30, 44, 193, 198, 199
La Loge Farm, 102
La Longueville, 83, 85
La Marette, 61
Lambert, 2nd Lt. P. F., 151, 153, 156; M.C., 164, 165, 166
Lambert, Sgt. E., M.S.M., 22 (1)
Lambton, Major-Gen. Hon. W., 146, 157
Lancashire Fusiliers, 2nd Bn., 145, 149, 153, 154, 156, 158, 161, 162, 163
Lancers, 9th, 84
  17th, 102, 103
Landing Farm, 170
Landrecies, 56, 86, 87, 88
Langdale, Capt. C. A. J. S., 111
Langemarck, 169
Lankhof Château, 130
Lanrezac, General, 59, 60
Laon-Fresnes line, 105
Laon–La Fère–St. Quentin line, 87
Lasswari, Battle of, 28, 29 *sqq.* (1)
Larcombe, 2nd Lt. A. H., 157, 164, 165, 166
Largny, 112
Lascelles, Viscount, 190

INDEX

Laughton, 2nd Lt. F. S., 164, 165
Law, 2nd Lt. J. H., 174
Lawless, Lt. A. W. H., 150
Lawson, Pte., D.C.M., 156
Leader, 2nd Lt. B. E., 142; Capt., 153, 154
Lean, Lt.-Col. and Bt. Col. K. E., 41, 46 (1)
Lebong, 15, 44, 45 (1)
　Life at (verse), 13 (1)
Le Cateau, 83, 85, 86, 87, 95
　Battle of, 88 *sqq.*, 110, 145
　Accounts of, by
　　De Sausmarez, 93
　　Ince, 88 *sqq.*, 90
　　O'Kelly, 90
　Retreat from, 91 *sqq.*
Le Cateau–Montay Road, 87
L'Eclase sector, 179
L'Ecleme, 174
Lee, 2nd Lt. R. W., 173
Lee-Enfield Rifle, 2nd Bn. armed with, 44, later with short magazine ditto, 45, and with S.L.E., 49
Leece, 2nd Lt. F. B., 151, 153
Le Gallais, Col., 8th Hussars, 41, 42
Leicestershire Regt., 15; 17th Bn., 35 (1)
Le Limon, 102
Lennon, Lt. J. A., M.C., 181; Capt., D.S.O., 184
Lens, 159
Le Quesnoy, 114
Lesbœufs, 153
　Attack on, 155, 156
Les Feuchères–Rougeville–Orly line, 101
Les Herbières, 61
Le Suich, 146
Leuze, 80
Lichfield, Rt. Rev. Bishop of, 46, 200
Lichfield, 45–6, 200
Liddell, Major (Lt.-Col.) E. M., 21 (1)
Liège, 58, 110
　Fall of, 57
Lierval–Chavignon–Terny line, 104
Lincolnshire Regt., 119

Little, 2nd Lt. H. W., 174, 175, 178
Little Hornu, 73
Liversidge, Sgt., M.M., 156
Livsey, Lt. H., 173; M.C., 183
Lloyd, Lt.-Col. G. E., C.B., D.S.O., 9, 11 (1)
Lobengula, 36, 37
Locke, 2nd Lt., 142
Locre, 124, 127, 129
Locre Hill, 124
Locre–Ypres Road, 118
Loire River, 99
Lomax, 2nd Lt. G. S., 173, 174
London, Rt. Rev. Bishop of, at Ypres, 131
London Dock Strike, and other strikes, duty during, 48
Longeuil, 112
Longley, Lt.-Col. J. R. (1st E. Surrey), 62
Longueval, 103
Loos, Battle of, 49, 143, 145
Lord, Lt. S. R., 150, 151
Lorraine, 102
　French Army of, 59
Louis Farm, 169
Louis XIV, 1, 2
Louis XVI, 5, 27
Louvencourt, 151
Lowe, 2nd Lt. A. S., 142
Lower Gharial, 16, 18 (1)
Lozinghem, 177
Ludendorff, Gen., Q.M.G., Push of, for Amiens, 174, and withdrawal, 179 *sqq.*
　Resignation of, 183
　On Artillery Barrages, 181
　On the British attacks on the Somme, 147
　On the Battle in the West in 1918, 172
Ludd, 21 (1)
Lumigny–Faremoutiers line, 100
Lunéville, 59
Lupton, Major B. C., M.C., 201
Luxembourg, 58, 59

MACLEOD, Capt. C., R.A.M.C., 150; M.C., 152
Macleod, Capt. K. A., 12 (1); Major, 70, 71, 72, 73, 75, 76, 78

McLeod, Major K. (a/Lt.-Col.), 111
Macloutsie, 37, 38
MacCracken, Lt.-Col. F. V. N., C.B., D.S.O., temp. Brig.-Gen. 7th Bde., 119, 123
McCrae, Lt.-Col. J., lines by ("In Flanders fields"), 116–17
McCulloch, 2nd Lt. G. T. M., 174
MacDonald, Lord, a 76th Regt. raised by, 26
Macdonalds in the 76th Regt., 26
MacDonnell, Major John, of Lochgarry, Lt.-Col., 76th Regt., 26
McDowall, 2nd Lt., R.A., 163, 173, 174
MacFarlane, 2nd Lt. W. G., 174
McGovern, Sgt. F., 11 (1)
McHugh, 2nd Lt. W., 179, 181–3
Macintosh, 2nd Lt. J. D. V., 156, 165, 166
Mackinnons, the, 26
Macnamara, 2nd Lt., 152, 155
MacRie, Brigadier, 30 (1)
Madras Cup won, 15 (1)
Madrell, 2nd Lt. S. K., 168
Mafeking, 36, 38
Maffett, Lt. R. E., 41; Major and Lt.-Col., 18, 22 (1)
Maharatta Campaign, 7, 28, 46, 193, 198, 199 (1)
"Mailed fist," the, 49
Mailly Maillet, 146
Maing–Querenaing–Artres line, 180
Maitland Cemetery, Cape Colony, 12
Maizière, 157, 163
Majuba Hill, 37
Malpoonah, 30 (1)
Malta, 32
Mametz, 143
Manchester Regt., 2nd Bn., 80, 83, 115, 124, 126
　4th Bn., 142
　12th Service Bn., 130

INDEX

Manoury, Gen., French Sixth Army, 94, 97, 98
Maples, 2nd Lt. W. E., 41; Major (Lt.-Col.), 21 (1), 189
Maricourt, 143, 149
Mariette, 71
Marks, Sgt. R., 11 (1)
Marlborough, John Churchill, 1st Duke of, 1, 129
Marlborough House, 202
Marne, Battle of the, 93, 98 *sqq.*, 110, 167
Marne River, crossing of, on rafts, 97, 102 *sqq.*
    Line of, 100, 101
    Valley of, 101
Marouilles, 56, 57, 59, 60, 67, 86, 87
Marshall, Lt. (later Capt.) Robert, 33, and his plays, 37-8
Marshall, Major F. M. H., 44; Lt.-Col., 44-5, 46
Marshall, Pte. W., 145; D.C.M., 177
Marshman, Lt. W. A., 192
Martin, Sir Richard, Imperial Commissioner, 38
Martinique, 26
Martinpuich, 153
Martyn, Lt.-Col. A., C.O., R.W. Kents, 70, 71, 72
Marwitz, Gen. von der, Cavalry Commander, 112
Mary, H.R.H. Princess, Viscountess Lascelles, 190
Mashonaland Campaign, 38, 40, 44, 46
Matabele Expedition of 1893, 36 *sqq.*
Matthews, R.S.M., War Service of, 20 (1)
Matoppo Hills, 40
Maubeuge, Fortress of, 59, 80, 83, 85, 86, 87
Maubeuge–Le Cateau–Hirson area, 56
Maunder, 2nd Lt. A. V., 147, 150, 151
Maurepas, 156
Maxse, Gen. Sir F. I., 186
Maxwell-Hyslop, Capt. R. G. B. M. (1st Dorsets), 73

s

Mayo, 6th Earl of, murder of, 44
Maude, Brig.-Gen., G.O.C. 14th Brigade, 124
Maynard, Brig.-Gen., G.O.C. 13th Brigade, 143
Maynard, Lt. W. E. (D.L.I.), 127
Meaux, 100
Meaux–Dammartin line, 97
Mecquignies, 61
Melun on Seine, 98
Memorial Chapel, York Minster, Dedication of, 186 *sqq.*
Menin, 117
Menin Road, 121
Méricourt L'Abbaye, 152, 156
Mesnil, 146
Messines, 128
Messines ridge, mines exploded at, and capture of, 166
Mesopotamia, 20, 21 (1)
Metcalf, C.M.S., D.C.M., 139; clasp to, 152
Metz, 58, 59; siege of, in 1870, 86
Meuse River, 58, 59, 60
Meuse and Sambre Rivers, salient along, 59
Mezières, 57
Middlesex Regt., 8th Bn., 152, 179
Middlewood, 2nd Lt. A., 165, 166
Milbank, Capt. R. P. C., 121, 122, 133, 137, 189
Military Tournament, Delhi, 16 (1)
Militia, the, 53
Militia Garrison Artillery, replacement of, 53
Miller, Capt. A. E., Adjt., 9th Bn., 142
Miller, Lt. (Somersetshire L.I.), 142
Miller, Lt. H. J. (E. Yorks), 139, 140
Miller, 2nd Lt. C. C. (3rd Somersets), 145
Millican, 2nd Lt. J. S., 147, 150, 151
Milln, Capt. K. J. (3rd Somersets), 145; Major, 146, 150, 151

Minto Centenary Fête, Calcutta, 15 (1)
Missy, 104 *sqq., passim*, 111
Missy–Chivres Road, 108
Missy–Condé Road, 108-9
Missy–Sermoise Bridge, 104, 106, 107
Mitchell, 2nd Lt. W. E., 156
Moberly, Lt.-Col. W. L., M.P. (76th Regt.), 198, 199
Mohmand tribe, the, 18 (1)
Monchaux-Verchain-Sommaing line, 180
Monchy, 165, 166, 167, 179
Monchy Ridge, 167
Mondidier, 94, 179
Molony, Major C. V., 105
Moltke, Gen. von, Chief, German General Staff, 102
Mons, 4 (1), 47, 52, 124, 183
Mons, Battle of, 61 *sqq.*, 67 *sqq.*, 82, 110, 127, 145
    Accounts of, by
        Ince, 67-8
        O'Kelly, 69
        Ozanne, 63 *sqq.*
    Events after, 82 *sqq.*
    Retreat from, 82 *sqq.*, end of, 98-9
Mons–Condé Canal line, 60, 61, 63, 78, 79, 82
Monson, Hon. Col., 29
Montgomery-Cunningham, —, 26
Montmirail, 100
Mont St. Eloi, 177
Montreuil, 102
Moody, Lt., a/Adjt., 170
Moore, Capt. N. H., 111, 114
Moore, Col.-Sgt. R. D., 11, 43
Moore, Sir John, 46
Moorhouse, Pte. M., 43
Morgan, 2nd Lt. A. K., 174
Morlancourt, 152
Morland, Major-Gen. Sir T. L. N., C.B., D.S.O., G.C.O. 5th Division, 116, 123, 142
Mornington, 2nd Earl of, Governor-General of India, 5, 6
Morris, 2nd Lt. H. M. (4th Manchesters), 142, 173, 177, 178, 179

Mortan, Cpl. W., 11 (1)
Mortcerf–La Celle-sur-Morin line, 100
Morval, 153
Moulin des Roches, 107, 108
Mounted Infantry, 38–9 (1), see also Burma M.I.
"M.I.," Kipling's lines on, 39
Mouy, 97
Mowat, Capt. J. W., M.C. (4th Bn.), 188
Mowatt, Lt.-Col. A. L., D.S.O., M.C., 201
Mudania, 23 (1)
Mulhausen, 59
Mungwe Pass, 37
Mur Copse, 181
Murree Hills, 16 (1)
Murrie, 2nd Lt. (E. Surreys), 142
Mysore Campaign, 5 sqq., 200 (1)

Namur, 57, 58, 59, 60
Nancy, 59
Nanteuil, 96, 101
Napoleon I, and Tippoo Sahib, 5
Natal, 37
National Reserve, the, 55
Naves, 180
Naylor, Lt. S., M.C., 192
Naylor, Pte., M.M. (posthumous), 174
Nery, 95
Nesbitt, Lt.-Col. E., 35, 36 (1)
Nesle, 94
Netherlands Campaign of 1794, 4–5 (1)
Neufchateau, 57
Neuve Chapelle, Battle of, 143
Neuve Eglise, 124, 125, 126, 129
Neuville, 156
Newman, Cpl. G., 11 (1)
Newroth, 2nd Lt. W. S., 142; Lt., 157; Capt., 174
New Year Honours, 1918, 173
Nive, 199
Nivelle, General, 158
Nogent, 101
Non-Co-operation movement in India, 17, 18

Norfolk Regt., 1st Bn., 84, 104, 125, 127, 142
North Staffordshire Regt., 3rd Bn., 142
Northumberland Fusiliers, 20 (1), 119
Nourse, Drummer (Mr. P. A. Nourse), 38
Nouvelles, 82
Noyelle, 112
Noyon, 86, 94, 143
Nova Scotia, discovery of, 33

Oakes, 2nd Lt., 41 (1)
Obies, 61
Offensive Committee, the, 56
Officer, Capt. W. G., 21 (1), 158; Major (temp. O.C.), 163, 170; Lt.-Col., 173–4
Official History of the War (Military Operations, France, and Belgium, 1914), *cited* on Army Reorganization, 52 sqq., on events of the Great War *passim*
Ogden, Sgt., D.C.M., 175
O'Gowan, Brig.-Gen. R. W., 141, 142, 143
Oise River, 94
Oise-Aisne Canal, 104
Oisy on Sambre, 183
O'Kelly, Lt. H. K., D.S.O., on the Battle of Mons and on the Retreat, 69 sqq., 76–7
On the Battle of Le Cateau and the subsequent Retreat, 90 sqq.
On the Capture of "Death's Head" Hussars, 95–6
O'Kelly, Pte., M.M., 156
Old Comrades' Association, 188
Oliphant, Lt. G. W., M.C., 78
Ollezy, 94
Open Warfare, training for, Oct. 1918, 180
Orly, 101
Ormond, Duke of, 1, 3 (1)
Osborne, Lt. G. (20th Hussars), 120, 121, 125
Ostend, 5, 54, 79, 80

Ouderdom, 130, 140, 142
Ourcq River, 100, 102
Owen, Capt. R. H. W., 192; Major, 19 (1)
Owen, Lt. R. H., 119, 130, 135, 138, 189
Ozanne, Lt. W. M., 139, 140; Capt. (M.G.O.), 63 sqq., 72, 78
On the Battle of Mons, 63 sqq.

Paardeberg, Battle of, 9, 11, 197 (1)
Pacaut Wood, raids on, 174, 175 sqq.
Pack-Beresford, Major C. G. (1st R.W.K'ts.), 75
How he met his death, 77
Padley, Cpl., 175
Paget, Lt.-Col. (7th Hussars), 38; Major-Gen., 9, 41 (1)
Palestine, 21, 22 (1)
Palmer, Sgt. J., M.S.M., 22 (1)
Paniput, 16 (1)
Panther, 49
Paris, 96, 97, 98, 100, 102, 110, 143, 166
Parry, Pte. J., D.C.M., 43
Parsons, Capt. E. M. K., 38
Passive Resistance movement, in India, 17
Passchendaele, 168
Patchett, 2nd Lt. N., 156, 164
Paton, Capt. D., 192
Paturages, 82
Paturages–Frameries line, 82
Pawlett, Lt.-Col. F. (Can. Army), O.C. 2nd Bn., 174, 179; D.S.O., bar to M.C., 183; temp. C.O. 4th Div., 185
Peace, German attitude to, Oct. 1918, 183
Pear Trench, 179
Pearce, C.S.M. L. J., 154; M.C., 156
Pegu ponies as pets, 41
Peishwa, the, 7 (1)
Pelves, 166
Peninsular War, the, 129, 198, 199 (1)

INDEX

Pennyfather, Gen. Sir J., Colours presented by, 198
Pension Fund, 186
Pernes, 177
Peronne, 179
Persia, 20 (1)
Persian Gulf, the, 55
Peruwelz, 79
Peselhoek, 168
Peshawar, 18 (1)
Pétain, Gen., 146, 147, 166
Petit Morin River, 100, 101
Pezarches–Lumigny line, 100
Phillips, Capt. G. F. (Duke of Cornwall's L.I.), 124
Phillips, 2nd Lt. C. St.T., 111, 115
Picardy, 143
Pickering, Bt. Lt.-Col. C. J., C.M.G., D.S.O., 190, 201
Pietermaritzburg, 37, 38
Pilkem, 168
Pimple, the, 181
Pitt, William, 5, 27
Plassey, H. T., 45
Plumb, 2nd Lt. E. S., 147, 150, 151
Plumer, F.M. the Lord, G.C.B., &c., 41; C.O.C. Second Army, 143, 169
Poelcappelle, 169
Pogson, Sgt. E., D.C.M., 119, 185
Pt. Hovvin, 177
Ponsonby's 37th Regt., 4
Pontoise, 94
Poperinghe, 152
Potize, 139
Pozières ridge, 145
Presidency Bde., the 2nd Bn. adjudged the best British Bn. in, 1905, 45
Preseau, 183
Pretoria, 11 (1), 41
Price, Lt. O., 79
Prince Imperial of France, 37
Prinsloo, 41
Prior, Cpl. H., M.M., 184
Prussian Guards' attack, Nov. 11, 137
Pullan, 2nd Lt. J., 156

Punjaub disturbances, 18 (1)
Pusieux ridge, 149

QUAREGNON-LA CORDELLETTE line, 71
Quatre-Bras, Battle of, 196
Queen's Bays, 121
Queen's Own Royal West Kent Regt., 1st Bn., 51, 61, 62, 63, 67, 70, 71, 72, 75, 80, 90, 104, 105, 106, 125, 127, 128, 130, 132, 133
Queen's Westminster Rifles, 152
Quentin Village, raid on, 177
Querenaing, 180
Quetta, 18, 19, 20 (1)
  Indian Staff College at, 52
Quievrain, 82

RAMSDEN, Pte., 170
Rangoon, 40, 41, 62
  Officers' Mess burnt down at, and Colours destroyed, 33, 43-4, 46, 193, 199, 200
Raniket, 15 (1)
Ransart, 146
Ravetsberg, 130
Rawalpindi, 16, 18 (1)
Rawalpindi Brigade, 21 (1)
Rawlinson, Lt.-Gen. Sir H., G.O.C. Fourth Army, 149
Rawnsley, 2nd Lt. E., 156
Rebais, 100, 101
Red Cross work at the Battle of the Somme, 154-5
Reed, Sgt. W., D.C.M., 183
Rees, 2nd Lt., 164, 165, 166
Reid, Sgt., 162, 163
Reninghelst, 142
Rennison, Pte. A., M.M., 175
Respirators, 142
Replunges, 101
Reumont, H. Q., 5th Div., 90
Reumont - Maurois, Roman Road, 90
Rheims, 104
Rheims–Amiens line, 94
Rhenoster Kop, 9, 11 (1)
Rhine, the, 58

Rhodesian Campaign of 1896-7, 38 *sqq.*
Richards, C.S.M., M.M., 156
Rhodes, 2nd Lt. J. F., 156, 165, 166
Rifle and bayonet fighting, Thomason on, 180
Rifle Bde., 1st Bn., 89, 151
Rippingille, Lt. F. A. (E. Yorks), 111, 120, 121, 125
Rivett-Carnac, Lt.-Col. P. T., 9, 12 (1)
Rivett-Carnac, Major, Bt. Lt.-Col., 40
Roberts, F.M. Earl, V.C., 12, 37
Roberts, W. R. Coleridge, Mayor of Lichfield, letter from, in praise of the Regiment, 48
Robertson, F.M. Sir W., 56
Robertson, 2nd Lt. C., 142
Robertson, 2nd Lt. T. W., 152
Robins, Capt. G. W. (E. Yorks), 139
  Poems by, and tributes to, 140
Rodgers, 2nd Lt. G., 156
Roll of Honour Book, 187-8
Rorke's Drift, 37
Rose, Major John, 3 (1)
Rosental Château, 130
Rouex Cemetery, 159
Rouex sector, 173
Rouveroy, 82
Rowlands, Gen. Sir Hugh, V.C., K.C.B., Colonel of the Regt., 46 (1)
Roy, 2nd Lt. W. H., 173, 174
Royal Army Medical Corps, efficiency of, 129
Royal Defence Corps, 55
Royal Engineers
  17th Fd. Coy., No. 2 Section, rafting troops over the Aisne, 105, 106, 107
  526 (Durham) Fd. Coy., 175
Royal Field Artillery, Brigades formed, 53
  Barrage by, Oct. 23/18, 181
  27th Battery, 84
  119th Battery, 84

INDEX

Royal Flying Corps, 146
Royal Fusiliers, 119, 151
Royal Garrison Artillery, 108th Battery, 88, 89
Royal Highlanders, 36, 37
Royal Horse Artillery, L Battery, 84, 95
Royal Horse Guards, 8
Royal Munster Fusiliers, 114
Royal Navy, the, 99
Royal Scots Fusiliers, 120, 121
Royal Sussex Regt., 121
Royal United Service Institution, Colours of the 33rd Regt. in, 196, and returned by, 197
Royal Warwickshire Regt., 46, 148; 1st Bn., 173, 174, 177, 181
Royal West Surrey Regt., 142
Rozoy, 100
Rue de Béthune, 116
Rue d'Hornu, 73
Rue de Marais, 115
Rue d'Ouvert village, 114, 115
Rundle, Lady, 12 (I)
Russell, Lt. L. E., 74, 75, 77, 79, 189
Russian Revolution of 1917, 166
Russo-Japanese War of 1904-5, Colours carried in, on both sides, 194
Rutherford, 2nd Lt. N. H., M.C., 156

SAACY, 101
Sailly-Laurette, 145
Sainsbury, 2nd Lt. P. S., 145; Lt., 150
St. Catherine, 177, 180
St. Cyr, 101
St. Eloi, 142
St. George's Harbour, Bermuda, 32
St. Ghislain, 61, 62, 65, 66, 67, 68, 70, 71, 80, 83, 93
St. Helena, 36
St. Hill, Major A. N., 21 (I); Lt.-Col., D.S.O., 21, 189
St. Jean Capelle, 124, 126, 127
St. Lucia, 35

St. Mary Magdalene Church, Taunton, 196
St. Nazaire, 99
St. Nicholas Church, Rouen, 187
St. Olle, 180
St. Omer, 59, 112
St. Pol, 112, 158, 179
St. Roch, 115
St. Quentin, 86, 87, 94
St. Sauveur-Verberie area, 94
St. Servin's Farm, 179, 183, 185
St. Waast, 84, 86
St. Waast-Amfroipret-Bermeries line, 85
St. Waast-Wargnies-Jenlain-Saultain line, 85
Salisbury, Rhodesia, 37
Salisbury Plain, 46
Salisbury Rifles, 40
Sambre River, 59, 86, 183
Sanderson, Pte. J., 43
Sanderson, 2nd Lt. C. R., 150, 151
Sandhurst Royal Military College, Chapel of, Memorial Panel in, 186
Sandringham House, 202
Saultain, 85
Saultzoir, 183
  Main line of Resistance behind, 180
Saultzoir sector, 180
Saxe, Marshal, 4 (I)
Scarpe River, 160, 174
Scindia, Maharajah, 7
Scott, Canon F. G., lines by, "On a Wayside Shrine in France," 131
Scott, Lt. R. A., 21 (I)
Scottish Rifles, 2nd Bn., 164
Schramm Barracks, 171
Schwaben Redoubt, 152
Seaforth Highlanders, 2nd Bn., 173, 177
Seikna, 12, 13 (I)
Seine River, 98
Semoy River gorges, 60
Sensee River, line along, 178
Septmonts, 103
Serches, 103
Seringapatam, siege of, 5, 6-7, 28, 31, 197 (I)
Sermoise, 105, 106, 107, 108, 111
Serre, 149, 150

Seven Years' War, 185
74th Regt., 28
75th Regt., 28
76th Macdonald's Highlanders, 26-7
76th Regt., 138
  Amalgamation of, with the 33rd Regt., as 2nd Bn., 8, 25, 198
  Area of Recruitment, 28
  Association with, of the "Iron Duke," 28, 31, 46
  Colours of, 44, 46, 192, 193, 197-8, 200
  Three earlier of this Number, 27-8
77th Regt., 28
Shaw, Capt. L., M.C., 173
Shaw, Cpl., 72
Shaw, 2nd Lt. V. R., 179
Shearne, Lt., M.C., 183
Shellabear, Pte., 70
Shenall, L./Cpl., M.M., 171
Shepherd, Lt. & Q.M. C., D.C.M., M.B.E., 185
Shepherd, Pte. J., 43
Shepherd, R.S.M. C., D.C.M., 152
Sheppard, 2nd Lt. L. C., 142
Shipton, ——, 29
S L E rifle, mark iv, and mark vii high velocity ammunition supplied, 49
Shoulder straps, change in, 49
Sialkote, 18 (I)
Sibi, 19 (I)
Siddle, Cpl., D.C.M., 139
Sikhs, 15th Bn., 116, 117
Simkins, 2nd Lt., 152, 153
Simner, Lt.-Col. P. R., D.S.O., 201
Simpson, 2nd Lt. A. B. T., 139, 140
Sims, Sgt. C., 43
Singapore, 32
Singer, Major E. W., R.E., 123
Siordet, Lt. F. J., 11 (I)
Sirhind Rifle Meeting Challenge Cup won, 15 (I)
Sitapur, 15 (I)
Skelton, Lt. C., M.C., 179
Skene, Lt.-General, 26
Slater, 2nd Lt. T. McD., 192

INDEX

Sleigh, Lt. G. P., 130, 151, 153, 154
Smith, Lt. T. S., 38
Smith, 2nd Lt., 142
Smith, Sgt., 64
Smith-Dorrien, Gen. Sir H. L., G.C.B., D.S.O., G.O.C. II Army Corps, B.E.F., 61, 82, 87, 88, 90, 91, 93, 94, 130
Snow, Major-Gen. (later Lt.-Gen.) T. D'O., G.O.C. 4th Div., 86, 89, 92
Soissons, 103, 104
Soissons-Compiègne line, 94
Solesmes, 86
Solon, 15, 16 (1)
Somerset Light Infantry, 3rd Bn., 142, 145, 146
Somme, Battle of the, 147 *sqq.*
   Ludendorff on, 147
   Typical day in, 153 *sqq.*
Somme River, 172
   Line on, held by 13th Brigade, 143
   Trenches along, mud and cold in, 156-7
Sonada, 13 (1)
Sordet, Gen., G.O.C. French Cavalry Corps, 57, 86, 94
Soult, Marshal, 46
South African War, 8, 9 *sqq.* (1), 37, 42, 46, 53, 54, 197
   Burma M.I. in, 40 *sqq.*
   Military Memorials, 10 *sqq.*
South Staffordshire Regt., 4th Bn., 142
Sowerby Brig, legend of, 4
Spalding, Pte. H., 43
Spanish Armada, the, 46
Spanish Succession, War of the, 1 *sqq.* (1)
Spanish Town, 196
Special Reserve, the, 53, 126, 190
Spectrum Trench, 156
Spellman, Pte. J., M.M., bar to, 184
Spence, Sgt., 77, 78
Sport as training for War, 10, 14
Spriggs, Sgt., M.M., 156

Starkey, 2nd Lt. W., 179; M.C., 184
Steenworde, 143
Stipe Copse, 172, 179
Stirling Castle, 27 (1)
Stocks, 2nd Lt., 174
Stopps, Pte., M.M., 156
Stowell, Lt.-Col. G., 203
Strafford, Major P. B., 67, 71, 72, 77, 78, 189
Strensall, 10 (1)
Sucrerie, 147, 150
Suez Camp, 168
Suffolk Regt., 2nd Bn., 89, 90, 151
Suft, Lt. H. C., 33 (1)
Sugden, Lt. G. H., 147, 150, 151, 153
Sunken Road, the, 155, 181
Susman, 2nd Lt. W., 173
Swadeshi movement, the, 17
Swan Château, 152
Swanson, Lt. F. H. H., 33; Capt., 38
Sykes, Capt. E. E., M.C., 189
Sykes, Capt. K., M.C., 201

Tatchell, Lt. (Lincolns), 42
Taunton, 196
Taupin Trench, 150
Taylor, Capt. E. R., 76, 124, 127, 135, 137, 189
   Escape of, 79-80
Taylor, 2nd Lt. A. E., 164
Taylor, Sgt., C.S.M., D.C.M., 119
Taylor, Sgt. T., 11 (1)
Taylor, Sgt. L., 43
Taylor-Smith, Bishop, Chaplain-General to the Forces, 190
Templemore, 198
Ternan, Colonel, 42
Territorial Artillery, Coast and Field, 53
Territorial System of Linked Battalions, 8
Territorial Regiments, organization of, 24
Territorial Troops, in India, 55
   Reorganization of, 53
Tertre Road, 62
Tetlow, Lt. L. M., 189

Thatcher, 2nd Lt. R. S., 142
Thackeray, Lt. F. R., 116, 120; a/Adjt., 121, 122, 124, 126, 136, 138; M.C., 189
Thelwell, 2nd Lt. H. R., 150, 151
Thiepval, 152
Thionville, 58
Thomas, 2nd Lt. G. R. (4th Manchesters), 142
Thomason, Capt. J. W., jnr., U.S. Marine Corps, on Red Cross work on the Somme, 154-5, and on rifle and bayonet fighting, 180
Thompson, Lt. J. H. L., 72, 73, 78, 79, 189
Thomson, Lt. D. H. W., 168
Thorneycroft, Colonel, 42
Thornton, Sgt., 163
Thorold, Major H. D., 38; Lt.-Col., 12, 15 (1)
Thrush, H.M. gunboat, 34
Thulin, 82, 84
Tidmarsh, Capt. R. M., 88, 98, 111; Major, 21; a/Lt.-Col., 22
Tidmarsh, Lt. J. M., 21 (1), 189
Tidswell, Pte. F., M.M., 175
Tidworth, 22 (1), 46, 48
Tilloy, 179
Tindaria, 13 (1)
Tippoo Sahib, 5-6, 27 (1)
Tirlemont, 57
Tobias, Lt. W. O., R.A.M.C., 138, 140, 141
Tokine, 44
Tollent, 158
Tournai, 79
Tournan, line E. and W. through, 98
   Retreat to, 95 *sqq.*
Tower Hill, clearing of, 19 (1)
Town, Major W. N., 201
Townsend, Major E. N., D.S.O. 68, 69, 71, 73, 76, 79, 88-9, 91
Tradition, value of, in the Army, 10
Travers, Capt. (R. Munster Fusiliers), 114; Major, 119
Travers, Major H. P., 189

Trelawny and Wulf trenches to Cat Street, sector, 151
Trench, Lt.-Col. S. J., 44, 187
Trench, Major (Lt.-Col.), M. V. le P., 21 (1)
Trench, Mrs. John, 187
Trench Feet, 129
Trench Warfare, 54, 88, 116
  Beginning of, 104, 107
Trenches, extent of, in the Great War, 54
  Flemish and French, 143
  on the Somme, 156-7
  in Winter, 1914-15, 129
Trinidad, 35
Troisvilles, 86
Trotter, Lt. W. K., 36
Tulloch, Capt. R. M. C. (1st Bn. R.W. Kents), 70, 72
Tulloch, Lt.-Col. J. A. S., C.R.E., 5th Div., 75
Tunstall, 2nd Lt. W., 174, 178
Turkey, birth of, as a nation, 22-3
Turner, Lt. H. N., 170
Turner, Lt. N. G. H., 33 (1); Capt., 11 (1), 42, 43
Turner, Lt. P. A., 36, 38, 40; Major, 21; Lt.-Col. (later Brig.-Gen.), 21, 132, 133, 134, 136, 137
Tustin, Cpl., D.C.M., 175
Tyler, Lt. A. J., 11, 38, 41, 43
Tyndall, Major W. E. M., D.S.O., 128, 129; a/O.C., 130, 133, 136-7, 189

UHLANS, 63-4, 67, 76
Umfreville, Capt. H. C., 111; Major, a/Lt.-Col., 111, 114, 120, 121
Uniforms, changes in, 24, 25, 49
Union Flag, the, in, and after 1801, 195-6
Union of South Africa, 37
United States of America, entry of, into the World War, 157, 166
Unwin, Capt. C. H. (E. Yorks), 126, 139, 144
Utrecht, Peace of, 33

VAILLY, 103, 104

Vaizy, 103
Valabrégne, General, 59
Valade Trench, B.H.Q. in, 151
Valenciennes, 105, 180
Valenciennes-Oisy line, Haig's Offensive on (Nov. 4, 1918), 183
Vaubricourt, 112
Vaudoy-Pezarches line, 100
Veldoek Château, 120, 121
Vellum Colour Book, the (1820), 196
Venizel, 103, 104
Verberie, 112
Verchain, 181, 183
Verdun, 102, 146, 147
Vermelles, 114, 145
Versailles, Peace of (1763), 26
Vesle River, 100, 103
Victoria, H.M. Queen, 25
Vickers, Miss, Colours deposited by, 196
Viebahn, General von, 112
Vile, 2nd Lt. H. L., 165, 166
Viljoen, General B., 9 (1)
Villeneuve, 98
Villers au Bois, 177
Villers Cottérêts, 94, 95, 97
Villers-sur-Morin-Villeneuve le Comte-Villeneuve St. Denis line, 100
Vimy Ridge, 143
  Taken by the Canadians, 158-9
Vint, Pte. G. W., 188
Violaines, 112, 114, 115
Virginian Company, the, 32
Visé, 57, 58
Vis en Artois, 177
Vismes, 156
Vlamertinge, 130
Vlamertinge-Ouderdom Road, 130
Volunteers, the, reorganization of, 53
"Voluntiers," raising of, 2-3
Voormezeele, 142
Vosges, the, 59
Vredenberg, 2nd Lt. V. F. de W. W., 167, 168

WALES, H.R.H. the Prince of, 124

Walker, Cpl. E., 184
Walker, Lt., 174
Walker, Lt. A., 21 (1)
Walker, Major P. L. E. (17th Hussars), temp. Lt.-Col., 2nd Bn., 173, 174
Walker, Major-Gen. M., V.C. C.B., Colours presented by, 197
Waller, Capt. H. N., 189
Waller, Sgt., M.M., 156
Wallis, Lt. A. F., 38; Capt., 11 (1)
Walmoden, Gen., 185
Walsh, 2nd Lt. P., 145; Lt., 146, 163
Walsh, 2nd Lt. T., 179
Wancourt, 171
Wapshare, Lt.-Gen. R., C.B., C.S.I., G.O.C. 4th (Quetta) Division, Special Divisional Order issued by, 20 (1)
War Council, the, 56
War Memorials
  Great War, 186 *sqq.*
  South African War, 10 *sqq.*
Ward, 2nd Lt. N. M., 156, 178
Wargnies, 85
Warluzel, 146
Warquinies, 84
Wasmes, 67, 70, 71, 72, 73, 78
Wasmes-Bois de Boussu line, 71
Wasmes to Hornu-Champ des Sarts line, 71
Waterloo, Battle of, 8, 14, 85, 196 (1)
Watkins, temp. Capt. G. D., R.A.M.C., D.S.O., M.C., bar to M.C., 184
Watmough, 2nd Lt. D. O., 179
Watson, Capt. W. M., 33, 37, 38; Major, 16, 49; Brig.-Gen. Rawalpindi, (Inf.) Bde., 18, 21; Colonel, 18
Watson, Mrs., and the Misses, 188
Watson, 2nd Lt. L. G., 152; Capt., 164
Wayside Shrine, A, Northern France, lines on (Scott), 131
Weedon, 197

INDEX

Wellesley, Major F. H. B., 21; a/Lt.-Col., 22 (1); O.C. 2nd Bn., 185
Wellesley, Lt.-Col. A., *see* Wellington, F.M., 1st Duke of
Wellington, Duke of, K.G., 45–6, 190, 200
Wellington, F.M., 1st Duke of, connection of, with the 33rd Regt., and career of, in Flanders, India, the Peninsula, and at Waterloo, 4 *sqq.*, 28, 31, 44, 129, 141, 185, 191; Colonel-in-Chief of the 33rd Regt., and Marquis, and Colonel of the Royal Horse Guards, 8; victory of, at Waterloo, 8; funeral of, 197
Weslie, Lt. Hon. A., *see* Wellington, F.M. Duke of
West Front, German defence on, crumbling, 183
West India Regt., 151
West Indies, the, 31, 35
West Kent Regt., *see* Queen's Own Royal West Kent Regt.
West Riding men, the Archbishop of York's tribute to, 191
West York Militia, 6th, 1st, and 2nd Bns., 202
West Yorkshire Regt., 139, 140, 174
Whale, Gen. Sir C., K.C.B., 197
Wheatley, 2nd Lt., 130
Wheeler, Lt. C., 21 (1)
White, Lt. F. S., 170
Whitefoot, Cpl. G., 43
Whittaker, 2nd Lt. C. F., 111, 116; Lt., 139, 140, 142
Whitwam, Capt. H. E., 189
Wildbourne, 2nd Lt., 173; Lt., 175
Willey, 2nd Lt. E. R. G., 163

William, Crown Prince of Prussia, at Verdun, 147
William II, German Emperor, 2, 9, 112, 172
William III of England, 1
Williams, Cpl. J. G., on the deaths of Lt. Russell and his platoon, 77
Williams, 2nd Lt. H. E., 156
Williamson, Lt. G., 111, 119, 189
Willey, 2nd Lt. E. R. G., 163
Wilmot, Pte. F., M.I., 12, 42, 43
Wilson, L./Cpl., 154
Wilson, Major J. H. P., 21 (1); Lt.-Col., 21, 189
Wilson, President, and Peace, 157, 183
Winburg, O. R. C., 11, 12, 42, 43
Witchdoctor's cave, the, 38–9
Wittebergen, medal clasp for, 41
Wittington, Lt. G. W., 142
Wolfenden, 2nd Lt. L., 179, 181
Wolseley, F.M. Viscount (Sir Garnet), 37
Wood, Capt., Cape Mounted Rifles, 36
Wood, F.M. Sir Evelyn, 37
Wood, Lt. H. W. W., 33; Capt., 38
Wood, Pte. R., M.M., 175
Wood, 2nd Lt. R., 163, 166
Wood Lane, 177
Woolley, Pte., M.M., 152
Woolridge-Gordon, Capt. (R. Highlanders), 36
Worge, Col., of the 76th, 26
Worge's Regiment, 26
World Crisis, the (Churchill), *cited*, 110
Wormald, L./Cpl. G. W., M.M., 184
Worsnop, L./Sgt., 11 (1)
Wulverghem, 124, 125, 126, 127, 129
Wulverghem–Messines Road, 129
Wynberg, Cape Colony, 36
Wytschaete, 127, 128

YATES, Lt., 111, 115
Yelland, 2nd Lt. E. Y., 156
Yeomanry reorganization, 53
York, Archbishop of, address by, at unveiling of the "Duke's" War Memorial, 190 *sqq.*
York, Dean of, Dr. Lionel Ford, 192 *sqq.*
York, H.R.H. General the Duke of, 185
York, quarters at, 9 *sqq.* (1)
Yorkshire S. African War Memorial at, 12
York and Lancaster Regt., 2nd Bn., 142
York Minster, War Memorial in, 10–11 (1), and Memorial Chapel, 186–7, 189 *sqq.*
Yorktown, 196
Young, Lt. B. K., 79
Young, 2nd Lt. C. T., 130, 138
Ypres, 116, 118, 123, 130, 132, 138
  Easter Day Service at, 1915, 131
  Inferno of, 133
Ypres, Battles of
  First, 111, 113 *sqq.*, 117 *sqq.*
  Second, first use of Gas by Germans in, 138, 139–40
  Third, 169 *sqq.*
Ypres Canal, 151
Ypres–Comines railway line, 132
Ypres–Menin Road, 119, 120
Ypres Road, 118, 122, 123
Ypres Salient, 151, 168
Yser Canal, 170
Yvrencheux, 146

ZEVECOTEN, 138, 142
Zillebeke, 130, 131, 133
Zillebeke Pond, 137
Zonnebeke front, the, 169
Zouave Infantry, 118, 119, 120
Zululand, 37
Zwarteleen ridge, 132

THE MAYFLOWER PRESS
WILLIAM BRENDON AND SON, LTD.
PLYMOUTH, ENGLAND

www.ingramcontent.com/pod-product-compliance
Lightning Source LLC
Chambersburg PA
CBHW082003150426
42814CB00005BA/205